Joseph Bruchac is the author of more than thirty books of poetry, fiction, and Native American folktales and legends. His writings have appeared in more than four hundred journals and anthologies and have been translated into several languages. In addition, Bruchac has edited or co-edited numerous anthologies of Native American folklore and Asian American poetry. He earned his doctorate from Union Graduate School in Ohio. The founding editor of the Greenfield Review Press, a respected publisher of Native American literature, he also serves on the editorial board of the journal *Studies in American Indian Literatures*.

Janet Witalec edits work on multicultural and environmental issues. Her previously published books include *Native North American Literature* and *Environmental Viewpoints*.

Sharon Malinowski earned her master's degree in English from the University of Michigan (Ann Arbor) and has completed studies toward a Ph.D. in American Culture. Among her previously published books are *Notable Native Americans* and *Gay & Lesbian Literature*.

NATIVE
NORTH
AMERICAN
LITERARY
COMPANION

Joseph Bruchac, Managing Editor

NATIVE NORTH AMERICAN LITERARY COMPANION

Janet Witalec, Editor
with Sharon Malinowski

VISIBLE INK PRESS

Detroit   New York   Toronto   London

The Native North American Literary Companion

Published by Visible Ink Press™
a division of Gale Research
835 Penobscot Building
Detroit, MI 48226-4094

Visible Ink Press™ is a trademark of Gale Research

Most Visible Ink Press books are available at special quantity discounts when purchased in bulk by corporations, organizations, or groups. Customized printings, special imprints, messages, and excerpts can be produced to meet your needs. For more information, contact Special Markets Manager, Gale Research, 835 Penobscot Bldg., Detroit, MI 48226. Or call 1-800-877-4253.

Cover Design: Mary Krzewinski, Page Design: Tracey Rowens

ISBN 1-57859-046-9

CONTENTS

dren's books who is known as one of the first Native women novelists in Canada.

☐ "We Are a People"

Brant is a Mohawk poet, short story writer, essayist, and editor who frequently addresses her identity as a Native American, woman, and lesbian in her works.

☐ "This Place"

A Lakota Sioux political activist and autobiographer, Brave Bird is best known for *Lakota Woman* and *Ohitika Woman*. *Lakota Woman*, which was written under the name Mary Crow Dog, won the American Book Award in 1991 and was a national bestseller.

☐ "Invisible Fathers"

A Shawnee and Cayuga poet and short story writer, Bush is noted for works that are imbued with a sense of outrage at both past and present injustices that white society has perpetuated against Native Americans.

☐ "Inherit the Blood"
☐ "Taking a Captive/1984"
☐ "Abbey of the Bear"

Campbell is a Métis autobiographer, author of children's books, playwright, scriptwriter, editor, and essayist who is best known for her autobiography *Halfbreed*, which relates her struggles as a Métis in Canadian society.

☐ *Halfbreed*

A Dakota Sioux poet, short story writer, and novelist, Cook-Lynn is especially concerned with the tension between white culture and Native American identity. She has stated that "writing is an essential act of survival for contemporary American Indians."

☐ *The Power of Horses*

blood, and her relationship to the landscape of the Great Plains.

- ☐ "Female Seminary, Tahlequah, Indian Territory, 1850–1905"
- ☐ "Here I Am Standing Beside Myself"
- ☐ "Regretfully"

JANET CAMPBELL HALE
197

A Coeur d'Alene novelist, poet, essayist, and autobiographer, Hale draws from her personal experiences to examine the adverse effects of poverty and alcoholism on Native Americans. Her novel *The Jailing of Cecilia Capture* was nominated for the Pulitzer Prize.

- ☐ "Return to Bear Paw"

JOY HARJO
211

Harjo is a Muskogee Creek poet whose works are often set in the American Southwest while emphasizing the plight of the individual and reflecting Creek values, myths, and beliefs. She has been consistently praised for her thematic concerns and the universal relevance of her verse.

- ☐ "The Woman Hanging From the Thirteenth Floor Window"
- ☐ "Remember"
- ☐ "Grace"
- ☐ "Autobiography"

LANCE HENSON
221

Henson is a Cheyenne poet whose verse is noted for its powerful imagery, economy of words, and universal appeal as well as its incorporation of Cheyenne philosophy and social commentary.

- ☐ "warrior nation trilogy"
- ☐ "buffalo marrow on black"
- ☐ "impressions of the cheyenne way"

TOMSON HIGHWAY
227

A Cree playwright, Highway is primarily known for his award-winning plays, *The Rez Sisters* and *Dry Lips Oughta Move to Kapuskasing*, both of which deal with life on the reservation.

- ☐ *The Rez Sisters*

X

x i

x i i i

issues and employs various poetic forms and multiple voices. He has stated that poetry "matters like hell" to Native Americans.

☐ "An Eagle Nation"
☐ "Close Encounters"

Of Hopi and Miwok descent, Rose is a poet who frequently examines the alienation of the halfbreed in both white and Native cultures. Her work is infused with overtones of pain, anger, and bitterness and is focused on spirituality, communion with the natural world, and the encroachment of white culture on Native society.

☐ "Julia"

Silko, a Laguna Pueblo novelist, poet, and short story writer, is among the foremost writers to emerge from the Native American literary renaissance of the 1970s. Her novels *Ceremony* and *Almanac of the Dead* have been praised for their vivid characterizations and inventive plots.

☐ *Ceremony*

Tapahonso's poems and short stories are highly autobiographical, infused and shaped by her beliefs and identity as a Navajo woman. She has been praised for her feminist and individualist sensibilities, her depiction of Navajo traditions and humor, and her ability to sensitively convey her multifaceted identity to diverse audiences.

☐ "In 1864"
☐ "Hills Brothers Coffee"

Vizenor is a prolific author whose novels, plays, essays, and stories draw heavily upon his experiences as a mixed-blood Chippewa. He frequently challenges conventional notions about Native American life in his essays and autobiographical memoirs, and his fiction is often described as postmodern because of his use of experimental narrative structures, word play, and complex symbols and imagery.

☐ "Santa Maria Casino"

Walters is a Pawnee and Otoe-Missouria novelist, essayist, short story writer, author of children's books, and poet, who has drawn on her Native American background to make tribal perspectives accessible to modern audiences. She has been praised for her effective blending of literary and artistic genres, her realistic depiction of Native American culture, and her focus on spiritual concerns.

☐ "The Warriors"

A Blackfeet and Gros Ventre novelist and poet, Welch is best known for his novels *Winter in the Blood,* which has received high praise for its treatment of modern concerns from a Native perspective, and *The Death of Jim Loney,* which focuses on a mixed blood's alienation from both white and Indian societies.

☐ "Thanksgiving at Snake Butte"
☐ *Winter in the Blood*

Whiteman, an Oneida poet, is noted for her collection *Star Quilt,* which has been praised for its simple and rhetorical language, vivid imagery, and sincere and distinctive voice.

☐ "Dream of Rebirth"
☐ "A Nation Wrapped in Stone"
☐ "Star Quilt"

FOREWORD

In many ways, the current interest in Native American literature and the mainstream success of many of its writers is both ironic and, perhaps, inevitable. In the early eighteenth century, it was proposed by serious scholars that Native Americans lacked real languages and were only questionably human. A century and a half ago, people still questioned the existence of literary traditions (or, quite frankly, any real culture) among the Native peoples of North America. The vast body of Native American oral traditions now being diligently studied by scholars around the world was either unknown or ignored. A generation of ethnologists, some of them (like Tuscarora J.N.B. Hewitt) Native Americans themselves, made considerable strides in recording and celebrating those oral traditions by the early part of the twentieth century. By then, however, the continued survival of Native American people and any aspect of their cultures was being seriously doubted. Genocidal policies of warfare and forced migration, the destruction of means of traditional subsistence (such as the buffalo in the western plains), the outlawing of Native American religious practices, and the continuing epidemics for which Native populations had no resistance, seemed to spell the end. The image of the "Vanishing Redman" became a common theme in North American popular culture and still remains prominent in cinematic depictions of Indians.

Yet, despite it all, Native American people survived. In the twentieth century the populations of Native people have gradually increased and their cultures have re-emerged, displaying amazing resiliance. Perhaps this may best be understood in the longer context of Native history. The North American continent has always been a place where many cultures have been in contact. Before the recorded arrival of Europeans, hundreds of different languages were spoken and widespread systems of communication and trade existed. The flexibility of Native American peoples was such that when new people and new technologies were encountered, processes of adoption and adaptation took place with great

The Gift Is Still Being Given

JOSEPH BRUCHAC

xvii

rapidity. European languages and European technology were quickly adopted if such adoptions contributed to individual and community survival. Thus the Native American nations of the Great Plains built a whole new culture around the horse. Had it not been for the enormouse impact of European diseases—wiping out as much as ninety percent of the populations in most parts of the Americas—Native adaptability was such that it is unlikely that this continent would have been so visibly dominated by European immigrants and their traditions.

Considering that adaptability, that ability to recognize and make use of new things, it should come as no surprise that Native Americans have not only mastered the literary forms of the West, but also drawn on their own oral traditions as they shaped those literary forms towards their own purposes. Further, though this anthology only presents contemporary voices, Native North Americans have been learning the craft of writing such European languages as English and seeing thier work in print for two centuries. The new Native American literature may seem to have burst suddenly upon the American scene with N. Scott Momaday's *House Made of Dawn* in 1969, but there was a long apprenticeship.

There are numerous ways to explain the current popularity of Native American writing. It has been suggested that North America has never gotten over (or grown beyond) its romance with the idea of the "Noble Savage." Some readers may come at first to Native American literature because they are desperately seeking James Fenimore Cooper. Though cultural separation remains the visible norm, Canada and the United States are profoundly multicultural. "Playing Indian" is so much a part of American life that it has been said that the average American male is an Indian until he is a teenager, at which point he becomes an African-American, only becoming White when he gets his first job. It has been noted that Indians are rediscovered every thirty years or so. We do see peaks of interest in publishing by Indians in the early 1900s with Zitkala-Sa and Charles Alexander Eastman, in the 1930s with John Joseph Mathews and D'Arcy McNickle, and in the 1960s beginning with Momaday. However, so many Native American authors have been published since the late 1960s that it seems this last cycle in popularity is not a fad likely to simply ebb away.

The dual heritage of the Natvie American author—a heritage composed of Western literary tradition and literary forms on the one hand and the content and purpose of the oral tradition on the other—has produced a body of literature that is strikingly original and compellingly relevant. Unlike the Western notion that "poetry makes nothing happen," the Native American writer "sings" to help insure survival—survival not only of Native people but of all life. Just as traditional storytellers used their tales to entertain on the one hand and offer moral instruction on the other, much of contemporary Native American writing has a similarly clear and powerful intent, bringing messages to the reader with subtlety and purpose. Further, just as Native American traditions universally stress the importance of spirituality, the world of the spirit is central in the works of most contemporary Native American writers. At a time when Western culture is engaged in questioning its faith and seeking meaningful direction, we find a kind of spiritual balance which is neither artificial nor otherworldly in the writing of such authors as Leslie Marmon Silko, Joy Harjo, Simon Ortiz, and numerous others. In a world of questions, Native American literature offers answers—not easy solutions, but ones charged with power.

In 1992, I was part of putting together a festival of North American Native writers, which we called **Returning the Gift.** Our abilities as writers—as novelists and poets, playwrights and essayists—are a gift given to us by the Creator. It is our obligation to return that gift, to make use of it in a way that serves the people and the generations to come. More than two hundred published Native American authors attended that four-day gathering in Norman, Oklahoma—land where the native nations of the southeast had been sent into forced exile and yet survived. Many of us came away from that gathering inspired not only with a sense of common purpose, but also with a respect for our differences, for the variey of traditions and voices that are behind each of us and which make up the mosaic that is contemporary North American Native writing today. And we came away with the belief that, as good as the work was that had been done thus far, there was much yet to come. The forty writers included in this collection are among the best known and most talented, but they represent only part of the still-growing body of work that is Native American literature. The gift is still being given.

INTRODUCTION

Smoke rising on the wind brings together the elements of earth, air, and fire. Does it signal an offering or a communication? Does it carry sacred or traditional meaning? Does it sting our eyes to tears or prompt the memory of a rhythm with its scent? The smoke is drawn out of a transformation by fire, visible yet without form, interpreting the wind for a brief moment before blending with the sky. What is it, and what does it mean? This is our metaphor for the literature offered in this collection.

The Native North American Literary Companion brings together writers whose singular experiences and distinctive voices give rise to such elemental themes as identity and meaning, heritage and marginalization, spirituality and ambivalence. A product of the rich and varied literary history of Native North Americans, this compelling collection focuses on thirty-seven Native American and Canadian voices.

More than a score of Native tribes are represented by the writers included in this book. While they may speak different languages, and encompass tremendous diversity in ethnic, geographic, and historical backgrounds, these authors share the experience of belonging to more than one nation. This duality provides fertile ground for the literature included here. We chose to focus on contemporary writers, providing a selection of new and well-known authors, to counter a tendency of works on Native issues to break off coverage in the historical era, stranded in the nineteenth century. This glimpse represents a jam-packed fraction of the Native literary tradition; we seek to give you a savory taste, and encourage further exploration.

More than a traditional anthology, this book is your companion to a literature and its craftspeople, presenting extensive details on the writers' lives and times as well as excerpts or complete selections from their works. Each profile features biographical information, a complete list of list of the author's published works, a comment in the author's own words, and a critical evaluation, along with a selection from the author's writing. An **Index** guides you to specific authors and their works covered in this volume.

ACKNOWLEDGMENTS

Information on the authors in this book was drawn in part from *Native North American Literature* and *Notable Native Americans*, two comprehensive reference works published by Gale Research Inc. We gratefully acknowledge the contributions of the advisory board for Native North American Literature: Catherine B. Bond, Conestoga High School, Berwyn, Pennsylvania; G. Edward Evans, Loyola Marymount University, Los Angeles, California; Linda Fritz, University of Saskatchewan Libraries, Saskatoon, Saskatchewan; Karl Kroeber, Columbia University, New York, New York; Kenneth M. Roemer, University of Texas at Arlington; A. LaVonne Brown Ruoff, University of Illinois at Chicago; James Ruppert, University of Alaska—Fairbanks; Dorthea M. Susag, English Teacher, Simms High School, Simms, Montana; Katharine Weiblen, Assistant Department Head, Humanities Division, Literature and Language Department, Minneapolis Public Library, Minneapolis, Minnesota.

For editorial contributions encompassing research, writing, keying, and proofreading, we thank Jeffery Chapman, Christopher Giroux, Marie J. MacNee, Kwelie Jomo, Kathleen J. Edgar, Eva Felts, Dean D. Dauphinais, Rebecca Nelson, Sharon Remington, and Julie Winklepleck. For persistent acquisition of text and picture permissions, we thank Kim Smilay and Margaret Chamberlain. For production assistance, we thank Barbara Yarrow, Pamela Hayes, Willie Mathis, and Mary Kelley. For inspired typesetting, we thank Marco Di Vita of the Graphix Group.

CREDITS

NATIVE
NORTH
AMERICAN
LITERARY
COMPANION

SHERMAN  ALEXIE

Sherman Alexie is one of the most exciting young Native American writers to emerge in the 1990s. The son of a Spokane father and a part-Coeur d'Alene mother, Alexie grew up on the Spokane Indian Reservation in Wellpinit, Washington. At 18 he left the reservation to attend college at Gonzaga University in Spokane. After two years he transferred to Washington State University in Pullman, where he majored in American Studies. He credits his creative writing instructor at Washington State, Alex Kuo, for encouraging him to seek publication for his writing. Alexie returned to the reservation during summer breaks from college, and life on the reservation— synonymous with poverty, unemployment, alcoholism, and despair— remains an important focus of his poetry and fiction.

Essay by

PAUL HADELLA

In 1990, Alexie's poems began to appear in literary magazines little known outside poetry circles. By 1993, the literary establishment was heralding him as the standard-bearer for a new generation of Native American writers: he had published four books; his chapbook, *I Would Steal Horses,* had won Slipstream Press' fifth annual chapbook contest; and leading magazines such as *Esquire* and *Vanity Fair* had featured his work. The Washington State Arts Commission awarded him a poetry fellowship in 1991, and the National Endowment for the Arts awarded him a creative writing fellowship in 1992.

This talented writer's rise from obscurity to national prominence is remarkable. A laudatory notice in the *New York Times Book Review* set

"I am a Spokane/Coeur d'Alene Indian from Wellpinit, Washington, where I live on the Spokane Indian Reservation. Everything I do now, writing and otherwise, has its origin in that."

the tone for a flood of reviews to come. Writing about *The Business of Fancydancing*, Alexie's 1992 debut collection of fiction and poetry, James R. Kincaid declared, "Mr. Alexie's is one of the major lyric voices of our time." As important as favorable reviews have been in establishing Alexie's reputation, his own tireless promotion of his books has also attributed to his success. In an interview in January of 1994, Alexie estimated that he had given 290 readings throughout the United States in 1992 and 1993, performing to audiences ranging in size from six to 1,000.

Timing has also been a factor in Alexie's rise. His emergence as an important writer coincided with the controversial five-hundredth anniversary of Columbus's discovery of the New World. With the literary establishment courting native reactions to the Quincentennial, the time was right for the appearance of a powerful new writer who would command the spotlight. *Old Shirts & New Skins*, which represents a veritable catalog of native grievances, contains the scathing poem, "Postcards to Columbus." This volume of poetry, with its militant tone, voices some of Alexie's most direct protests against the 500 years of oppression that Native Americans have endured. In *Old Shirts & New Skins*, Alexie targets his anger at incidents such as the nineteenth-century Sand Creek massacre, Hollywood's treatment of Native Americans, as well as life on the reservation.

The Element of Humor

In *The Lone Ranger and Tonto Fistfight in Heaven*, Alexie's 1993 collection of short fiction, he writes: "Survival = Anger x Imagination. Imagination is the only weapon on the reservation." Also necessary for survival is the ability to laugh at most of life's miseries. As intense as Alexie's writing often is, none of his books is devoid of humor. Two works particularly reveal his comic sensibility: *The Lone Ranger and Tonto Fistfight in Heaven* and *The Business of Fancydancing*. In his 1969 *Custer Died for Your Sins*, Native American essayist, Vine Deloria, Jr., challenged the stereotype of the "granite-faced grunting redskin . . . perpetuated by American mythology," claiming that "Indian people are exactly opposite of the popular stereotype." Although it may be true, as Deloria pointed out, that laughter is a defining element of everyday American Indian life, no native writer before Alexie has consistently brought this element to the forefront.

Spokane/Coeur d'Alene poet and fiction writer.

Born: October 7, 1966, in Spokane, Washington.

Education:, Attended Gonzaga University, 1985–1987; Washington State University, B.A., 1991.

Career: Writer.

Address: P.O. Box 376, Wellpinit, WA 99040.

"Indians have found a humorous side of nearly every problem . . . ," writes Deloria. "The more desperate the problem, the more humor is directed to describe it." Problems as desperate as racist state troopers, commodity food, the Bureau of Indian Affairs (BIA), and cancer are all given the comic treatment in Alexie's work.

13/16

From *The Business Of Fancydancing*, Hanging Loose Press, copyright © 1992 by Sherman Alexie

1.
I cut myself into sixteen equal pieces
keep thirteen and feed the other three
to the dogs, who have also grown

tired of U.S. Commodities, white cans
black letters translated into Spanish.
"Does this mean I have to learn

the language to eat?" Lester FallsApart asks
but directions for preparation are simple:
a. WASH CAN; b. OPEN CAN; c. EXAMINE CONTENTS

OF CAN FOR SPOILAGE; d. EMPTY CONTENTS
OF CAN INTO SAUCE PAN; e. COOK CONTENTS
OVER HIGH HEAT; f. SERVE AND EAT.

2.
It is done by blood, reservation mathematics, fractions:
father (full-blood) + mother (5/8) = son (13/16).

It is done by enrollment number, last name first, first name last:
Spokane Tribal Enrollment Number 1569; Victor, Chief.

S H E R M A N   **A L E X I E**

3

It is done by identification card, photograph, lamination:
IF FOUND, PLEASE RETURN TO SPOKANE TRIBE OF INDIANS,
    WELLPINIT, WA.

3.
The compromise is always made
in increments. On this reservation
we play football on real grass
dream of deserts, three inches of rain

in a year. What we have lost:
uranium mine, Little Falls Dam
salmon. Our excuses are trapped
within museums, roadside attractions

totem poles in Riverfront Park.
I was there, watching the Spokane River
changing. A ten-year-old white boy asked
if I was a real Indian. He did not wait

for an answer, instead carving his initials
into the totem with a pocketknife: J.N.
We are what we take, carving my name
my enrollment number, thirteen hash marks

into the wood. A story is remembered
as evidence, the Indian man they found dead
shot in the alley behind the Mayfair.
Authorities reported a rumor he had relatives

in Minnesota. A member of some tribe or another
his photograph on the 11 o'clock news. Eyes, hair
all dark, his shovel-shaped incisor, each the same
ordinary identification of the anonymous.

4.
When my father disappeared, we found him
years later, in a strange kitchen searching
for footprints in the dust: still

untouched on the shelves all the commodity
cans without labels—my father opened them
one by one, finding a story in each.

The Business of Fancydancing, Hanging Loose Press, 1992.

First Indian on the Moon, Brooklyn, Hanging Loose Press, 1993.

The Lone Ranger and Tonto Fistfight in Heaven, Atlantic Monthly Press, 1993.

Old Shirts & New Skins, UCLA American Indian Studies Center, 1993

THE LONE RANGER AND TONTO FISTFIGHT IN HEAVEN

From *The Lone Ranger and Tonto Fistfight in Heaven*, HarperPerennial, copyright © 1993 by Sherman Alexie

Too hot to sleep so I walked down to the Third Avenue 7-11 for a Creamsicle and the company of a graveyard-shift cashier. I know that game. I worked graveyard for a Seattle 7-11 and got robbed once too often. The last time the bastard locked me in the cooler. He even took my money and basketball shoes.

The graveyard-shift worker in the Third Avenue 7-11 looked like they all do. Acne scars and a bad haircut, work pants that showed off his white socks, and those cheap black shoes that have no support. My arches still ache from my year at the Seattle 7-11.

"Hello," he asked when I walked into his store. "How you doing?"

I gave him a half-wave as I headed back to the freezer. He looked me over so he could describe me to the police later. I knew the look. One of my old girlfriends said I started to look at her that way, too. She left me not long after that. No, I left her and don't blame her for anything. That's how it happened. When one person starts to look at another like a criminal, then the love is over. It's logical.

"I don't trust you," she said to me. "You get too angry." She was white and I lived with her in Seattle. Some nights we fought so bad that I would just get in my car and drive all night, only stop to fill up on gas. In fact, I worked the graveyard shift to spend as much time away from her as possible. But I learned all about Seattle that way, driving its back ways and dirty alleys.

Sometimes, though, I would forget where I was and get lost. I'd drive for hours, searching for something familiar. Seems like I'd spent my whole life that way, looking for anything I recognized. Once, I ended up in a nice residential neighborhood and somebody must have been worried because the police showed up and pulled me over.

5

SHERMAN ALEXIE

"What are you doing out here?" the police officer asked me as he looked over my license and registration.

"I'm lost."

"Well, where are you supposed to be?" he asked me, and I knew there were plenty of places I wanted to be, but none where I was supposed to be.

"I got in a fight with my girlfriend," I said. "I was just driving around, blowing off steam, you know?"

"Well, you should be more careful where you drive," the officer said. "You're making people nervous. You don't fit the profile of the neighborhood."

I wanted to tell him that I didn't really fit the profile of the country but I knew it would just get me into trouble.

"Can I help you?" the 7-11 clerk asked me loudly, searching for some response that would reassure him that I wasn't an armed robber. He knew this dark skin and long, black hair of mine was dangerous. I had potential.

"Just getting a Creamsicle," I said after a long interval. It was a sick twist to pull on the guy, but it was late and I was bored. I grabbed my Creamsicle and walked back to the counter slowly, scanned the aisles for effect. I wanted to whistle low and menacingly but I never learned to whistle.

"Pretty hot out tonight?" he asked, that old rhetorical weather bullshit question designed to put us both at ease.

"Hot enough to make you go crazy," I said and smiled. He swallowed hard like a white man does in those situations. I looked him over. Same old green, red, and white 7-11 jacket and thick glasses. But he wasn't ugly, just misplaced and marked by loneliness. If he wasn't working there that night, he'd be at home alone, flipping through channels and wishing he could afford HBO or Showtime.

"Will this be all?" he asked me, in that company effort to make me do some impulse shopping. Like adding a clause onto a treaty. *We'll take Washington and Oregon and you get six pine trees and a brand-new Chrysler Cordoba.* I knew how to make and break promises.

"No," I said and paused. "Give me a Cherry Slushie, too."

"What size?" he asked, relieved.

"Large," I said, and he turned his back to me to make the drink. He realized his mistake but it was too late. He stiffened, ready for the gunshot or the blow behind the ear. When it didn't come, he turned back to me.

"I'm sorry," he said. "What size did you say?"

"Small," I said and changed the story.

"But I thought you said large."

"If you knew I wanted a large, then why did you ask me again?" I asked him and laughed. He looked at me, couldn't decide if I was giving him serious shit or just goofing. There was something about him I liked, even if it was three in the morning and he was white.

"Hey," I said. "Forget the Slushie. What I want to know is if you know all the words to the theme from 'The Brady Bunch'?"

He looked at me, confused at first, then laughed.

"Shit," he said. "I was hoping you weren't crazy. You were scaring me."

"Well, I'm going to get crazy if you don't know the words."

He laughed loudly then, told me to take the Creamsicle for free. He was the graveyard-shift manager and those little demonstrations of power tickled him. All seventy-five cents of it. I knew how much everything cost.

SHERMAN ALEXIE

"Thanks," I said to him and walked out the door. I took my time walking home, let the heat of the night melt the Creamsicle all over my hand. At three in the morning I could act just as young as I wanted to act. There was no one around to ask me to grow up.

In Seattle, I broke lamps. She and I would argue and I'd break a lamp, just pick it up and throw it down. At first she'd buy replacement lamps, expensive and beautiful. But after a while she'd buy lamps form Goodwill or garage sales. Then she just gave up the idea entirely and we'd argue in the dark.

"You're just like your brother," she'd yell. "Drunk all the time and stupid."

"My brother don't drink that much."

She and I never tried to hurt each other physically. I did love her, after all, and she loved me. But those arguments were just as damaging as a fist. Words can be like that, you know? Whenever I get into arguments now, I remember her and I also remember Muhammad Ali. He knew the power of his fists but, more importantly, he knew the power of his words, too. Even though he only had an IQ of 80 or so, Ali was a genius. And she was a genius, too. She knew exactly what to say to cause me the most pain.

But don't get me wrong. I walked through that relationship with an executioner's hood. Or more appropriately, with war paint and sharp arrows. She was a kindergarten teacher and I continually insulted her for that.

"Hey, schoolmarm," I asked. "Did your kids teach you anything new today?"

And I always had crazy dreams. I always have had them, but it seemed they became nightmares more often in Seattle.

In one dream, she was a missionary's wife and I was a minor war chief. We fell in love and tried to keep it secret. But the missionary caught us fucking in the barn and shot me. As I lay dying, my tribe learned of the shooting and attacked the whites all across the reservation. I died and my soul drifted above the reservation.

Disembodied, I could see everything that was happening. Whites killing Indians and Indians killing whites. At first it was small, just my tribe and the few whites who lived there. But my dream grew, intensified. Other tribes arrived on horseback to continue the slaughter of whites, and the United States Cavalry rode into battle.

8

The most vivid image of that dream stays with me. Three mounted soldiers played polo with a dead Indian woman's head. When I first dreamed it, I thought it was just a product of my anger and imagination. But since then, I've read similar accounts of that kind of evil in the old West. Even more terrifying, though, is the fact that those kinds of brutal things are happening today in places like El Salvador.

All I know for sure, though, is that I woke from that dream in terror, packed up all my possessions, and left Seattle in the middle of the night.

"I love you," she said as I left her. "And don't ever come back."

I drove through the night, over the Cascades, down into the plains of central Washington, and back home to the Spokane Indian Reservation.

When I finished the Creamsicle that the 7-11 clerk gave me, I held the wooden stick up into the air and shouted out very loudly. A couple lights flashed on in windows and a police car cruised by me a few minutes later. I waved to the men in blue and they waved back accidentally. When I got home it was still too hot to sleep so I picked up a week-old newspaper from the floor and read.

There was another civil war, another terrorist bomb exploded, and one more plane crashed and all aboard were presumed dead. The crime rate was rising in every city with populations larger than 100,000, and a farmer in Iowa shot his banker after foreclosure on his 1,000 acres.

A kid from Spokane won the local spelling bee by spelling the word *rhinoceros.*

When I got back to the reservation, my family wasn't surprised to see me. They'd been expecting me back since the day I left for Seattle. There's an old Indian poet who said that Indians can reside in the city, but they can never live there. That's as close to truth as any of us can get.

Mostly I watched television. For weeks I flipped through channels, searched for answers in the game shows and soap operas. My mother would circle the want ads in red and hand the paper to me.

"What are you going to do with the rest of your life?" she asked.

"Don't know," I said, and normally, for almost any other Indian in the country, that would have been a perfectly fine answer. But I was special, a former college student, a smart kid. I was one of those Indians who was supposed to make it, to rise above the rest of the reservation like a fucking eagle or something. I was the new kind of warrior.

9

SHERMAN **ALEXIE**

For a few months I didn't even look at the want ads my mother circled, just left the newspaper where she had set it down. After a while, though, I got tried of television and started to play basketball again. I'd been a good player in high school, nearly great, and almost played at the college I attended for a couple years. But I'd been too out of shape from drinking and sadness to ever be good again. Still, I liked the way the ball felt in my hands and the way my feet felt inside my shoes.

At first I just shot baskets by myself. It was selfish, and I also wanted to learn the game again before I played against anybody else. Since I had been good before and embarrassed fellow tribal members, I knew they would want to take revenge on me. Forget about the cowboys versus Indians business. The most intense competition on any reservation is Indians versus Indians.

But on the night I was ready to play for real, there was this white guy at the gym, playing with all the Indians.

"Who is that?" I asked Jimmy Seyler.

"He's the new BIA chief's kid."

"Can he play?"

"Oh, yeah."

And he could play. He played Indian ball, fast and loose, better than all the Indians there.

"How long's be been playing here?" I asked.

"Long enough."

I stretched my muscles, and everybody watched me. All these Indians watched one of their old and dusty heroes. Even though I had played most of my ball at the white high school I went to, I was still all Indian, you know? I was Indian when it counted, and this BIA kid needed to be beaten by an Indian, any Indian.

I jumped into the game and played well for a little while. It felt good. I hit a few shots, grabbed a rebound or two, played enough defense to keep the other team honest. Then that white kid took over the game. He was too good. Later, he'd play college ball back East and would nearly make the Knicks team a couple years on. But we didn't know any of that would happen. We just knew he was better that day and every other day.

The next morning I woke up tired and hungry, so I grabbed the want ads, found a job I wanted, and drove to Spokane to get it. I've been working at the high school exchange program ever since, typing and answering phones. Sometimes I wonder if the people on the other end of the line know that I'm Indian and if their voices would change if they did know.

One day I picked up the phone and it was her, calling from Seattle.

"I got your number from your mom," she said. "I'm glad you're working."

"Yeah, nothing like a regular paycheck."

"Are you drinking?"

"No, I've been on the wagon for almost a year."

"Good."

The connection was good. I could hear her breathing in the spaces between our words. How do you talk to the real person whose ghost has haunted you? How do you tell the difference between the two?

"Listen," I said. "I'm sorry for everything."

"Me, too."

"What's going to happen to us?" I asked her and wished I had the answer for myself.

"I don't know," she said. "I want to change the world."

These days, living alone in Spokane, I wish I lived closer to the river, to the falls where ghosts of salmon jump. I wish I could sleep. I put down my paper or book and turn off all the lights, lie quietly in the dark. It may take hours, even years, for me to sleep again. There's nothing surprising or disappointing in that.

I know how all my dreams end anyway.

11

PAULA GUNN | ALLEN

Paula Gunn Allen's heritage is a mixture of various ethnicities and nationalities, but at her heart she is Native American. Branches of her family tree come from the Laguna Pueblo and Sioux cultures, and it is this American Indian past that informs and directs her work. In a 1989 telephone interview with Robin Pogrebin for the New York Times Book Review, *Allen characterizes Native Americans as "something other than victims—mostly what we are is unrecognized." To help remedy this situation, Allen compiled* The Sacred Hoop: Recovering the Feminine in American Indian Traditions, *a collection of 17 essays covering topics that range from the status of lesbians in Native American cultures to literature's roots in the soil of tradition and ritual.*

Essay by

ANNETTE VAN DYKE

In 1989 Allen edited *Spider Woman's Granddaughters: Traditional Tales and Contemporary Writing by Native American Women,* giving space not only to contemporary authors such as Vickie L. Sears but also to legends of old deities such as the Pueblos' mother goddess of corn. She also includes the words of Pretty Shield, a Crow Indian who told her life story to ethnographer Frank B. Linderman early in the twentieth century.

Allen's only novel, 1983's *The Woman Who Owned the Shadows,* received a generally favorable review from Alice Hoffman in the *New York Times Book Review.* "In those sections where the author forsakes the artifice of her style," declares the critic, "an absorbing, often fascinating world is created." The novel's heroine, Ephanie, is emotionally wounded

1 3

Laguna Pueblo/Sioux novelist, poet, and professor.

Born: 1939, in Cubero, New Mexico.

Education: Received B.A., M.F.A., and Ph.D.

Career: Writer; former lecturer at San Francisco State University, University of New Mexico, and

Fort Lewis College. *Memberships:* registered member of the Laguna Pueblo tribe.

Address: c/o University of California, Berkeley, Berkeley, CA 94720.

Agent: Diane Cleave.

as a young girl and struggles to mend her fractured core "guided," according to Hoffman, "by the traditional tales of spirit women."

Allen has also gained recognition as a poet. Her first published collection of poems, *The Blind Lion*, appeared in 1974. Her most recent, *Skin and Bones*, was published in 1988.

THE SACRED HOOP: A CONTEMPORARY PERSPECTIVE

From *The Sacred Hoop: Recovering the Feminine in American Indian Traditions*, Beacon Press, copyright © 1986 by Paula Gunn Allen

Literature is one facet of a culture. The significance of a literature can be best understood in terms of the culture from which it springs, and the purpose of literature is clear only when the reader understands and accepts the assumptions on which the literature is based. A person who was raised in a given culture has no problem seeing the relevance, the level of complexity, or the symbolic significance of that culture's literature. We are all from early childhood familiar with the assumptions that underlie our own culture and its literature and art. Intelligent analysis becomes a matter of identifying smaller assumptions peculiar to the locale, idiom, and psyche of the writer.

The study of non-Western literature poses a problem for Western readers, who naturally tend to see alien literature in terms that are familiar to them, however irrelevant those terms may be to the literature under consideration. Because of this, students of traditional American Indian literatures have applied the terms "primitive," "savage," "childlike," and "pagan" to these literatures. Perceiving only the most superficial aspects of American Indian literary traditions, Western scholars have labeled the whole body of these literatures "folklore," even though the term specifically applies only to those parts of the literatures that are the province of the general populace.

I 4

The great mythic and ceremonial cycles of the American Indian peoples are neither primitive, in any meaningful sense of the word, nor necessarily the province of the folk; much of the literature, in fact, is known only to educated, specialized persons who are privy to the philosophical, mystical, and literary wealth of their own tribe.

Much of the literature that was in the keeping of such persons, engraved perfectly and completely in their memories, was not known to most other men and women. Because of this, much literature has been lost as the last initiates of particular tribes and societies within the tribes died, leaving no successors.

Most important, traditional American Indian literature is not similar to western literature because the basic assumptions about the universe and, therefore, the basic reality experienced by tribal peoples and by Western peoples are not the same, even at the level of folklore. This difference has confused non-Indian students for centuries. They have been unable or unwilling to accept this difference and to develop critical procedures to illuminate the materials without trivializing or otherwise invalidating them.

For example, American Indian and Western literary traditions differ greatly in the assumed purposes they serve. The purpose of traditional American Indian literature is never simply pure self-expression. The "private soul at any public wall" is a concept alien to American Indian thought. The tribes do not celebrate the individual's ability to feel emotion, for they assume that all people are able to do so. One's emotions are one's own; to suggest that others should imitate them is to impose on the personal integrity of others. The tribes seek—through song, ceremony, legend, sacred stories (myths), and tales—to embody, articulate, and share reality, to bring the isolated, private self into harmony and balance with this reality, to verbalize the sense of the majesty and reverent mystery of all things, and to actualize, in language, those truths that give to humanity its greatest significance and dignity. To a large extent, ceremonial literature serves to redirect private emotion and integrate the energy generated by emotion within a cosmic framework. The artistry of the tribes is married to the essence of language itself, for through language one can share one's singular being with that of the community and know within oneself the communal knowledge of the tribe. In this art, the greater self and all-that-is are blended into a balanced whole, and in this way the concept of being that is the fundamental and sacred spring of life is

My poetry has a haunted sense to it and it has a sorrow and a grievingness in it that comes directly from being split, not in two but in twenty, and never being able to reconcile all the places that I am.

—**Paula Gunn Allen, in** *Survival This Way: Interviews with American Indian Poets,* **by Joseph Bruchac, 1987.**

I 5

PAULA GUNN **ALLEN**

given voice and being for all. American Indian people do not content themselves with simple preachments of this truth, but through the sacred power of utterance they seek to shape and mold, to direct and determine, the forces that surround and govern human life and the related lives of all things.

An old Keres song says:

I add my breath to your breath
That our days may be long on the Earth
That the days of our people may be long
That we may be one person
That we may finish our roads together
May our mother bless you with life
May our Life Paths be fulfilled.

In this way one learns how to view oneself and one's tradition so as to approach both rightly. Breath is life, and the intermingling of breaths is the purpose of good living. This is in essence the great principle on which all productive living must rest, for relationships among all the beings of the universe must be fulfilled; in this way each individual life may also be fulfilled.

This idea is apparent in the Plains tribes' idea of a medicine wheel or sacred hoop. The concept is one of singular unity that is dynamic and encompassing, including all that is contained in its most essential aspect, that of life. In his introduction to Geronimo's autobiography, Frederick Turner III incorrectly characterizes the American Indian cultures as static. Stasis is not characteristic of the American Indians' view of things. As any American Indian knows, all of life is living—that is, dynamic and aware, partaking as it does in the life of the All Spirit and contributing as it does to the continuing life of that same Great Mystery. The tribal systems are static in that all movement is related to all other movement—that is, harmonious and balanced or unified; they are not static in the sense that they do not allow or accept change. Even a cursory examination of tribal systems will show that all have undergone massive changes while retaining those characteristics of outlook and experience that are the bedrock of tribal life. So the primary assumptions tribespeople make can be seen as static only in that these people acknowledge the essential harmony of all things and see all things as being of equal value in the scheme of things, denying the opposition, dualism, and isolation (separateness) that characterize non-Indian thought. Christians believe that God is separate from humanity and does as he wishes without the creative assistance of any of his creatures, while the non-Christian tribal person assumes a place in creation that is dynamic, creative, and responsive. Further, tribal people allow all animals, vegetables, and minerals (the entire biota, in short) the same or even greater privileges than humans. The Indian participates in destiny on all levels, including that of creation. Thus this passage from a Cheyenne tale in which Maheo, the All Spirit, cre-

Novels
The Woman Who Owned the Shadows, San Francisco, Spinsters/Aunt Lute Books, 1983.

Poetry
The Blind Lion, California, Thorp Springs Press, 1974.
Coyote's Daylight Trip, New Mexico, La Confluencia, 1978.
A Cannon Between My Knees, Strawberry Hill Press, 1981.
Star Child, Marvin, South Dakota, Blue Cloud Quarterly, 1981.
Shadow Country, University of California Indian Studies Center, 1982.
Wyrds, Taurean Horn, 1987.

Skin and Bones, New Mexico, West End Press, 1988.

Editor
From the Center: A Folio; Native American Art and Poetry, Strawberry Hill Press, 1981. *Studies in American Indian Literature: Critical Essays and Course Design,* Modern Language Association, 1983.
Spider Woman's Granddaughters: Traditional Tales and Contemporary Writing by Native American Women, Fawcett, 1990.
The Voice of the Turtle: American Indian Literature 1900–1970, Ballantine Press, 1994.

Other
Sipapu: A Cultural Perspective, New Mexico, University of New Mexico Press, 1975.
The Sacred Hoop: Recovering the Feminine in American Indian Traditions, Beacon Press, 1986.
Grandmothers of the Light: A Medicine Woman's Sourcebook, Beacon Press, 1991.
Indian Perspectives, Southwest Parks and Monuments Association, 1992.

---

ates out of the void four things—the water, the light, the sky-air, and the peoples of the water:

> "How beautiful their wings are in the light," Maheo said to his Power, as the birds wheeled and turned, and became living patterns against the sky.
>
> The loon was the first to drop back to the surface of the lake. "Maheo," he said, looking around, for he knew that Maheo was all about him, "You have made us sky and light to fly in, and you have made us water to swim in. It sounds ungrateful to want something else, yet still we do. When we are tired of swimming and tired of flying, we should like a dry solid place where we could walk and rest. Give us a place to build our nests, please, Maheo."
>
> "So be it," answered Maheo, "but to make such a place I must have your help, all of you. By myself, I have made four things . . . Now I must have help if I am to create more, for my Power will only let me make four things by myself."

In this passage we see that even the All Spirit, whose "being was a Universe," has limited power as well as a sense of proportion and respect for the powers of the creatures. Contrast this spirit with the Judeo-Christian God, who makes everything and tells everything how it may and may not function if it is to gain his respect and blessing and whose commandments make no allowance for change or circumstance. The American Indian universe is based on dynamic self-esteem, while the Christian universe is based primarily on a sense of separation and loss. For the American Indian, the

1 7

PAULA   GUNN   **ALLEN**

ability of all creatures to share in the process of ongoing creation makes all things sacred.

In Paradise, God created a perfect environment for his creatures. He arranged it to their benefit, asking only that they forbear from eating the fruit of one particular tree. In essence, they were left with only one means of exercising their creative capacities and their ability to make their own decisions and choices. Essentially, they were thus prevented from exercising their intelligence while remaining loyal to the creator. To act in a way that was congruent with their natural curiosity and love of exploration and discovery, they were forced to disobey God and thus be exiled from the perfect place he had made for them. They were severely punished for exercising what we might call liberty—Eve more than Adam, for hers was the greater sin (or so the story goes):

> And the Lord God commanded the man, saying, Of every tree of the garden thou mayest freely eat:

> But of the tree of the knowledge of good and evil, thou shalt not eat: for in the day that thou eatest thereof thou shalt surely die. (Gen. 2:16–17)

The Cheyennes' creator is somewhat wiser. He gives his creatures needs so that they can exert their intelligence and knowledge to satisfy those needs by working together to solve common problems or attain common goals. Together Maheo, the creator, and the water beings create the earth, and with the aid of these beings, Maheo creates first man and first woman and the creatures and environment they will need to live good and satisfying lives. These creation stories demonstrate the basic ordering principles of two different cultures. The Judeo-Christian view is hierarchical. God commands first; within the limits of those commands, man rules; woman is subject to man, as are all the creatures, for God has brought them to Adam for him to name (Gen. 2:18–24, 3:16). In this scheme, the one who is higher has the power to impose penalties or even to deny life to those who are lower:

> And the Lord God said, Behold, the man is become as one of us, to know good and evil; and now, lest he put forth his hand, and take also of the tree of life, and eat, and live for ever;

> Therefore, the Lord God sent him forth from the garden of Eden to till the ground from whence he was taken. (Gen. 3:22–23)

The sin Adam and Eve committed in the Garden of Eden was attempting to become knowledgeable. Their attempt opened the further possibility that, with knowledge, they might become immortal. This, apparently, was not acceptable, not because knowledge and immorality were sinful but because the possession of them by human beings would reorder the hierarchical principles on which the Judeo-Christian universe is posited. Those reared in a Christian society are inclined to perceive social relationships—

18

and literary works—in this context; they order events and phenomena in hierarchical and dualistic terms. Those reared in traditional American Indian societies are inclined to relate events and experiences to one another. They do not organize perceptions or external events in terms of dualities or priorities. This egalitarianism is reflected in the structure of American Indian literature, which does not rely on conflict, crisis, and resolution for organization, nor does its merit depend on the parentage, education, or connections of the author. Rather, its significance is determined by its relation to creative empowerment, its reflection of tribal understandings, and its relation to the unitary nature of reality.

The way the loon prays in the Cheyenne creation story is indicative of that difference. The loon looks around him as he addresses Maheo, "for he knew that Maheo was all about him," just as earlier in the story the snowgoose addressed Maheo in these words: "I do not know where you are, but I know you must be everywhere."

Another difference between

Much of Allen's work is a search for meaning, an attempt to understand natural harmony and to place the individual in that fusion of person, land, and spirit [that I call "mythic space"]. Each moment is placed on a web of history, natural harmony and traditional understanding. Through this perceptive act, the moment is given significance. . . . Allen's stance is a highly meditative one wherein she forges connections between mundane and mythic space. Making these connections is frequently referred to as "going home," for we see the physical journey often combined with the mythic journey and the personal search.

—Jim Ruppert, *"Paula Gunn Allen and Joy Harjo: Closing the Distance between Personal and Mythic Space,"* in **American Indian Quarterly,** Spring 1983.

these two ways of perceiving reality lies in the tendency of the American Indian to view space as spherical and time as cyclical, whereas the non-Indian tends to view space as linear and time as sequential. The circular concept requires all "points" that make up the sphere of being to have a significant identity and function, while the linear model assumes that some "points" are more significant than others. In the one, significance is a necessary factor of being in itself, whereas in the other, significance is a function of placement on an absolute scale that is fixed in time and space. In essence, what we have is a direct contradiction of Turner's notion about the American Indian universe versus that of the West: the Indian universe moves and breathes continuously, and the Western universe is fixed and static. The

Christian attitude toward salvation reflects this basic stance: one can be "saved" only if one believes in a Savior who appeared once and will not come again until "the end of time." The idea "once a saint, always a saint" is another expression of the same underlying perception and experience.

The notion that nature is somewhere over there while humanity is over here or that a great hierarchical ladder of being exists on which ground and trees occupy a very low rung, animals a slightly higher one, and man (never woman)—especially "civilized" man—a very high one indeed is antithetical to tribal thought. The American Indian sees all creatures as relatives (and in tribal systems relationship is central), as offspring of the Great Mystery, as cocreators, as children of our mother, and as necessary parts of an ordered, balanced, and living whole. This concept applies to what non-Indian Americans think of as the supernatural, and it applies as well to the more tangible (phenomenal) aspects of the universe. American Indian thought makes no such dualistic division, nor does it draw a hard and fast line between what is material and what is spiritual, for it regards the two as different expressions of the same reality, as though life has twin manifestations that are mutually interchangeable and, in many instances, virtually identical aspects of a reality that is essentially more spirit than matter or, more correctly, that manifests its spirit in a tangible way. The closest analogy in Western thought is the Einsteinian understanding of matter as a special state or condition of energy. Yet even this concept falls short of the American Indian understanding, for Einsteinian energy is believed to be unintelligent, while energy according to the Indian view is intelligence manifested in yet another way.

Many non-Indians believe that human beings possess the only intelligence in phenomenal existence (often in any form of existence). The more abstractionist and less intellectually vain Indian sees human intelligence as rising out of the very nature of being, which is of necessity intelligent in and of itself, as an attribute of being. Again, this idea probably stems from the Indian concept of a circular, dynamic universe in which all things are related and are of one family. It follows that those attributes possessed by human beings are natural attributes of *all* being. The Indian does not regard awareness of being as an abnormality peculiar to one species, but, because of a sense of relatedness to (instead of isolation from) what exists, the Indian assumes that this awareness is a natural by-product of existence itself.

In English, one can divide the universe into two parts: the natural and the supernatural. Humanity has no real part in either, being neither animal nor spirit—that is, the supernatural is discussed as though it were apart from people, and the natural as though people were apart from it. This necessarily forces English-speaking people into a position of alienation from the world they live in. Such isolation is entirely foreign to American Indian thought. At base, every story, every song, every ceremony tells the Indian that each creature is part of a living whole and that all parts of that whole are related to one another by virtue of their participation in the whole of being.

In American Indian thought, God is known as the All Spirit, and other beings are also spirit—more spirit than body, more spirit than intellect, more spirit than mind. The natural state of existence is whole. Thus healing chants and ceremonies emphasize restoration of wholeness, for disease is a condition of division and separation from the harmony of the whole. Beauty is wholeness. Health is wholeness. Goodness is wholeness. The Hopi refer to a witch—a person who uses the powers of the universe in a perverse or inharmonious way—as a two-hearts, one who is not whole but is split in two at the center of being. The circle of being is not physical, but it is dynamic and alive. It is what lives and moves and knows, and all the life forms we recognize—animals, plants, rocks, winds—partake of this greater life. Acknowledgement of this dynamic unity allows healing chants such as this from the Night Chant to heal (make a person whole again):

Happily I recover.
Happily my interior becomes cool.
Happily I go forth.
My interior feeling cool, may I walk.
No longer sore, may I walk.
As it used to be long ago, may I walk.
Happily, with abundant dark clouds, may I walk.
Happily, with abundant showers, may I walk.
Happily, with abundant plants, may I walk.
Happily, on a trail of pollen, may I walk.
Happily, may I walk.

Because of the basic assumption of the wholeness or unity of the universe, our natural and necessary relationship to all life is evident; all phenomena we witness within or "outside" ourselves are, like us, intelligent manifestations of the intelligent universe from which they arise, as do all things of earth and the cosmos beyond. Thunder and rain are specialized aspects of this universe, as is the human race. Consequently, the unity of the whole is preserved and reflected in language, literature, and thought, and arbitrary divisions of the universe into "divine" and "worldly" or "natural" and "unnatural" beings do not occur.

Literature takes on more meaning when considered in terms of some relevant whole (like life itself), so let us consider some relationships between specific American Indian literary forms and the symbols usually found in them. The two forms basic to American Indian literature are the ceremony and the myth. The ceremony is the ritual enactment of a specialized perception of a cosmic relationship, while the myth is a prose record of that relationship. Thus, the wiwanyag wachipi (sun dance) is the ritual enactment of the relationship the Plains people see between consecration of the human spirit and Wakan Tanka as manifested as Sun, or Light, and Life-Bestower. Through purification, participation, sacrifice, and supplication, the participants act as instruments or transmitters of increased power and wholeness, which bestows health and prosperity, from Wakan Tanka.

The formal structure of a ceremony is as holistic as the universe it purports to reflect and respond to, for the ceremony contains other forms such as incantation, song (dance), and prayer, and it is itself the central mode of literary expression from which all allied songs and stories derive. The Lakota view all the ceremonies as related to one another in various explicit and implicit ways, as though each were one face of a multifaceted prism. This interlocking of the basic forms has led to much confusion among non-Indian collectors and commentators, and this complexity makes all simplistic treatments of American Indian literature more confusing than helpful. Indeed, the non-Indian tendency to separate things from one another—be they literary forms, species, or persons—causes a great deal of unnecessary difficulty with and misinterpretation of American Indian life and culture. It is reasonable, from an Indian point of view, that all literary forms should be interrelated, given the basic idea of the unity and relatedness of all the phenomena of life. Separation of parts into this or that category is not agreeable to American Indians, and the attempt to separate essentially unified phenomena results in distortion.

For example, to say that a ceremony contains songs and prayers is misleading, for prayers are one form of address and songs are another. It is more appropriate to say that songs, prayers, dances, drums, ritual movements, and dramatic address are compositional elements of a ceremony. It is equally misleading to single out the wiwanyag wachipi and treat is as an isolated ceremony, for it must of necessity include the inipi (rite of purification) and did at one time contain the hanblecheyapi (vision quest), which was how the Lakota learned about it in the first place. Actually, it might best be seen as a communal vision quest.

The purpose of a ceremony is to integrate: to fuse the individual with his or her fellows, the community of people with that of the other kingdoms, and this larger communal group with the worlds beyond this one. A raising or expansion of individual consciousness naturally accompanies this process. The person sheds the isolated, individual personality and is restored to conscious harmony with the universe. In addition to this general purpose, each ceremony has its own specific purpose. This purpose usually varies from tribe to tribe and may be culture-specific. For example, the rain dances of the Southwest are peculiar to certain groups, such as the Pueblos, and are not found among some others tribes, while war ceremonies, which make up a large part of certain Plains tribes' ceremonial life, are unknown among many tribes in California. But all ceremonies, whether for war or healing, create and support the sense of community that is the bedrock of tribal life. This community is not made up only of members of the tribe but necessarily includes all beings that inhabit the tribe's universe.

Within this context the dynamic characteristics of American Indian literature can best be understood. The structures that embody expressed and implied relationships between human and nonhuman beings, as well as the symbols that signify and articulate them, are designed to integrate the various orders of consciousness. Entities other than the human participants are present at ceremonial enactments, and the ceremony is composed for their participation as well as for that of the human beings who are there. Some tribes understand that the human participants include members of the tribe who are not physically present and that the community as a community, not simply the separate persons in attendance, enact the ceremony.

Thus devices such as repetition and lengthy passages of "meaningless" syllables take on significance within the context of the dance. Repetition has an entrancing effect. Its regular recurrence creates a state of consciousness best described as "oceanic," but without the hypersentimental side effects implied by that term. It is hypnotic, and a hypnotic state of consciousness is the aim of the ceremony. The participants' attention must become diffused. The distractions of ordinary life must be put to rest and emotions redirected and integrated into a ceremonial context so that the greater awareness can come into full consciousness and functioning. In this way the participants become literally one with the universe, for they lose consciousness of mere individuality and share the consciousness that characterizes most orders of being.

In some sense repetition operates like the chorus in Western drama, serving to reinforce the theme and to focus the participants' attention on central concerns while intensifying their involvement with the enactment. One suits one's words and movements (if one is a dancer) to the repetitive pattern. Soon breath, heartbeat, thought, emotion, and word are one. The repetition integrates or fuses, allowing thought and word to coalesce into one rhythmic whole, which is not as jarring to the ear as rhyme.

Margot Astrov suggests that this characteristic device stems from two sources, one psychic and one magical:

> . . . this drive that forces man to express himself in rhythmic patterns has its ultimate source in psychic needs, for example the need of spiritual ingestion and proper organization of all the multiform perceptions and impressions rushing forever upon the individual from without and within . . . Furthermore, repetition, verbal and otherwise, means accumulation of power.

23

Astrov finds evidence that the first, the need to organize perception, predominates in the ceremonies of some tribes, such as the Apaches, and that the second, a "magically creative quality," is more characteristic of others, such as the Navajo. In other words, some tribes appear to stress form while others stress content, but either way a tribe will make its selection in terms of which emphasis is most likely to bring about fusion with the cosmic

PAULA   GUNN   **ALLEN**

whole in its group and environment. This fusion depends on the emphasis that is most congenial to the aesthetic and psychic sense of the tribe.

One should remember, when considering rhythmic aspects of American Indian poetic forms, that all ceremony is chanted, drummed, and danced. American Indians often refer to a piece of music as a dance instead of a song because song without dance is very rare, as is song without the use of a drum or other percussion instrument. One must also note that the drum does not "accompany" the song, for that implies separation between instrument and voice where no separation is recognized. Words, structure, music, movement, and drum combine to form an integral whole, and accompaniment per se is foreign to the ceremony, though it is common in Western music. The ceremony may be enacted before people who are neither singing nor dancing, but their participation is nevertheless assumed. Participation is a matter of attention and attunement, not of activity.

Repetition is of two kinds, incremental and simple. In the first, variations will occur. A stanza may be repeated in its entirety four times—once for each of the directions—or six times—once for each lateral direction plus above and below—or seven times—once for each direction plus the center "where we stand." Alternatively, the repetition may be of a phrase only, as in the Yei be chi, or of a phrase repeated four times with one word—the ceremonial name for each of four mountains, say, or the names of significant colors, animals, or powers—inserted in the appropriate place at each repetition, as in this Navajo Mountain Chant:

> Seated at home behold me,
> Seated amid the rainbow;
> Seated at home behold me,
> Lo, here, the Holy Place!
>   Yea, seated at home behold me.
> At Sisnajinni, and beyond it,
>   Yea, seated at home behold me;
> The Chief of Mountains, and beyond it,
>   Yea, seated at home behold me;
> In Life Unending, and beyond it,
>   Yea, seated at home behold me;
> In Joy Unchanging, and beyond it,
>   Yea, seated at home behold me.
>
> Seated at home behold me,
> Seated amid the rainbow;
> Seated at home behold me,
> Lo, here, the Holy Place!
>   Yea, seated at home behold me.
> At Tsodschl, and beyond it,
>   Yea, seated at home behold me;

The Chief of Mountains, and beyond it,
    Yea, seated at home behold me;
In Life Unending, and beyond it,
    Yea, seated at home behold me;
In Joy Unchanging, and beyond it,
    Yea, seated at home behold me.

Seated at home behold me,
Seated amid the rainbow;
Seated at home behold me,
Lo, here, the Holy Place!
    Yea, seated at home behold me.
At Doko-oslid, and beyond it,
    Yea, seated at home behold me;
The Chief of Mountains, and beyond it,
    Yea, seated at home behold me;
In Life Unending, and beyond it,
    Yea, seated at home behold me;
In Joy Unchanging, and beyond it,
    Yea, seated at home behold me.

Seated at home behold me,
Seated amid the rainbow;
Seated at home behold me,
Lo, here, the Holy Place!
    Yea, seated at home behold me.
At Depenitsa, and beyond it,
    Yea, seated at home behold me;
The Chief of Mountains, and beyond it,
    Yea, seated at home behold me;
In Life Unending, and beyond it,
    Yea, seated at home behold me;
In Joy Unchanging, and beyond it,
    Yea, seated at home behold me.

Some critics have said that this device results from the oral nature of American Indian literature, that repetition ensures attention and makes the works easy to remember. If this is a factor at all, however, it is a peripheral one, for nonliterate people have more finely developed memories than do literate people. The child learns early to remember complicated instructions, long stories—often verbatim—multitudes of details about plants, animals, kinship and other social relationships, privileges, and responsibilities, all "by heart." For a person who can't run to a bookshelf or a notebook to look up either vital or trivial information, reliance on memory becomes very important in everyday life. This highly developed everyday memory is not

PAULA   GUNN   **ALLEN**

likely to fail on ceremonial occasions, so the use of repetition for ease of memorization is not significant.

Astrov, in her discussion of the "psychic" basis of the device, touches on another reason folklorists give for the widespread use of repetition in oral ceremonial literature:

> A child repeats a statement over and over for two reasons. First, in order to make himself familiar with something that appears to him to be threateningly unknown and thus to organize it into his system of familiar phenomena; and, second, to get something be wants badly.

Astrov implies that repetition is childish on two counts: that it (rather than rational thought) familiarizes and defuses threat and that the person, irrationally, believes that oral repetition of a desire will ensure its gratification. Let us ignore the obvious fact that shamans, dancers, and other adult participants in the ceremony are not children and concentrate on actual ceremonies to see whether they contain factors that are or might appear "threatening" to the tribe or whether they simply repeat wishes over and over. Nothing in the passages quoted so far could be construed as threatening, unless beauty, harmony, health, strength, rain, breath, life unending, or sacred mountains can be so seen. Nor are any threatening unknowns mentioned in the songs and chants Astrov includes in her collection; there are threats implicit in death or great powers, but while these constitute unknowns to many civilized people, they are familiar to the tribes. And, by Astrov's own admission, the works approach death or severe illness in positive ways, as in this death song:

> From the middle
> Of the great water
> I am called by the spirits.

"Light as the last breath of the dying," she comments, "these words flutter out and seem to mingle with the soft fumes and mists that rise from the river in the morning"—hardly a threatening description. She continues:

> It is as though the song, with the lightness of a bird's feather, will carry the departing soul up to where the stars are glittering and yonder where the rainbow touches the dome of the sky.

Nowhere in her discussion of Indian songs does Astrov indicate that the singers feel threatened by the chants. Instead, she points out that they express serenity and even joy in the face of what might seem frightening to a child. Nor do there appear any passages, in her extensive collection, that are the equivalent of "Lord, Won't You Buy Me a Color TV," and the absence of such material weakens the childhood-magic theory of repetition. In fact, the usual American Indian perception of humanity (collectively, not individually) as cocreator discourages the people from perceiving the deity as a sort of cosmic bellhop who alone is responsible for their personal well-being. This perception simultaneously discourages people from setting themselves up as potentates, tyrants, dictators, or leaders of any other kind.

The failure of folklorists to comprehend the true metaphysical and psychic nature of structural devices such as ceremonial repetition is a result of the projection of one set of cultural assumptions onto another culture's customs and literatures. People of the Western cultures, particularly those in professions noted for their "objectivity" and intellectual commitment to Freudian tenets, are likely not to interpret psychic components of ceremonial literature in its extramundane sense but rather in its more familiar psychological sense. The twin assumptions that repetition serves to quiet childish psychological needs and to assure participants in a ceremony that they are exerting control over external phenomena—getting something they want badly—are projections. The participants do indeed believe that they can exert control over natural phenomena, but not because they have childishly repeated some syllables. Rather, they assume that all reality is internal in some sense, that the dichotomy of the isolate individual versus the "out there" only appears to exist, and that ceremonial observance can help them transcend this delusion and achieve union with the All Spirit. From a position of unity within this larger Self, the ceremony can bring about certain results, such as healing one who is ill, ensuring that natural events move in their accustomed way, or bringing prosperity to the tribe.

The westerner's bias against nonordinary states of consciousness is as unthinking as the Indian's belief in them is said to be. The westerner's bias is the result of an intellectual climate that has been carefully fostered in the west for centuries, that has reached its culmination in Freudian and Darwinian theories, and that only now is beginning to yield to the masses of data that contradict it. This cultural bias has had many unfortunate side effects, only one of which is deep misunderstanding of tribal literatures that has for so long marked the learned and popular periodicals that deal with tribal culture.

In his four-volume treatise on nonordinary reality, Carlos Castaneda has described what living in the universe as a shaman is like. Unfortunately, he does not indicate that this experience is rather more common to ordinary than to extraordinary people, that the state of consciousness created through ceremony and ritual and detailed in mythic cycles is exactly that of the "man of knowledge," or sage. He makes the whole thing sound exotic, strange, beyond the reach of most persons, yet the great body of American Indian literature suggests quite a different conclusion. This literature can best be approached as a psychic journey. Only in the context of the consciousness of the universe can it be understood.

American Indian thought is essentially mystical and psychic in nature. Its distinguishing characteristic is a kind of magicalness—not the childish sort described by Astrov but rather an enduring sense of the fluidity and malleability, or creative flux, of things. This is a reasonable attitude in its own context, derived quite logically from the central assumptions that characterize tribal thought. The tribal person perceives things not as inert but as viable and alive, and he or she knows that living things are subject to processes of growth and change as a necessary component of their aliveness. Since all that exists is alive and since all that is alive must grow and change, all existence can be manipulated under certain conditions and according to certain laws. These conditions and laws, called "ritual" or "magic" in the West, are known to American Indians variously. The Sioux refer to them as "walking in a sacred manner," the Navajo as "standing in the center of the world," and the Pomo as "having a tradition." There are as many ways of referring to this phenomenon as there are tribes.

The symbolism in American Indian ceremonial literature, then, is not symbolic in the usual sense; that is, the four mountains in the Mountain Chant do not stand for something else. They are those exact mountains perceived psychically, as it were, or mystically. The color red, as used by the Lakota, doesn't stand for sacred or earth, but it is the quality of a being, the color of it, when perceived "in a sacred manner" or from the point of view of the earth itself. That is, red is a psychic quality, not a material one, though it has a material dimension, of course. But its material aspect is not its essential one. As the great metaphysician Madame Blavatsky put it, the physical is not a principle; or, as Lame Deer the Lakota shaman suggests, the physical aspect of existence is only representative of what is real:

> The meat stands for the four-legged creatures, our animal brothers, who gave of themselves so that we should live. The stream [from the stewpot] is living breath. It was water; now it goes up to the sky, becomes a cloud again . . .

> We Sioux spend a lot of time thinking about everyday things, which in our mind are mixed up with the spiritual. We see in the world around us many symbols that teach us the meaning of life. We have a saying that the white man sees so little, he must see with only one eye. We see a lot that you no longer notice. You could notice if you wanted too, but you are usually too busy. We Indians live in a world of symbols and images where the spiritual and the commonplace are one. To you symbols are just words, spoken or written in a book. To us they are part of nature, part of ourselves, even little insects like ants and grasshoppers. We try to understand them not with the head but with the heart, and we need no more than a hint to give us the meaning.

Not only are the "symbols" statements of perceived reality rather than metaphorical or poetic statements but the formulations that are characterized by brevity and repetition are also expressions of that perception. One sees life as part of oneself; a hint as to which particular part is all that is needed to convey meaning. This accounts for the "purity" and simplicity" that apparently characterize traditional American Indian literatures. The works are simple in that they concern themselves with what is known and familiar, not in that they are childlike or unsophisticated.

In a sense, the American Indian perceives all that exists as symbolic. This outlook has given currency to the concept of the Indian as one who is close to the earth, but the closeness is actual, not a quaint result of savagism or childlike naiveté. An Indian, at the deepest level of being, assumes that the earth is alive in the same sense that human beings are alive. This aliveness is seen in nonphysical terms, in terms that are perhaps familiar to the mystic or the psychic, and this view gives rise to a metaphysical sense of reality that is an ineradicable part of Indian awareness. In brief, we can say that the sun or the earth or a tree is a symbol of an extraordinary truth.

This attitude is not anthropomorphic. No Indian would regard personal perception as the basic, or only, unit of universal consciousness. Indians believe that the basic unit of consciousness is the All Spirit, the living fact of intelligence from which all other perceptions arise and derive their power:

I live, but I will not live forever.
Mysterious moon, you only remain,
Powerful sun, you alone remain,
Wonderful earth, you remain forever.
All of us soldiers must die.

This attitude is not superstitious, though it can degenerate into superstition when the culture disintegrates. It is based very solidly on experience, and most members of the tribe share that experience to some degree. The experience is verified by hundreds and thousands of years of experience and is a result of actual perception—sight, taste, hearing, smell—as well as more indirect social and natural phenomena. In the West, if a person points to a building and says, "There is a building," and if other people looking in the direction indicated agree, and if that building can be entered, walked through, touched, then the building is said to be really there.

In the same way, traditional American Indians encounter and verify metaphysical reality. No one's experience is idiosyncratic. The singer who tells of journeying to the West and climbing under the sky speaks of a journey that many have taken in the past and will take in the future. Every traveler will describe the same sights and sounds and will enter and return in like fashion.

Generations of Western observers have noticed this peculiarity of psychic travel, and many attempt to explain it in psychoanalytic terms, referring to Jung's "collective unconscious," for example, or to Freud's notion of the projection of repressed conflict. Nevertheless, the evidence, however one interprets it, suggests that the psychic life of all humanity is the same. West-

2 9

P A U L A   G U N N   **A L L E N**

ern sophisticates presume that the experiences—sights, sounds, and beings encountered on psychic journeys—are imaginary and hallucinatory; they are equally inclined to presume that thoughts are idiosyncratic events of no real consequence. Nowhere in the literature on ceremonialism have I encountered a Western writer willing to suggest that the "spiritual and the commonplace are one." Many argue that these "hallucinations" are good, others that they are the product of diseased minds, but none suggests that one may *actually* be "seated amid the rainbow."

Symbols in American Indian systems are not symbolic in the usual sense of the word. The words articulate reality—not "psychological" or imagined reality, not emotive reality captured metaphorically in an attempt to fuse thought and feeling, but that reality where thought and feeling are one, where objective and subjective are one, where speaker and listener are one, where sound and sense are one.

The many kinds of American Indian literature can be categorized in various ways, but, given the assumptions behind the creation and performance of the literature, a useful division might be along functional lines rather than along more mechanical ones.

It might be said that the basic purpose of any culture is to maintain the ideal status quo. What creates differences among cultures and literatures is the way in which the people go about this task, and this in turn depends on, and simultaneously maintains, basic assumptions about the nature of life and humanity's place in it. The ideal status quo is generally expressed in terms of peace, prosperity, good health, and stability. Western cultures lean more and more heavily on technological and scientific methods of maintenance, while traditional cultures such as those of American Indian tribes tend toward mystical and philosophical methods. Because of this tendency, literature plays a central role in the traditional cultures that it is unable to play in technological ones. Thus, the purpose of a given work is of central importance to understanding its deeper significance.

We can divide traditional literature into two basic genres: ceremonial and popular, as opposed to the Western prose and poetry distinction. Ceremonial literature includes all literature that is accompanied by ritual actions and music and that produces mythic (metaphysical) states of consciousness and/or conditions. This literature may appear to the westerner as either prose or poetry, but its distinguishing characteristic is that it is to some degree sacred. The word *sacred,* like the words *power* and *medicine,* has a very different meaning to tribal people than to members of technological societies. It does not signify something of religious significance and therefore believed in with emotional fervor—"venerable, consecrated, or sacrosanct," as the Random House dictionary has it—but something that it is filled with an intangible but very real power or force, for good or bad. Lame Deer says in his discussion of symbolism:

Four is the number that is most wakan, most sacred. Four stands for Tatuye Tope—the four quarters of the earth. One of its chief symbols is Umane, which looks like this:

It represents the unused earth force. By this I mean that the Great Spirit pours a great unimaginable amount of force into all things—pebbles, ants, leaves, whirlwinds—whatever you will . . .

This force is symbolized by the Umane. In the old days men used to have an Umane altar made of raised earth in their tipis on certain special occasions. It was so *wakan* you couldn't touch it or even hold your hand over it.

PAULA   GUNN   **ALLEN**

Lame Deer is not saying that one was forbidden to touch the altar; he is saying that one *could not* touch it. The Umane does not represent the power; it is the power. *Sacred, power,* and *medicine* are related terms. Having power means being able to use this extra force without being harmed by it. This is a particular talent that human beings possess to greater or lesser degree, and *medicine* is a term used for the personal force through which one possesses power. Medicine is powerful in itself, but its power can be used only by certain persons, under certain conditions, and for certain purposes.

Ceremonial literature is sacred; it has power. It frequently uses language of its own: archaisms, "meaningless" words, or special words that are not used in everyday conversation. It can be divided into several subcategories, some of which appear in some tribes but not in others, and others that can be found throughout Indian America. Ceremonial literature includes songs for many occasions: healing; initiation; planting, harvesting, and other agricultural pursuits; hunting; blessing new houses, journeys, and undertakings. There are also dream-related songs; war songs; personal power songs; songs for food preparation, purification, and vision seeking. The subjects of the major ceremonial cycles include origin and creation, migration, celebration of new laws, and commemoration of legendary or mythic occurrences. Each serves to hold the society together, create harmony, restore balance, ensure prosperity and unity, and establish right relations within the social and natural world. At base the ceremonials restore the psychic unity of the people, reaffirm the terms of their existence in the universe, and validate their sense of reality, order, and propriety. The most central of these perform this function at levels that are far more intense than others, and these great ceremonies, more than any single phenomenon, distinguish one tribe from another.

Every tribe has a responsibility to the workings of the universe; today as yesterday, human beings play an intrinsic role in the ongoing creation. This role is largely determined by the place where the tribe lives, and the role changes when the tribe moves. In the Southwest, for example, the Zuñi dance Shalako every winter at the solstice so that the sun will turn in its course and move once again toward summer. Cosmic cycles such as Shalako or Wúwuchim relate to life processes on earth and, by virtue of natural relationship, within the universe. They aim toward forces far bigger than the community or the individual, though each is inescapably dependent on the other—"circles within circles," as Lame Deer says, "with no beginning and no end."

The greater and lesser symbols incorporated into the ceremonies take their meaning from the context of the ceremony—its purpose and its meaning. Attempts to understand ceremonial literature without knowledge of this purpose often have ludicrous results. The symbols cannot be understood in terms of another culture, whether it be that of Maya or of England, because

3 2

those other cultures have different imperatives and have grown on different soil, under a different sky within the nexus of different spirits, and within a different traditional context. "Owl" in one situation will have a very different significance from "owl" in another, and a given color—white or blue—will vary from place to place and from ceremony to ceremony in its significance, intensity, and power. In other words, the rules that govern traditional American Indian literatures are very different from those that govern western literature, though the enormity of the difference is, I think, a fairly recent development. Literature must, of necessity, express and articulate the deepest perceptions, relationships, and attitudes of a culture, whether it does so deliberately or accidentally. Tribal literature does this with a luminosity and clarity that are largely free of pretension, stylized "elegance," or show. Experiences that are held to be the most meaningful—from those that completely transcend ordinary experience to those that are commonplace—are celebrated in the songs and ceremonial cycles of the people.

The more commonplace experiences are celebrated in popular tales and songs, which may be humorous, soothing, pedagogical, or entertaining. In this category are lullabies, corn-grinding and ditch-digging songs, jokes, pourquoi tales, "little" stories, and stories with contemporary settings. Included here, too, are those delightful dances called '49s. All but the '49s appear in collections of Indian lore, sometimes masquerading as true myths or simple songs. This masquerade, of course, does little to clear up misunderstandings regarding American Indian literature, for frequently those "myths" that seem childlike are forms developed for children and bear only a slight resemblance to the true mythic chants from which they derive.

Between the trivial, popular forms and the ceremonial works are songs and stories such as various games; incantations and other simple forms of magic; prose cycles such as the Trickster tales recorded by Paul Radin; and some journey and food-related songs and legends.

Individual songs may be difficult to classify, though the level of symbolism they contain and the amount of prescribed ritual and associated ceremony, the number and special qualifications of the celebrants, and the physical setting and costume can help distinguish one kind from another. To classify any given song, though, one needs more than a nodding acquaintance with the locality and the tribe whose song or story is under consideration.

Another important factor to consider in classification of a song is the relative secrecy of parts or all of the ceremony, especially when tourists, cameras, or tape recorders are present. The amount of secrecy will vary to some extent from tribe to tribe, some being more open than others, but some secrecy is nearly always the rule.

Another such indicator, particularly valuable for classroom work, is the source of the song or story. Only very erudite tomes are likely to have much that is really sacred, and even those have usually been altered in some way.

PAULA   GUNN   **ALLEN**

Popular books are likely to carry mainly popular literature, with a few selections from the next more powerful category. It would be well to mention, in this connection, that the use of really sacred materials by ordinary mortals and publishers is generally forbidden. Also, these works do not make good classroom materials for a variety of reasons: they are arcane; they are usually taboo; they tend to confuse non-Indian students; they may cause resentment among Indian students; and they create questions and digressions that are usually beyond the competence of the teacher or of the academic setting. Frequently they lead to ridicule, disrespect, and belittlement; non-Indian students are not inclined by training or culture to view the sacred as that which has power beyond that of economics, history, or politics.

Underlying all their complexity, traditional American Indian literatures possess a unity and harmony of symbol, structure, and articulation that is peculiar to the American Indian world. This harmony is based on the perceived harmony of the universe and on thousands of years of refinement. This essential sense of unity among all things flows like a clear stream through the songs and stories of the peoples of the western hemisphere. This sense is embodied in the words of an old man:

> There are birds of many colors—red, blue, green, yellow—yet it is all one bird. There are horses of many colors—brown, black, yellow, white—yet it is all one horse. So cattle, so all living things—animals, flowers, trees. So men: in this land where once were only Indians are now men of every color—white, black, yellow, red—yet all one people. That this should come to pass was in the heart of the Great Mystery. It is right thus. And everywhere there shall be peace.

So Hiamove said, more than fifty years ago. It remains for scholars of American Indian literature to look at this literature from the point of view of its people. Only from this vantage can we understand fully the richness, complexity, and true meaning of a people's life; only in this way can we all learn the lessons of the past on this continent and the essential lesson of respect for all that is.

JEANNETTE ARMSTRONG

The first Native woman novelist in Canada, Armstrong was born on the Okanagan Reserve in British Columbia. A member of the Penticton band, she learned the traditions of the Okanagan people from her parents and elders and also attended local schools. During the sixties and seventies she participated to a limited extent in the American Indian Movement. Following the completion of her education in 1978—Armstrong received a Diploma of Fine Arts from Okanagan College and a Bachelor of Fine Arts from the University of Victoria—she worked as a researcher and writer at the En'owkin Center, a cultural and educational organization operated by the Okanagan Nation, and since 1985 has served as the center's director. In 1989 she helped to found the En'owkin School of International Writing. Affiliated with the University of Victoria, the En'owkin School is the first credit-giving creative writing program in Canada to be managed and operated expressly by and for Native people.

A grandniece of Mourning Dove, the first Native American woman novelist, Armstrong has stated that one of her goals in writing is to educate young people about Native culture and history. In conjunction with the Okanagan Indian Curriculum Project, Armstrong has produced two works of juvenile fiction designed for use in the school system. *Enwhisteetkwa: Walk on Water* covers one year in the life of an Okanagan girl in the mid-

I've been criticized by non-Native critics in terms of character development in [Slash]. I know that. I see the weaknesses in the novel as anyone does. . . . But, in terms of the characters and the character development of Slash as a character in the novel, in the writing process I couldn't isolate the character and keep the character in isolation from the development of the events in the community, and the whole of the people. . . . I know what I should have been doing, but I know what I couldn't do and make the story for my people. The question of his connectedness to his family, to his friends, to his people, and to the outer world always entered in, all the time!

—Jeannette Armstrong, in an interview with Hartmut Lutz, in *Contemporary Challenges: Conversations with Canadian Native Authors,* **Fifth House, 1991.**

1800s and provides a detailed account of daily and seasonal rituals and tasks; *Neekna and Chemai* likewise gives an account of traditional life from the perspective of two young girls.

Armstrong's novel *Slash* centers on the experiences of Thomas Kelasket, a young Okanagan man who becomes deeply involved in the American Indian Movement as he tries to come to terms with the racism of white society and his own identity as a Native Canadian. In his travels between the United States and Canada during the 1960s and 1970s, he comes in contact with many perspectives on Native affairs, ranging from assimilation to radical political action. While recovering from alcohol and drug addiction in a detoxification center, Thomas realizes that the key to his recovery and the future prosperity of the Native community is acceptance and understanding of the traditional ways of Native peoples. Variously identified as historical fiction, a fictional biography, and a young adult novel, *Slash* has been highly successful, though occasionally criticized for its overreliance on stream-of-consciousness narration and lack of information regarding specific historical events and figures. Critics have additionally faulted Armstrong's fiction for lacking in character development, but concur that her works succeed in documenting and exploring her people's past. Patty Lawlor has written of *Slash* that the novel "gives the readers insight into the implications of the assimilation policies practised in Canada and the United States, and it acknowledges the confusion, power struggles, and despair among the native peoples as they attempt to come to terms with the realities of the present and the likely realities of the future."

3 6

Okanagan novelist, poet, short story writer, and author and illustrator of children's books.

Born: 1948, on Okanagan Reserve, near Penticton, British Columbia, Canada.

Education: Okanagan College, Diploma of Fine Arts; University of Victoria, B.F.A.

Career: En'Owkin Cultural Center, staff member, 1978–, director, 1985–. Penticton Band, member of council. University of Victoria, co-founder and director of En'Owkin School of International Writing, 1989–.

WE ARE A PEOPLE

From *Slash*, Theytus Books, copyright © 1992 by Jeannette C. Armstrong

Late that summer we heard that some F.B.I. agents were slain in South Dakota. We learned that some AIM people being blamed were on the run. I left on the long trail again after that. Somehow it had all seemed to tie in with other things that were beginning to go wrong.

Sometime during that summer, things slowed down as people felt the impact of no funds. With no easy ways to get money on the reserves except through the funds, payments that had to be made weren't made. People's cars and other stuff were repossessed. It was hard on the people that there simply was not any funds for jobs at the offices.

People found many reasons why the funds should be reaccepted. There seemed to be a big split where there was none before in the thinking of the leaders about the rejection of funds and the mandate of the Chiefs.

Around August, most of the blockades had been abandoned, and most of the sit-ins were over. Many Bands took their funds back because of a growing number of people who had expressed concern over "those on social assistance."

Some Bands were outright in their statements that they would gladly take the share of those Bands who still refused their funds. It was a time of deep depression and a growing chaos. Everyone was suspicious of everyone else.

3 7

The leaders were busy blaming one another over everything that went wrong. Many people accused the Movement renegades of acting without direction from duly elected Chiefs and Councils.

D.I.A. had a grand time making deals with whomever would listen, wherever there was a chance to breed further division and suspicion. An interim office to service the Central District Bands was set up in Vancouver at regional Indian Affairs office.

J E A N N E T T E   **A R M S T R O N G**

Things turned sour all over the place. Nobody seemed to be feeling strong and confident like they had earlier that year. I had thought a lot of it was because of the inaction, but then I realized it had been more than that. People had wanted something to happen. At the same time, all decisions made had been against violence. People, including the press and the public, had been waiting for something violent to happen. When nothing had, it was a real letdown.

One of the main reasons had been that the Bands which had organized the most well attended demonstrations had signed an agreement with the provincial government. The agreement was not to hold any further demonstrations while negotiations over the cut-off lands were held.

Most of the Bands in the Okanagan had been involved with those negotiations, so they had to stop demonstrations. When that had happened, the other Bands which were holding out for settlement of the overall land claims question didn't get the same support for their actions. The actions stopped and there seemed to be nothing to do. A lot of young people were pretty dissatisfied and didn't understand what had happened.

With the reason for the demonstrations gone in the Okanagan, there was no reason to continue the rejection of funds stand, especially since some of the Bands had already talked with D.I.A. about taking funds back.

All kinds of internal upheaval happened with the leadership in the Union of Chiefs during that time, as well, over the whole issue surrounding the rejection of funds. It was pretty clear who had won the round by the time August rolled around. It sure wasn't the Indians.

About that time all the militant youth drifted away from the camp. Somehow they knew that they were no longer needed or even wanted by those leaders who, just months earlier, had driven them around and treated them like celebrities.

Somehow that had bugged me the most. To me it had been like using people and then discarding them when they weren't needed anymore. When tough-looking Indians with the militant image that could sing the drum songs and put the scare on the honkies had been needed it had been fine to have them around. When the confrontation was over, and the agreements had been signed that had spelled out a lot of money, then suddenly the question had been "What are those people hanging around here for? Welfare checks?" Some of those same leaders, who had taken to wearing long hair, blue jeans, army cast-off jackets and red bandanas, had cut their hair and bought three-piecers in order to "look presentable" to government negotiators.

I figured it was a good time to leave. My Mom and Pops had been doing good again since Josie had decided to leave the kids permanently with them. I felt like staying and being with little Kelly, but I felt that I didn't have anything to teach him, while there were some things I had to learn myself.

I didn't know how or where to start, so I left with a couple of guys and a girl from Alberta. They were headed there for a conference on Indian religion. It sounded pretty interesting and I decided to go. I thought maybe I would hear from some of the people from down in South Dakota, where there was that shoot-out in which two F.B.I. agents were killed.

We had been all glad to be on the road again, camping and hustling wherever we stopped. Nobody was into drinking or drugs that I travelled with and that had been good.

During that summer, there had been a growing number of those that insisted that it wasn't Indian to be doing that stuff. At the rallies and blockades those young people had stuck together and demanded that there be no drinking and no drugs at those things. They had asked they be respected for their fight against those things.

I had grown to know quite a few of them and I had a lot of respect for them. I hated it when some of the political leaders overruled those wishes and brought in booze and drugs to some of those gatherings. However, there was a strong and quiet determination by those young people that pitied and despised those leaders for them things.

I lost a lot of respect for some of them leaders during that time, and gained some for others who I felt were the real leaders but were never recognized because they spoke with actions and not words. The group I travelled with was like that.

At the conference, we were given a teepee to camp in and told there would be food served twice a day. I was surprised, there were hundreds of people there. Some were very old and some were young and obviously on the move like ourselves. Many things were new to me.

An arbor was set up where a fire was kept burning continuously by some medicine men. Sweat lodges were going on almost continuously for people to cleanse their bodies and minds. Ceremonies of all different kinds from different areas were going on at night. Most interesting were the talks during the day in the arbor.

Armstrong is a woman of strong sympathies and warm passions. Her poetry is direct, unequivocal, and assertive, even aggressive. One can always rely on her to grapple with the grim realities of the contemporary Native Canadian experience and tell the uncomfortable truths. No one has portrayed the Native dilemma more energetically or with more emotional intensity.

—Penny Petrone, "1980–1989," in her *Native Literature in Canada: From the Oral Tradition to the Present,* Oxford University Press, Canada, 1990.

J E A N N E T T E   A R M S T R O N G

Medicine men talked to the youth continuously about returning to the medicine ways of their people. It was said that it was important if they were to conquer the disease that was eating away at the foundations of our reserves. The young people were urged to continue their struggle in finding their true identity.

One old man made a lot of sense to me. It was almost as if he were speaking to me. He said, "Many of you are talking about losing out to the white man. You talk about losing your culture. I will tell you something about that. It is not the culture that is lost. It is you. The culture that belongs to us is handed down to us in the sacred medicine ways of our people. Our strength lies there because it is our medicine ways that feeds the spirit of our people so that they will be healthy. That is not lost. It is here all around us in the mountains and in the wild places. It is in the sound of the drum and the sound of the singing of the birds. We got to go back to them things to feed our spirit. We are the ones who are lost, in alcohol and drugs and in cities in the rat-race. We will soon be as extinct as the buffalo if we don't get back to them things. Our spirits will starve and the only thing to fill the empty hole inside will be alcohol, drugs or greed for money. That's what happened to our people and what is happening right now."

I listened and heard some of the same things that my Uncle Joe had tried to talk to me about some years ago. It seemed to make better sense than before.

I wanted, from that point on, to try to find out as much as I could about the things the Old Man talked about. I travelled again but with a new head space. Throughout the rest of that summer and fall, I followed a group of young people who gathered for the same reasons.

As far as politics were concerned, there was a growing depression everywhere, as agreements were reached with confrontation groups and others were battled out in courts and lost. Still others were brutally squashed with military-like violence. It was clear that the government had been busy rallying it's bureaucratic support because there was always some prominent Indian businessman, or other "white success" story, making some statements about "those few radicals" not really representing anybody.

By the time winter had come around things had degenerated to mostly internal bickering. Everybody I talked to seemed deeply disillusioned. It seemed like the worst had happened. I had hoped for a resurgence of the strong feelings of the year before.

I waited for it, thinking that a new internal strength would be a part of it. With that in mind, I went home that winter to take part in the Indian dance put on by my family, but things back there were appalling. Most of the reserves were embroiled in internal upheaval as Chiefs and Councils were challenged by younger members who were unhappy and disillusioned with the seeming lack of action through the summer.

A certain idealism had still been apparent in the peoples' actions. The attitude seemed to be that since we had control over our own affairs, we had to shape things up.

People had different ideas about how that should be done. All kinds of committees were busy meeting and making recommendations about everything under the sun. Education and a lot of new approaches to social services were on the top of the list. A lot of controversy developed over proposed development schemes. Young people were agreeing with some of the old people that it wasn't good to have developments that didn't fit with our idea of fitting people resources together with the economy. They felt that we could just compound the social problems that were there already.

People seemed to have a renewed sense of community awareness, but there was an obsessive quality to the whole thing. In that way, it seemed like a few good things had come out of the last couple of years. Not some of the things people had aimed at, of course, but some hidden things. A stronger sense of community and the vigor with which everything was attacked and criticized was good. The process was painful, however, because of the internal conflicts that arose.

It was a time of building in the community those things that could be done only by the people. Indian control was what it was about. No D.I.A. people were allowed on the reserves them times without being invited. Very few were invited no matter how hot the internal fighting got. It was a healthy sign, whether people understood what it meant or not. I sure didn't want to stick around and get involved with that stuff, however, no matter how necessary it was. I knew I couldn't handle it.

With the first signs of spring, I headed out. This time it was down into the States again. I figured that if I travelled down there I might run into what I was looking for.

When I hit Seattle, it was like something from out of my past reached out and took hold of me. I don't know how it happened.

I had gone to the AIM house to crash and visit and get caught up on the news. The guys there were many of the same people I had known from the caravan and from other places. I slipped easily into their casual talk about waiting for something to happen.

Things were pretty tense because one of the people wanted in the F.B.I. killings had moved through the area and had been arrested in Canada. A defense committee had been drawn up to try to fight his extradition back to the States.

As I listened to the stories of what had happened, I wondered how in hell the courts would handle it. There were a lot of different stories of what went down during that F.B.I. attack on those AIM people, when the killings happened there at the house on Pine Ridge. Most of the stories in the papers were so out of whack, they didn't even make sense. One thing I saw was that there had been definitely some kind of move to get as many AIM people as possible. I saw that, from the way things had been done whenever something went on.

I wondered how they were going to determine who shot who, when I heard there had been lots of guns inside and outside that had been blazing. Anyway, people there said that one guy had been set up as a scapegoat. I believed that.

I listened to the talk and felt the frustration and the weariness in the voices of the people who were organizing the defense. I felt the hatred start to stir inside of me again. It seemed to me like, all of a sudden, all of the stuff about taking things cool and non-violent just didn't work. It seemed Indians were being pushed so far down that they couldn't do anything about it. Things seemed so hopeless. The whole past year of participating in a quiet way, without a lot of violence, had just piled up the frustration more and more inside of me.

I went out and got loaded with the Bro's who were into that while we discussed everything going on. I fell flat on my face with it.

After that, I drifted around that city for a long while that way. I didn't care anymore. You don't seem to know how fast time goes, when one day and one week just meshes into one another.

I kept saying that I was going to head out next week, but I just didn't make it. The city is like that when you're drifting. It draws you to its lights and music and you lose yourself in it.

Sometimes I went up to the AIM house to get word on stuff that was happening. A lot of people had just drifted out of the scene right after the courts up there had decided the guy up in Canada held for those F.B.I. deaths was going to be extradited. He had to face new charges in the U.S.A. Everything was depressing. There didn't seem to be anything to sober up for.

Summer was deathly hot and muggy in that city. I had heard stuff about a woman who had been found earlier in the year, supposedly dead of exposure, in the States somewhere. The woman was from Canada and she had been a pretty well known activist. People said that the F.B.I. were probably responsible for their death and that her people had asked for a second autopsy. From what I heard there had been a lot of really brutal things like that which were carried out to neutralize the AIM.

Later I heard that there was a second autopsy held and that the body of that woman had been found with a bullet hole in it. Somebody said that Trudeau had promised to "look into the matter."

I also heard that a really good friend of mine up there in Canada had been found dead. He had also been a known activist. The report made, we

Enwhisteetkwa: Walk on Water (juvenile fiction), Friesen Printers, 1982.
Neekna and Chemai (juvenile fiction), Theytus Books, 1984.

Slash (novel), Theytus Books, 1985; revised edition, 1988.

Author of poems and short stories.

heard, was that he had committed suicide and had left a note demanding an investigation of the D.I.A. and the removal of the head Indian Agent in Ottawa. Trudeau had mentioned his intention to look into that matter, too.

Man, that had just blown me away! It had hit me over the head so hard that I couldn't think clear. It just hadn't made sense to me. I didn't believe it. Somehow it had hurt me, way inside, the way Mardi's disappearance had. I never went up for the burial but I saw reports of it that were broadcast and it reminded me of that famous painting called "END OF THE TRAIL." Somehow his death had given me the same feeling inside.

I had a kind of defeatist attitude about everything I felt after that. The way I heard, it was the same way almost everywhere with everybody. I could imagine what it was like back home. Same old ham and eggs, as I had heard somebody up there say. Same old conferences, same old bitch sessions, same old resolutions, same old speeches. Same old problems growing worse and worse added with a definite backlash toward all activists, even by some Indians themselves.

I knew a few groups and some people would be hanging in there with the old idealism burning. They would continue at all odds to try to set some things right and keep things moving, but things would just happen to stomp those people out or negotiate them out or buy them out.

Sometimes I picked up the Indian papers to see how right I was. I wasn't far off target at anytime. Them times, I never really cared too much about anything when I woke up and straightened up for awhile. Those intervals grew shorter and shorter. Sometimes in those intervals I called home or picked up a letter from my little sister Jenny, who thought I was some kind of hero because I knew some big name AIMers. She filled me in on the stuff going on politically at home. For one awful year and a half things were the same at home as with me. Things just kind of drifted and deteriorated.

Something about the city was just like a slow rot inside my brain. I guess what I felt was close to total defeat, almost suicidal. Like there was nothing left to try for anymore. I felt like the only chance we had going for us had slipped away like a fog. One day it was there and real and the next it was just gone.

I sank farther and farther into that shadow world of drink and drugs; a world where things can be made to vanish like magic; a world where there is little feeling and less caring.

43

J E A N N E T T E   A R M S T R O N G

Sometimes I surfaced for awhile and then I would begin to think about the total hopelessness of everything. I looked around me and saw the stink and the filth of the others around me. Many were Indians like me. I looked at the city and what it stood for. Sometimes I shook my fist at it and shouted, "Screw you, you can't suck me in. I'm free. I always will be. I'm like the buffalo, man. You'll never own me because I resist. I won't join the stink that you are. I'm a dirty, drunken Indian, probably full of lice and that's how I resist. That's the only thing that makes you look at it and see that I will not be what you are. I refuse. I'll die a dirty, drunken Indian before I become a stinking, fat hog."

Sometimes, I thought of going home and tried to get myself together. I thought of the food sometimes, when all I had eaten for days was some bologna and bread at somebody's dump. I thought of the sweet fat on smoked deer meat and thick pieces of fry bread dripping with butter. Sometimes my stomach would hurt like somebody was drilling a hole from the inside. But I couldn't think about going home seriously. I felt like a stranger whenever I thought of Mom and Pops and my people.

One time, I was sitting at this bar, drinking cheap wine, when I saw the face of a guy sitting directly in front of me. Somehow, the guy's face looked familiar but his eyes, that stared straight at me, were like those of a gorilla I had once seen at a zoo. The eyes were hard, bitter and alien, but deep behind them was a pain and a question that asked, "Why?" I had looked at the guy for a long time before I realized I was looking into a mirror.

I drank anything and everything. I scraped pennies together with the other winos to buy bay rum and shaving lotion. I ended up in the drunk tanks and detox centers and ate whenever I thought of it at the Salvation Army. I don't remember too much, but sometimes, when I woke up in jail or in the D, I got flashes of things that I had done. Sometimes I didn't remember a thing for weeks. That was frightening but somehow comforting, too. Frightening because of what I might have done and didn't know about, and comforting that I didn't have to bear those days. They were just gone, forever.

Summer, fall and winter passed like flashes across a screen. Each only meaning that I had to find a different place to hang out.

4 4

The end of that road stands out clear though. It was spring again and I was sick as a dog. I woke up down by the wharves. I had been lying there listening to the water crashing and I felt the sun, warm on my face. I looked up when I heard a friend of mine from back home say, "Here, have a drink." I sat up and reached for it. I looked around and nobody was there, but I heard laughter echo and echo in my ears. There were some driftwood piles and big boulders scattered around. All of them looked black and ugly with slime. I looked again and some guys were sitting there. They all dripped slime, oozing and grey. They were the guys that had been talking to me. There was a stench all over everything that smelled like dead bodies. The waves were oily looking and seemed to do things water doesn't do. It formed into shapes that dripped slime and oozed with green and black sludge.

Those guys sat there and kept talking to me. I couldn't hear what they said, but they laughed with gaping toothless grins at me. I started answering them in a conversational way and the next minute they were gone. I was shaking and felt hot all over like my skin was on fire. I looked down. There was slime stuck all over me, too. It seemed like it ate into my skin right down into my bones and my flesh rotted away in gobs. That's what I smelled. I jumped up and ran, screaming. The other guys ran after me, laughing and shouting and offering me a drink. Every few steps I took, my feet and legs gave way and I looked down and thought they were rotting away. I saw I was leaving big wet marks in the sand from the slime that slid down my legs. I remember falling and feeling the stuff slowly spreading over me. I fought it, but it was like quicksand sucking me farther and farther down. I screamed and screamed for what seemed like days. I really don't know how long it was. I'll never forget the pain all over my body and the horror. It was real, more real than anything I had felt for a long time.

I got over it though. I woke up in another detox and wished I had died. I looked out at the grey sky and the grey room and the grey food, and wished I had another drink.

After staying at the detox a while, I was moved to a dry-out place that catered mostly to Indians.

One time, this guy, an Ojibway from Ontario, talked with me. I knew he had been trying to get me to think about drying out for real and not just to escape the DT's like I had done before. He told me he had just come from a place where I could go to get help for what was wrong with me.

I looked at him and laughed. I said, "Joe, it ain't what's wrong with me, you know. It's what's wrong with the stinking world. I can sober up, Joe, but for what? Ninety percent of my people are dying a slow death. I can't stand to see what's happening to the ones that ain't."

He sat there and looked down at his feet, then he said real low, like he was talking to himself, "That's what they want you to think. Them ain't the only choices. There is another way. It's always been there. We just got to see it ourselves though. There are some people who help people who are looking for another way to live as an Indian person. You know we don't have to cop out and be drunks and losers. We don't have to join the rats either. There is another way. Slash, there is one place you should check out, if you do nothing else that makes sense. I don't know of any other way you are going to get out of this mess except to go for help to that kind of place. We could take you. There are another couple of guys who want to go from here. Think about it."

JEANNETTE ARMSTRONG

I did. I had really liked Joe when he came to the dry-out to visit some of the guys. He was different than some of the workers there, who had a kind of missionary attitude about their work. They were reformed alkies, you could tell. Joe wasn't jumpy and over-happy like them either. Some of that really put me off, like it was a forced act. Almost a desperate attempt to prove that being sober was just hunky-dory.

Joe was quiet and talked easily with anyone. He somehow made you feel good, just by being around him. I felt that he was deeply religious in the Indian way. He had a gentle strength and a peaceful way, that other people seemed to lack.

Once, as he prayed with his pipe for the Thanksgiving meal, he talked with real emotion about being happy to be there sharing with us. You felt his caring even though everyone there was from different parts of the country. It was real. It wasn't a put-on. I wanted to be like Joe. I wanted to feel again, to care, to love.

I decided I would find out if what he was like was connected to that place he mentioned. I had a feeling it did, from the way he talked about it.

I went to that place. I was afraid, but I was desperate. I knew for me it meant life or death.

When I got there with the other two guys, we were given the low-down. We were told that this was a camp where young people could find sanctuary from the concrete jungle. We were told that this was a place where we could learn about Indian ways so we could become strong again. I wasn't sure what that meant, but I knew my only hope was to try to stick with it.

They put us through sweats, every day for ten days. Those were the hardest ten days of my life. Those were the hardest sweats I have ever had to endure. Sometimes after the sweats, all I could do was crawl out and lay on the ground, for a long time so weak and drained I felt like a noodle. I had known that there was a lot of stuff I had to clean out of my system before I would ever be strong again. I prayed hard them times, during the sweats. I stuck close to the main man around the camp, hoping I could draw strength from him not to take off and lose myself again. I knew I couldn't make it on my own.

I stayed at that camp for six long months. During that time, I had a lot of time to think. I also had a lot of time to ask the questions I needed to ask.

There was a medicine man who came to the camp during that time. He had been travelling through to other places where he had to help people who were sick or troubled.

I had never met anyone quite like him. He never dressed up in garb that others called Indian stuff. He wasn't old, probably middle-aged. His hair was a little long and he didn't wear braids. He was a Plains Indian, and looked it.

4 6

The day he came to the camp everybody had seemed really excited. The women around the camp cooked all kinds of stuff. All the men who knew him took turns and sat talking with him. The rest of us sat back and wondered what all the commotion was about.

This man was very unassuming, but you could feel the warmth and love everybody had for him. You saw it in the eyes of the people, that this was a very special person. He was quiet and joked a little, while people talked to him about things that were happening around the country and in their personal lives.

He set up a ceremony that night for the people at the camp, to help them in the things they were there for. I went. It was a lot like that night in jail some years ago. What happened to me was the single most profound experience in my life.

Something touched me deep inside and I came out of there a new person. It was like suddenly waking up, like what those people say about being born again. All the questions that were unanswered for years, suddenly seemed so simple. I knew with my whole self that this was what being Indian was all about. From one moment to the other, I suddenly knew I would never despair again, in the way that I did before, no matter how hard things got, because I knew it wasn't a matter of belief. It was more, it was knowing for sure. I realized I would be able to make it then because there was something worthwhile to live for.

When I came out I felt so light and happy, it was a genuine high. For the first time in years, I felt warm inside. I felt like I wanted to hug everybody and shout and dance around. I felt good, so good it's hard to describe.

He talked to us for the next few days that he was there. One of the things he said sticks in my mind all the time. He said, "It's hard to be Indian. Most of you know that by now. Right now you feel good. It's always like that after a ceremony, but you have to realize in order to stay that way you have to keep to this path. It's hard to do that sometimes. Everything pulls you away from it. I don't mean you have to quit the whole society. I mean you don't have to take part in the things that destroy you. The kind of jobs you work at, for instance. The things you get involved in for Indian rights, too. The kind of recreation you get into is important. You see, there are certain things that are good for us, things we need to keep our balance. The drum and songs are important to us. We need to work with those things around us and work under the instructions handed down to our people. That way, we can live good and be a help to them others around us. That speaks louder than any grand speeches of politicians."

He continued, "The next generations, and how we survive as Indians, depends on that. It's something that can't be changed by any legislations or politicians. You young people are the real leaders, whether you know it or

47

not. It is you that will make the biggest changes for people in what you do. Remember this, nobody says it's going to be easy. The responsibility is heavy and you will be tested hard at every turn, but every test will make you stronger."

He seemed to be talking just to me. He seemed to know the things that were in my mind and the questions I had about what to do from here on. I knew then that I would stay to work with these ways a while longer, until I knew more about it. Then I would go home.

I met a lot of people during that time and talked to a lot of people in the same space as me. It was a good time, full of peace and good experiences.

When I finally felt I was strong enough to face the world without falling flat on my face again, I left. By then, I had met a large circle of people involved in the same things, from all around the country. I had met them through the camp.

I found out that there were places like that springing up all across the country. Most of them were not advertised around. A wider and wider circle of people knew about them. At these places there was sameness in the ways things were done. The use of the pipe and sweats were common to all. All kinds of ceremonies and traditional practices were revived. Some of the things were held open to people of all tribes to participate in. Survival gatherings and survival schools, working with those concepts, started up in almost every part of the country.

I went to a lot of places where really old medicine people were. I found out something very important. In every area there were those people who, for some reason, kept to the old ways regardless of what other influences had been. All I had to do was to look and I found them. They were always willing to help you in whichever way they could. It seemed to me a new world had opened up. At the same time I knew it had always been there and had never gone anywhere. I knew then what that old man at that Alberta gathering had spoken about.

I learned many things during that time, about the strength those ways gave the people. I learned about the goodness, the caring and the sharing. Most of all, I learned about me. I learned that, being an Indian, I could never be a person only to myself. I was part of all the rest of the people. I was responsible to that. Everything I did affected that. What I was affected everyone around me, both then and far into the future, through me and my descendants. They would carry whatever I left them. I was important as one person but more important as a part of everything else. That being so, I realized, I carried the weight of all my people as we each did.

I understood then that the great laws are carried and kept in each of us. And that the diseases in our society came because those great laws remained in only very few people. It was what my Pops had meant when he had said, paper laws weren't needed if what you have in your head is right. I saw then that each one of us who faltered was irreplaceable and a loss to all. In that way, I learned how important and how precious my existence was. I was necessary.

I realized then that it had been something that had been missing all my life. And that it was missing from a lot of peoples lives. I saw how people went looking for it in various ways, some good and some bad. Many filled that gap with things that made you feel good for a little while, but was a far cry from finding what I had just found.

49

It was as though a light was shining for my people. I felt that we were moving toward it faster and faster. There was a rightness about it that the past few years didn't have. Yet I realized, without the past few years, I would not have made it to this point. I knew that as a certainty. I would have ended up like Danny.

Sometimes, as I went from place to place, I wondered how things were at home. I had heard some new young Chiefs had been elected in the Okanagan and they were more moderate in their approach to things. I had heard the Union of Chiefs had reformed under a new leader. I was surprised when I learned that the man was once the head of the national organization.

I had kind of kept up with situations up there, while I made my way around the country. I hadn't been ready to head home, though. I heard that an inquiry over the pipeline up North got a lot of support for the Indians concern over the damage to the environment and their culture. I knew, too, that a bigger and bigger group of Indian people became very vocal about stuff like that. Almost everywhere, you picked up the newspapers, you read about a Tribe that was opposing this development, or that mining explorations proposal, because of concern for damage to fishing and wildlife and people's health. I knew that there was a total abhorrence for the exploration for minerals like uranium and proposed coal burning plants among our people. Much of the opposition was based on a greater concern for the health of the people that lived near those areas.

Many people who surfaced at such meetings were people who were aware of their responsibilities as Indian people. At most of the gatherings I went to there was serious discussion about the responsibility of Indian people to educate the ignorant non-Indians about our role as human beings on this earth. I felt I understood so little of what was meant. I was satisfied to listen and learn.

When I decided to head home again, it was winter time. Almost two years had passed since I left. I had been down in Oregon at a camp there. Things got kind of boring for me. I was attending the same kinds of meetings to "strengthen ourselves" and going to the same kinds of ceremonies to help us with our personal problems. I talked to one of the men there who sometimes came to visit and counsel. I told him that I thought I was ready to head home. I told him how hard it had been for me to put aside my drinking and toking, and that I was halfways afraid it might hit me in the face again if I wasn't with the circle of people that were a strong support group. I told him what had happened before and how I had lost myself even when I thought I was strong.

He looked intently at my face as I talked. When I got done he nodded and said, "Slash, you know all the things we talked about. Well, the most important of them is to know you are in control of what you do. You can ask for help anytime things go wrong. You can help yourself anytime, anywhere. Them Indian ways belong to you; to each one of us. You don't need somebody to pray for you or help you all the time. Most of the time if you live right, you can deal with everything that comes along yourself, no matter how hard it is. As long as you stick to that you'll be okay."

Softly, he continued, "There comes a point when you got to start giving help yourself instead of relying on people to lean on. You got to start to be a support for others. Go home and be what you are supposed to be. A good strong Indian that don't tear people down but builds them up. You'll do okay."

He sat quietly for a while then said, "You know, in every Indian family, it don't matter how modernized the family has become, there is always one who is a keeper of the ways. That person is drawn to Indian ways like a magnet. That person sometimes suffers the worst because of it, but inside that person knows the rightness of it. I can't explain it too good, but I have seen it to be true, no matter where in the country you go as long as there are Indians, it is true. These ones find their way eventually, to the things that they need to help them be what they are intended to be. Some of them don't even know it and spend much of their lives in frustration because things pull them in other directions. You are one of those."

"You'll be okay, though." He added, "You still got some learning to do when you get home. Just remember, don't spend your time criticizing people in their weakness, spend your time instead, getting them up in their thinking. You don't have to act like a missionary. Respecting people and being a good teacher just by your actions is enough. That talks louder than any speeches shouted at the top of the lungs. You'll be okay, you got a good mind and a big heart, and the spirit is in you."

I hitch-hiked all the way home. I got a few rides, but sometimes I walked for miles in the raw cold. I came into the valley from the south end, after having left Omak. The weather had been kinda warm and a soft snow fell. There had been no cars for a long ways. Just the quiet snow and my tracks. I looked back and I saw that my tracks stretched far away into the white, white distance. Flakes fell into my tracks and my tracks were soon gone. I looked ahead and the white snow stretched for miles ahead of me. I had felt the silence, alive around me. I stopped and stretched my arms up toward the soft white flakes that danced around me. I felt the feeling rise inside my head. Like a quiet explosion that spread ripples to all my body. I felt the singing music that the swirling snow danced to. I felt it take hold and I danced to the sound that swirled in white cascades around me, and covered the earth with a promise. A promise that the flowers would bloom again for my people. I knew I was home, really home and my land welcomed me.

51

JEANNETTE ARMSTRONG

BETH  BRANT

Essay by

LINDA CULLUM

Writer Beth E. Brant, who uses the name Degonwadonti, garnered acclaim in the 1980s for the distinctive voice presented in her fiction and poetry. Brant is of Mohawk ancestry and openly lesbian, two elements that play an important thematic role in her body of work. She was born in suburban Detroit and raised both there and in Canada; she continues to live part-time in each country. After a marriage to an abusive, alcoholic husband ended in divorce, Brant came to terms with her own sexuality at the age of thirty-three. It took her even longer to accept her vocation as a writer, which she recognized after being visited with a vision concordant with her Mohawk ancestry. Nearing the age of forty, she was on vacation, driving with her partner Denise Dorsz, when a bald eagle flew in front of the car and told Brant that she was to be a writer. When she returned home, Brant began to set her thoughts to paper.

5 3

Brant's first published volume, *Mohawk Trail,* is a collection of short stories that reflect the multifaceted nature of her life. Her Mohawk heritage is the predominant theme behind many of the works, such as the one incorporating the Coyote "trickster" tales of traditional Native American folklore; yet Brant's coyote is female. One of the works, "Her Name Is Helen," is a long narrative poem, and other pieces recall her early family life and sexual experiences as a teenager. Brant's themes also address issues faced by Native Americans living in the contemporary world, such

Since I didn't begin to write until I turned forty years of age, I look upon my writing as a marvelous gift that has changed my life. I write because I have a great commitment to the communities of which I am a member—Indian, gay and lesbian, working-class—and the larger community of Earth and Her many inhabitants. My work is charged with a political and nationalist consciousness, that of a Mohawk lesbian who believes in the power and beauty of language to heal and to open hearts and minds.

as the tale of a woman whose children are removed from her custody by a government agency.

Food and Spirits, Brant's second collection, consists of stories that address sometimes-painful issues facing contemporary Native Americans. Brant writes of abusive relationships, the AIDS epidemic, returning to ancestral lands, and entering adulthood. "These are things I've seen and experienced, people I've known, stories and history that have been with my people forever," the author told *Advocate* writer Victoria A. Brownworth. The title story involves a Native American grandfather who journeys to see his granddaughters in Detroit. He waits in a bar, learning to play video games and becoming acquainted with the largely African American clientele. Other stories move in the opposite direction—a young man dying of AIDS returns to the reservation. Brant also utilizes traditional imagery in the pieces, in one case transforming the Mohawk creation tale into a love story about two women. Like much of Brant's work, though, the tales in *Food and Spirits* attempt to enlighten readers about contemporary Native American culture and counterculture. "White people are not speaking out for justice if they don't take my writing or any other Indian writer's work and spread that word and make changes," Brant told the *Advocate*. "We become aware from our hearts easier than our minds. When human beings feel, it changes things."

54

THIS PLACE

From *Food and Spirits*, Firebrand Books, copyright © 1991 by Beth Brant

"Mother, I am gay. I have AIDS." The telephone call that it almost killed him to make.

The silence. Then, "Come home to us."

Mohawk poet, short story writer, essayist, and editor.

Born: May 6, 1941, in Melvindale, Michigan.

Partnerships: divorced.

Career: Writer; part-time teacher of creative writing and native women's writing.

Memberships: National Writers Union (United States and Canada), Turtle Clan.

Address: 18890 Reed, Melvindale, MI 48122.

David came home because he was dying. He expected to see his place of birth in a new way, as if he were a photographer capturing scenes through diverse lenses. *Scene one: through a living man's eyes. Scene two: through a dying man's eyes.* But the beauty remembered was the beauty that still existed. Nothing had changed in ten years. The water of the bay just as blue and smooth. The white pines just as tall and green. The dirt roads as brown and rutted as the day he had left. His mother as small and beautiful, her dark hair with even more grey streaks running through the braid she wrapped around her head.

Had nothing changed but him?

He had left this place and gone to the city to look for other men like himself. He found them. He found a new life, a different life. He found so much. Even the virus that now ate at him. David came home and was afraid of death.

David could feel the virus changing his body, making marks on his insides. Outside, too, his body was marked: by the tumors growing on his face and the paleness of his skin. He worried that the virus was somehow taking away his color, bleaching the melanin that turned him polished copper in the summer and left him light terra cotta in winter. He could feel the virus at war with the melanin and he could not check the battle. He couldn't hold this virus in his fist and squeeze the death out of it. He could only wait and look in the mirror to see the casualty of this war. David was afraid.

"Mother, am I turning white?"

"No, my baby son. You are dark and beautiful. Your hair is black and shiny as ever. Your eyes are tired, but still as brown and strong as the day you left this place."

He knew she lied to him. Mothers lie about their children's pain. *It will go away,* they say. *I'll make it better,* they say. *Oh, Mother, make it better, make it go away. I'm afraid of death.*

He felt the virus eating his hair. It fell out in clumps as he combed it. His forehead got broader and receded further. The blackness of the strands had dulled to some nondescript color. His braid was thin and lifeless, not as

5 5

it used to be, snapping like a whip across his back, or gliding down his back like a snake.

David's sister brought her children to see him. They crawled on his lap and kissed him. He was afraid for them. Afraid the virus would reach out of his body and grab these babies and eat at them until they, too, disappeared in its grip. The virus put a fear in him—a fear that he could wipe out his people by breathing, by talking, by living. David saw, in his dreams, the virus eating away at this place until it was gone.

His dreams were also about a place called death. Death seemed to be a gaping hole in the world where David looked and there was nothing. He would wake from these dreams sweating, his limbs filled with pain. He had lived his life so well, so hard, clutching it to him like food, swallowing and being nourished. He wanted to greet death like that, opening his arms to it, laughing and embracing that other world. But he was afraid.

"Mother, I am afraid of death."

"Joseph is coming to visit."

On a day when David was seated in his chair before the window, looking out at the way the bright sun had turned everything in the yard golden, he heard the pickup truck making its way down the dirt road to the house. He also heard a voice singing. David laughed out loud. The song being sung was "All My Exes Live in Texas," and he knew that Joseph was on his way to him.

The truck came to a screeching, convulsive stop. David's mother went out to greet the man who jumped from the truck laughing, "Where's the patient?" As David watched, Joseph extracted a brown paper bag and an orange-striped cat from the truck. "Meet my friend, the Prophet. You can call her Prophet." David's mother reached for the cat who nudged at her breast and looked into her face. Joseph kissed Grace on the cheek. Prophet licked Grace's face. David wondered at the fact that Joseph looked the same as he had when David was a child. Dressed in faded jeans and a flannel shirt, Joseph's face was lean and unlined. His nose was sharp and slightly curved at the end, like a bird's beak. His eyes were black and round, reminding David again of a bird, perhaps a kestrel or a falcon. Joseph wore long, beaded earrings that draped across the front of his shirt. His hair, black and coarse, was tied back with a leather string. His fingers were covered with silver-and-garnet-studded rings, his hands delicate but used. Joseph looked at the young man in the window and lifted his hand in a greeting. Then he smiled and his face took on the unfinished look of a child. David waved back, feeling excitement—the way he used to feel before going to a party.

"This ain't goin' to be like any party you ever went to," Joseph remarked as he stepped through the doorway. "Here, have a Prophet," and he lifted the orange cat from Grace's arms onto David's lap.

5 6

Works

Mohawk Trail, Ithaca, Firebrand Books, 1985.

(Editor) *A Gathering of Spirit: A Collection by North American Women*, Firebrand Books, 1988.

Food & Spirits: Stories, Firebrand Books, 1991.

"Giveaway: Native Lesbian Writers," *Signs: Journal of Women in Culture and Society*, 18, summer 1993; 944–947.

"Grandmothers of a New World," *Women of Power*, 16, spring 1990; 40–47.

Writing As Witness, *Women's Press*, 1995.

Contributor of short stories to numerous anthologies, including Songs from the Earth on Turtle's Back: Contemporary American Indian Poetry, *edited by Joseph Bruchac, Greenfield Review Press, 1984; Early Ripening: Poetry by Women, edited by Marge Piercy, Pandora Books, 1987; New Voices from the Longhouse: Contemporary Iroquois Writing, edited by Bruchac, Greenfield Review Press, 1989; Talking Leaves: Contemporary Native American Short Stories, edited by Craig Lesley, Dell, 1991; and Getting Wet: Lesbian Tales of Seduction, Women's Press, 1992. Some works written under name Degonwadonti.*

Prophet looked intently at David's face, then kneaded his lap and settled herself on it, where she purred. David stroked the orange fur and scratched the cat's head. She burrowed deeper in his lap. "I would get up to greet you, but I think Prophet's got something else in mind."

Joseph laughed. "We wouldn't want to disturb her highness. David, we have not seen each other in many years." He bent down to kiss the young man on his forehead. "You don't look so good." Joseph eyed him critically.

"Thanks. But you look the same as ever."

"You in a lot of pain, " Joseph said in a statement, not a question.

"Yeah, a lot of pain. I take about fifty pills a day. They don't seem to make that much of a difference." David continued to stroke Prophet.

"You think I can cure you?"

"No."

"Good, because I can't. All of us are afraid of death, though. We don't know what to expect, what to take with us." He looked in his paper sack. "Maybe I got the right things here."

Grace went into the kitchen, and Joseph pulled up a chair and sat beside David. Looking at Prophet asleep on David's lap, Joseph remarked, "Cats is smart. This one had a brother looked just like her. I called him Tecumseh. One morning I woke up and he was gone. I asked the Prophet if she knew where her brother went. She looked at me and blinked, then turned her head away like I'd said somthin' rude. I went outside to look for Tecumseh and I found him, layin' dead under a rose bush. It was a good year for the roses, they was bloomin' to beat the band. He had chosen the red roses to die under. That was a good choice, don't you think? I buried him under that red rose bush. The old man knew what *he* wanted, but he had to let me know, me not bein' as smart as a cat. Prophet came out and sat on the grave. She sat

B E T H   **B R A N T**

there for three days and nights. Cats are different from us. We worry about fittin' things to our own purpose. Cats don't worry about them things. They live, they die. They get buried under a red rose bush. Smart, huh?"

"You got any spare rose bushes? Only make mine flaming pink!" David laughed, then began coughing, blood spattering the Kleenex he held to his mouth.

The Prophet jumped from David's lap and sat on the floor, her back to him.

"Now I've done it," David gasped. "Come back. Here kitty, kitty, kitty."

The Prophet turned and gave him a look of contempt, her back twitching her tail moving back and forth on the floor.

"Huh," Joseph said. "She ain't comin' back for a while. Don't like the name Kitty."

Grace came in to announce dinner. David grabbed his cane and shuffled to the table. He sat down, gasping for breath. "Takes longer every time. I think I'm losing feeling in my right leg, but what the hell, I'd crawl to the table for Mother's beef stew." He half-heartedly lifted the spoon to his mouth. "My appetite's still pretty good, isn't it Mother?"

Grace smiled at her son. "The day your appetite goes is the day I go."

She had made fresh bread to eat with the stew and set dishes of pickles and cheese on the table. Joseph rubbed his hands together in glee. "This looks good!" They ate, talking local gossip, the Prophet sitting daintily beside Joseph's chair. David's hands shook as he barely fed himself, spilling stew on his blue shirt. Grace fussed and tied a napkin around his neck. David smiled. "Next, she'll be feeding me or giving me a bottle." He winked at his mother and blew a kiss across the table to her. She caught it and put it on her cheek.

Joseph watched while he fed bits of meat to Prophet. He looked in his sack and pulled out a dish covered in waxed paper. "I made these this mornin'. Butter tarts. The flakiest crust you'll find anywhere. You gotta use lard, none of that shortenin'. Lard is what makes a crust that'll melt in your mouth. It's my gift to you, David."

As David bit into the sweetness of the tart, he looked at Joseph, his earrings swinging against his shoulders, his hands making patterns in the air as he described the making of the tarts, and David thought, *He acts like a queen.* He looked harder at Joseph, thinking, if you put him in a city, in a gay bar, the old nelly would fit right in. David laughed out loud.

Grace looked startled, but Joseph grinned and nodded his head. "Catchin' on, my young friend?"

As he helped clear the table, David smiled with his new knowledge. Collapsing into his reclining chair, David swallowed his medicine and laid his head back, closing his eyes. He could hear the murmurs between Joseph and Grace, his mother always a living, vivid presence in his life—his reason for hanging on so long to life. "I love you, Mother," he whispered. He opened his eyes to the dry touch of Joseph's fingers on his face. His mother was bringing out the moccasins she had made from rabbit hide and had beaded the nights they sat and watched TV. She presented them to Joseph. He unlaced his red hightops and slipped the beautiful moccasins on his feet. He put his feet out in front of him in admiration. He got up and walked in them. He jumped and clicked his heels together. "Thank you, Grace. You haven't lost your touch, have you? Now it's time for you to go. Don't come back till mornin'."

Grace gathered her things together and stood looking at David. Her face shifted with emotions: sorrow, pride, fear, love. She kissed her son and hugged Joseph. They watched her leave.

Joseph turned and asked David, "You tryin' to be brave for your mom? Let me tell you somethin' about mothers. They know everything. She feels what you're goin' through. Can't hide it, even though you try."

"No! I don't want her to know how bad it gets. I can see it in her face, she gets crazy not knowing what to do for me. But this is the real crazy part, I don't want to let go of her. That death . . . that place . . . she won't be there."

The Prophet jumped on Joseph's lap and began washing herself. "That's true. Her time isn't here yet. David, you have lived your life in the way that was best for you. You think Grace didn't know why you left here? Think she didn't know you was gay? You can't tell someone like Grace not to go crazy when her son is dyin'. You can't tell her how to mourn you. And you can't be draggin' her along with you when you leave this place."

"I don't want to do that. I feel like a little kid when I was scared of a nightmare. Mother would make it go away. Death is like that nightmare. I gotta meet it on my own, but I'm scared."

"Yes, I know you are," and Joseph reached for David's hand. David's bony fingers closed over Joseph's.

"When I lived in the city, I used to get so homesick for this place. I'd picture the way it looked—the sky, the trees, my relatives. I'd dream it all up in my mind, but I never thought I would come back. I made my life in the city, thinking that I couldn't come back here. My people don't want queers, faggots living among them. But now, some of us are coming home to die. Where else would we go but back to our homes, our families? What a joke, eh? They couldn't deal with my life, now they gotta deal with my death. God, I think about the guys that really can't go home. They have to die alone in some hospital, or even on the street. There was a guy I knew, Ojibwe, and he died outside his apartment. I heard about it after it happened and

I got in this rage! People just walking by him probably thinking, oh here's another drunk Indian, just walking by him! And him, getting cold and no one would touch him." Tears were moving down David's face. He lofted his hand to wipe his face. "That's when I hated being an Indian. My own people, hateful to that guy. He was scared to go home. Probably thought they'd throw him out again, or stone him or something."

"Well, Indians got no immunity from hatefulness or stupidity, David. Maybe he had made his choice to die alone. Maybe he didn't have a home to go to."

David looked shocked. "No, that can't be true. I know what it's like. I grew up here, remember? It seemed like I had to make a choice, be gay or be an Indian. Some choice, eh? So I moved to the city." David sighed, then began to cough.

Joseph stroked Prophet, whose ears were twitching. "Even a city can't take the Indian part away. Even a virus can't do that, my young friend." He dipped into his sack and held out a piece of metal to David. "Look in this. What do you see?"

David held the piece of metal to his face. He saw a blurred image of himself, tumors covering his face. When he tilted the piece of tin, he saw himself laughing and dressed in his finest clothes, dancing in the bar in the city. He tilted it yet another way and saw himself dancing at a pow wow, his hair fanning out as he twirled and jumped. In another tilt, he saw himself as a child, sitting on Grandmother's lap.

"Which one is you?" Joseph asked.

"All of them."

"When the Prophet was a kitten," Joseph said, petting the now sleeping cat, "she used to keep me awake at night. She'd jump on my head just as I was dozin' off. I'd knock her away and turn over, but just when that sweet moment of sleep was callin' me, she'd jump on my head again. I thought maybe she was hungry and I'd get up to feed her. She'd eat, then start the whole routine all over again. She even got Tecumseh in the act. While she'd jump on my head, he'd get under the covers and bite my feet. I finally gave up and got out of bed and went outside and looked at the sky. About the fifth night of these carryin' ons, I *really* looked at the sky. I saw all the stars as if they was printed on the insides of my eyes. I saw the moon like she really was. And I started to pray to Sky Woman, blinkin' and shinin' up there. She answered me back, too, all because the cats was smarter than me. Nothin' hides in front of old Sky Woman. You might think *she's* hidin' when you can't see her, but she's there, checkin' everything out. People can't hide from her. And people can't hide from themselves."

"Is that what I've done?" David asked, his face sad. "I've always been proud of being Mohawk, of being from here. I *am* proud of being gay even though everywhere I turned, someone was telling me not to be either. In the city they didn't want me to be Native. In this place, they don't want me to be gay. It can drive you crazy! *Be this. Be that. Don't be this way.* So you get to be like an actor, changing roles and faces to please somebody out there who hates your guts for what you are." David laughed. "When I was diagnosed I thought, well, now I don't have to pretend anymore. It's all out in the open. I'm going to die, and why did I waste my time and tears worrying about all this other stuff? I got real active in AIDS work. I wanted to reach out to all the Indian gays I knew, form support groups, lean on each other. 'Cause the other guys just didn't understand us. I was a fireball for two years, real busy, but then I got too sick to do much of anything. My friends were good, but they couldn't take care of me anymore. I came home. Here I sit, Grandfather, waiting for death, but scared shitless.

Joseph began to hum and sing, "Crazy . . . I'm crazy for feelin' so lonely." He stuck his hand inside the sack and handed David a piece of paper.

We, as the original inhabitants of this country, and sovereigns of the soil, look upon ourselves as equally independent and free as any other nation or nations. This country was given to us by the Great Spirit above; we wish to enjoy it, and have our passage along the lake, within the line we have pointed out. The great exertions we have made, for this number of years, to accomplish a peace and have not been able to obtain it; our patience, as we have observed, is exhausted. We, therefore, throw ourselves under the protection of the Great Spirit above, who will order all things for the best. We have told you our patience is worn out, but that we wish for peace and whenever we hear that pleasing sound, we shall pay attention to it. Until then, you will pay attention to us.

"My ancestor. Quite a man." David held the paper in his thin hands.

"Yes, he was. Diplomats, they called him and his sister. We call them warriors."

David read the words again. "Grandfather, I would like to be a warrior like this man. I would like to see death coming and run to meet it, not afraid, not hiding behind my mother."

"Who says you ain't a warrior? David, the bravest people I know were the ones that lived and kept on livin'. Those two, Tyendinaga and Molly, they fought to keep us alive as a people. Looks to me like you're as fine a warrior as they was. David, you lived!"

The Prophet suddenly came awake and stretched to her full length. She sat up and washed her face. She blinked at David, her yellow eyes staring at him until he looked away. She jumped off Joseph's lap and settled herself in front of David's feet.

6 1

BETH **BRANT**

"Trust the Prophet to interrupt the proceedings. Let's go outside and sit on the porch." Joseph stood up and stretched his arms and shook his legs.

David reached for his cane, his body curved and stooped. Joseph got a blanket to wrap him in against the cool night air. David made his way toward the front door. Joseph went to the kitchen and brought out two mugs of coffee and the rest of the butter tarts. They settled on the porch steps.

"David, look at the moon. When she's a crescent like that, I think Sky Woman's smilin' at us. More than likely, laughin'. She has big jobs to do like pullin' in the tides, and we sit here yappin' about life and death."

"The moon is beautiful. Somehow, it never seemed to shine like that in the city." David began coughing again, his body shaking and throbbing.

Joseph held onto him until the shaking stopped. "David, you're just a rez boy, ain't you? Nothin' look as good as here, eh? But I think so too. One time, a long time ago, I thought about leavin' here."

"Why didn't you? It can't have been easy for you. Or were things different then? Maybe not so homophobic, not so much hatred?"

"Oh, things was bad. But not in that way. There was hatred, alright. The kind that makes people turn to the bottle or put a gun in their mouth and shoot." David winced, remembering his father's death. Joseph continued. "That kind of hatred, self-hatred. I stayed because I was supposed to. I fought it, but I had to stay. It was my job." He began a song. *"Your cheatin' heart will tell on you. You'll cry and cry, the way I do.* Sing with me, David." And they sang until the last words were finished and Joseph hugged David.

"I thought medicine men were supposed to chant and cast spells, not sing old Hank Williams' songs," David teased.

Joseph looked surprised. "Oh, some do. Some do. But how many medicine people you know, David?"

"Only one, Grandfather."

"Well then, there you go. What you see is what you get."

6 2

"When my father died, I remember being shut out from what was going on. I know they were all trying to protect me and Sister, but we were scared. One day he was there, the next day he wasn't. He wasn't the greatest dad, but he was ours! You were there, Grandfather. Why did he do it?"

Joseph took a deep breath and let it out. It lingered in the night air like a puff of smoke. "Because he didn't know any other way. Are you judgin' him, David? 'Cause if you are, you can forget it. Too many people made a judgment on your father all his life. He doesn't need yours to add to it." Joseph's face became angry, then softened as he took David's hand again.

"Children get scared. We fail you because we fail ourselves. We think *you'll* get over it because you're younger and have fewer memories. Grownups are fools, David. Your father didn't know what else to do with his life, a life he thought was worthless. So he shot it away."

David wept. "I've thought about shooting mine away, like him. Like father, like son, isn't that what the people would say? So, I didn't all because I didn't want to be mentioned in the same breath with him. Pride, that's all that kept me going. And I couldn't do the same thing to my mother and sister that he did to us."

"You're a lot like your dad. Sweet, like he was. Oh yes," Joseph looked at David's disbelieving face, "a sweet man. When we was at residential school together, he's the one that took me under his wing. He fought the grownups and the other kids that ganged up on me. He was always my friend. He didn't fail me, ever. And I tried not to let him down, but I wasn't enough to keep that gun out of his hand. Nobody was enough, David. Not you, or your mom or your sister. Don't you judge him. He wouldn't have judged you." Joseph raised his face to the crescent moon and closed his eyes.

David felt a small piece of pain dislodge from inside him. It floated away in the night's darkness. "Thank you for telling me that, Grandfather. I always loved him."

Joseph smiled, his crooked teeth shining white in the moon's light. "Love is a funny thing, David. It stays constant, like her," he pointed to the crescent. "When you cut through all the crap, the need and greed part, you got the good, lastin' stuff. She knew that," and he pointed again to he moon. "She put herself up there to remind us of her love, not to admire her pretty shine. Of course, the pretty shine doesn't hurt, does it?" And they laughed together.

David said, "I met my pretty shine in the city. He will always be the love of my life, even though he doesn't feel that way about me. We're still friends . . . . God, the city was so different for me—I loved it! Excitement. All those gorgeous men. If I'd stayed here, I wouldn't have known the world was full of gay people. If I'd stayed here though, maybe I wouldn't have gotten AIDS." David pulled the blanket closer around himself and shivered.

Joseph squeezed David's wasting fingers. "Do you regret any of it?"

"No. I've thought about that a lot. I only wish I could have stayed, but I thought I had to make the choice and don't know what would have happened if I hadn't left."

Joseph rustled in his sack. "Who can read the future? Well, maybe I can, but can you read the past as well? Here, take this."

David held out his hand. A dry snakeskin was deposited into his dry palm. The skin was faded but still showed orange-and-black markings.

6 3

BETH **BRANT**

"I saw this snake shed her skin. I was walking in the bush and heard a very small noise. I watched her wriggle out of her old life, just like she was removin' an overcoat. It took this snake a long time, but then, there she was in her new overcoat, her old skin just lyin' there waitin' for me to pick it up and give it to you."

"Thank you, Grandfather. It's beautiful." David touched the snakeskin and looked into Joseph's face. "I think it would be wonderful if we could shed ourselves like this and have a brand-new, beautiful skin to face the world. Or maybe, to face death."

"We do, David. A snake doesn't put on a new skin with different colors. She has the same one, just layers of it. She doesn't become a new snake, but older and wiser with each shedding. Humans shed. We don't pay attention to it, though. We get new chances all the time. A snake makes use of her chances; that's why she's a snake and we're not. We never know when we got a good thing goin'."

"That's true! Mother used to tell me I was lucky, I had it good compared to other little boys. She was right, of course." David giggled into his hand. "She is always right. Why is that, Grandfather?"

"Now you got me. That's something I'll never know either!"

They laughed, the sound filling the night air. Prophet scratched at the door to be let out. "The Prophet's afraid she's missin' out on something. Those butter tarts, maybe." Joseph got up to open the door.

The Prophet streaked out the open door and ran to the cluster of apple trees. She climbed one and sat on a branch. David could see the yellow glow of her eyes as she watched the men drink their coffee and bite into the tarts.

Joseph remarked between bites, "Prophet does it every time. I'd sit around all night talkin' if she didn't remind me why I was here."

David started to shake. "I'm afraid, Grandfather."

"Yes, I know, David. We'll go inside, and you can lay down while I make some special tea. I'm here with you, David. I won't leave you."

David clutched the snakeskin in his hand and struggled to his feet. He made his way into the house and to the couch where he started coughing and spitting up blood. Joseph cleaned David's face and wrapped the blanket tightly around his skinny body. He went to the kitchen, and David could hear him singing, "I fall to pieces . . . each time I see you again." David smiled, the voice reassuring to him.

"The Prophet's still in that apple tree, starin' at the house," said Joseph, as he brought a steaming mug of liquid to David.

David sipped the tea and made a face. "What is this stuff? It tastes like wet leaves!"

"It is wet leaves. Drink up. It's good for what ails you."

"Yeah, right," David smiled, "I notice you're not drinking any."

"Well, I'm not the sick one, am I?"

David drank the brew, watching Joseph walk around the room, picking up books and stacking them neatly, straightening a picture hanging on the wall, tidying a lamp table. "There's a dust rag in the broom closet. The rug could use a shake and the windows need a wash," David said teasingly.

"You're a regular Henny Youngman, ain't you?"

"Who?"

"All finished?" Joseph pointed to the mug. "If you want more, you can't have it. I only brought enough for one cup."

David pushed the mug toward Joseph. "Please, no more. I think I'll survive without it."

"Ah, survival. Let me tell you about that one." Joseph sat on the couch at David's feet.

David felt heavy in his body. He tried to lift his hand, but it was too much of an effort. He tried to speak, but his voice wouldn't move out of him. He looked at Joseph who was talking, but his voice was thin and far away. He saw that Prophet had come back into the house and was sitting on Joseph's lap. The Prophet stared at David with her yellow eyes and smiled at him. Was that a smile? What was that tea? Wet leaves . . . and David was falling was falling back into wet leaves and it was autumn the air smelled like winter he was a boy a boy who jumped up from wet leaves and ran he ran he was chasing something he felt so good so good this is what childhood is you run you laugh you open your mouth you feel the wind on your tongue the sun on your head the apple trees were giving up their gifts of fruit you picked an apple you feel you taste the juice running down your throat the apple made a loud crunch as you bit and the swallows in the tree were waiting for the core to be thrown down so they could share the fruit of the tree the geese were flying you ran you ran into the cornfield and scared the pheasant who was picking at the seed you laughed you laughed it was a perfect day you picked up a feather and put it in your pocket the day was perfect when you were a child you ran you laughed you played you were loved you loved you were a child it was good so good to be a child in this place this place this place never changed this place this place.

David opened his eyes. The Prophet was washing her tail. Joseph held a turtle rattle in his left hand. He was talking . . . *and then the church people sent their missionaries here to teach us to be christian but we . . .*

David was falling he fell into the sound of the turtle's rattle he fell into the turtle's mouth he shook his body shook and . . . *fought them* . . . he fell into the sound of the rattle he was the rattle's sound the music the music he was dancing dancing with the first man he ever loved they were dancing holding holding the music the music the turtle's music was in them through them in them . . . *killed us* . . . he went home he went with the first man he ever loved the music was beating was beating their hearts the rattle the music they fell onto the bed the music the music touched them the turtle touched them the rattle touched them they touched they touched the touching was music was music his body singing music his body the rattle of the turtle the first man he loved . . . *we fought back* . . . their bodies singing shaking joining joining everything was music was music so good so good good the first man he loved Thomas Thomas . . . *they kept killing us off* . . . Tommy Tommy singing sighing joining . . . *but we* . . . singing our bodies singing Tommy David Tommy Tommy . . . *survived* . . . .

David's eyes opened. The room was dark. The Prophet was staring, smiling, her eyes brilliant yellow. Joseph was staring also, his eyes sending out shafts of brilliance, laser beams into his soul.

"Grandfather."

Joseph held up the rattle and sang a song with no words, a song in a high, quivering voice. Joseph's face changed shape. He became a cat. The Prophet sat smiling, her teeth white in the dark room. Joseph sang and became a wolf, lemon-yellow eyes steady on David. Joseph sang and he became a snake hissing his song, his eyes sending out shards of light. Joseph sang and shook the turtle. He sang.

"Grandfather."

David was falling he fell into the song of the cat the song of the wolf the song of the snake the song of the turtle he fell he fell into the turtle's mouth the turtle's song he was shaking was shaking his grandmother was singing was singing a song a song in Indian his grandmother was singing singing he was singing with Grandmother he was sitting on Grandma's lap her lap she was holding him close so close . . . *our people survived* . . . she sang his mother sang his sister sang his father sang he sang he was singing in Indian Indian the voices the songs in Indian . . . *the sicknesses came* . . . singing singing his grandmother holding him his mother his father singing . . . *measles, smallpox* . . . Grandmother talking singing in Indian the language the song of Indian the people the song Grandma's hair brushing against his face as she whispered and told him he . . . *AIDS* . . . was an Indian Indian Mohawk singing songs Mohawk the voices Kanienka 'ha'ka the song the song of this place this Indian place this place.

The rattle was silent. The Prophet was sitting in a hump, the fur around her neck electric, like an orange ruff. Joseph sat, his laser eyes bright in the face of an old, old man. He spoke, his voice not audible, the words not recognizable, and David heard.

"They took parts of us and cut them up and threw them to the winds. They made lies we would believe. We look for the parts to put ourselves back together. To put the earth back together. It is broken. We look for truth to put us all together again. There is a piece here. A part there. We scavenge and collect. Some pieces are lost. We will find them. Some parts are found, and we do not see them yet. We gather the pieces and bring them together. *We* bring them together. *We* make the truth about ourselves. *We* make the truth."

David was falling was falling he fell he fell into the sound of the ancient voice the ancient words he was falling into the sounds of screaming screaming in his face dirty Indian faggot fucking faggot the voices screaming you dirty Indian you the sound of fists of fists the sound of hate the sound of hate you dirty Indian you dirty faggot the sound of hate the sound of blood the taste of blood in his mouth the taste the hate the hate . . . *we collect the parts that have been damaged* . . . the hate the pain as they raped him you dirty Indian faggot the hate the blood the rape the sound of rape . . . *we hunt for the pieces* . . . the hate the pain the fear the dirty Indian faggot . . . *we gather it all together* . . . you filthy Indian scum you dirty you dirty you dirty . . . *we are resisters, warriors* . . . you dirty Indian you dirty faggot the rape the sound of you dirty filthy . . . *we do not believe the lies they* . . . the taste the taste the taste of hate in his mouth.

David cried out. Joseph stroked his thinning hair, the turtle held over his body. "They hurt us in so many ways. The least of what they did was to kill us. They turned us into missing parts. Until we find those missing parts we kill ourselves with shame, with fear, with hate. All those parts just waitin' to be gathered together to make us. *Us.* A whole people. The biggest missing piece is love, David. *Love!"*

The Prophet leapt in the air and hissed. She leapt again and knocked the turtle rattle into Joseph's lap.

"The Prophet says we are not finished. Who am *I* to argue with *her?"*

David tugged at the man's arm. "Joseph. Grandfather. I am so thirsty, so thirsty."

David was falling was falling into the shake of the rattle he fell he fell into the turtle's mouth he fell he was flying he flew he was inside the turtle the turtle shook he fell into voices voices asking him are you ready his heart his heart was beating are you ready his heart grew larger his heart was beating his heart the turtle asked him are you ready his grandmother held out her hand and touched him are you ready are you ready his grandmother touched his heart are you ready his father touched his heart are you ready the people hold out their hands are you ready he reached for their hands his heart was beating inside the turtle a drum a drum are you ready Turtle touched his heart are you ready he fell he put out his arms he held out his arms I am ready they touched him I am ready I am ready I am ready.

David opened his eyes. The taste of tears was in his mouth. "I saw it." Prophet jumped delicately on David's chest and licked the salt tears from his face. She sat back on her haunches and watched David speak. "I saw my grandmother, my father. They touched me." He began coughing again, retching blood.

Joseph held a towel to David's mouth and touched the young man's face. "You found your parts, your pieces." Digging into his sack, he pulled out a white feather. "This is from a whistling swan. They stop here in the spring before goin' on to Alaska. The thing about them—they never know what they'll find when they get there. They just know they got to get there. When our bodies are no longer here, *we* are still here." He stood up, his joints creaking and snapping. "Your mother is comin.' The sun is real bright today. It's a good day to go." He scooped Prophet up from David's lap and draped her across his shoulder.

"Thank you, Grandfather," David whispered, his breath coming in ragged bursts.

David heard him go out the front door. He couldn't see, but he heard Joseph talking to the Prophet. He heard the truck door slam and the engine start its rattling and wheezing. David moved his hands on the blanket to find the tin, the snakeskin, his ancestor's words, the feather. He touched them and felt Joseph's presence. The sound of his mother's car made him struggle to sit up. He heard the door open and the footsteps of his mother coming into the room. He felt her standing by him, her cool fingers touching his face and hands.

He opened his mouth to say good-bye.

MARY  BRAVE BIRD

Born in 1953 on the Rosebud reservation in South Dakota, Brave Bird is
known for her autobiographies Lakota Woman *and* Ohitika Woman,
both of which she wrote with Richard Erdoes. In Lakota Woman, *which*
was published under the name Mary Crow Dog, Brave Bird recounts her
impoverished childhood on the reservation, her rebellious youth, her growing
awareness of her heritage, and her marriage to political activist Leonard
Crow Dog. This work, which won the American Book Award in 1991, has
been praised for it observant account of the hardships of reservation life and
its first-hand portrayal of the American Indian Movement of the 1960s and
1970s, including the 1973 siege of Wounded Knee in South Dakota.

Essay by

RUTH ROSENBERG

Ohitika Woman begins in 1977, where *Lakota Woman* concluded, and
delineates Brave Bird's participation in the Native American Church, her
deteriorating relationship with her husband, and her struggles with poverty and alcoholism. Critical reaction to *Ohitika Woman* was generally positive, with reviewers praising the work's realism and insights into contemporary Native American life. Pat Monaghan has stated: "[We] learn of the
difficulties facing Native American woman today: the domestic brutality,
the abandonments, the assaults. But we learn as well of the medicine and
rituals that strengthen women of Native American heritage."

Lakota Sioux political activist and autobiographer.

Born: 1953 on the Rosebud reservation, South Dakota.

Partnerships: married Leonard Crow Dog, 1973 (divorced); three children.

Career: Political activist and autobiographer. Joined American Indian Movement (AIM) in 1971; took part in AIM takeover of Bureau of Indian Affairs office in Washington, DC, 1972; was active in siege of Wounded Knee, SD, 1973.

INVISIBLE FATHERS

From *Lakota Woman*, Harper Perennial, copyright © 1990 by Mary Brave Bird

The father says so–E'yayo!
The father says so–E'yayo!
You shall see your grandfather!
You shall see your kindred–E'yayo!
The father says so.
A'te he'ye lo.

Child let me grasp your hand,
Child let me grasp your hand.
You shall live,
You shall live!
Says the father.
A'te he'ye lo.
—*Ghost Dance song*

Our people have always been known for their strong family ties, for people within one family group caring for each other, for the "helpless ones," the old folks and especially the children, the coming generation. Even now, among traditionals, as long as one person eats, all other relatives eat too. Nobody saves up money because there is always some poor relative saying, "Kanji, I need five bucks for food and gas," and he will not be refused as long as there is one single dollar left. Feeding every comer is still a sacred duty, and Sioux women seem always to be cooking from early morning until late at night. Fourth and fifth cousins still claim relationship and the privileges that go with it. Free enterprise has no future on the res.

At the center of the old Sioux society was the tiyospaye, the extended family group, the basic hunting band, which included grandparents, uncles,

aunts, in-laws, and cousins. The tiyospaye was like a warm womb cradling all within it. Kids were never alone, always fussed over by not one but several mothers, watched and taught by several fathers. The real father, as a matter of fact, selected a second father, some well-thought-of relative with special skills as a hunter or medicine man, to help him bring up a boy, and such a person was called "Father" too. And the same was true for the girls. Grandparents in our tribe always held a special place in caring for the little ones, because they had more time to devote to them, when the father was out hunting, taking the mother with him to help with the skinning and butchering.

The whites destroyed the tiyospaye, not accidentally, but as a matter of policy. The close-knit clan, set in its old ways, was a stumbling block in the path of the missionary and government agent, its traditions and customs a barrier to what the white man called "progress" and "civilization." And so the government tore the tiyospaye apart and forced the Sioux into the kind of relationship now called the "nuclear family"– forced upon each couple their individually owned allotment of land, trying to teach them "the bene-fits of wholesome selfishness without which higher civilization is impossi-ble." At least that is how one secretary of the interior put it. So the great brainwashing began, those who did not like to have their brains washed being pushed farther and farther into the back country into isolation and starvation. The civilizers did a good job on us, especially among the half-bloods, using the stick-and-carrot method, until now there is neither the tiyospaye nor a white-style nuclear family left, just Indian kids without parents. The only thing reminding one of the old Sioux family group is that the grandparents are playing a bigger role than ever. With often no mother or father around, it is the old folks who are bringing up the kids, which is not always a bad thing.

My father, Bill Moore, was part Indian, but mostly white, French with a little Spanish mixed in—Spanish not chicano. He was in the navy and later became a trucker. He lives in Omaha—I think. All that's left of him is his picture on the mantel piece showing him in navy uniform, a lean-faced, sharp-eyed man. He stayed around just long enough until mom got pregnant with me. Then he split, telling my mother he was tired of all that baby shit. He just left. He was not interested in us, nor in the kids he had with another wife whom he did not want either and placed on welfare. I don't know what became of them. So there is just that one picture left to remind me that I, too, had a father like everybody else. My mother never talked of him; my grandfather—his own father—never talked of him. So all I know is that he wanted no part of me and liked to drink. That's the only things I was ever told about him.

I saw him twice in the flesh. He came back when I was eleven in order to ask his father for some money. The second time I saw him was when he came for his brother's funeral. He looked right through me as if I had not been there. His eyes were dead. He did not even ask who I was. As a matter of fact he did not talk at all, just grinned when some jokes were told and looked uncomfortable in his tight, new cowboy boots. After the funeral he just shook hands all around, without uttering a word, in a hurry to be off again. My mother divorced him in 1954 when I was one year old.

When I was nine or ten my mother married again. This stepfather was even worse than my real father, who at least was not around. My stepfather was. He was a wino and started us kids drinking when I was barely ten years old. After my mother married this man I did not want to be around. I did not like the way he stared at me. It made me uncomfortable. So I just kept away from my mother's place. I rather was on my own, took care of myself, hating myself for having allowed him to teach me to drink. On the rare occasions when I went home I always got into arguments with my mother, telling her, "Why did you marry that man? He's no dad. He doesn't love us. He does nothing for us."

So I and my mother did not get along then. I was a natural-born rebel. They were married and I could do nothing about it. So I drank and ripped off as I got older, living like a hobo, punishing my mother that way. I had to mature. My mother had to mature also. We get along now, really like and respect each other. I realize that I was very intolerant. My mother could not help herself. The little settlements we lived in—He-Do, Upper Cut Meat, Parmelee, St. Francis, Belvidere—were places without hope where bodies and souls were being destroyed bit by bit. Schools left many of us almost illiterate. We were not taught any skills. The land was leased to white ranchers. Jobs were almost nonexistent on the reservation, and outside the res whites did not hire Indians if they could help it. There was nothing for the men to do in those days but hit the bottle. The men were psychologically crippled and thus my mother did not have much choice when it came to picking a husband. The men had nothing to live for, so they got drunk and drove off at ninety miles an hour in a car without lights, without brakes, and without destination, to die a warrior's death.

There were six of us kids. A seventh had died as a baby. First, my oldest sister, Kathie, then my brother Robert, then Barbara, who is closest to me in life-style and has had experiences almost exactly like mine. Then came Sandra, and then myself, the youngest. After me came a little boy. We adopted him. This came about when my mother visited his parents for some reason or other. She found nobody at home except this baby boy, dirty, bawling with hunger, and soaking wet, in a box under the dresser. All alone. Everybody gone. Barhopping, most likely. It got my mother mad and somehow she worked it out so we could adopt the baby. He was very spoiled. Everything he wanted he got. So at least one kid in the family got pampered.

After father left, mother became our sole financial support. In order to earn a living she went to be trained as a nurse. When she had finished her training the only job she could find was in Pierre, some hundred miles away. There was nobody there to take care of us while she worked, so she had to leave us behind with our grandparents. We missed her at times. We would see her only rarely. She did not have many chances to come home because she had no transportation. She could not afford a car and it was impossible to get around without one. So she was not there when we needed her because she had to care for white patients. It was only after I was almost grown-up that I really became acquainted with her.

Like most reservation kids we wound up with our grandparents. We were lucky. Many Indian children are placed in foster homes. This happens even in some cases where parents or grandparents are willing and able to take care of them, but where the social workers say their homes are substandard, or where there are outhouses instead of flush toilets, or where the family is simply "too poor." A flush toilet to a white social worker is more important than a good grandmother. So the kids are given to wasicun strangers to be "acculturated in a sanitary environment." We are losing the coming generation that way and do not like it.

We were lucky, having good, warm-hearted grandparents until we, too, were taken away to a boarding school. My grandma was born Louise

Flood and she was a Sioux. Her first husband's name was Brave Bird. I have tried to find out about this ancestor of mine. I looked in all the Lakota history books. There were Brave Bears, and Brave Bulls, and Brave Wolves, but no Brave Birds listed. I should have asked when grandma was still alive. They lived on their allotted land way out on the prairie. When grandma was young the whole tribe lived on commodities. Every head of household had a ration card, keeping this precious object in a small, beautifully beaded pouch around his neck, the kind which now costs collectors as much as three hundred dollars. Once a month everybody had to go for their supplies—coffee, sugar loaves, sacks of flour, bacon—mostly starch but filling enough while it lasted, and if we were not cheated out of part of it. Sometimes there was a beef issue of living cattle, the stringiest, skinniest beasts imaginable. This meat-on-the-hoof was driven into a huge corral and then our men were allowed to play buffalo hunters for a couple of hours and ride after them and shoot down those poor refugees from the glue factory and butcher them. This was always a big occasion, good entertainment one could talk about. One day, Grandfather Brave Bird hitched up his wagon and team to drive six hours to town to get his government issue. He went all by himself. On the way home he ran into a thunderstorm. Lightning spooked the horses. They raced off at a dead run, upsetting the wagon. The box seat got ripped off with Brave Bird still in it, entangled in the reins. The horses dragged him through the brush, over rocks, and finally for a couple of miles along a barbed-wire fence. He was dead when they found him.

At that time my grandmother had two girls and two boys. These uncles of mine got TB as they grew up, were taken to an institution, and died from this disease. Tuberculosis is still a problem with us, striking men more often than women. At least they died when they were grown-up, not as children as often happens. At least my grandmother thinks that is where and how they died. She never got any records. All she got was a box to bury.

There was a man called Noble Moore. He had a family and his wife died, and grandma had a family and her husband had died. So the widow and the widower got together and married. By this time my mom was already grown-up. Now Moore had a son of the same age called Bill. One thing led to another and mom married Bill, our absentee head of family, the ex-navy trucker in Omaha. Grandma had the father and my mother wound up with the son. In this kind of lottery grandma won the big prize, because the old man was as good and sober and caring as his son was the opposite.

Grandpa and Grandma Moore were good to us, raising us ever since we were small babies. Grandfather Noble Moore was the only father I knew. He took responsibility for us in his son's place. He gave us as good a home as he could. He worked as a janitor in the school and had little money to take care of a large family, his own and that of his son. Nine people in all plus always some poor relatives with no jobs. I don't know how he managed, but somehow he did.

The old couple raised us way out on the prairie near He-Dog in a sort of homemade shack. We had no electricity, no heating system, no plumbing. We got our water from the river. Some of the things which even poor white or black ghetto people take for granted we did not even know existed. We knew little about the outside world, having no radio and no TV. Maybe that was a blessing.

Our biggest feast was Thanksgiving because then we had hamburgers. They had a wonderful taste to them which I still remember. Grandpa raised us on rabbits, deer meat, ground squirrels, even porcupines. They never seemed to have money to buy much food. Grandpa Moore and two of his brothers were hunting all the time. It was the only way to put some fresh, red meat on the table, and we Sioux are real tigers when it comes to meat. We can't do without it. A few times grandpa came back from fishing with a huge mud turtle and threw it in the pot. That was a feast for him. He said one could taste seven different kinds of meat flavors in a turtle stew—chicken, pork, beef, rabbit, deer, wild duck, antelope, all these. We also got the usual commodities after OEO came in.

Our cabin was small. It had only one room which served as our kitchen, living room, dining room, parlor, or whatever. At night we slept there, too. That was our home—one room. Grandma was the kind of woman who, when visitors dropped in, immediately started to feed them. She always told me: "Even if there's not much left, they gonna eat. These people came a long ways to visit us, so they gonna eat first. I don't care if they come at sunrise or at sundown, they gonna eat first. And whatever is left after they leave, even if it's only a small dried-up piece of fry bread, that's what we eat." This my grandmother taught me. She was Catholic and tried to raise us as whites, because she thought that was the only way for us to get ahead and lead a satisfying life, but when it came to basics she was all Sioux, in spite of the pictures of Holy Mary and the Sacred Heart on the wall. Whether she was aware of how very Indian she had remained, I cannot say. She also spoke the Sioux language, the real old-style Lakota, not the modern slang we have today. And she knew her herbs, showing us how to recognize the different kinds of Indian plants, telling us what each of them was good for. She took us to gather berries and a certain mint for tea. During the winter we took chokecherries, the skin and the branches. We boiled the inside layers and used the tea for various sorts of sicknesses. In the fall she took us to harvest chokecherries and wild grapes. These were the only sweets we had. I never discovered candy until much later when I was in school. We did not have the money for it and only very seldom went to town.

We had no shoes and went barefoot most of the time. I never had a new dress. Once a year we would persuade somebody to drive us to the Catholic mission for a basement rummage sale. Sometimes we found something there to put on our feet before it got cold, and maybe a secondhand blouse or skirt. That was all we could afford. We did not celebrate Christmas, at least not the kind of feast white people are used to. Grandma would save a little money and when the time came she bought some crystal sugar—it looked like small rocks of glass put on a string—some peanuts, apples, and oranges. And she got some kind of cotton material, sewing it together, making little pouches for us, and in each put one apple, one orange, a handful of peanuts, and some of that crystal sugar which took forever to melt in one's mouth. I loved it. That was Christmas and it never changed.

I was too small to know about racism then. When I was in third grade some relative took me to Pine Ridge and I went into a store. It was not very big, a small country grocery. One of my teachers was inside. I went right to the vegetable and fruit bins where I saw oranges just like the one I always got on Christmas. I sure wanted one of them. I picked the biggest one. An uncle had given me a nickel to go on a wild spree with and I wanted to use it paying for the orange. The store owner told me, "A nickel ain't enough to pay for one of them large Sunkist navel oranges, the only ones I got. Put it back." I still remember that. I had to put that damned orange back. Next to me, the wasicun teacher saw me do it and she made a face saying out loud, so that everyone in the store could hear it: "Why can't those dirty Indians keep their hands off this food? I was going to buy some oranges, but they put their dirty hands on them and now I must try to find some orange elsewhere. How disgusting!" It made a big impression on me, even though I could not understand the full meaning of this incident.

Grandma told me: "Whatever you do, don't go into white people's homes. 'Cause when they come into our homes they make fun of us, because we are poor." When we were growing up at He-Dog there were a few Indian shacks and the garage for buses and the filling station and that was totally it. Then the government started to move us to Parmelee where they put up new OEO houses, small, matchstick structures without cellars which the people called "poverty houses. " A school was also built and a few white teachers moved there. I made friends with a little white girl. She said, "Come to my house," I answered, "No, I ain't supposed to go to nobody's house." She said, "My ma ain't home. She's visiting neighbors. Just come!" So I sneaked over there without grandma knowing it. The white girl had many toys, dolls, a dollhouse. All the things I used to admire in the *Sears, Roebuck Catalogue* which I always studied in the outhouse. She had everything. She said, "Sit down and play with my toys." I did. I thought she was my friend. Suddenly I heard the door banging, banging, banging. It was the little girl's mother and she was yelling, "You open this door! You got some nerve coming into my home. You locked me out." She was screaming and I was shaking. I did not know what to do. I told her, "I did not lock you out. I did not even know that door was locked." She yelled, "Where is my whip?" She went into the hallway and got hold of a big, thick leather belt. She said, "Get over here!"

I ran as fast as I could back to my grandmother's house. I told her. "That white woman is going to whip me."

"What did you do?"

"Nothing. I just went into her house and she wants to whip me. Her little girl got me into trouble. I didn't do nothing. Hide me, grandma!" I was so scared.

By about that time the lady was coming. Grandma told me, "You stay here!" Then she got her big butcher knife. She went out standing in the doorway and told the woman, "You goddam white trash, you coming any closer and I'll chop your ears off." I never saw anybody run as fast as did that white lady.

In South Dakota white kids learn to be racists almost before they learn to walk. When I was about seven or eight years old, I fought with the school principal's daughter. We were in the playground. She was hanging on the monkey bar saying, "Come on, monkey, this thing is for you." She also told me that I smelled and looked like an Indian. I grabbed her by the hair and yanked her down from the monkey bar. I would have done more, but I saw the principal coming.

As I said, grandma spoke Sioux fluently. So does my mother. But we were not allowed to speak it and we were not taught. Many times I asked my grandmother, "Why don't you teach me the language?" Her answer always was: "'Cause we want you to get an education, to live a good life. Not have a hard time. Not depend on nobody. Times coming up are going to be real hard. You need a white man's education to live in this world. Speaking Indian would only hold you back, turn you the wrong way."

She thought she was helping me by not teaching me Indian ways. Her being a staunch Catholic also had something to do with it. The missionaries had always been repeating over and over again: *"You must kill the Indian in order to save the man!"* That was part of trying to escape the hard life. The missions, going to church, dressing and behaving like a wasicun—that for her was the key which would magically unlock the door leading to the good life, the white life with a white-painted cottage, and a carpet on the floor, a shiny car in the garage, and an industrious, necktie-wearing husband who was not a wino. Examples abounded all around her that it was the wrong key to the wrong door, that it would not change the shape of my cheekbones, or the slant of my eyes, the color of my hair, or the feelings inside me. She had only to open her eyes to see, but could not or would not. Her little dream was nourished and protected by the isolation in which she lived.

Grandma had been to mission school and that had influenced her to abandon much of our traditional ways. She gave me love and a good home, but if I wanted to be an Indian I had to go elsewhere to learn how to become one. To grandma's older sister, Mary, for instance, the one who is married to

Charlie Little Dog. I call them grandfather and grandmother, too, after the Sioux manner. He is a hundred and four years old now and grandma Little Dog about ninety-eight. They are very traditional people, faithful to the ancient rituals. They still carry their water from the river. They still chop wood. They still live like the Sioux of a hundred years ago. When Charlie Little Dog talks, he still uses the old words. You have to be at least sixty or seventy years old to understand what he is talking about—the language has changed that much. So I went to them if I wanted to hear the old tales of warriors and spirits, the oral history of our people.

I also went to grand-uncle Dick Fool Bull, the flute maker, who took me to my first peyote meeting, and to people like the Bear Necklaces, the Brave Birds, Iron Shells, Hollow Horn Bears, and Crow Dogs. One woman, Elsie Flood, a niece of grandma's, had a big influence upon me. She was a turtle woman, a strong, self-reliant person, because a turtle stands for strength, resolution, and long life. A turtle heart beats and beats for days, long after the turtle itself is dead. It keeps on beating all by itself. In traditional families a beaded charm in the shape of a turtle is fastened to a newborn child's cradle. The baby's navel cord is put inside this turtle charm, which is believed to protect the infant from harm and bad spirits. The charm is also supposed to make the child live to a great old age. A turtle is a strength of mind, a communication with the thunder.

I loved to visit Aunt Elsie Flood to listen to her stories. With her high cheekbones she looked like grandma. She had a voice like water bubbling, talking with a deep, throaty sound. And she talked fast, mixing Indian and English together. I had to pay strict attention if I wanted to understand what she told me. She always paid her bills, earning a living by her arts and crafts, her beautiful work with beads and porcupine quills—what she called "Indian novelties." She was also a medicine woman. She was an old-time woman carrying her pack on her back. She would not let a man or younger woman carry her burden. She carried it herself. She neither asked nor accepted help from anybody, being proud of her turtle strength. She used turtles as her protection. Wherever she went, she always had some little live turtles with her and all kinds of things made out of tortoiseshell, little charms and boxes. She had a little place in Martin, halfway between Rosebud and Pine Ridge, and there she lived alone. She was very independent but always glad to have me visit her. Once she came to our home, trudging along as usual with the heavy pack on her back and two shopping bags full of herbs and strange things. She also brought a present for me—two tiny, very lively turtles. She had painted Indian designs on their shells and their bottoms. She communicated with them by name. One she called "Come" and the other "Go." They always waddled over to her when she called them to get their food. She had a special kind of feed for them, leaving me whole bags of it. These small twin turtles stayed tiny. They never grew. One day the white

(Under name Mary Crow Dog with Richard Erdoes) *Lakota Woman* (autobiography), Grove Weidenfeld, 1990; republished by Harper Perennial, 1991.

(Under name Mary Brave Bird with Richard Erdoes) *Ohitika Woman* (autobiography), Grove Press, 1993.

principal's son came over and smashed them. Simply stomped them to death. When she heard it my aunt said that this was an evil sign for her.

The turtle woman was afraid of nothing. She was always hitchhiking, constantly on the road thumbing her way from one place to the other. She was a mystery to some. The Indians held her in great respect, saying that she was "wakan," that she was some sort of holy person to whom turtles had given their powers. In the summer of 1976 she was found beaten to death in her home. She was discovered under the bed, face down and naked, with weeds in her hair. She had never hurt anyone or done an unkindness to anybody, only helped people who needed it. No Indian would have touched a single hair on her head. She died that way. I still grieve for her. Her death has never been investigated. The life of an Indian is not held in great value in the State of South Dakota. There is no woman like her anymore.

So many of my relations and friends who were ever dear to me, or meant something to me, or meant something to the people, have either been killed or found dead on some out-of-the-way road. The good Indians die first. They do not grow old. This turtle aunt of mine was one of the traditionally strongest women of her generation. To bring back what knowledge she had is going to take time. It will take another generation or two to bring it back.

In spite of our grandparents trying so hard to be good Christians, some Indian beliefs rubbed off on them. I remember when I was little, if someone was sick, Grandfather Moore would fill one of the tubs used for watering the cattle and put live ducks in it, saying: "If those birds stay in and swim awhile, swim around, that sick person is gonna be all right. But if the ducks just jump out and leave, the sick one won't get better." He never explained it, just expected everybody to take it on faith. Much later, when my sister Barbara lost her baby, some relatives and friends held a peyote meeting for her. Barb asked our mother and grandmother to come and they actually did. They must have been a little uneasy among all these heathenish goings-on, but they lasted all night and behaved well, as if they had been doing it all their lives. I am sure they worried that the priest would hear about it. I also remember having been told that once, when a person living in a tent behind our shack fell ill, grandfather got a medicine man to doctor him and suck the evil poisons out of his system.

M A R Y   B R A V E   **B I R D**

I lived the simple life at He-Dog until I had to go to boarding school. We kids did not suffer from being poor, because we were not aware of it. The few Indians nearby lived in the same kind of want, in the same kind of dilapidated shacks or one-room log cabins with dirt floors. We had nothing to compare our life to. We existed in a vacuum of our own. We were not angry because we did not know that somewhere there was a better, more comfortable life. To be angry, poverty has to rub shoulders with wealth, as for instance ghetto people in squalid tenements living next door to the rich in their luxury apartments as I have seen during my visits to New York. TV has destroyed the innocence, broken through the wall that separates the rich whites from the poor nonwhites. The "boob tube" brainwashes people, but if they are poor and nonwhite, it also makes them angry seeing all those things advertised that they can never hope to have—the fancy homes and cars, the dishwashers and microwaves, the whole costly junk of affluent America. I wonder whether the advertisers who spend a hundred thousand dollars on a commercial are aware of broadcasting a revolutionary message.

As we had no electricity we also had no "idiot box" and therefore felt no envy. Except for that one incident in the white lady's home, I had not yet encountered racism in its varied forms, and that one event I had not fully comprehended. It left me afraid of white people, though, that and some stories I had heard. As I hardly met any white people, they did not bother me. I liked the food I got; I did not know any other, and hunger is a good cook. I liked our shack. Its being overcrowded only meant womblike security to me. Again, except for that white lady's house, I only knew the kind that looked like ours, except for the filling station, but that was not a home. I had food, love, a place to sleep, and a warm, potbellied, wood-fed stove to sit near in the winter. I needed nothing more. Finally, I had something white kids don't usually have—horses to ride. No matter how poor we Sioux are, there are always a few ponies around. When I was a small girl you could buy a nice-looking pinto for ten dollars. So I was riding from as early an age as I can remember. I liked the feel of a horse under me, a feeling of mastery, of freedom, of wildness, of being Indian. It is a feeling shared by everybody on the reservation. Even the most white-manized Sioux is still half horse. I never particularly wished for anything during my earlier childhood except to own an Appaloosa, because I had seen a picture of one in a magazine and fell in love with it. Maybe one day, if I live, I'll get my wish.

Grandfather Moore died in 1972. He passed away peacefully in his sleep. I was glad he had such an easy death. He was a good, loving man, a hard-working janitor. I miss him. I miss grandma. They protected us as long as they were able, but they could not protect us from being taken away to boarding school.

BARNEY FURMAN  BUSH

Essay by

RUTH ROSENBERG

Although born and raised in southern Illinois, Bush generally claims Oklahoma as his home, arguing that his "relatives who remain strongly attached to [their Native American] identity live there." After completing high school, Bush hitchhiked across the United States for several years before attending Fort Lewis College in Durango, Colorado, from which he graduated in 1972 with degrees in art and history. Following graduation, he became involved in the American Indian Movement, helped to establish the Institute of the Southern Plains (a Cheyenne Indian School in Oklahoma), and taught subjects relating to Native American culture at the University of Wisconsin in Milwaukee and several other colleges. In 1980 he earned a master's degree in English and fine arts from the University of Idaho.

Since 1975 Bush has published four volumes of poetry: *Longhouse of the Blackberry Moon*, *My Horse and a Jukebox*, *Petroglyphs*, and *Inherit the Blood*, which also contains a short story. Lyricism, narrative intensity, vivid images, and a realistic attention to detail characterize the style of Bush's poetry. Frequently imbued with a sense of outrage at past and present injustices that white society has perpetrated against Native Americans and the natural environment, Bush's works focus on themes of identity, cultural conflict, social struggle, and the disintegration of traditional values. Although criticized for sometimes weighing down his poetry with anger and sentimentality, most commentators concur that Bush possesses a distinctive poetic voice that dramatizes the suffering and aspirations of Native Americans.

Shawnee and Cayuga poet and short story writer.

Born: August, 27, 1946 (some sources say 1945).

Education: Fort Lewis College, Durango, CO, B.A., 1972; University of Idaho, M.A., 1980.

Career: University of Wisconsin, Milwaukee, WI, Native American specialist, 1973–74; National Indian Youth Council, Albuquerque, NM, and Institute of the Southern Plains, Hammond, OK, educational specialist, 1974–75; Milwaukee Area Technical College, Milwaukee, WI, instructor in American Indian literature.

Memberships: National Society of Poets, Rio Grande Writer's Association, Poets and Writers (New York City).

Address: P.O. Box 52, Herod, IL 62947.

INHERIT THE BLOOD

From *Inherit the Blood*, Thunder's Mouth Press, copyright © 1985 by Barney Bush

Last nights moon   opened
power of seeds   rich earth
Ohio and Mississippi River
villages bring forth the
sacred objects
On flat topped mounds   wise
elders confer   bless the
seeds in moonlight
Moons power   songs of our
elders   are handsome male
and female spirit
Wet bottomlands   thick with
budding limbs   night peepers
crickets   wind of rushing
water   stir with morning
sun   grandfather the
nourisher   the mid husband for
children about to be born

Greedy Ones   as you leave
take your sacred icons
statue of liberty   nuclear
cores   draglines   cancer
the gold in Ft Knox   take
your names with you   to

8 4

Poetry

Longhouse of the Blackberry Moon, 1975.

My Horse and a Jukebox, American Indian Studies Center, 1979.

Petroglyphs, with drawings by Meenjit Tatsii, Greenfield Review Press, 1982.

Inherit the Blood: Poetry and Fiction, Thunder's Mouth Press, 1985.

Work represented in several anthologies, including *The Remembered Earth,* Red Earth Press; *The First Skin Around Me,* Territorial Press; *Brother Songs,* Holy Cow Press; and *Harper's Anthology: Native American Poetry,* Harper & Row, 1987. Contributor to numerous periodicals, including *Beloit Poetry Journal, Denver Quarterly, Suntracks, Concerning Poetry, Coyote's Journal, Scree,* and *Quetzal.* Has also released a music album, *Oyate,* Nato Records, France, 1990.

your world beyond the stars
and   with madlike laughter
know your manifest destiny is
not complete   until each
planet bears your flag
i remember wind   i remember
last nights moon   songs in
the circle of my silhouette
i remember etching these
symbols onto this
conch shell disk   i
remember the origin of our
world   what foreigners in
forty years will scientifically
say is   inherited in the
blood.

TAKING A CAPTIVE/1984

for Mike Gavlak

A light drizzle falling   off
and on for days
Kentucky hills   yellow leaves
matted to damp black   your
pensive eyes in smokey hollows
My son   you are born by

B A R N E Y   F U R M A N   **B U S H**

mistake in another world where

your vision lingers

too long

too long to teach those who

seek wisdom from the future

Three generations back   in

my village you would be

painted   have a name

Waylahskese

You would carry flute of

polished cedar   inlaid with

finest abalone shell   bound

with soft white buckskin

On humid evenings i would

hear your cavernous melodies

rolling off limestone bluffs

above Spaylawa Theepi

You would grow into manhood

bringing fresh meat to the

door of your grandmothers

weegiwa   carry

your opahwahka in the

oracle of your heart

Stalking figures yet roam

shadows of colonial america

yet drawing breath   continuous

memory absorbed into blood

Your ivoried tiger form spoors

its way to my heart   not as

a killer but as   one of grace

Here in my center   M'qua seeks

power to bring you home   sniffs

the air for winter

Too soon   Shemegana pepoou

Your real name awaits

Come into your dreams   my young

captive   hear the hawk shriek

as he soars outside your window

Come into the lodge of winter

dreams   hibernate with the

bear.

Spaylaway Theepi Ohio River
Weegiwa house
Opahwahka Medicine
M'qua Black bear
Shemegana pepoou Foreign cold, threat of winter

ABBEY OF THE BEAR

for Ursule Molinaro with much affection

Hard years in Euroamerica's alien world have brought Omar back to the headwaters of White Bird Creek. Childhood familiarity blends with his stagnant odor, sloshes over mirrored rocks that dissolve the forest edge, spills into the canyon's decaying wetness. The flood pours into the bell of Omar's worlds. His body is almost six feet of naked summer, hardened with prison tattoos, sheened in Oklahoma humidity. Omar is a veteran . . . not of the Viet Nam War that has just ended . . . but of the streets. A squinting icon in the afternoon sun, he feels the rapid beating of his heart, the rupturing of honky-tonk nights that dull his memory. He steps reverently into the cool river, kneads the sandy bottom with his toes, senses the blue hill water edging up his calves. He scoops the liquid, allows it to pour between his fingers, swallows it like whiskey of which there was never enough. His scream shatters the wall of cedar and black oak air as he abandons himself into the depths of White Bird Creek.

Around the corner of the log house, she carries her willow basket filled with plump blackberries and dewberries that she has picked from hillside briars. Old Annie possesses acute eyes that jet from side to side inside a face that bears the plum's lot of remaining in the sun too long. On summer mornings before the red sun devours the smokey mist, she wanders the dank hollows, harvesting plants and singing prayers. It is the whites who call her Old Annie. Among older native people, she is known as Gonawah

Hequawi, Rainbow Woman. Many young people in the district call her Nohkohmis, Grandmother, as it is her leathered hands that pulled their mucoused bodies into this world. And this she is, by blood, to Omar. With bears and rainbows she exchanges secrets of earth and sky, of the spirit world and of the plants that reveal themselves to her. During winter nights elders tell stories of the times when the Southwind People first lived along the Spaylaway Theepi, Ohio River, and of the brave men and women who fought and died resisting the Greedy Ones. How diseases, alcohol, and murders of children and elders had destroyed their respect for the Greedy Ones as human beings. But the favorite story is told by hunters who have seen Old Annie conversing with P'qway, a gigantic female black bear, who lives somewhere in the bluffs above White Bird Creek. Eyes of children widen and sparkle when they hear that black bears used to be human beings.

Setting her basket down by the well, Annie sinks the bucket with one twisting jerk, distorting her shimmering image into whirlpools of darkness. She pours the entire contents through her harvest. The berries glitter like tiny clumps of midnight sky. This pleases her even though her eyes are fixed with concern, squinting perhaps more from the sunlight than the visit yesterday. Attorneys representing the Ozark Mining Company had approached her about testing her land for coal. She straightens her back and ponders over her garden patch. The corn is doing good. She wonders why she had heard Semyalwa, the owl, hooting down by the creek this morning. Hesitating on her weathered porch, she looks across the garden to the hills beyond. Some few berries roll from her basket as she turns, allowing the screen door to slam behind her.

He is near the valley and can hear cicadas humming their familiar way, familiar time of midsummer when it's even too hot to snag. The rolling meadows of his boyhood unfold before him. It is a land not too unlike the Ohio Valley of his grandparents. This was the final removal area, the last land that the Greedy Ones didn't want. And those who had not hidden in remote pockets of the east had come to call it home. To the west, the tribes who had followed the buffalo were settled on the open plains. Omar touches gently the large white pine under which he used to sit. There were always aunts and uncles and kids around the house of his nohkohmis. He remembers his mother always leaving him there with her, for days on end. His Uncle Adrian, Annie's brother, had stood in for the father he never knew. The other kids had teased him, saying his father was some old white drunk that his mother never called by name. This is a puzzle Omar has yet to put together. His Uncle Adrian had taught him to track deer, trap rabbits, and had helped to translate his visions. Leaning against the mnemonic tree, Omar wonders how his Nohkohmis will react when she knows he is home. He doesn't know that she has saved his sporadic letters from over the years, the ones written from jails and rooms above flashing lights; but she has saved them and reads them like books with pages missing. He expels the pine needle from between his teeth and begins walking resignedly down the hill.

While she prepares the berries for Ptakuwha, sour bread, steam from boiling deer meat permeates the house and makes sweat on the windows. Her purple hands work the dough, over and over. The same way her own mother and grandmother had done it. Her hands stop. For an instant she closes her eyes as if she could feel her face being brushed lightly with a feathered wing. Before submerging her hands in old dishwater, she mechanically glances out the window. She stands solemnly on the porch. Tears appear between the long grey braids that frame her face.

Omar munches on Ptakuwha and daqualaquay, closing his eyes with each bite. Nohkohmis light the lamp. She begins a long recapitulation into a starry night once dominated by whippoorwills, owls, and coyotes. Omar's lips stumble over his first language. The good feel of the words thaw on his tongue, warming him like the closeness of Nohkohmis and the whitewashed log walls around them.

[Bush's] poetry is distinctly contemporary. Rather than identifying in the older traditions with a single tribal origin and fixed sense of place, Bush works toward an Indian consciousness of tribes and places that would bind Native Americans together. He seems, first of all, a human being who reaches down for definition as an Indian—but with a present-tense twist, a traveler's knowing of the way things are in country and city nowadays. His traditional past is set against city time and the descents of history, nascent in tribal names, family ties, Indian places, powwows in "Milwaukee, Chicago, Minneapolis," city names all in their origins Indian.

She lets him sleep this morning, until the humidity becomes too uncomfortable. Omar awakens, smearing the cool dampness over his body. He stretches his shoulders, rubs his face as if he were waking with a hangover. Realizing that he is at home, he lies still for a few moments longer, relieved. Omar knows it is hotter outside. He senses that his grandmother is not in the house. Putting on his pants, he walks to the screendoor, scans the summer light, sees her hoeing her rows of near mature corn. On her face, the sun reflects tiny beads of sweat. He can feel the sound of the hoe breaking the crust of rich bottomland earth and the clanging of steel when she strikes a rock. Remembering her words from the night, "Na quisah, my son, do you know why you have come home?" He didn't. And today is no different, not yet anyway. And one does not answer an elder haphazardly.

BARNEY FURMAN **BUSH**

Besides, Annie is from a generation that requires words straight from the heart. Their eyes cause lies to stumble.

Through the night hours, like pails of soil from a cave, she filled his absent seasons with past events: who had died, married, children born, feuds, illnesses, who was in jail, who got out, who moved away, moved home, powows, stomp dances, ball games, Green Corn Ceremonies, who was drinking, who had quit, who was off to college, who weren't raising their children right. All this before telling him about the lawyers from Tulsa, "The Greedy Ones are coming again."

They had told her that they were representatives of the Ozark Mining Company and that their mineralogists had tested the swampy bottoms for coal. The rich vein that they had found ran the whole length of the valley. Omar recalls her spitting motion as she related their promises of wealth to the Southwind People and all their descendants, if only they would sell their land for stripmining.

In his mind, Omar visualizes the nervous twitching of the attorneys as his grandmother patiently rebukes their attempts at cajoling her. She told them of the importance of the land, the children, and the ceremonies, ". . . . but their greed would not let them hear this truth." Mechanically, the attorneys repeated over and over the advantages that wealth could bring to a people. The attorneys, too, had tried to be patient. They raised their voices as if they were talking to a deaf person, one who could not hear that they were talking big bucks.

"The revenue from the coal will provide a lot of jobs for your people. Industry needs this coal. Take a little more time to think this over. We don't think you realize the magnitude of this situation. Other tribes have gladly sold leases to mine coal. They want to help out their country. They want businesses moving in on their reservations," said the one attorney whose fingers and neck were laden with turquoise jewelry.

"Yes," Annie had said, "Greed has affected lives among all the tribes. We heard Crows, Cheyennes, and Navajoes tell us stories about the coalmines. They say the big machines came and devoured the earth like angry monsters, spit out the remains and left orange water in their holes. They say their homes are gone, and their children are sick from the invisible enemy, their old people are turning to alcohol to bury the sorrow of their weaknesses, their ignorance in allowing this awful thing to happen. When our people make deals with you, there is only death. Your own history says it is so, yet you continue without regard for the balance of life. The sparkle of gold and silver is the light of your eyes. Go somewhere else and deceive some other people, like your fathers and mothers, but you will buy no land from the Southwind People." The red-faced attorneys had risen from their seats as if having been dealt a challenge rather than a refusal.

"Lady, we can see you need time to think this over. Here is some literature on coalmining. The land can be made to look as good as new and you can move back on it when the coal is dug out," said the turquoised one trying to control his thoughts.

"Now you speak of graveyards. Our home is alive now, and we will not sell our mother," Annie had spoken.

Truly frustrated, the attorneys stomped out the door promising Annie that they would be back with a more agreeable offer. She knew this was just the beginning. Omar shakes the conversation from his head.

Nohkohmis stands, the hoe supporting her folded hands, watching Omar leave the porch for the well. He has not forgotten how to sink a bucket and lift cold spring water to his lips. He sets the bucket down, splashes his face and chest. No words are necessary now. Nohkohmis knows. Omar knows. Behind the smokehouse, he takes a piss, watching the mid-day breeze play across the top of the sagegrass. It is the real world, the quiet world of beauty and daydreams. Omar thinks perhaps it is too quiet.

II

Days come and go, each one seeming to intensify with the heat. Omar passes time with his nohkohmis, with the intimacy of a first born grandson imitating the hands of his female blood. There is a noticeable absence of visitors that Omar attributes to the scalding heat, and does not verbally question this absence. But with his eyes, he questions her use of all these herbs that she is constantly collecting. Omar recalls many from his youth but has never realized the reasons for all the continual harvesting. Annie explains to him slowly and assuredly how to prepare the plants for medicine, that everything in this life is medicine if one knows how to use it properly.

"Even a small mistake may cause great harm to the user, and the one who prepares it. Many of the plants offer themselves at only one time during the seasons and if one is to use them, they must be taken at that time. One must never forget that, like all life, plants are male and female too, each giving according to its design. To take the plants or animals properly, you must know which side of you is required. . . . .," Annie says, directing her statement deeply into Omar's presence, ". . . . This is the balance that Matche prevents others from knowing."

Omar becomes preoccupied with this balance. Even away from her, on White Bird Creek, swimming in the cold murky depth, "Each of us is male and female," she had said. Lying back in the shade of the bank, he stares into the river's hypnotic movement until he becomes an animate part of the beauty around him. A heated wind welters through the cottonwoods, shaking the willows as if someone were walking in them. It is the wind, and the heat and lack of rain that have lowered the creek.

It was like this, as a child, when his Uncle Adrian, other male relatives, and himself, would put seines at opposite ends of the creek, walk and swim them toward each other. Everyone would strip off their clothes, and with burlap sacks, dive into the water. Bodies would surface, yelling, "Hoyah, hoyah!" and laughing, everyone was always laughing, holding, grappling with bags of catfish, bass, and bluegill. Always at such gatherings, someone could be heard to say, "Giteen hili lewe! P'laytha hisip kihe!" P'laytha, the eagle, would always be circling, at first a mere speck in the humid sky, screaming, closer, watching, blessing. A fish from each bag was always left for P'laytha.

"Ah, yes, P'laytha," Omar remembers. It was about second or third grade, at the mission school. He was on these creek banks, in a confusion bordering on fear. He had been whipped again for quoting his methoshena, grandfather, "We don't need the Greedy Ones to tell us about our Creator. Great Eagle is our messenger between earth and sky. The Greedy Ones teach fear and hate. Our Creator is not such a one." The teachers had taken their turns whipping the young pagan into submissiveness.

With this recollection, Omar yet cringes. He can still feel the inward attack on his beliefs, his relatives, and shakes at the memory of the uncontrollable crying that overcame him when he looked to the sky to see many eagles circling. He remembers P'qway had been watching him from the opposite bluff. Omar's Methoshena Elmer had been fishing in the clearing above the willows, and had heard Omar's crying, "Miyon ne lahne, young man, what is the matter? Don't let P'qway hear you cry. It will make her sad." At that moment, P'qway had reared up on her haunches, her gentle black face appearing to smell the sky. Settling back on all four, she wandered the edge of the bluff, staring into the creek, until she was out of sight.

Omar gets up with his daydreams, wanders into the willows at the creek's edge. Stooping, he gouges out a ball of the blood red clay, and rolls it between his palms. . . . remembering his grandfather's stories of being at Carlisle Indian School in Pennsylvania where he had read the Bible. Elmer's teachers had smiled, well-satisfied that they were sending another heathen convert back to the wilds of Indian Territory. They became dismayed, however, to find that Elmer Blue Jacket, in reading the Bible, had only confirmed that the Creator of native people was the same one who had created the whiteman. The Creator had given to everyone, a place to live, and ceremonies that were in harmony with the homeland. That was why everyone was different. Aghast, the missionaries finally sent Elmer home, an unchangeable patron of Satan.

Through his remaining days, Omar's methoshena acted as a mediator between the Christian Indians and the traditional Round House people explaining that the Creator never intended for anyone to quarrel over religion, or to make war over interpretation. Omar recalls his grandfather's last speech at Green Corn, to peoples of both religions. "The elders speak of a time when we will live in peace and harmony with one another, again. They say our Creator will send the White Plumed Spirit back among us. In Europe's Bible, Jesus says, 'For as the lightning comes from the east and shines as far as the west, so will be the coming of the Son of man. Wherever the body is, there the eagles will be gathered together.'"

The ball of clay is nearly dry. "Omar!" Annie's voice interrupts his reminiscing. The clay ball rolls from Omar's long fingers into the creek, and dissolves. "Omar, the people are stomp dancing over in Bowleg's Hollow tonight. If you feel like it, we'll go. People have heard that you are home and have asked for you to come."

It is too sudden, the idea of going among the people. Other scenes flash through his head: hitchhiking into Newtown, to the night spots where white farmers elude Christian wives, where "Satin Sheets" is playing on the blue jukeboxes, guzzling beers over a pooltable . . . shit! Annie eyes him, back and forth, waiting for his reply.

"Damn!" he mumbles to himself. "How will we get there, Nohkohmis?"

"Your Uncle Adrian. He is coming in his truck, with his family. They all want to see you. They may come before dark, so come help me. There are things to do," she says, assuming an affirmation. The planning in Omar's eyes has not passed by her.

Western sky is fiery red when Omar hears the first whippoorwill near the house. A childhood excitement. Getting ready for a dance, almost like getting ready to go out to the bars. Omar feels slick. Just barely hanging over the collar of his white cowboy shirt, his sunburned black hair is parted in the middle and combed back behind his ears. He has two turquoise posts in his ears that were pierced by his grandmother when he was four. His sleeves are rolled to his elbows, exposing the tattoos on his forearms. On the right arm is an Indian with a western headdress, and the Initials A.I.M. underneath; the left arm reveals the names, Roseanne, Naomi, Carol T., and a jumbling of initials, and scars that were desperate attempts at removing old initials, before adding new ones. His new looking blue jeans are boot cut and reach to the heel of beige colored boots with pointed brown tips like Navajos wear.

Annie, too, is busy. Moving about the house with premeditated opening and closing of drawers and cabinet doors. She holds first one shawl up to the remaining light, than another, with no pretense of hiding her excitement of attending the stomp dance with her beloved grandson . . . that his return might provide some kind of balance to their clan, and to this new threat from the stripmines, but for tonight, it is a dance. She continues with no other thought except for the wrapping of items that are without English names, into cloths of various colors. . . . "Omar, fold all those blankets and shawls that are in the front room closet, and put them into those garbage bags," she instructs him by pointing with her lips.

At that moment, Omar hears the motor rumbling across the field, iron breaking against stone. He sees the headlights bouncing through the pines lining the rocky dirt road. Down into the dry wash and up, billows of red dust trailing into the yard, camouflaging headlights that have come to a dead stop. The back of the dark pickup is filled with kids, young men, and women, yelling and laughing at the wild horse ride.

Shadows dart about in the headlights. Omar walks into view. Shadows stand still. Silence. Omar, his hands in his back pockets, is nervously seeking familiarity. The driver's door opens and into view is Omar's Uncle Adrian. Silent words through eyes and smiles. Adrian Little Light, Kesauthwau, younger brother of Gonawah Hequawi, had assumed her husband's role of teacher for young Omar, after Elmer had died.

Omar searches his uncle's smooth brown face, the alert eyes that illuminate his tall, heavy, frame. His ungrayed black hair is short. Short, short, from boarding school days over sixty-one years ago. In the silence that occupies the space between Omar and Adrian, the power of Bear Clan reenters this circle, and it is like a dream that reverses reality. Omar remembers the habits of two legs, four legs, and no legs, how their spirits return for food, for power, and how many others seek this knowledge to further control the lives of humans as well as animals, how Matche tries to weaken the clans so as to misuse their power. From all sides, come the odors of sage, sweetgrass, cedar, and Adrian's big hands and arms embracing Omar's stout body. In the firm embrace, Omar is finally connected with the old tobacco smell of his uncle, and the songs melt away the seasons of his thirty-two years.

9 4

Wanda, who is married to Adrian, gives the female embrace. She had provided shawls, food, and encouragement when Omar, as a child, had first danced. She is a mother who lines the road of harmony, whose face is always seen in the ring of firelight.

And the ancient presence that is inscribed into pottery and conch shell disks, that presided over councils atop archaic mounds lives inside Gonawah Hequawi. She stands, magenta Pendleton blanket, edged with black fringe, over her arm. On her feet are puckered style deerskin moccasins with a floral design in cut beads, barely perceptible beneath her long, blue broadcloth, transitional dress, edged with red, yellow, and green ribbon work. A handworked German-silver concho belt holds her waist. Her hair, unbraided, is wrapped behind her neck and hanging loosely past her waist. From each pierced ear hangs a German-silver waterbird. Suspended on a twisted string of sinew around her neck in a single bear's claw, usually worn only by males. There is neither modesty nor loftiness in her countenance, nor in Wanda's, or Adrian's, but Omar is inwardly trying to struggle loose.

He senses that there is something in tradition, in human memory that cannot be passed on without ceremony, cannot be recorded for history, but passes into the winds, into the soil and rivers until that time that someone must pick it up again, must use it to dignify survival, to give life to beauty. Omar cannot, does not allow himself to complete his thoughts. He feels nauseous, like he must sit down. . . .

Adrian comforts him, holding his arm under Omar's, "I understand, Na quisah. It's been a long time . . . Maybe, let's go fishing tomorrow, in old White Bird, huhhh! Let's get everybody in the truck." Off to the side, yet embracing Omar, Adrian says to him, "You know, I bet we have to cut switches to keep those Creek women off you tonight. Aieeeee!"

Annie rides up front with Adrian, Wanda, and one small grandson crying to ride in the back. Omar sits on blankets in the truck bed with the younger relatives and their kids. By tradition they are all brothers and sisters, nephews and nieces, to Omar, but the years of absence brings only surface conversation. Omar is glad to ride quietly through the summer night, feeling the cool wind and looking up at the stars. After leaving the dirt road, the truck turns onto a county maintained gravel road along the foot of the hills. The humid darkness rushes in on Omar reminding him of the first time he hit Oklahoma City. "Damn! I wish I had a good long swig of Jack Daniels," he says in English to himself.

III

Woodsmoke permeates the air. The haunting swamp voice of the lead singer, the steady rhythm of shakers, nostalgic tremors possess Omar, momentarily, and again he realizes that he dreams in someone else's sleep sometimes never knowing which nightmare is real.

The grounds are lit with fires. German silver pendants sparkle in the procession of dancers. Bright scarves hang from necks, and suspend from clothing. Metal shakers, attached to the legs of dancers, keep a constant beat with singing and drumming.

Kids hurtle from the truck, and enjoy a momentary wild abandon scrambling between trucks and cars that have been battered by dirt roads and wired together beyond use by white people. Annie's family of Bear Clan people stand just long enough to groom themselves, and instruct the children before entering the grounds.

The song ends. Whispered conversations slow to a deafening silence. Children stop dead in their tracks to gape at the arriving delegation. The congregation observes with awe and admiration for one whose spiritual ties are unquestionable, and with curiosity for the mysterious grandson. An elder woman steps forward to shake hands with Gonawah Hequawi, then the others of her family. Other elders, mothers, fathers, and young people follow the elder lady in line, shaking hands with Bear Clan People, and welcoming Omar home. There are members of many tribes at this dance—Miamis, Creeks, Seminoles, Peorias, Delawares, Cherokees, Senecas, Shawnees— whose ancient homelands were east of the Mississippi River, until the resistance and removal days, all concentrated here in northeast Indian Territory. Now bound by blood ties and changing ceremonies.

In his mind, Omar realizes that his body and eyes move in "street fashion." He is glad to be here, but he is uneasy. He feels an odd sensation in his neck. The reverence shown for his grandmother, for him, is confusing. He wonders why he agreed to come. He shakes hands, tries to smile and return respect. As the greeters pass by, they begin resuming places. Adrian touches Omar's shoulder and motions with his lips toward a log bench.

Water drums begin warming up. Dancers file in two by two. Songs permeate veins of the forest until Omar gasps inside his former world. Drums resound inside his head, his chest, from times surviving in warrior hearts. At eighteen he had simply shrugged when his friends had spoken of joining the army . . . to become warriors. His grandfather, Elmer, had said that he thought young people in these days had begun to believe what the whites had written in their history books about Indians. All that bullshit. Why should a real warrior offer his life to defend the enemy, Matche, who continued to drain the very life from his own people, and the land? Omar is a warrior. Deep in his blood, he has always known it, but the frustration of not knowing what all this blood means. . . .

"What does it mean to be a warrior?" he had asked his grandfather.

"To be honorable," his grandfather had said, "and to pray for honor among all our relatives."

What was honor? Omar had left home for reasons not even known to himself. The ambiguous term, job relocation, had gotten lost in the gloomy shadows of bars, and in the people who lived in those bars. Many times while drunk, Omar had tried to figure it out. He told himself that this was why he stayed drunk so often. Then he would use it as an excuse for sobering up, then use it for getting drunk again.

9 6

Omar recalls that in desperate moments of his street world, drunk and screaming hopelessly for a touch of recognition, he would fall into his stinking sweat, wake up in dark rooms bare of surroundings. In the corner of darkness, he would hear grunting and snorting, a bear licking its paws as if they were greasy. In pounding silence, he would attempt to focus on the bear's figure, but he can never recall being awake when the dank gamboling animal approached him.

Adrian's hand rests reassuringly on Omar's. "Son, you're home. Stay here with us. Your grandmother needs you at home. She is getting on in her days, worries about those lawyers." Omar quickly changes the subject with, "Uncle, who was my father? Why has no one ever spoke of him to me? I'm grown man. What kind of secret can change my life at this time?"

"Because I only know what others tell me regarding those days, you must seek this information from your nohkohmis . . . the story is too unclear for me to attempt to clear your mind on who your father was," Adrian concluded. Omar stares at his uncle with a smiling resignation and gets up to walk around the dance grounds.

Groups of young girls who had timidly shaken hands with Omar, are now following him as he walks. He turns abruptly, grunting out, "Yahhhh-eh!" The girls scream. . . . laughing. . . .

And boldly whisper to each other and yell loudly, "Aieeeee . . . " They do this over and over. Someday one of these girls will snag him. They think.

Omar shakes hands with old school chums, cousins, their children and appears to be talking intimately with some of the guys, and those young girls still flashing black shining eyes back and forth. Annie, visiting with a group of shawled older women on the other side of the dance, watches everything.

Leaving her friends with an indication of return, Annie catches up to Omar, and instructs him to aid his uncle in bringing up the plastic bags from the truck.

Wanda, Adrian, Omar, and cousins bring the bags of blankets, shawls, food, and lay them near the big fire. Wanda and Annie spread thin cotton blankets on the ground. All the blankets and shawls are stacked nearly on top with several bags of food, including chunks of fresh beef from Adrian's herd, laid out on the plastic.

97

All singing has stopped. The headman of the dance grounds calls for all family members of Gonawah Hequawi and Kesauthwau to come forward and assist their relatives in the give away. Annie instructs the standing positions of everyone. Her brother Kesauthwau and his family on her left. Omar stands on her right. Annie begins, "Na quisah, Omar, has come home to be with his people. Since this is so, it is the way of our clan that we show our happiness in this fashion. Kesauthwau will call out the names to come up and receive a gift from our family. When we have called all the names, those visitors and ones who did not hear their names will please come and accept the remaining gifts."

Each recipient passes, shaking hands first with Omar, then each member on down to the youngest child. After all the gifts are taken, the lead singer begins a song accompanied by other singers and the drummers and dancers. Omar and his family must lead. This is familiar to Omar, who has forgotten all about wanting a drink, and is feeling the drum in his feet. Males, side by side, followed by females. . . . in the center of night . . . seeming tireless . . . like the singers whose voices are more explicit as daylight, pale and irrefutable, appears above hills to the east, edging into the starry sky.

The morning star hears the laughing, last minute visiting . . . shines into the open mouths of children whose eyes are sealed. . . . blankets shake into morning air. . . . teasing . . . laughter. Hosts of the stomp dance grounds smother the fires. Annie quietly packs a sleeping child into the truck and gets in beside him. First light of sun breaks through the dust and onto the stomp grounds. Silence. The embers are dead, but the earth is resonating long after everyone is gone. It is another humid day.

MARIA  CAMPBELL

Campbell is best known for her autobiography Halfbreed, *which relates her struggles as a Métis woman in Canadian society. A best-seller in Canada, the book has been described by Hartmut Lutz as "the most important and seminal book authored by a Native person from Canada." Of Scottish, Indian, and French descent and the eldest daughter in a family of seven children, Campbell was born in northern Saskatchewan. After her mother's death, Campbell was forced to quit school at age twelve to take care of her younger siblings. At age fifteen she married an alcoholic, abusive white man in order to prevent her brothers and sisters from being placed in an orphanage. Her attempt to keep her family united, however, was unsuccessful; her husband reported her to the welfare authorities, and her siblings were placed in foster care.*

After moving to Vancouver, where her husband deserted her, Campbell became a prostitute and drug addict. After two suicide attempts and a nervous breakdown, she was hospitalized and entered Alcoholics Anonymous. She began writing *Halfbreed* in an attempt to deal with her anger, frustration, loneliness, and the pressure to return to a life of drugs and prostitution: "I had no money, and I was on the verge of being kicked out of my house, had no food, and I decided to go back out in the street and work. I went out one night and sat in a bar. And I just couldn't, because I knew if I went back to that, I'd be back on drugs again. . . . I started writing a letter [to myself] because I had to have somebody to talk to, and there was nobody to talk to. And that was how I wrote *Halfbreed*."

Relating the first thirty-three years of her life, *Halfbreed* recounts on a personal level the discrimination and racism to which the Métis have historically been subjected. Infused with a strong undercurrent of anger and bitterness, the book documents Campbell's search for self-identity, her attempts to overcome the harshness of Métis life, and finally, albeit briefly, her work as a political activist. Considered a sociological tract as well as a moving historical account, the book has been praised for its humor, its documentation of Métis patois and rituals, and its tender portrait of Campbell's loving relationship with her grandmother, Cheechum.

Campbell is additionally known for such children's works as *People of the Buffalo: How the Plains Indians Lived* and *Riel's People*, which relate Métis traditions and history, and for *The Book of Jessica: A Theatrical Transformation*, which documents her attempt to produce a stage adaptation of *Halfbreed* with Linda Griffiths. Commenting on the significance of *Halfbreed* to cross-cultural communication, Agnes Grant has observed: "Though the book was written for non-Natives Maria keeps them at a distance. She writes of things she knows, which she believes her readers do not know. The humor and irony are very effective in pointing out to the readers that, indeed, Maria is right. There are things that we did not know. Until she wrote the book, `halfbreed' was nothing but a common derogatory term; now it means a person living between two cultures."

HALFBREED

Saturday Review Press, copyright © 1973 by Maria Campbell

Introduction

The house where I grew up is tumbled down and overgrown with brush. The pine tree beside the east window is dried and withered. Only the poplar trees and the slough behind the house are unchanged. There is a family of beavers still there, busy working and chattering just as on that morning, seventeen years ago, when I said good-bye to my father and left home.

The graveyard down the hill is a tangle of wild roses, tiger lilies and thistle. The crosses are falling down and gophers scurry back and forth over the sunken graves. The old Roman Catholic church still needs repainting but because of the poverty of the congregation it continues to wait until another year.

The blacksmith shop and cheese factory across the road have long since been torn down and only an old black steam-engine and forgotten horseshoes mark the place where they once stood. The store is still there,

Métis autobiographer, author of children's books, playwright, scriptwriter, editor, and essayist.

Born: April, 1940, in Saskatchewan, Canada.

Partnerships: Divorced; four children.

Career: Writer.

old and lonely, looking like the country around it, and, like the people it serves, merely exists. The French owners who came from Quebec are dead and their families have gone. It is as if they were never there.

Grannie Campbell's house is gone. The Halfbreed families who squatted on the road allowances have moved to nearby towns where welfare hand-outs and booze are handier, or else deeper into the bush as an escape from reality. The old people who were so much a part of my childhood have all died.

Going home after so long a time, I thought that I might find again the happiness and beauty I had known as a child. But as I walked down the rough dirt road, poked through the broken old buildings and thought back over the years, I realized that I could never find that here. Like me the land had changed, my people were gone, and if I was to know peace I would have to search within myself. That is when I decided to write about my life. I am not very old, so perhaps some day, when I too am a grannie, I will write more. I write this for all of you, to tell you what it is like to be a Halfbreed woman in our country. I want to tell you about the joys and sorrows, the oppressing poverty, the frustrations and the dreams.

Chapter 5

There was an annual Trappers Convention is northern Saskatchewan every summer which Daddy attended faithfully. He would come home and be up half the night telling us what had happened. I remember crying each year because I wanted to go with him, for no particular reason except it was usually held in Prince Albert, and a city meant all sorts of exciting things to a little girl.

One day he came home and said that we could all go with him. I was getting ready for bed after the excitement of packing when Daddy told me to be sure and take all our fishing gear. Pack fishing gear to go to a city? I couldn't sleep, so finally I had to ask him where we were going to fish. He answered, "Montreal Lake, that's where we're going this year." I felt terribly

101

MARIA CAMPBELL

Halfbreed (autobiography), Saturday Review Press, 1973.
People of the Buffalo, Douglas & McIntyre, 1976.

Little Badger and the Fire Spirit, McClelland & Stewart, 1977.

Author of "The Red Dress," a film released by National Film Board, 1977. Author of radio plays. Contributor to magazines, including *Maclean's*, and newspapers.

let down. Who wanted to go to Montreal Lake where there was nothing but dogs and Indians?

However, next morning the prospects of such a long trip by car were just too exciting for an eight-year-old to waste time in pouting. Daddy had hired the storekeeper's son, Laroque, to drive us there. The car was a Model T convertible without a top, but I couldn't imagine going to the Convention in grander or more dashing style. The trip was to take us three days so we were really loaded down. Daddy, the driver and Jamie sat in front, Mom, Cheechum and I in the back with the tent, grub box, camping equipment and some traps. The traps were to be left in a cache somewhere by the road so that Daddy would not have to pack them in when he went trapping that fall.

We must have looked hilarious in that old red and green car with me perched on top of the load. The sun shone and what could be seen of the countryside was beautiful. The first thirty miles were so dusty that soon Mom put a handkerchief over her nose and mouth. The wind whipped at Cheechum's hair and she choked from the dust. She covered herself with a shawl and blasted Dad for wanting to travel like a white man.

We spent the first night with friends at Waskesiu, which was filled with tourists at that time of year. Daddy said that some of them were "Long Knives" (Americans). We stopped at a restaurant for Mom to buy some ice cream. She got as far as the door and came back, looking as if she had seen something awful. Dad went in and came out with the ice cream, grinning from ear to ear. He wanted Grannie to see something special, so we waited a few minutes while Mom spoke angrily to him in Cree. I was nearly falling off my perch with curiosity to see what was inside when two white-haired ladies came out. They were both wearing two-piece bathing suits. One was quite fat and the other was well built and falling out all over.

Cheechum covered her face saying, *"Ayee ee. Tan-sa ay se yat chich o-kik."* ("What's wrong with these women?") Mom looked straight ahead. One of the women came over and asked if she could take a picture of us. They wanted a picture of Cheechum too, but she would not uncover her head, so they left, laughing and talking. Cheechum hit Laroque hard on the back with her cane to get him going, and as the car lurched forward I lost my ice cream. Normally I would have complained until my ice cream was

102

replaced, but I was too astounded by the sight of those almost naked women who dared to walk among people and not be shy. That was my first impression of American women.

The road from Waskesiu was very bad, more like a wagon trail through muskeg and sand. There were rough stretches of corduroy - poles laid side by side across the road to keep travellers from sinking into the muskeg. It started to rain when we were half way there and we got stuck so many times that we lost count. We arrived late, soaked to the bone and dirty.

I will never forget my first sight of Montreal Lake. It was the biggest lake I had ever seen, dark and stormy-looking even though the sun was shining. It was dotted with islands and the shore had stretches of sandy and rocky beaches with miles of dense pine, tamarack and spruce. I had heard many stories of this lake from old trappers and Indians who had visited our home. I knew it had a monster fish that the Indians had seen many times over the years, and that many people had been drowned in storms and never found. Also, in the middle of this lake my Grandpa Campbell had seen lightning strike dead a man who had robbed the Sundance tree. There is nothing unusual about being struck by lightning except that in this case it happened in the middle of January.

The log houses were small, mostly one-roomed, and they seemed to blend in with their surroundings. There was a little whitewashed R.C. church and a Hudson's Bay store and various other buildings. There were children everywhere, and with the children were packs of grey and black dogs, big, husky animals, some of which were tied up, looking vicious and hungry. Daddy said that these people never used horses, they used dogs for everything. The smell was unbelievable. Every single thing smelled of fish, even the people. Their sole diet was fish, smoked or boiled, bannock and

I don't think of myself as a writer. My work is in the community. Writing is just one of the tools that I use in my work as an organizer. If I think that something else would work better, then I do it. So it's multimedia kinds of things! I do video, I do film, and I do oral storytelling. I do a lot of teaching. Well, I don't like calling it "teaching," it's facilitating. And I work a lot with elders. . . . I get quite embarrassed when I have to speak from the point of view of a writer, because I really don't know what that is. I know what a storyteller is. A storyteller is a community healer and teacher. There's lots of work in my community, which is important.

MARIA CAMPBELL

tea. The dogs, too, ate fish. The yards were littered with fish bones and heads. Everywhere there were little fires with racks over them where fish were spread to dry and smoke. These fires were tended by grannies like Cheechum with failing sight and no teeth. Working with them were little girls of my age who carried the wood and kept the dogs away.

Cheechum and Jamie and I went for a walk while camp was being set up and it was not long before Cheechum had made herself comfortable in front of one of the fires and had started visiting with an old lady. Jamie and I sat down on a log to listen and to eat a piece of smoked fish. When Cheechum finished her tea the old lady offered her a snuff box. She declined, but the little girl who was tending the firewood took a pinch and offered us some. We were too surprised to say anything so Cheechum said, "No they don't chew." That little girl could spit snuff dead on wherever she aimed, so I tried to copy her; but it was impossible for me to develop a taste for it.

The old ladies and little girls did all the work in the village. They did the cleaning and cooking, looked after the babies and mended the fish nets. The other women seemed to do nothing but sit around and talk or gamble. The little boys raced and played while the older boys and the men sat in groups and talked, or gambled, or slept.

We walked past one group seated on blankets, playing poker. Another group were playing the "hand game." This is a form of gambling with many variations, accompanied by Indian singing and drums. The players sit in two rows, facing each other, with a blanket between them. They have little bones under the blanket and the opposing sides have to guess which hand they are in.

Cheechum told me that we used to live in much the same way before the white people came. She said it was the job of the old women and little girls to tend to the housework and the fires. The older women were good trappers and hunters, better in some cases than the men. They went out on the traplines and helped their men in all the work. Boys never did much until they were older.

The women really impressed me for they were so free, although Mom with her convent background felt that they were quite shameless. They wore long bright skirts and blouses of satin in reds, blues and purples. Their long hair was oiled and braided with many barrettes, gay pins and ribbons, and the jewelery on their necks and arms jangled as they walked. I thought they were gorgeous, and the fact that many of them were blue-eyed made me feel that I had finally found my kin.

Blue eyes were unusual where I came from and we were teased by our brown- and black-eyed relatives. Cheechum said that these people were descendants of the first Hudson's Bay Scots to come to our North, and that despite the fact that they were treaty Indian they were more Halfbreed than we were—probably spawns of the Campbells, Simpsons and McLaughlins. As a child I believed that any Indian unfortunate enough to have blue eyes must have the devil Scot in him or her, and I would think, "There goes another spawn of Satan." I was very disappointed when the first Scot I met was brown-eyed, short and meek-looking instead of the legendary figure I envisioned—a bearded giant with wild hair and blazing blue eyes.

When we arrived back at our camp to change and clean up, Cheechum made me hurry as we had been invited out for supper. She oiled her hair with bear grease and braided it, then oiled and neatly braided mine as well. She put on her best purple blouse, black skirt and shawl, and away we went. We must have reeked of bear fat, but I guess we were in style for when we reached the house everyone crowded around to kiss us and shake our hands. The home was very small with a packed dirt floor and a fireplace made of clay or mud and willow sticks. There was a table but we all ate outside. I loved fish and ate until I burst. An old man sitting across from me was eating so quickly that it was hard to keep up with him, and as fast as he ate the bones flew out of the side of his mouth. We visited there until late at night, then watched the people powwow until almost morning.

The Convention officially started that day, but I have only one memory of it. Two men were trying to out-shout Daddy who was very angry about the trapline boundaries. They were almost ready to fight when the meeting was brought to order. The man who had the most to say against Daddy was sitting in front of Cheechum. When the meeting started again, Dad brought up his point once more and again the man jumped up and started yelling.

Maria Campbell presents a compelling picture of her own life as a Halfbreed. As a Métis woman she is subject to the general stereotypes produced by the cultural mix of Canada. She is outspoken, and this is attributed to her "white" blood by Treaty Indians: "'It's the white in her.' Treaty Indian women don't express their opinions; Halfbreed women do". . . . Throughout her life Campbell wrestled with the question of her own identity. To identify herself as Indian, or Halfbreed, meant to accept the stereotypes, to expose herself to prejudice and discrimination. To reject the label, however, meant to turn her back on the love and warmth of her family, the traditions of the culture. . . .

—Gretchen M. Bataille and Kathleen Mullen Sands, "The Long Road Back: Maria Campbell," in their *American Indian Women: Telling Their Lives,* University of Nebraska Press, 1984.

1 0 5

Cheechum took a safety pin from her blouse, stretched it open and when the man sat down she pushed it into his backside. The poor man jumped to his feet and started to say something, but with one look at Cheechum he sat down and never said another word for the rest of the afternoon.

There was one thing that was special about Montreal Lake and that was the medicine. I had often heard the old people talk about Montreal Lake and the strength of the people there. I listened to these stories and asked Cheechum to explain what I did not understand. Many native people practised medicine, but Montreal Lake was renowned for its bad medicine. The men used it on their traplines so they would have good hauls. They would also go onto other people's lines and take their fur. No one dared to fight back. They could cast spells and even kill with it. They used it on each other sometimes, after fights, and they could catch any man or woman they wanted with special love spells.

When we arrived at Montreal Lake I knew about the medicine, but was too young to care about it. However, little as I was, I felt it as soon as we got there. It is hard to describe or explain as it is something you cannot see or hear, only feel and smell. It is so frightening at first that your hair almost stands up on end, then the effect levels out and while you remain aware of it all the time, it is not so intense.

The smell is unlike anything else: heavy and musky and almost human. Sometimes it's almost overpowering, and then suddenly it's gone like it was not even there. The night of the powwow I saw a woman under a love spell. She was about Mom's age and very pretty. She was with an older man and followed him everywhere, never taking her eyes off him. She had a husband and children but acted as if she didn't know them or see them. There was one woman whose face looked as though someone had grabbed her and twisted the skin and eyes. She had taken someone's husband and the wife had put a spell on her. One man was unable to walk because someone had used bad medicine on his trapline and caused him to lose the use of his legs. He almost froze to death but managed to crawl back to his camp.

I became curious and wanted to talk to different people, but Cheechum warned me severely against it. Cheechum and Dad always impressed upon us this one thing: never ever fool around with anyone who uses medicine. If someone used medicine on you, you had to find a more powerful medicine man or woman to either remove or return the spell.

Whenever Grannie Dubuque planned to visit us we became excited as we anticipated the boxes of goodies, clothing, bedding and toys that we knew would come with her. But we seldom saw her as she lived in Prince Albert. She cleaned for well-to-do families in Prince Albert and the things she brought were all cast-offs given to her by employers.

Momma would tell us to mind our manners and to take care not to ruin our good clothes, which we always wore while Grannie was there.

106

Daddy never said much during these visits. He would become quiet, and he and Cheechum would often leave for a few days. Grannie always arrived in style, usually in an old Model T Ford that she hired in town. She wore nice silk dresses trimmed with white lace and a white lacey handkerchief tucked into her belt. She also wore a small hat with a veil, gloves, and shoes with heels while carrying a real handbag. She was the only woman I remember in my childhood who used face powder and perfume. She would hug and kiss Momma and the children, inspecting us carefully. Once settled in the house she watched while we tore through the boxes and tried on the wonderful assortment of clothes. Then came our presents, usually dolls, china dishes, trucks and trains. Momma would receive a special gift, maybe a new dress or shoes. But most of all I remember the pretzels. Being the oldest and her favourite, she would give a huge box of them to me which I shared with the others.

Grannie generally stayed for a week and in that time our lives changed. We used a table cloth and ate bread instead of bannock. Momma took special pains in cooking the game and somehow we managed to have cakes with our wild fruit preserves. Cheechum, who grudgingly came back after the

MARIA CAMPBELL

excitement died down, looked on disapprovingly but said nothing. I would be really spoiled by the time Grannie left and, as Daddy said, impossible to live with until straightened out with the help of a willow switch.

The year I was seven Grannie Dubuque brought a different kind of gift for her special granddaughter. At dinner, after her arrival, she announced a surprise. She had made arrangements for me to go to a residential school in Beauval. It sounded exciting, but looking at Dad's shocked face, Mom's happy one, and Cheechum's stony expression—a sure sign of anger—I was confused. Dad went out after dinner and did not return until the next day. Meanwhile Momma and Grannie planned my wardrobe. I remember only the ugly black stockings, woolly and very itchy, and the little red tam I had to wear and how much I hated it.

I can recall little from that part of my life besides feeling lonely and frightened when I was left with the Sister at the school. The place smelled unpleasantly of soap and old women, and I could hear my footsteps echoing through the building. We prayed endlessly, but I cannot recall ever doing much reading or school-work as Momma had said I would—just the prayers and my job, which was cleaning the dorms and hallways. I do recall most vividly a punishment I once received. We weren't allowed to speak Cree, only French or English, and for disobeying this, I was pushed into a small closet with no windows or light, and locked in for what seemed like hours. I was almost paralyzed with fright when they came to let me out. I remember the last day of school, and the sense of freedom I felt when Dad came for me. He promised that I would never have to go back, as a school was being built at home.

ELIZABETH ✦ COOK-LYNN

Born on a Sioux reservation in South Dakota, Cook-Lynn identifies her family's literary and political background, her Dakota heritage, the northern plains landscape, and Kiowa novelist N. Scott Momaday's writings as her greatest influences. Her grandmother, who wrote for a newspaper, and her grandfather, who helped develop an early Dakota dictionary, along with her father's and grandfather's experiences as tribal council members, contributed to her identity as both a writer and a Dakota. She began writing in college, but received little attention for her work until Then Badger Said This *was reissued in 1983. In this work she implements a variety of perspectives and forms, including verse, personal narrative, oral history, story, and essay, to depict life on the reservation and affirm her Dakota heritage.*

Essay by

JENNIFER GRAY

REDDISH

109

The novel *From the River's Edge* similarly focuses on Dakota values and familial relationships as well as the effects of damming the Missouri river. Cook-Lynn is especially concerned with the effects of, and the tension between, white culture and Native American identity. She has commented that "writing is an essential act of survival for contemporary American Indians. I'm not interested in some kind of melancholy reminiscence. . . . I'm interested in the cultural, historical, and political survival of Indian nations, and that's why I write and teach."

Dakota Sioux poet, short story writer, novelist, and educator.

Born: November 17, 1930, in Fort Thompson, South Dakota.

Partnerships: married Melvin Traversie Cook, 1953 (divorced, 1970); married Clyde J. Lynn (a teacher), 1975; children: (first marriage) David, Mary, Lisa, Margaret.

Education: South Dakota State College (now South Dakota State University), B.A., English and Journalism, 1952; graduate study at New Mexico State University, 1966, and Black Hills State College, 1968; University of South Dakota, M. Ed., 1972; doctoral study at University of Nebraska, Lincoln, 1977–78; attended Stanford University.

Career: High school teacher in South Dakota and New Mexico; Eastern Washington University, Cheney, began as associate professor of Native American studies, 1971, became associate professor emeritus, 1993.

Memberships: University of Washington, Seattle, member of Council of Editors of Learned Journals; Authors Guild.

Address: Route 8, Box 510, Dakotah Meadows, Rapid City, SD 57702.

THE POWER OF HORSES

From *The Power of Horses and Other Stories*, Arcade Publishing, copyright © 1990 by Elizabeth Cook-Lynn

The mother and daughter steadied themselves, feet planted squarely, foreheads glistening with perspiration, and each grasped a handle of the large, steaming kettle.

"Ready?"

"Un-huh."

"Take it, then," the mother said. "Careful." Together they lifted the tub of boiled beets from the flame of the burners on the gas stove and set it heavily on the table across the room. The girl let the towel which had served as a makeshift pot holder drop to the floor as the heat penetrated to the skin, and she slapped her hand against the coolness of the smooth, painted wall and then against her thigh, feeling the roughness of the heavy jeans with tingling fingers. To stop the tingling, she cupped her fingers to her mouth and blew on them, then raised her apologetic eyes and looked at her mother. Without speaking, as if that was the end of it, she sank into the chrome chair and picked up the towel and began wiping the sweat from her face. The sun came relentlessly through the thin gauze curtains, and the hot wind blew gently across the stove, almost extinguishing the gas flames of the burners, making the blue edges turn yellow and then orange and then white. The towel was damp now and stained purple from the beets, and the girl leaned back in the chair and laid the towel across her face, feeling her own hot breath around her nose and mouth.

"Your hands get used to it, Marleen," the mother said, not even glancing at the girl, nor at her own rough, brown hands, "just have to keep at it," saying this not so much from believing it as from the need to stop this feeling of futility in the girl and the silence between them. The mother gingerly grasped the bleached stems of several beets and dropped them into a pan of cold water, rolling one and then another of the beets like balls in her hands, pushing the purple-black skins this way and that, quickly, deftly removing the peel and stem and tossing the shiny vegetable into another container. Finishing one, she hurriedly picked up another, as if by hurrying she could forestall the girl's rebellion.

Anger is what started me writing. Writing, for me, then, is an act of defiance born of the need to survive. I am me. I exist. I am a Dakotah. I write. It is the quintessential act of optimism born of frustration. It is an act of courage, I think. And, in the end, as Simon Ortiz says, it is an act that defies oppression.

—Elizabeth Cook-Lynn, in *I Tell You Now: Autobiographical Essays by Native American Writers*, University of Nebraska Press, 1987.

The woman's arms, like her hands, were large, powerful. But, despite the years of heavy work, her sloping shoulders and smooth, long neck were part of a tender femininity only recently showing small signs of decline and age. The dark stains on her dark face might have seemed like age spots or a disfigurement on someone else, but on the woman they spread delicately across her cheeks, forehead, and neck like a sweep of darkened cloud, making her somehow vulnerable and defenseless.

"Your hands'll get used to it, Marleen," she repeated, again attempting to keep the girl's unwillingness in check, and an avenue to reasonable tolerance and cooperation open.

The brief rest with the towel on her face seemed to diminish the girl's weariness, and for an instant more she sat silently, breathing peacefully into the damp towel. As the girl drew the towel across her face and away from her eyes, something like fear began to rise in her, and she peered out the window, where she saw her father standing with a white man she had never seen before. Her father was looking straight ahead down the draw where the horses stood near the corral. They always want something from him, she thought, and as she watched the white man put a cigarette in his mouth and turn sideways out of the wind, the flame of his lighter licking toward his bony profile, she wondered what it was this time. She watched the man's quick mannerisms, and she saw that he began to talk earnestly and gesture toward his green pickup truck, which was parked close to the barbed-wire fence encircling the house and yard.

I I I

ELIZABETH COOK-LYNN

The girl was startled out of her musings at the sound of her mother's *"yu-u-u-u,"* the softly uttered indication of disapproval, insistent, always compelling a change in the girl's behavior. And she turned quickly to get started with her share of the hot beets, handling them inexpertly, but peeling their hot skins away as best she could. After a few minutes, during which the women worked in silence, only the monotonous hiss of the burning gas flame between them, the girl, surprised, thought: her sounds of disapproval aren't because I'm wasting time; instead, they are made because she is afraid my father and the white man will see me watching them. Spontaneously, defensively, she said. "They didn't see me." She looked into the brown-stained face but saw only her mother's careful pretense of being preoccupied with the beets, as she picked up a small knife to begin slicing them. All last winter, every time I came home, I spied on him for you, thought the girl, even riding my horse over to Chekpa's through the snow to see if he was there. And when I came back and told you that he was, you acted as if you hadn't heard anything, like now. So this is not the beginning of the story, nor is it the part of the story that matters, probably, thought the girl, and she started to recognize a long, long history of acrimony between her parents, thinking, in hindsight, that it would have been better if she had stayed at Stephen Mission. But then, she remembered her last talk with Brother Otto at the Mission as he sat before her, one leg languidly draped over the other, his collar open, showing his sparse red chest hairs, his watery, pale eyes looking at her searchingly, and she knew that it wasn't better to have stayed there.

He had sat quivering with sympathy as she had tried to tell him that to go home was to be used by her mother against her father. I rode over to Chekpa's, she told him, hating herself that she was letting out the symptoms of her childish grief, despising him for his delicate white skin, his rapt gaze, the vicariousness of his measly existence, and *Até* was there, cutting wood for the eldest of the Tatiopa women, Rosalie, the one he was supposed to marry, you know, but, instead, he married my mother. My mother sent me there, and when I rode into the yard and saw him, he stood in uncertainty, humiliated in the eyes of Chekpa, his old friend, as well as all of those in the Tatiopa family. Worse yet, she knew, humiliated in the eyes of his nine-year-old daughter.

In her memory of that awful moment, she didn't speak, nor did her father, and so she had ridden out of the yard as abruptly as she had come and home at a dead gallop, standing easily in the stirrups, her face turned toward her right shoulder out of the wind, watching the slush fly behind the horse's hooves. She didn't cut across Archie's field as she usually did, but took the long way, riding as hard as she could alongside the road. When she got to the gate she reined in, dismounted, and led her horse through the gate and then, slowly, down the sloping hill to the tack shed. She stood for a long time with her head against the wide, smooth leather of the stirrup shaft, her eyes closed tightly and the smell of wet horse hair in her nostrils. Much later she had recited the event as fully as she could bear to the mission school priest, much as she had been taught to recite the events of her sinful life: I have taken the Lord's name in vain, I have taken the Lord's name in vain, I have tak . . .

Damn beets, damn all these damn beets, the girl thought, and she turned away from the table back to the stove, where she stirred the second, smaller, pot of sliced beets, and she looked out through the gauze curtains to see if her father and the white man were still there. They had just run the horses into the corral from the small fenced pasture where they usually grazed when they were brought down to the place.

"He must be getting ready to sell them, is he?" she asked her mother.

Her mother said nothing.

"How come? I didn't know he was going to sell," the girl said slowly, noticing that her horse, two quarter-horse brood mares, and a half-Shetland black-and-white gelding she had always called "*Shota*" had been cut out of the herd and were standing at the far corner of the pasture, grazing. The heat shimmered above the long buffalo grass, and the girl's thoughts drifted, and, vaguely, she heard her mother say, "You'd better spoon those sliced ones into these hot jars, Marleen," and then, almost to herself, her mother started talking as if in recognition of what the girl did not know about the factual and philosophical sources from which present life emerges. "I used to have land, myself, daughter," she began, "and on it my grandfather had many horses. What happened to it was that some white men from Washington came and took it away from me when my grandfather died because, they said, they were going to breed game birds there; geese, I think.

"There was no one to do anything about it," she continued, "there was only this old woman who was a mother to me, and she really didn't know what to do, who to see, or how to prevent this from happening.

"Among the horses there on my land was a pair of brood mares just like those two out there." She pointed with her chin to the two bays at the end of the pasture. And, looking at the black-and-white horse called *Shota,* she said, "And there was also another strange, mysterious horse, *su'ka wak*

E L I Z A B E T H   C O O K - L Y N N

a'," *i-e-e,* she had used the word for "mysterious dog" in the Dakotah language. And the mother and daughter stood looking out the window at the *shota* horse beside the bays, watching them pick their way through the shimmering heat and through the tall grass, slowly, unhurried. The beets were forgotten, momentarily, and the aging woman remembered the magic of those horses and especially the one that resembled the *shota* horse, thinking about that time, that primordial time when an old couple of the tribe received a gift horse from a little bird, and the horse produced many offspring for the old man and woman, and the people were never poor after that. Her grandfather, old Bowed Head, the man with many horses, had told her that story often during her childhood when he wished to speak of those days when all creatures knew one another . . . and it was a reassuring thing. "I wish this tribe to be strong and good," the mysterious horse had told the old man, "and so I keep giving my offspring every year and the tribe will have many horses and this good thing will be among you always."

"They were really fast horses," said the mother, musing still, filling in the texture of her imagination and memory, "they were known throughout our country for their speed, and the old man allowed worthy men in the tribe to use them in war or to go on a hunt with them. It is an old story," the woman concluded, as though the story were finished, as though commenting upon its history made everything comprehensible.

As the girl watched her mother's extraordinary vitality, which rose during the telling of these events, she also noted the abruptness with which the story seemed to end and the kind of formidable reserve and closure which fell upon the dark, stained features as the older woman turned again to the stove.

"What happened to the horses?" the girl wanted to know. "Did someone steal them? Did they die?"

After a long silence her mother said, "Yes, I suppose so," and the silence again deepened between them as they fell to filling hot jars with sliced beets and sealing hot lids upon them, wiping and stroking them meticulously and setting them one by one on a dim pantry shelf.

The girl's frustration was gone now, and she seemed mindless of the heat, her own physical discomfort, and the miserableness of the small, squalid kitchen where she and her mother moved quietly about, informed now with the wonder of the past, the awesomeness of the imagination.

The sun moved west and the kitchen fell into shadow, the wind died down, and the mother and daughter finished their tedious task and carried the large tub of hot water out through the entryway a few feet from the door and emptied its contents upon the ground. The girl watched the red beet juice stain the dry, parched earth in which there was no resistance, and she stepped away from the redness of the water, which gushed like strokes of a painter's brush, suddenly black and ominous, as it sank into the ground. She looked up to see the white man's green pickup truck disappear over the rise, the dust billowing behind the heavy wheels, settling gently in the heat.

The nameless fear struck at her again and she felt a knot being drawn tightly inside her and she looked anxiously toward the corral. Nothing around her seemed to be moving, the air suddenly still, the sweat standing out in beads on her face and her hands, oddly, moist and cold. As she ran toward the corral, she saw her mother out of the corner of her eye, still grasping one handle of the boiler tub, strangely composed, her head and shoulders radiant in the sun.

At the corral, moments later, she saw her father's nearly lifeless form lying facedown in the dirt, his long gray hair spread out like a fan above him, pitifully untidy for a man who ordinarily took meticulous care with his appearance. He had his blue cotton scarf which he used as a handkerchief clutched tightly in his right hand, and he was moaning softly.

For Cook-Lynn, the past is not a cold stone tablet; it is a living vital force. As she watches the changes of the present world, it becomes easier for her, and subsequently for us, to understand and believe the changes of history and legend. The personal leads to understanding and confirmation of the mythic, for they are not as separate as some would think. . . . [W]e are warned to open our minds, ears and eyes to the insight, clear in oral cultures, that history also consists of memory and imagination. To understand history is to imagine, but also it is to hear, to listen. . . .

—James Ruppert, "The Uses of Oral Tradition in Six Contemporary Native American Poets," in *American Indian Culture and Research Journal,* Vol. 4, No. 4, 1980.

The odor of whiskey on his breath was strong as she helped him turn over and sit up, and in that instant the silent presence of the past lay monumentally between them, so that he did not look at her nor did he speak. In that instant she dimly perceived her own innocence and was filled with regret that she would never know those times to which *Até* would return, if he could, again and again. She watched as he walked unsteadily toward the house, rumpled and drunk, a man of grave dignity made comic and sad and helpless by circumstances which his daughter could only regard with wonderment.

ELIZABETH COOK-LYNN

WRITINGS
"You May Consider Speaking about Your Art . . . ," in *I Tell You Now: Autobiographical Essays by Native American Writers*, edited by Brian Swann and Arnold Krupat, University of Nebraska Press, 1987.

The Power of Horses and Other Stories, Arcade-Little, Brown, 1990.
From the River's Edge, Arcade-Little, Brown, 1991.
Seek the House of Relatives, South Dakota, Blue Cloud Quarterly, 1993.

Then Badger Said This, Washington, Ye Galleon Press, 1983.
"As a Dakotah Woman," in *Survival This Way: Interviews with American Indian Poets*, edited by Joseph Bruchac, University of Arizona Press, 1987; 57–71.

Keyapi: Late one night, when the old man had tied the horses near his lodge, someone crept through the draw and made ready to steal them; it was even said that they wanted to kill the wonderful horses. The mysterious gift horse called to the sleeping old man and told him that an evil lurked nearby. And he told the old man that since such a threat as this had come upon them and all the people of the tribe, the power of the horses would be diminished, and no more colts would be born and the people would have to go back to their miserable ways.

As her father made his way to the house, walking stiffly past her mother, who pretended to be scrubbing the black residue from the boiler, the girl turned and walked quickly away from the corral in the opposite direction.

I must look: she thought, into the distance, and as she lifted her eyes and squinted into the evening light, she saw the Fort George road across the river, beyond the bend in the river, so far away that it would take most of the day for anyone to get there from where she walked. I must look: at the ground in front of me where my grandmothers made paths to the ti(n)psina beds and carried home with them long braided strands over their shoulders. I must look: she thought, into the past for the horse that speaks to humans.

1 1 6

She took long strides and walked into the deepening dusk. She walked for a long time before returning to the darkened house, where she crept into her bed and lay listening to the summer's night insect sounds, thinking apocalyptic thoughts in regard to what her mother's horse story might have to do with the day's events.

She awoke with a start, her father shaking her shoulder. "You must ride with me today, daughter, before the horse buyer comes back," he said. "I

wish to take the horses way out to the far side of the north pasture. I am ready to go, so please hurry."

The girl dressed quickly, and just as dawn was breaking, she and her father, each leading two horses, with the others following, set out over the prairie hills. These were the hills, she knew, to which the people had come when the Uprising was finished and the U.S. Cavalry fell to arguing with missionaries and settlers about the "Indian problem." These were the hills, dark blue in this morning light, which she knew as repositories of sacred worlds unknown to all but its most ancient tenants.

When they reached the ridge above Dry Creek, the girl and her father stopped and let the horses go their way, wildly. The *shota* horse led them down the steep prairie hills and into the dry creek bed and, one by one, the horses of the herd disappeared into the stand of heavy cottonwood trees which lined the ravine.

She stood beside her father and watched them go. "Why were you going to sell them?" she asked abruptly.

ELIZABETH   COOK-LYNN

"There are too many," he replied, "and the grass is short this summer. It's been too hot," he said, wiping his face with the blue handkerchief, and he repeated, "The grass is short this summer."

With that, they mounted their horses and rode home together.

VINE  DELORIA, JR.

"Among his people Vine Deloria, Jr., has achieved a status somewhat similar to that of Sitting Bull's leadership of the Sioux tribes a century ago," writes Dee Brown in the New York Times Book Review. *A Standing Rock Sioux lawyer and educator, Deloria is perhaps the most prominent spokesman in the country for native American nationalism. Brought to public attention in 1969 with the publication of his first book,* Custer Died for Your Sins: An Indian Manifesto, *Deloria, says Douglas N. Mount of* Publishers Weekly, *"wants to be the red man's Ralph Nader." To that end, in addition to having served as executive director of the National Congress of American Indians and chairman of the Institute for the Development of Indian Law, he has written several books which serve as legal and historical sourcebooks as well as sharply defined statements of Indian nationalism.*

Essay by

KAREN P. ZIMMERMAN

119

Custer Died for Your Sins: An Indian Manifesto is both a scathing indict-ment of white America's treatment of Indians and an articulation of the goal of Indian activists: an existence that is culturally but not economi-cally separate. J. A. Phillips of *Best Sellers* notes that if this book "is indicative of Deloria's methods, he's more interested in results than in being tactful. Nauseated by the traditional Indian image, he asserts the worth if not the dignity of the redman and blasts the political, social, and religious forces that perpetuate the Little Big Horn and wigwam stereo-typing of his people." A *Time* critic writes that what Deloria really wants to talk about, aside from the origins of scalping and the differences between Black and Indian nationalism, is something "few white Americans know anything about—termination and tribalism." Termination is a government policy designed to cut federal aid to Indians, close down reservations, and blend all remaining Indians into the American economic and cultural mainstream. The *Time* critic says that in Deloria's opinion, "the termination policy, which implies integration of Indians, is a loser's game."

Deloria sees tribalism—whereby peoplehood, land, and religion form a single covenantal relationship that gives each community unique character—as the key to the whole Indian struggle, but adds that it may also be the Indians' greatest liability. In an interview with Mount, he describes tribalism as "a way of life, a way of thinking, . . . a great tradition which is timeless, which has nothing to do with the sequence of events. This creates a wonderful relaxing atmosphere, a tremendous sense of invulnerability." But he cautions that it also fosters the impression that the white man will just go away and leave the Indian alone.

Tribalism is also the subject of Deloria's second book, *We Talk, You Listen: New Tribes, New Turf*. Examining what he considers to be the deteriorating core of contemporary technological society, Deloria attacks the corporate patterns of American life, advocates a return to tribal social organization, and describes the tribal characteristics he perceives in American minority groups. Cecil Eby of *Book World* writes that in this book, as well as in *Custer Died for Your Sins*, Deloria "describes the thrust of the Red-Power movement without annointing himself as its oracle or its official spokesman. . . . [He] brings into focus the moods and habitat of the contemporary Indian as seen by a Standing Rock Sioux, not by a research anthropologist or a jobber in the basketry trades. He peels away layers of tinsel and feathers heaped upon the Indian by misinformed whites . . . and he reveals an uncanny ability for impaling them on the fine points of their own illogic." However, N. Scott Momaday, writing in the *New York Review of Books*, considers Deloria's portrayal of the contemporary Indian weak: "Deloria is a thoughtful man, and he is articulate as well; but [*Custer Died for Your Sins* and *We Talk, You Listen*] are disappointing in one respect: they tell us very little about Indians, after all. In neither book is there any real evocation of that spirit and mentality which distinguishes the Indian as a man and as a race. . . . This seems all the more regrettable in view of the fact that he really knows something about the subject by virtue of blood as well as experience."

In *God Is Red: A Native View of Religion*, Deloria, the son of an Indian Episcopalian clergyman and himself seminary-trained, not only attempts to evoke that spirit and mentality which is unique to the Indian but argues that its theological basis in tribal religions seems to be "more at home in the modern world than Christian ideas and Western man's traditional concepts." Asserting that Christianity inculcates and justifies imperialism, rootlessness, and ecocide, Deloria maintains that America can survive only if there is a revolution in theological concepts. Peter Mayer says in *Best Sellers* that "Deloria could have made his point—that Indian religious practices are far more in accord with the necessities of contemporary life than are Christian—without dredging up the many failures of the sons of the Church upon the earth. . . . But read the book; I found it hard to put down."

Serving as an Indian treaties expert, Deloria was the first witness for the defense in the Wounded Knee trial of 1974, held in St. Paul, Minnesota. His book *Behind the Trail of Broken Treaties* "is not only the best account yet written of events leading to Wounded Knee 1973," writes Dee Brown in the *New York Times Book Review*, but "it is also a compelling argument for a reopening of the treaty-making procedure between Indian tribes and the U.S. Government." L.A. Howard of *Best Sellers* echoes Brown's assessment: "Step by step, argument by argument, [Deloria] refutes those who would label treaty-making as an implausible way at best for the United States to conduct its relations with the American Indians." L. E. Oliva of *Library Journal* notes that Deloria does not consider this proposal "as a panacea but simply as a necessary first step" to insure the survival of Indian tribes, their lands, and their ways of life. What Deloria hopes for is a new treaty relationship which will give Indian tribes the status of quasi-international independence, with the United States acting as protector.

> *I think New Age shamanism is very interesting. Whites want to take our images, they want to have their Indian jewelry; at the same time, they need our valley to flood for a dam. People are desperately trying to get some relationship to Earth, but it's all in their heads. Whites have a psychological problem with regard to their own authenticity.*

—Vine Deloria, Jr., *The Progressive*, April 1990.

SACRED PLACES AND MORAL RESPONSIBILITY

From *God Is Red: A Native View of Religion*, Fulcrum Publishing, copyright © 1994 by Vine Deloria, Jr.

When the tribes were forced from their aboriginal homelands and confined to small reservations, many of the tribal religious rituals were prohibited by the BIA in the 1870s and 1880s because of an inordinately large

Sioux nonfiction writer and editor.

Born: March 26, 1933, in Martin, South Dakota.

Partnerships: Married Barbara Jeanne Nystrom, June 14, 1958; children: Philip, Daniel, Jeanne.

Education: Iowa State University, B.S., 1958; Lutheran School of Theology, Rock Island, Ill., M.Th., 1963; University of Colorado, J.D., 1970.

Career: United Scholarship Service, Denver, Colo., staff associate, 1963–64; National Congress of American Indians, Washington, D.C.,executive director, 1964–67; Institute for the Development of Indian Law, Golden, Colo., chairman, 1970–76; University of Arizona, Tucson, professor of political science, 1978–, chairman of American Indian studies, 1979–82. Lecturer at Western Washington State College (now University), 1970–72, and University of California, Los Angeles, 1972–74. Member, Board of Inquiry on Hunger and Malnutrition in the United States, 1967–68, executive council of Episcopal Church, 1969–70, and National Office for Rights of the Indigent. Consultant to U.S. Senate Select Committee on Aging.

Memberships: Amnesty International, American Bar Association, American Judicature Society, Authors Guild, Authors League of America, Advocates for the Arts, American Indian Resource Association (vice-chairman, 1973–75), Colorado Authors League.

Address: Home—Tucson, Ariz. 85710. Office—Department of Political Science, University of Arizona, Tucson, Ariz. 85721.

number of Christian zealots as Indian agents. We read in chapter 14 how traditional people had to adopt various subterfuges so that their religious life could be continued. Some tribes shifted their ceremonial year to coincide with the whites' holidays and conducted their most important rituals on national holidays and Christian feast days, explaining to curious whites that they were simply honoring George Washington and celebrating Christmas and Easter. Many shrines and holy places were located far away from the new reservation homelands, but because they were not being exploited economically or used by settlers, it was not difficult for small parties of people to go into the mountains or to remote lakes and buttes and conduct ceremonies without interference from non-Indians.

Since World War II, this situation has changed dramatically. We have seen a greatly expanding national population, the introduction of corporate farming practices that have placed formerly submarginal lands under cultivation, more extensive mining and timber industry activities, and a greatly expanded recreation industry—all of which have severely impacted the use of public lands in the United States. Few rural areas now enjoy the isolation of half a century ago, and as multiple use of lands increased, many of the sacred sites that were on public lands were threatened by visitors and subjected to new uses. Tribal religious leaders were often able to work out informal arrangements with federal and state agencies to allow them access to these places for religious purposes. But as the personnel changed in state and federal agencies, a new generation of bureaucrats, catering to developers, recreation interest, and the well-established economic groups who have always used public lands for a pittance, began to restrict Indian access to sacred sites by establishing increasingly narrow rules and regulations for managing public lands.

In 1978, in a symbolic effort to clarify the status of traditional religious practices and practitioners, Congress passed a Joint Resolution entitled the American Indian Religious Freedom Act. This act declared that it was the policy of Congress to protect and preserve the inherent right of American Indians to believe, express, and practice their traditional religions. The resolution identified the problem as one of a "lack of knowledge or the insensitive and inflexible enforcement of Federal policies and regulations." Section 2 of the resolution directed the president to require the various federal departments to evaluate their policies and procedures, report back to Congress on the results of their survey, and make recommendations for legislative actions.[1]

The white man may be the political owner of the land, but the red man is still its spiritual owner. America can survive only if the white man becomes an Indian, learns to revere the sacred spaces of this land and put his bones into the earth so they become his roots. The treaty of red and white man must be a covenant with nature as well. Only then can they sign a treaty which will not be broken; which shall stand "as long as the grass shall grow and the rivers flow."

Rosemary Radford Ruether, in *The New Republic*, January 5–12, 1974.

Many people assumed that this resolution clarified the federal attitude toward traditional religions, and it began to be cited in litigation involving the construction of dams, roads, and the management of federal lands. Almost unanimously, however, the federal courts have since ruled that the resolution did not protect or preserve the right of Indians to practice their religion and conduct ceremonies at sacred sites on public lands.[2] Some courts even hinted darkly that any formal recognition of the existence of tribal practices would be tantamount to establishing a state religion,[3] and interpretation that, upon analysis, is a dreadful misreading of American history and the Constitution and may have been an effort to inflame anti-Indian feelings.

A good example for making this claim was the 1988 Supreme Court decision in the *Lyng v. Northwest Indian Cemetery Protective Association* case that involved protecting the visitation rights of the traditional religious leaders of three tribes to sacred sites in the Chimney Rock area of the Six Rivers National Forest in Northern California. The Forest Service proposed to build a 6-mile paved road that would have opened part of the area to

123

commercial logging. This area, known by three Indian tribes as the "High Country," was the center of their religious and ceremonial life. The lower federal courts prohibited the construction of the road on the grounds that it would have made religious ceremonial use of the area impossible. Before the Supreme Court could hear the appeal, Congress passed the California Wilderness Act that made the question of constructing the road moot for all practical purposes. But the Supreme Court insisted on hearing the appeal of the Forest Service and deciding the religious issues. It turned the tribes down flat, ruling that the Free Exercise clause did not prevent the government from using its property in any way it saw fit and in effect rolling back the religious use of the area completely.

Most troubling about the Supreme Court's decision was the insistence on analyzing tribal religions within the same conceptual framework as western organized religions. Justice O'Connor observed,

> A broad range of government activities—from social welfare programs to foreign aid to conservation projects—will always be considered essential to the spiritual well-being of some citizens, often on the basis of sincerely held religious beliefs. Others will find the very same activity deeply offensive, and perhaps incompatible with their own search for spiritual fulfillment and with the tenets of their religion.[4]

Thus, ceremonies and rituals that had been performed for thousands of years were treated as if they were popular fads or simply matters of personal preference based upon the erroneous assumption that religion was only a matter of individual aesthetic choice.

Justice Brennan's dissent vigorously attacked this spurious line of reasoning, outlining with some precision the communal aspect of the tribal religions and their relationship to the mountains. But his argument failed to gather support within the Court. Most observers of the Supreme Court were simply confounded at the majority's conclusion that suggested that destroying a religion "did not unduly burden it" and that no constitutional protections were available to the Indians.[5]

When informed of the meaning of this decision, most people have shown great sympathy for the traditional religious people. At the same time, they have had great difficulty understanding why it is so important that these ceremonies be held, that they be conducted only at certain locations, and that they be held in secrecy and privacy. This lack of understanding highlights the great gulf that exists between traditional Western thinking about religion and the Indian perspective. It is the difference between individual conscience and commitment (Western) and communal tradition (Indian), these views can only be reconciled by examining them in a much broader historical and geographical context.

Justice Brennan attempted to make this difference clear when he observed, "Although few tribal members actually made medicine at the most powerful sites, the entire tribe's welfare hinges on the success of individual practitioner."[6] More than that, however, the "World renewal" ceremonies conducted by the tribes were done on behalf of the earth and all forms of life. To describe these ceremonies as if they were comparable to Oral Roberts seeking funds or Jimmy Swaggart begging forgiveness for his continuing sexual misconduct or Justice O'Connor's matters of community aesthetic preference is to miss the point entirely. In effect, the Court declared that Indians cannot pray for the planet or for other people and other forms of life in the manner required by their religion.

Two contradictory responses seem to characterize the non-Indian attitudes toward traditional tribal religions. Some people want the traditional healers to share their religious beliefs in the same manner that priests, rabbis, and ministers expound publicly the tenets of their denominations. Other people feel that Indian ceremonials are simply remnants of primitive life and should be abandoned. Neither perspective understands that Indian tribes are communities in ways that are fundamentally different than other American communities and organizations. Tribal communities are wholly defined by the family relationships; the non-Indian communities are defined primarily by residence, by an arbitrary establishment of political jurisdiction, or by agreement with generally applicable sets of intellectual beliefs. Ceremonial and ritual knowledge is possessed by everyone in the Indian community, although only a few people may actually be chosen to perform these acts. Authorization to perform ceremonies comes from higher spiritual powers and not by certification through an institution or any formal organization.

A belief in the sacredness of lands in the non-Indian context may become the preferred belief of an individual or group of people based on their experiences or on an intensive study of preselected evidence. But this belief becomes the subject of intense criticism and does not, except under unusual circumstances, become an operative principle in the life and behavior of the non-Indian group. The same belief, when seen in the Indian context, is an integral part of the experiences of the people—past, present, and future. The idea does not become a bone of contention among the people for even if someone does not have the experience or belief in the sacredness of lands, he or she accords tradition the respect that it deserves. Indians who have never visited certain sacred sites nevertheless know of these places from the community knowledge, and they intuit this knowing to be an essential part of their being.

Justice Brennan, in countering the arguments raised by Justice O'Connor that any recognition of the sacredness of certain sites would allow traditional Indian religions to define the use of all public lands, suggested that the burden of proof be placed on the traditional people to demonstrate why some sites are central to their practice and other sites, while invoking a sense of reverence, are not as important. This requirement is not unreasonable, but it requires a willingness on the part of non-Indians and the courts to entertain different ideas about the nature of religion—ideas which until the present have not been a part of their experience or understanding.

If we were to subject the topic of the sacredness of lands to a Western rational analysis, fully recognizing that such an analysis is merely for our convenience in discussion and does not represent the nature of reality, we would probably find four major categories of description. Some of these categories are overlapping because some groups might not agree with the description of certain sites in the categories in which other Indians would place them. Nevertheless, it is the principle of respect for the sacred that is important.

The first and most familiar kind of sacred lands are places to which we attribute sanctity because the location is a site where, within our own history, something of great importance has taken place. Unfortunately, many of these places are related to instances of human violence. Gettysburg National Cemetery is a good example of this kind of sacred land. Abraham Lincoln properly noted that we cannot hallow the Gettysburg battlefield because others, the men who fought there, had already consecrated it by giving "that last full measure of devotion." We generally hold these places sacred because people did there what we might one day be required to do—give our lives in a cause we hold dear. Wounded Knee, South Dakota, has become such a place for many Indians where a band of Sioux Indians were massacred. On the whole, however, the idea of regarding a battlefield as sacred was entirely foreign to most tribes because they did not see war as a holy enterprise. The Lincoln Memorial in Washington, D.C., might be an example of a nonmartial location, and, although Justice O'Connor felt that recognizing the sacredness of land and location might inspire an individual to have a special fondness for this memorial, it is important to recognize that we should have some sense of reverence in these places.

Every society needs these kinds of sacred places because they help to instill a sense of social cohesion in the people and remind them of the passage of generations that have brought them to the present. A society that cannot remember and honor its past is in peril of losing its soul. Indians, because of our considerably longer tenure on this continent, have many more sacred places than do non-Indians. Many different ceremonies can be and have been held at these locations; there is both an exclusivity and an inclusiveness, depending upon the occasion and the ceremony. In this classification the site is all important, but it is sanctified each time ceremonies are held and prayers offered.

A second category of sacred lands has a deeper, more profound sense of the sacred. It can be illustrated in Old Testament stories that have become the foundation of three world religions. After the death of Moses, Joshua led

Custer Died for Your Sins: An Indian Manifesto, Macmillan, 1969.

We Talk, You Listen: New Tribes, New Turf, Macmillan, 1970.

(Compiler) *Of Utmost Good Faith*, Straight Arrow Books, 1971.

God Is Red: A Native View of Religion, Grosset, 1973; second edition, North American Press, 1992.

Behind the Trail of Broken Treaties, Delacorte, 1974.

The Indian Affair, Friendship, 1974.

Indians of the Pacific Northwest, Doubleday, 1977.

The Metaphysics of Modern Existence, Harper, 1979.

(With Clifford Lytle) *American Indians, American Justice*, University of Texas Press, 1983.

(With Clifford Lytle) *The Nations Within: The Past and Future of American Indian Sovereignty*, Pantheon, 1984.

The Aggressions of Civilization: Federal Indian Policy Since the 1880s, Temple University Press, 1984.

American Indian Policy in the Twentieth Century, University of Oklahoma Press, 1985.

Editor

(And author of introduction) *Jennings Cooper Wise, The Red Man in the New World Drama*, Macmillan, 1971.

The Aggressions of Civilization, Temple University Press, 1984.

A Sender of Words, Howe Brothers, 1984.

American Indian Policy in the Twentieth Century, University of Oklahoma Press, 1984.

Work in Progress

Research on Indian legends concerning the creation of mountains, rivers, and other natural phenomena; research on Indian treaties, social problems, and political history.

the Hebrews across the River Jordan into the Holy Land. On approaching the river with the Ark of the Covenant, the waters of the Jordan "rose up" or parted and the people, led by the Ark, crossed over on "dry ground," which is to say they crossed without difficulty. After crossing, Joshua selected one man from each of the Twelve Tribes and told him to find a large stone. The twelve stones were then placed together in a monument to mark the spot where the people had camped after having crossed the river successfully. When asked about this strange behavior, Joshua then replied, "That this may be a sign among you, that when your children ask their fathers in time to come, saying 'What mean ye by these stones?' Then you shall answer them: That the waters of Jordan were cut off before the Ark of the Covenant of the Lord, when it passed over Jordan."[7]

In comparing this site with Gettysburg, we must understand a fundamental difference. Gettysburg is made sacred by the actions of men. It can be described as exquisitely dear to us, but it is not a location where we have perceived that something specifically other than ourselves is present, something mysteriously religious in the proper meaning of those words has happened or been made manifest. In the crossing of the River Jordan, the sacred or higher powers have appeared in the lives of human beings. Indians would say something holy has appeared in an otherwise secular situation. No matter how we might attempt to explain this event in later historical, political, or economic terms, the essence of the event is that the sacred has become a part of our experience.

Some of the sites that traditional religious leaders visit are of this nature. Buffalo Gap at the southeastern edge of the Black Hills of South Dakota marks the location where the buffalo emerged each spring to begin

127

the ceremonial year of the Plains Indians, and it has this aspect of sacred/secular status. It may indeed be the starting point of the Great Race that determined the primacy between two-legged and four-legged creatures at the beginning of the world. Several mountains in New Mexico and Arizona mark places where the Pueblo, Hopi, and Navajo peoples completed their migrations, were told to settle, or where they first established their spiritual relationships with bear, deer, eagle, and other peoples who participate in the ceremonials.

Every identifiable region has sacred places peculiar to its geography and as we extend the circle geographically from any point in North America, we begin to include an ever-increasing number of sacred sites. Beginning in the American Southwest we must include the Apache, Ute, Comanche, Kiowa, and other tribes as we move away from the Pueblo and Navajo lands. These lands would be sacred to some tribes but secular to the Pueblo, Hopi, and Navajo. The difference would be in the manner of revelation and what the people experienced. There is immense particularity in the sacred and it is not a blanket category to be applied indiscriminately. Even east of the Mississippi, though many places have been nearly obliterated, people retain knowledge of these sacred sites. Their sacredness does not depend on human occupancy but on the stories that describe the revelation that enabled human beings to experience the holiness there.

In the religious world of most tribes, birds, animals, and plants compose the "other peoples" of creation. Depending on the ceremony, various of these "peoples" participate in human activities. If Jews and Christians see the action of a deity at sacred places in the Holy Land and in churches and synagogues, traditional Indian people experience spiritual activity as the whole of creation becomes active participants in ceremonial life. Because the relationship with the "other peoples" is so fundamental to the human community, most traditional practitioners are reluctant to articulate the specific elements of either the ceremony or the locations. Because some rituals involve the continued prosperity of the "other peoples," discussing the nature of the ceremony would violate the integrity of these relationships. Thus, traditional people explain that these ceremonies are being held for "all our relatives" but are reluctant to offer any further explanations. It is these ceremonies in particular that are now to be denied protection under the Supreme Court rulings.

It is not likely that non-Indians have had many of these kinds of religious experiences, particularly because most churches and synagogues have special rituals that are designed to cleanse the buildings so that their services can be held there untainted by the natural world. Non-Indians have simply not been on this continent very long; their families have rarely settled in one place for any period of time so that no profound relationship with the environment has been possible. Additionally, non-Indians have engaged in the senseless killing of wildlife and utter destruction of plant life. It is unlikely that they would have understood efforts by other forms of life to communicate with humans. Although, some non-Indian families who have lived continuously in isolated rural areas tell stories about birds and animals similar to the traditions of many tribes indicating that lands and the "other peoples" do seek intimacy with our species.

The third kind of sacred lands are places of overwhelming holiness where the Higher Powers, on their own initiative, have revealed Themselves to human beings. Again, we can illustrate this in the Old Testament narrative. Prior to his journey to Egypt, Moses spent his time herding his father-in-law's sheep on or near Mount Horeb. One day he took the flock to the far side of the mountain and to his amazement saw a bush burning with fire but not being consumed by it. Approaching this spot with the usual curiosity of a person accustomed to the outdoor life, Moses was startled when the Lord spoke to him from the bush, warning, "Draw not hither; put off thy shoes from thy feet, for the place where on thou standest is holy ground."[8]

This tradition tells us that there are places of unquestionable, inherent sacredness on this earth, sites that are holy in and of themselves. Human societies come and go on this earth and any prolonged occupation of a geographical region will produce shrines and sacred sites discerned by the occupying people, but there will always be a few sites at which the highest spirits dwell. The stories that explain the sacred nature of these locations will frequently provide startling parallels to the account about the burning bush. One need only look at the shrines of present-day Europe. Long before Catholic or Protestant churches were built in certain places, other religions had established shrines and temples on that spot. These holy places are locations where people have always gone to communicate and commune with higher spiritual powers.

This phenomenon is worldwide and all religions find that these places regenerate people and fill them with spiritual powers. In the Western Hemisphere these places, with few exceptions, are known only by American Indians. Bear Butte, Blue Lake, and the High Places in the *Lyng* case are all well known locations that are sacred in and of themselves. People have been commanded to perform ceremonies at these holy places so that the earth and all its forms of life might survive and prosper. Evidence of this moral responsibility that sacred places command has come through the testimony of traditional people when they have tried to explain to non-Indians at various times in this century—in court, in conferences, and in conversations—that they must perform certain ceremonies at specific times and places in order that the sun may continue to shine, the earth prosper, and the stars remain in the heavens. Tragically, this attitude is interpreted by non-Indians as indicative of the traditional leader's personal code or philosophy and is not seen as a simple admission of a moral duty.

VINE   DELORIA,   JR.

Skeptical non-Indians, and representatives of other religions seeking to discredit tribal religions, have sometimes deliberately violated some of these holy places with no ill effects. They have then come to believe that they have demonstrated the false nature of Indian beliefs. These violations reveal a strange non-Indian belief in a form of mechanical magic that is touchingly adolescent, a belief that an impious act would, or could trigger an immediate response from the higher spiritual powers. Surely these impious acts suggest a deity who jealously guards his or her prerogatives and wreaks immediate vengeance for minor transgressions—much as some Protestant sects have envisioned God and much as an ancient astronaut (see chapter 9) wanting to control lesser beings might act.

It would be impossible for the thoughtless or impious acts of one species to have an immediate drastic effect on the earth. The cumulative effect of continuous secularity, however, poses a different kind of danger. Long-standing prophecies tell us of the impious people who would come here, defy the creator, and cause the massive destruction of the planet. Many traditional people believe that we are now quite near that time. The cumulative evidence of global warming, acid rain, the disappearance of amphibians, overpopulation, and other products of civilized life certainly testify to the possibility of these prophecies being correct.

Of all the traditional ceremonies extant and actively practiced at the time of contact with non-Indians, ceremonies derived from or related to these holy places have the highest retention rate because of their extraordinary planetary importance. Ironically, traditional people have been forced to hold these ceremonies under various forms of subterfuge and have been abused and imprisoned for doing them. Yet the ceremonies have very little to do with individual or tribal prosperity. Their underlying theme is one of gratitude expressed by human beings on behalf of all forms of life. They act to complete and renew the entire and complete cycle of life, ultimately including the whole cosmos present in its specific realizations, so that in the last analysis one might describe ceremonials as the cosmos becoming thankfully aware of itself.

Having used Old Testament examples to show the objective presence of the holy places, we can draw additional conclusions about the nature of these holy places from the story of the Exodus. Moses did not demand that the particular location of the burning bush become a place of worship for his people, although there was every reason to suppose that he could have done so. Lacking information, we must conclude that the holiness of this place precluded its use as a shrine. If Moses had been told to perform annual ceremonies at that location during specific days or times of the year, world history would have been entirely different.

Each holy site contains its own revelation. This knowledge is not the ultimate in the sense that Near Eastern religions like to claim the universality of their ideas. Traditional religious leaders tell us that in many of the ceremonies new messages are communicated to them. The ceremonies enable humans to have continuing relationships with higher spiritual powers so that each bit of information is specific to the time, place, and circumstances of the people. No revelation can be regarded as universal because times and conditions change.

The second and third kinds of sacred lands result from two distinctly different forms of sacred revelations where the sacred is actively involved in secular human activities and where the sacred takes the initiative to chart out a new historical course for humans. Because there are higher spiritual powers who can communicate with people, there has to be a fourth category of sacred lands. People must always be ready to experience new revelations at new locations. If this possibility did not exist, all deities and spirits would be dead. Consequently, we always look forward to the revelation of new sacred places and ceremonies. Unfortunately, some federal courts irrationally and arbitrarily circumscribe this universal aspect of religion by insisting that traditional religious practitioners restrict their identification of sacred locations to places that were historically visited by Indians, implying that at least for the federal courts, God is dead.

In denying the possibility of the continuing revelation of the sacred in our lives, federal courts, scholars, and state and federal agencies refuse to accord credibility to the testimony of religious leaders. They demand evidence that a ceremony or location has *always* been central to the beliefs and practices of an Indian tribe and impose exceedingly rigorous standards of proof on Indians who appear before them. This practice allows the Supreme Court to command what should not be done, it lets secular institutions rule on the substance of religious belief and practice. Thus, courts will protect a religion that shows every symptom of being dead but will create formidable barriers if it appears to be alive. Justice Scalia made this posture perfectly clear when he announced in *Smith,* that it would be unconstitutional to ban the casting of "statues that are used for worship purposes" or to prohibit bowing down before a golden calf.

We live in time and space and receive most of our signals about proper behavior from each other and the environment around us. Under these circumstances, the individual and the group *must* both have some kind of sanctity if we are to have a social order at all. By recognizing the various aspects of the sacredness of lands as we have described, we place ourselves in a realistic context in which the individual and the group can cultivate and enhance the sacred experience. Recognizing the sacredness of lands on which previous generations have lived and died is the foundation of all other sentiment. Instead of denying this dimension of our emotional lives, we should be setting aside additional places that have transcendent meaning. Sacred sites that higher spiritual powers have chosen for manifestation

VINE DELORIA, JR.

enable us to focus our concerns on the specific form of our lives. These places remind us of our unique relationship with the spiritual forces that govern the universe and call us to fulfill our religious vocations. These kinds of religious experiences have shown us something of the nature of the universe by an affirmative manifestation of themselves and this knowledge illuminates everything else that we know.

The nature of tribal religion brings contemporary America a new kind of legal problem. Religious freedom has existed as a matter of course in America *only* when religion has been conceived as a set of objective beliefs. This condition is actually not freedom at all because it would be exceedingly difficult to read minds and determine what ideas were being entertained at the time. So far in American history religious freedom has not involved the consecration and setting aside of lands for religious purposes or allowing sincere but highly divergent behavior by individuals and groups. The issue of sacred lands, as we have seen was successfully raised in the case of the Taos Pueblo people. Nevertheless, a great deal more remains to be done to guarantee Indian people the right to practice their own religion.

A number of other tribes have sacred sanctuaries in lands that have been taken by the government for purposes other than religion. These lands must be returned to the respective Indian tribes for their ceremonial purposes. The greatest number of Indian shrines are located in New Mexico and here the tribal religions have remained comparatively strong. Cochiti Pueblo needs some 24,000 acres of land for access to and use of religious shrines in what is now Bandelier National Monument. The people also have shrines in the Tetilla Peak area. San Juan Pueblo has also been trying to get lands returned for religious purposes. Santa Clara Pueblo requested the Indian Claims Commission to set aside 30,000 acres of the lands that have religious and ceremonial importance to its people but are presently in the hands of the National Forest Service and Atomic Energy Commission.

In Arizona the Hopi people have a number of shrines that are of vital importance to their religion. Traditionals regard the Black Mesa area as sacred, but it is being leased to Peabody Coal by the more assimilative tribal council. The San Francisco Peaks within the Coconino National Forest are sacred because they are believed to be the homes of the Kachinas who play a major part in the Hopi ceremonial system. The Navajo have a number of sacred mountains now under federal ownership. Mount Taylor in the Cibola National Forest, Blanca Peak in southern Colorado, Hesperus Peak in the San Juan National Forest, Huerfano Mountain on public domain lands, and Oak Creek canyon in the Coconino National Forest are all sites integral to the Navajo tradition. Part of the Navajo religion involves the "mountain chant" that describes the seven sacred mountains and a sacred lake located within these mountains. The Navajo believe their ancestors arose from this region at the creation. Last, but certainly not least, is the valiant struggle now being waged by the Apache people to prevent the University of Arizona from building several telescopes on Mount Graham in southern Arizona.

In other states several sacred sites are under threat of exploitation. The Forest Service is proposing to construct a major parking lot and observation platform at the Medicine Wheel site near Powell, Wyoming, that is sacred to many tribes from Montana, the Dakotas, and Wyoming. Because the only value of this location is its relationship to traditional Indian religions that need isolation and privacy, it seems ludicrous to pretend that making it accessible to more tourists and subject to increasing environmental degradation is enhancing it. The Badger Two Medicine area of Montana, where oil drilling has been proposed, is a sacred area for traditional Blackfeet who live in the vicinity. The Pipestone Quarry in southwestern Minnesota was confiscated from the Yankton Sioux in the closing decades of the last century when some missionaries pressured the federal government to eliminate Indian access to this important spot.

Finally, there is the continuing struggle over the Black Hills of South Dakota. Many Americans are now aware of this state thanks to the success of the movie *Dances with Wolves* that not only depicted the culture of the Sioux Indians but also filled the screen with the magnificent landscape of the northern Great Plains. Nineteen ninety-one was a year of great schizophrenia and strange anomalies in South Dakota. Local whites shamelessly capitalized on the success of the movie at the same time they were frothing at the mouth over the continuing efforts of the Sioux people to get the federal lands in the Black Hills returned to them. Governor George Mickelson announced a "Year of Reconciliation" that simply became twelve months of symbolic maneuvering for publicity and renewal of political images. When some of the Sioux elders suggested that the return of Bear Butte near Sturgis would be a concrete step toward reconciliation, non-Indians were furious that reconciliation might require them to make good-faith effort to heal the wounds from a century of conflict.

The question that must be addressed in the issue of sacred lands is the extent to which the tribal religions can be maintained if sacred lands are restored. Would restoration of the sacred Pipestone Quarry result in more people seeking to follow the traditional religious life or would it result in continued use of the stone for tourism and commercial purposes? A small group of Sioux people have made a living during this century from making ashtrays and decorative carvings from this sacred rock; they refuse to stop their exploitation. A major shift in focus is needed by traditional Sioux people to prepare to reconsecrate the quarry and return to the old ways of reverence.

A very difficult task lies ahead for the people who continue to believe in the old tribal religions. In the past, these traditions have been ridiculed by disbelievers, primarily missionaries and social scientists. Today injuries nearly as grievous are visited on traditional religions by the multitude of non-Indians who seek entrance and participation in ceremonies and rituals. Many of these non-Indians blatantly steal symbols, prayers and teaching by laying claim to alleged offices in tribal religions. Most non-Indians see in tribal religions the experiences and reverence that are missing in their own heritage. No matter how hard they try, they always reduce the teachings and ceremonies to a complicated word game and ineffectual gestures. Lacking communities and extended families, they are unable to put the religion into practice.

Some major efforts must be made by the Indians of this generation to demonstrate the view of the world that their tradition teaches has an integrity of its own and represents a sensible and respectable perspective of the world and a valid means of interpreting experiences. There are many new studies that seem to confirm certain tribal practices as reasonable and sometimes even as sophisticated techniques for handling certain kinds of problems. It might be sufficient to show that these patterns of behavior are indicative of a consistent attitude toward the world and includes the knowledge that everything is alive and related.

134

Sacred places are the foundation of all other beliefs and practices because they represent the presence of the sacred in our lives. They properly inform us that we are not larger than nature and that we have responsibilities to the rest of the natural world that transcend our own personal desires and wishes. This lesson must be learned by each generation; unfortunately the technology of industrial society always leads us in the other direction. Yet it is certain that as we permanently foul our planetary nest, we shall have to learn a most bitter lesson. There probably is not sufficient time for the non-Indian population to understand the meaning of sacred lands and incorporate the idea into their lives and practices. We can but hope that some protection can be afforded these sacred places before the world becomes wholly secular and is destroyed.

Notes

1. 92 Stat 469, 42 U.S.C. §1996.

2. See *Wilson v. Block*, 708 F 2d. 735 (D.C. Cir 1983). Hopi and Navajo sacred sites and shrines on San Francisco peak were destroyed by the U.S. Forest Service to make room for a new ski lift. In *Fools Crow v. Gullet*, 706 F. 2d. 856 (8th Cir 1983) the court upheld intrusions by the U.S. Park Service on Sioux vision quest use of Bear Butte. In *Badoni v. Higginson*, 638 F. 2d.172 (10th Cir 1980) the court allowed the destruction of a Navajo sacred site at Rainbow Bridge in the Grand Canyon area.

3. The majority decision in *Lyng* even suggested that to recognize traditional Indian religious freedom would make it seem as if the Indians owned the federal lands. No disrespect for these practices is implied when one notes that such beliefs could easily require de facto beneficial ownership of some rather spacious tracts of public property. Even without anticipating future cases, the diminution of the government's property rights, and the concomitant subsidy of the Indian religion, would in this case be far from trivial . . . . 108 S. Ct 1319, 1327 (1988)

4. At 1327

5. Justice Brennan's dissent makes this point specifically,The Court today, however, ignores *Roy's* emphasis on the internal nature of the government practice at issue there, and instead construes that case as further support for the proposition that governmental action that does not coerce conduct inconsistent with religious faith simply does not implicate the concerns of the Free Exercise Clause. That such a reading is wholly untenable, however, is demonstrated by the cruelly surreal result it produces here: *governmental action that will virtually destroy a religion is nevertheless deemed not to 'burden' that religion.* (at 1337) (Emphasis added.)

6. At 1332

7. Joshua 4:6–7

8. Exodus 3:5

MICHAEL  DORRIS

Essay by

RUTH ROSENBERG

An author of a diverse body of work in different genres, Dorris is praised for his sensitive and intelligent treatment of Native American concerns. Dorris, who is part Modoc, grew up on reservations in Montana and Kentucky. In college he studied English, history of the theater, and the classics, and eventually developed a strong interest in cultural anthropology. Dorris accepted a teaching position at Dartmouth College in the early 1970s, and became chairman of the Native American studies department in 1979.

It was at Dartmouth that he met his wife, the Chippewa author Louise Erdrich, whom he married in 1981. Critics have often discussed Dorris's productive collaboration with Erdrich under the joint pseudonym Milou North, especially their novel *The Crown of Columbus*. In the novel, the authors—utilizing elements of romance novels, detective stories, thrillers, and revisionist histories—tell the story of two lovers trying to uncover the truth about Columbus and his treatment of Native Americans.

Discussing his novel *A Yellow Raft in Blue Water* and the short fiction collection *Working Men*, critics have noted Dorris's deft use of detail and complex characterization. In his nonfiction book *The Broken Cord: A Family's Ongoing Struggle with Fetal Alcohol Syndrome*, Dorris chronicles the effects of FAS (Fetal Alcohol Syndrome) on his adopted son and the devastation alcoholism has caused in the Native American community. The work has garnered critical acclaim for its intensely personal portrayal of frustration and courage, and along with the rest of his fiction and nonfiction, the complex and sensitive treatment of human relationships and foibles.

Modoc novelist, short story writer, poet, nonfiction writer, author of children's books, essayist, scriptwriter, and songwriter.

Born: January 30, 1945, in Dayton, Washington.

Partnerships: Married Louise Erdrich (a writer); children: Reynold Abel, Jeffrey Sava, Madeline Hannah, Persia Andromeda, Pallas Antigone, Aza Marion.

Education: Georgetown University, B.A., 1967; Yale University, M.Phil., 1970.

Career: University of Redlands, Johnston College, Redlands, CA, assistant professor, 1970; Franconia College, Franconia, NH, assistant professor, 1971–72; Dartmouth College, Hanover, NH, instructor, 1972–76, assistant professor, 1976–79, associate professor, 1979, professor of anthropology, 1979–88, adjunct professor, 1989–, chair of Native American studies department, 1979–, chair of Master of Arts in Liberal Studies program, 1982–85. University of New Hampshire, visiting senior lecturer, 1980. Director of urban bus program, Summers, 1967, 1968, and 1969. Society for Applied Anthro-

pology, fellow, 1977–; Save the Children Foundation, board member, 1991–92, advisory board member, 1992–; U.S. Advisory Committee on Infant Mortality, member, 1992–. Consultant to National Endowment for the Humanities, 1976–, and to television stations, including Los Angeles Educational Television, 1976, and Toledo Public Broadcast Center, 1978. Has appeared on numerous radio and television programs. *Memberships:* PEN, Author's Guild, Writer's Guild, Modern Language Association of America (delegate assembly and member of minority commission, 1974–77), American Anthropological Association, American Association for the Advancement of Science (opportunities in science commission, 1974–77), National Indian Education Association, National Congress of American Indians, National Support Committee (Native American Rights Fund), Research Society on Alcoholism, National Organization for Fetal Alcohol Syndrome, Phi Beta Kappa, Alpha Sigma Nu.

Address: Home—Cornish, N.H. Office—Department of Native American Studies, Dartmouth College, Box 6152, Hanover, N.H. 03755.

A Yellow Raft in Blue Water

Henry Holt and Company, copyright © 1987 by Michael Dorris

2

Three gallons of Gulf gas start the Volaré's motor going and we get back to Seattle from Tacoma about midnight. Once she decides we're going to Aunt Ida's, Mom sees no reason to delay. There aren't many things, or many people, she wants a last look at, and I think the hardest thing for her to abandon in Seattle is her lifetime membership at Village Video.

A week before she went into the hospital this last time, she saw the ad in the paper. I thought she was checking out the classifieds like she did every morning, hoping to improve her prospects, but she had browsed too long in the Arts and Leisure.

"Look at this," she said, excited. "For only ninety-nine cents you can join this club for life, with all the privileges!"

"We don't have a VCR," I reminded her. "We don't even have a TV that works."

"Well, you never know. If we ever do get one we'd kick ourselves if we passed on this deal. Listen: you get movies for a dollar off on Tuesdays and Wednesdays. You can reserve ahead. You get a free subscription to their literature."

Mom put down the paper and went to the kitchen drawer for her scissors. She cut out the ad in a neat square and folded it twice before putting in into her purse. She was always one for a bargain.

The next time we were out in the Volaré, she drove to a shopping mall on the north side of the city. We worked our way through Sears and Kmart and into an immense building full of stores that sold shoes and cards and sports equipment and dresses with Japanese writing on them. Finally we came to Village Video, a small glass room with racks of cassettes lining the walls. Two people, a man and a woman, were ahead of us, and the manager was talking to them.

Native American literature is about as descriptive a term as non-Native American literature. If by definition non-Native American literature is about and by people who are not Native Americans, fine; except that doesn't tell you a great deal. I think what [Louise Erdrich, my wife], and I do is either within the tradition of a particular tribe or reservation or it is within the context of American literature. . . . I don't think that either of us, by any extension of the imagination, could presume or even dare to speak for or write about themes that were important for Navajos or for Iroquois or for people from other regions or other tribal backgrounds.

—**Michael Dorris, in *North Dakota Quarterly*, Winter 1987.**

"Ninety-nine cents is what it says in black and white and that's what I'm sticking to," he said. "Village Video does not go back on its word."

"But I paid twenty-five dollars for the same thing four days ago," the woman complained. Mom gave me a look with her eyebrows raised, as if to say "See!"

"I know, I know," the manager said. He seemed truly sad, but helpless. He shrugged his heavy shoulders in despair. "I can't do anything about that. We have competition coming into this mall." He looked from right to left out the door as if expecting to see competition arriving any minute. "We have to build our membership."

M I C H A E L   D O R R I S

It is a cliché about Americans that one of the first things we ask a new acquaintance is "What do you do?" In Europe, the question would be considered unpardonably rude. Michael Dorris taps into this essential aspect of American life, that we are what we do, and most of the stories in Working Men *center on a moment of self-revelation connected with work. . . . The stories share a concern with how ripples from the world of work spread into and even define a character's emotional and family lives.*

Tony Eprile, in *The New York Times Book Review,* October 17, 1993.

"But . . . " the woman said.

"No retroactive," the manager cut in before she could go on. "I understand, I really do, but that's just the way it has to be."

Mom was delighted. The woman's loss was her gain. I could tell she felt proud that she had not come in here last week and plunked down twenty-five dollars. It would have done me no good to point out that the thought to do so would have never entered her head.

"How long does it last?" said the other customer, a man wearing a tan shirt with little straps that buttoned on top of his shoulders. He looked as if he was comparing all the pros and cons before shelling out ninety-nine cents. You could see he thought he was pretty shrewd.

"It lasts for as long as you live," the manager said slowly. There was a second of silence while we all thought about that. The man in the tan shirt drew his head back, tucking his chin into his neck. His mind was working like a house on fire.

"What about other people?" he asked. "The wife? The kids?"

"They can use your membership as long as *you're* alive," the manager said, making the distinction clear.

"Then what?" the man asked, louder. He was the type who said things like "You get what you pay for" and "There's one born every minute" and was considering every angle. He didn't want to get taken for a ride by his own death.

"That's it," the manager said, waving his hands, palms down, like a football referee ruling an extra point no good. "Then they'd have to join for themselves or forfeit the privileges."

"Well then, it makes sense," the man said, on top of the situation now, "for the youngest one to join. The one that's likely to live the longest."

"I can't argue with that," said the manager.

The man chewed his lip while he mentally reviewed his family. Who would go first. Who'd survive the longest. He cast his eyes around to all the cassettes as if he'd see one that would answer his question.

The woman had not gone away. She had brought along her signed agreement, the one that she paid twenty-five dollars for. "What is this accident waiver clause?" she asked the manager.

"Look," he said, now exhibiting his hands to show they were empty, nothing up his sleeve, "I live in the real world. I'm a small businessman, right? I have to protect my investment, don't I? What would happen if, and I'm not suggesting *you'd* do this, all right, but some people might, what would happen if you decided to watch one of my movies in the bathtub and a VCR you rented from me fell into the water?"

The woman retreated a step. This thought had clearly not occurred to her before.

"I don't want to be sued by your estate, do I? By your orphaned children?" The manager continued, now leaning his elbows on the counter and putting his weight on them. "I don't want to be held responsible for you if you electrocute yourself by mistake."

The woman put her expensive contract into her purse and drifted off. At first she pretended to browse through New Selections, but actually she was working her way toward the door and when she thought no one was watching, she cut out.

Mom stepped up to the counter in her place and pulled out a dollar bill.

"I'm joining this thing!" she announced brightly, "and I want you to know," she said to the manager, "that I intend to get my money's worth!"

"That's good, that's good," he said, handing her a blank contract card.

"What if I live for fifty years?" Mom asked.

"You're covered," he nodded.

"What if I put it in her name," Mom said, jerking her head in my direction, "and she lives for a hundred years. You know, medical science."

"You can both use it during her lifetime," the manager answered, giving me an appraising look. "As long as you continue to share the same domicile."

"She wouldn't evict me, would you, baby?" Mom said. "And this way, if the worst happens to me, you can still rent tapes at the members' rate. It's like something I'd leave you."

"This low offer may not be repeated," the manager agreed.

MICHAEL DORRIS

"Well, that's that," Mom decided. She wrote my name on the dotted line and had me sign on the bottom. "Till death," she said proudly.

I can't explain how I felt, but it was as though a part of my life was over. As far as video clubs went, this deal would last as long as I did, no matter what else ever happened to me. No surprises. Someday, if I was lucky, I would still be a name in the records of Village Video, an old lady whose charter membership had never expired.

"Remember," the manager said as we left the store, "I'm not responsible. What you do with your cassettes is your ball game."

"We are not idiots." Now that she was the mother of a lifetime member Mom could afford to be more herself. "Some of your people may watch shows in their bathrooms, but not us."

"We don't watch them anywhere," I reminded her as we searched for our car in the huge parking lot. "We don't have anything to watch them on. Our TV barely has sound."

"Go ahead and be smart," she said. "But you'll be laughing out the other side of your mouth if we ever get one of those players and can watch all the movies we want at the special prices."

At the time I didn't say it was unlikely that we'd be getting a VCR soon, or that, even if we did, it was a sure bet we wouldn't come all the way out to the suburbs to rent films for it. I figured we'd never lay eyes on Village Video again. Then, the next week, Mom checked into the hospital and I forgot the whole thing.

Now, while it's still night, we clean out our closet and pack Mom's scrapbooks and the odds and ends that we want to keep from our apartment. The building manager is asleep with the TV on downstairs, so we tiptoe. After Mom's flirtation with suicide, she's in no mood to stay around arguing about the rent we owe or the security deposit we have borrowed against. She changes out of her candy striper uniform, and holds it in front of her.

"I'm just going to run this over to Charlene so she can return it," she says, and rushes from the apartment. I hear her knock on the door down the hall.

Finally Charlene answers.

"Do you know what time it is?" she shouts in a whisper you could hear on the next block, but then it hits her that Mom is standing there and not asleep in the hospital. "What are you doing? You're sick in bed."

"We're taking off," Mom says. "I'm going home."

Books

Native Americans: Five Hundred Years After, photographs by Joseph Farber, Thomas Y. Crowell, 1977.

(With Arlene Hirschfelder and Mary Lou Byler) *A Guide to Research on North American Indians*, American Library Association, 1983.

A Yellow Raft in Blue Water, Henry Holt, 1987.

The Broken Cord, Harper & Row, 1989.

(With Louise Erdrich) *The Crown of Columbus*, HarperCollins, 1991.

(With Louise Erdrich) *Route Two*, California, Lord John Press, 1991.

Morning Girl, Hyperion Books, 1992.

Rooms in the House of Stone, Minnesota, Milkweed Editions, 1993.

Working Men (short stories), Henry Holt, 1993.

Paper Trail, HarperCollins, 1994.

Essays

"The Grass Still Grows, the Rivers Still Flow: Contemporary Native Americans," *Daedalus*, spring 1981; 43–70.

(With Louise Erdrich) "Sea to Sea on Route 2," *New York Times*, March 15, 1987; 530.

"The Best of Pen Pals: Corresponding with People around the World," *Seventeen*, August 1987; 128.

"Why Mister Ed Still Talks Good Horse Sense: An Anthropologist Explains How Reruns, Like Old Tribal Tales, Can Link Generations and Teach Enduring Values," *TV Guide*, May 28, 1982; 34–37.

"Rite of Passage: A Man's Journey into Fatherhood Echoes His Son's Entry into Adolescence," *Parents'*, June 1989; 246–248.

"A Desparate Crack Legacy," *Newsweek*, June 25, 1990; 8.

"What Men Are Missing," *Vogue*, September 1991; 511–513.

Adaptations

The Broken Cord: A Family's Ongoing Struggle with Fetal Alcohol Syndrome was produced for television by Universal Television and ABC-TV, 1992.

A Yellow Raft in Blue Water and *The Broken Cord: A Family's Ongoing Struggle with Fetal Alcohol Syndrome* were released on audiocassette by HarperAudio in 1990; *The Crown of Columbus* was released on audiocassette by HarperAudio in 1991.

Film rights to *The Crown of Columbus* were sold to Cinecom.

Work in Progress

Amory Goes Wild, a book for young adults, for Hyperion, 1995.

"I don't believe they checked you out." Charlene hisses back.

"They didn't. I sprung myself wearing this."

I imagine her displaying the red-and-white-striped dress. I wait for Charlene to scream her shocked approval. But there is just a pause and then Charlene almost sounds sad. "You're crazy, Christine. You're killing yourself."

"Not if you be my friend," Mom says. Something rattles. "Here's my address. You can get more medicine from the pharmacy. Send it to me here. But don't let *anybody* know where I've gone."

I recognize the sound I heard: pills loose in a plastic bottle.

"I could lose my job for that," Charlene says. "They check inventory once a week."

"Well, don't then. I don't need the fucking stuff anyway."

I hear Mom coming back. Her steps are fast and close together, proud. Just as she reaches our door, Charlene's voice catches her.

"All right then. Some. But you go see a doctor out there. I can't keep ripping off Percocet without getting caught."

Mom's feet turn and she rebounds to Charlene.

We pack everything that matters in four jumbo green plastic garbage bags that we find in the kitchen cabinet. Each one gets labeled with masking tape: two with "Christine," one with "Ray," and one with "Junk." We have to squeeze them into the backseat of the Volaré, since the trunk is permanently wedged shut. It's five A.M. by the time we're done. I'm all set for the long drive, but not Mom.

"We can't go yet," she says. "We have to wait till the stores open."

"Stores?" We're low on cash, as always.

"Village Video. We can't blow into Aunt Ida's like deadbeats, alone and empty-handed. We'll rent a couple of movies at members' prices and take them along for a surprise."

"To Montana?" I say. "It's probably a federal offense to take stolen videotapes across state lines." I remember that the membership is in my name. I'll be the one the cops come after.

"They won't be stolen," Mom corrects me. "They'll be rented for life. It's completely legal. You just have to read the contract the right way."

The manager is rolling back a metal gate, opening his store, and Mom greets him like an old friend. "My daughter is still alive," she announces, pointing to me. "We're just going to exercise our privileges and borrow some tapes."

"Fine, fine," the manager says.

"What if we are a little late bringing them back?" Mom's voice is casual, cagey.

"Oh, not to worry. A little fine, reduced to almost nothing because of your charter membership. It happens all the time."

Mom presses her foot on my toe to show she has been right.

After five minutes of browsing, she picks a movie about a jealous old car named Christine that murders people. She loved the ads when the film came to a theater in Seattle.

"Look at this," she said that day, shoving the Amusement section under my nose, and then reading the ad: "I am Christine. I am pure evil." She cut the slogan out and stuck it on the refrigerator with a magnet, and was thrilled to get the same thing printed on a bumper sticker the third time she saw the movie.

For the second tape, after a lot of considering, she picks *Little Big Man*.

"I dated a guy who played an Indian in that movie," she whispers at me.

She tells the manager an almost similar story when she has me sign for the tapes.

"This one is special to me," she brags. "I was once engaged to the star."

"Dustin Hoffman?"

Mom smiles as if she knows a secret, but doesn't say yes or no. "Did you see his face?" she asks when we're out of the store.

But I just think that now he'll remember who we are.

The gray sky has started to sprinkle. The two tapes, in a yellow plastic bag decorated with a red v.v., are on the seat between us, in for a long haul. I let the noise and steady motion of the windshield wipers hypnotize me, lull me into drowsiness. Mom is talking, telling me what to expect in Montana, whom we're going to meet, what a rotten drive she had the last time we made this trip in winter when I was a baby. I nod whenever she pauses for breath. Her words rinse through my thoughts, clear as water, disconnected as rain.

Mom insists that we take a two-lane highway instead of the Interstate because, she says, she knows the way. The traffic is light and in between naps I watch the scenery roll by. Compared to western Washington the land on the other side of the mountains is at first dry and flat and then thick forest, but always empty of people. There are miles between towns so small that I can see their whole length as we approach. Late the first afternoon, a pair of black eagles circle above the road and Mom almost veers onto the shoulder with trailing them. I try to convince her to rest. All along the side in Montana you see little white metal crosses that mark the spots where people died in accidents, and I don't want our trip to end with two more, but she has energy to spare and drives all night, humming with the radio, learning new songs.

We grow accustomed to the car's ticking and clanks. Mom compensates for the steering wheel's tendency to pull to the right by bearing down on the left. We come to ignore the blinking emergency lights of oncoming cars. We *know* that one of our headlamps is out and there's nothing much we can do about it. When the service station attendants fill the tank and frown at our old credit card, its expiration date smoothed out with Mom's penknife, we ask them to check the tires. That changes the subject fast, since every one of them figures they can convince us that if we keep going on our smooth tubes the next mile might be our last. By the time they realize we aren't buying, we're already rolling.

The car is just one of the things Mom worries about. Her relations are her main concern.

"Do you remember Aunt Ida?" Mom wakes me in the middle of the night to inquire. Our speeding light illuminates a sign that says we're in the Kootenai National Forest. I think before I answer.

Aunt Ida is nobody's aunt, at least that I know of, but she wasn't married when Mom came along, so rather than have her only daughter remind her of this fact, she settled on being an aunt. By the time Mom's brother Lee was born it was natural that he'd call her that too. People get used to anything. I made the mistake of using "Grandma" when she came to Seattle. She was mixing flour for fry bread in a yellow basin, and her hands stopped in the wet dough. "Aunt Ida," she said, staring me down. "Aunt Ida."

Even after eight years, I flinch at the memory of her tone, and answer Mom's question with one of my own. "Are you anxious to see her?"

"Oh I'm looking forward to it," Mom says. "About as much as snow in March."

When Mom and I have conversations, they mostly involve subjects not personal to our lives. We discuss the cost of shoes, the marriages and divorces of TV stars, the plot of "Hill Street Blues." Mom tries not to ask me questions, and I'm not supposed to mind her business either. But sometimes she forgets, and chats with me as though I'm a girlfriend like Charlene. Very late, once in a while, she'll have a glass of wine and start complaining about her latest job, or how the guy she went out with was too rough, or how she's heard Dad has been seen with the same woman more than once.

I listen, eavesdropping into her life, while she lights Kent after Kent and the room fills with smoke while she kills the bottle. Those evenings always end with Mom's thoughts returning either to the day in Tacoma that Dad proposed to her, or to something about her brother, Lee, who was killed in Vietnam. She confuses who I am and asks me if I knew him, asks me if he had any last words for her. Those nights I help her to bed.

On this night, though, as we clatter over Route 2 and try to find good stations on the radio, Mom wants to hear about me.

"Are you going to miss anybody in Seattle?" she wonders, but before I can answer, she goes on. "No you won't. Bunch of punks. You wait. Out on the rez it'll be different."

She's right in a way, there isn't anybody to miss except the hope of Dad that I used to have. As we've moved around from one apartment to another I've changed schools so often that I never get past being the new girl. Too big, too smart, not Black, not Indian, not friendly. Kids keep their distance, and most teachers are surprised, then annoyed, that I know the answers on their tests. I'm not what they expect. About once a year I get discovered, get called a diamond in the rough. Some eager young counselor has big plans for me, but before they pan out, we're gone, living in another neighborhood, and the whole shooting match starts all over.

"Me neither," Mom goes on. "Charlene's been okay, but she's no mental giant. And screw the rest of them."

She means Dad.

"I shouldn't have stayed so long. When I was a kid, I thought Seattle was Hollywood. I was going to hit it big. I applied for relocation and before I turned around I had a husband and you. And then just you."

I don't ask Mom what she plans to do with herself back on the reservation. I know she doesn't know. She makes her plans from one day to the next, always sure that a happy ending is just out of sight. I try and imagine what it would be like if we settled in one of the places we drive through. Each of them was the end of the line for people who took off from their homes somewhere else and beat a path to Shelby or Pinnacle or Dunkirk. We could do that too, move anywhere, be anybody.

MICHAEL DORRIS

1 4 7

The Volaré almost makes it. All the next day, descending the Rockies through fields of wheat and lentils and mint, we parallel a black ribbon of railroad track, underlining scattered patches of short mountains to the north. Clouds seem low, within reach, larger than life. Distance is measured by hours instead of miles and sea gulls patrol the pavement like vultures. Once we reach the high plains where Mom grew up, the car seems to relax, and quiets down. The worst is over, it seems to realize, and it's a straight coast the rest of the way. After a Conoco station east of Havre, Mom turns to me, shaking her head.

"Maybe we should have done us all a favor and let that hippie pump jockey unload some new tires on us. I don't want Aunt Ida to think I'm down on my luck."

Mom calls every man with a ponytail a hippie. "What were you planning to use for cash?" I ask.

She pats her green purse where it rests against her thigh on the seat. "If that old card will fill the tank for a thousand miles, I got to believe it will replace our tires too," she says. "Besides, that guy was so out of it he didn't even try to check the expiration date."

She seems about to turn back but reconsiders and keeps driving. "Four retreads would just make the rest of this car stand out old," she decides.

We whiz through the small towns, ignoring their offers of a real country breakfast, a fill-up, or a Dairy Queen, and come, about one o'clock, to the turn-off that leads to the reservation.

Mom is so relieved to be close to a place she can stop, she gets careless and forgets about potholes and flood washes that have been baking unrepaired in the spring heat. Less than a mile away from Aunt Ida's, she drives straight into a dip and the Volaré stalls, then dies. It sounds as sounds as if something falls off the bottom of the car and hits the gravel below, but Mom and I are not in a mood to check.

"Maybe it threw a rod," Mom says.

"What does that mean?"

"Who the hell knows? But it's beyond my powers of fixing and we're close enough to walk. I'll tell Dayton the car's out here and he can look."

Dayton is her friend from high school, a mixed-blood living on lease land close to Aunt Ida's. He's the person she says will be glad to see her after all these years, the person she talks about connecting with. "Dayton and Lee were real close," she says. "He was a pallbearer. Do you remember him?" She sets her mouth as if she's recalling something she would rather forget.

"I was only two," I say, but Mom is already standing by the road, stretching her arms, arching her stiff back.

We are almost directly next to a faint track that Mom says leads over a rise to Aunt Ida's house, so we start out. Mom carries the two "Christine" garbage bags, and her big carved-leather purse. Crammed inside it, keeping the flap from snapping, are the two videocassettes she has rented for life. I carry the two other plastic bags: the "Junk" and my own. Mom doesn't want to leave anything in the car.

"This is a poor place," she says.

It's hard for me to imagine that anything we own would tempt anybody.

As soon as we clear the top of the ridge, Aunt Ida comes into view. Her house, its boards warped and turned gray by too much weather, is the only structure you can see in any direction, and Aunt Ida is in front of it. She's not an unusually tall woman, but her arms and legs are long. A black bouffant wig is tacked on her head by bobby pins that shine in the sunlight, and beneath men's bib overalls, a dark blue bra dents deeply into her back and shoulders. Her skin is a darker brown than Mom's, though not as deep as Dad's or mine. Behind her sunglasses, her eyes are invisible.

Aunt Ida is pushing an old lawn mower back and forth across a plot of scrub grass. As we get closer I can see that it's not doing any cutting. Either the blades are dull or the grass it too tough: the stems flatten as the mower passes over, and then spring back. But she isn't aware of it, or of us. The speakers of the Walkman we sent her last Christmas are plugged into her ears. Her craggy, accented voice, surprisingly familiar to me, is off-key but loud as she accompanies the tape.

"I've been looking for love in all the wrong places," she booms out, and then something makes her notice us. At first she pretends not to have seen anything out of the ordinary, and goes back to her pushing.

"Looking for love in too many faces," she shouts, then stops again and drops her forearms on the handle of the mower. Finally she glances over her shoulder and sighs as she pulls off the headset.

"Well, what did the cat drag in," she says in Indian, in a voice as scratchy and knotted as a fir tree. "My favorite thing, a surprise visitor."

"I came home, Aunt Ida." Mom stands in the yellow field, her hair blowing across her face like dark string, the green garbage bags full of Seattle clothes at her feet. She's nervous. The wind rises, filling her blouse like a kite and outlining her short, square body. I have a sudden, sure sense that for Mom this is an important moment, a beginning or an end of something, and she's scared to find out which. I have the idea to walk over to her, punch her on the

M I C H A E L   D O R R I S

arm, and tell her to lighten up, but I stay put and watch as though I'm seeing this scene on an old movie and a commercial could come along any time.

The music leaking out of Aunt Ida's earphones is tinny and low, but it fills the air around us and we listen. I think it's the Oak Ridge Boys or a group like that, but it's a song I don't know. Hearing that tune gives us all something to do, though, while we wait for what Aunt Ida will say. She's taking her time, giving Mom a chance to put in another word more if she wants.

"Give me three good reasons why I should be glad to see you." Aunt Ida's forehead bends into a frown. She pulls a red kerchief from her hip pocket and wipes her mouth.

Mom doesn't move. She doesn't even relax her scared smile. She tenses as though she's thought of an answer but she's not sure it's right. Then she gives it a try anyway, as if this is a quiz show and she's out to stump the stars.

"One, Mother, I'm your daughter, your only living child."

Aunt Ida doesn't like to hear this. Her face twists as if Mom has punched her below the belt or whacked her from behind when she wasn't looking.

"Two, I need someplace to stay."

Aunt Ida's expression changes fast. She has hit upon some good comeback, something that will start with "Ha!" and not quit until "I told you so" is thrown in.

"Three . . . " Mom hesitates. She has been watching Aunt Ida too and knows that the minute she finishes her answer, no matter what it is, Aunt Ida's going to let go with something mean. As long as she doesn't say the third reason she's safe, Aunt Ida's hands are tied. Mom's eyes are bright. She looks from side to side, not seeing anything. Her fingers are shredding the top of one of the "Christine" bags, stretching and punching holes in the dark plastic. She seems to see something on the ground and stares at it, pries at it with the toe of her boot. Nobody breathes.

"Three," Mom says, looking up straight at Aunt Ida. "Three, go fuck yourself anyway."

Mom picks up the bags in her fists and turns away, walking, and then, off balance, doing a jerky run down the hill toward the car. Her feet start landslides of pebbles, storms of dust. Aunt Ida's mouth is open now. She is shocked, she's amazed, she can't believe her ears. She's reacting like there's an audience ready to laugh or hoot, but there's only the noise of the whispering tape and of Mom's jagged steps, running, tripping, the bags slapping against her legs.

She's almost to the car before I remember that I'm really here, that this is really happening. I turn to Aunt Ida, expecting her to do something, to call

Mom back, but her expression says she's just heard bad news or the worst joke in the world. She puts on the earphones, silencing the tiny speakers. I grab the other bags and start down the hill and build speed as I go.

"Wait a minute," I yell. "Hold on."

Mom doesn't look back, doesn't slow down, even when the sack with the videotapes spills from her purse. She hits the dirt road and doesn't pause as she passes the Volaré.

The land folds and slopes around me as I chase after her. I can see for miles. The "Junk" bag snaps on the gray remains of a tree stump, ripping a gash in the bottom and spilling a trail of towels and postcards and half-read magazines. I stop to try and scoop them up, but the bag is useless and my arms won't contain them. Everytime I collect one object, two others fall, and finally I let everything drop.

Mom has reached the main road, far below, and she's still moving. Her body is small and tight, crouched in a low jog. Nobody would guess that three days ago she had been flat on her back in the hospital. She can't keep going, I figure. I have time to catch her, to become part of her plan, but as I think this I see dust disturbed on the road further away. A blue pickup, jarring through the rain ruts, is heading in our direction. It stops next to Mom but she doesn't slack her pace, so it starts again, slowly lurching beside her. She's talking to the guy behind the wheel, talking and running, dragging her garbage bags, and finally the door opens and she hops in. The truck gathers speed, kicking gravel. It gets lost in its own dust.

My head is buzzing. I'm not used to running. I hear my heartbeat inside my ears. I look down, The earth is ugly. The way the grass grows out of the tan soil reminds me of a photograph I saw of a bald man who had a hair transplant. His scalp was a wide empty place with dark stalks poking out of little black holes. A Barbie doll scalp. The ground seems to me the most disgusting thing in the world. It makes my skin crawl. I drop to my knees, surrounded by our blowing junk, and pull weeds out by their roots, scratch them out with my fingernails. I must make the soil smooth, even, without bristles. No matter how much I pull there's more. I will never clean it all, and yet I can't stop. I pound at the earth with my flat hands, pushing it pure, scraping it loose. Nothing else matters to me. Nothing but fixing this dirt.

I know Aunt Ida is close by me but I pay no attention until her hands seize my wrists and hold them still. I won't look at her when she moves before me. I could never explain about the grass. My muscles strain against her arms, strain and pull until they cramp, and still my fingers arch into rakes.

MICHAEL **DORRIS**

I'm no match for her. I try to tell her to let go, but instead of saying words I am screaming, howling like a crazy person, and she hangs on. She hauls me in like a trapped salmon and imprisons me. I am kneeling into her, my face forced into the warm, damp skin about her bra, her breasts against my neck. I can't move, no matter how I struggle, and finally I surrender. The strength goes out of me, the hate I feel for the ground leaves as completely as a day-old dream. I press against her fine grass-smelling skin, sink into the basket of her arms.

She lets me stay that way for some space of time. It seems long because I keep dreading it will end, and finally it does. Her grip relaxes on my wrists and there's room between us as she steps back. I life my face but the sun is behind her and shows me only the outline of her head, round and clean as a street lamp.

"Save your belongings before they blow away," she says, and turns for the house.

But I don't save them. I am afraid to look down, and so feel and step around them with my feet as I follow her up the hill, over the crest, out of sight of the road.

LOUISE  ERDRICH

Award-winning author Louise Erdrich published her first two books—Jack-light, a volume of poetry, and Love Medicine, *a novel—at the age of thir-ty. The daughter of a Chippewa Indian mother and a German-American father, the author explores Native American themes in her works, with major characters representing both sides of her heritage.*

Essay by

BRIGHAM NARINS

Love Medicine, which traces two Native American families from 1934 to 1984 in a unique seven-narrator format, was extremely well-received, earning its author numerous awards, including the National Book Critics Circle Award in 1984. Since then, Erdrich has gone on to publish *The Beet Queen, Tracks,* and *The Bingo Palace*—three more novels in a four-part series—which explore the roots of *Love Medicine's* characters, as well as those of their white neighbors. These four novels, which are related through recurring characters and themes, all became national best-sellers.

Erdrich's interest in writing can be traced to her childhood and her heritage. She told *Writer's Digest* contributor Michael Schumacher, "People in [Native American] families make everything into a story. . . . People just sit and the stories start coming, one after another. I suppose that when you grow up constantly hearing the stories rise, break, and fall, it gets into you somehow." The oldest in a family of seven children, Erdrich was raised in Wahpeton, North Dakota. Her Chippewa grandfather had been the tribal chair of the nearby Turtle Mountain Reservation, and her parents worked at the Bureau of Indian Falls boarding school. Erdrich once told *Contemporary Authors* of the way in which her parents encouraged her writing: "My father used to give me a nickel for every story I wrote, and my mother wove strips of construction paper together and stapled them into book covers. So at an early age I felt myself to be a published author earning substantial royalties."

Erdrich's first year at Dartmouth, 1972, was the year the college began admitting women, as well as the year the Native American studies department was established. The author's future husband and collaborator, anthropologist Michael Dorris, was hired to chair the department. In his class, Erdrich began the exploration of her own ancestry that would eventually inspire her novels. Intent on balancing her academic training with a broad range of practical knowledge, Erdrich told Miriam Berkley in an interview with *Publishers Weekly*, "I ended up taking some really crazy jobs, and I'm glad I did. They turned out to have been very useful experiences, although I never would have believed it at the time." In addition to working as a lifeguard, waitress, poetry teacher at prisons, and construction flag signaler, Erdrich became an editor for the *Circle*, a Boston Indian Council newspaper. She told Schumacher, "Settling into that job and becoming comfortable with an urban community—which is very different from the reservation community—gave me another reference point. There were lots of people with mixed blood, lots of people who had their own confusions. I realized that this was part of my life—it wasn't something that I was making up—and that it was something I wanted to write about." In 1978, the author enrolled in an M.A. program at Johns Hopkins University, where she wrote poems and stories incorporating her heritage, many of which would later become part of her books. She also began sending her work to publishers, most of whom sent back rejection slips.

After receiving her master's degree, Erdrich returned to Dartmouth as a writer-in-residence. Dorris—with whom she had remained in touch—attended a reading of Erdrich's poetry there, and was impressed. A writer himself, he decided then that he was interested in working with Erdrich and getting to know her better. When he left for New Zealand to do field research and Erdrich went to Boston to work on a textbook, the two began sending their poetry and fiction back and forth with their letters, laying a groundwork for a literary relationship. Dorris returned to New Hampshire in 1980, and Erdrich moved back there as well. The two began collaborating on short stories, including one titled "The World's Greatest Fisherman." When this story won five thousand dollars in the Nelson Algren fiction competition, Erdrich and Dorris decided to expand it into a novel—*Love Medicine*. At the same time, their literary relationship led to a romantic one. In 1981 they were married.

The titles Erdrich and Dorris have chosen for their novels—such as *Love Medicine* and *A Yellow Raft in Blue Water*—tend to be rich poetic or visual images. The title is often the initial inspiration from which their novels are drawn. Erdrich told Schumacher, "I think a title is like a magnet: It begins to draw these scraps of experience or conversation or memory to it. Eventually, it collects a book." Erdrich and Dorris's collaboration process begins with a first draft, usually written by whoever had the original idea for the book, the one who will ultimately be considered the official author. After the draft is written, the other person edits it, and then another draft is written; often five or six drafts will be written in all. Finally, the two read the work aloud until they can agree on each word. Although the author has the original voice and the final say, ultimately, both collaborators are responsible for what the work becomes.

Erdrich's novels *Love Medicine, The Beet Queen, Tracks,* and *The Bingo Palace* encompass the stories of three interrelated families living in and around a reservation in the fictional town of Argus, North Dakota, from 1912 through the 1980s. The novels have been compared to those of William Faulkner, mainly due to the multivoice narration and nonchronological storytelling which he employed in works such as *As I Lay Dying.* Erdrich's works, linked by recurring characters who are victims of fate and the patterns set by their elders, are structured like intricate puzzles in which bits of information about individuals and their relations to one another are slowly released in a seemingly random order, until three-dimensional characters—with a future and a past—are revealed. Through her characters' antics, Erdrich explores universal family life cycles while also communicating a sense of the changes and loss involved in the twentieth-century Native American experience.

Erdrich's involvement with *The Crown of Columbus* represents a significant departure from that world. Although *The Crown of Columbus* involves interpreting and finding new meaning in history, the Argus characters are themselves living out history and guiding the reader through its changes. As she once told the *New York Times Book Review,* "I can't stand not knowing what's happening . . . [because] there's an ongoing conversation with these fictional people. Events suggest themselves. You have no choice."

My first audience that I would write for, that [my husband Michael Dorris and I] write for, as a couple, is American Indians, hoping that they will read, laugh, cry, really take in the work. One of the problems is the distribution of literature. For instance, how many Indians can afford to buy Love Medicine *right now? It's pretty expensive and it's the way publishing unfortunately goes on. One of our hopes was to have it available in a nice, cheap edition everywhere, so that people could get it easily.*

—**Louise Erdrich, in an interview in Laura Coltelli's** *Winged Words: American Indian Writers Speak,* **University of Nebraska Press, 1990.**

155

Chippewa novelist, poet, short story writer, essayist, and critic.

Born: June 7, 1954, in Little Falls, Minnesota.

Partnerships: Married Michael Anthony Dorris (a writer and professor of Native American studies), October 10, 1981; children: Reynold Abel, Jeffrey Sava, Madeline Hannah, Persia Andromeda, Pallas Antigone, Aza Marion.

Education: Dartmouth College, B.A., 1976; Johns Hopkins University, M.A., 1979.

Career: Writer. North Dakota State Arts Council, visiting poet and teacher, 1977–78; Johns Hopkins University, Baltimore, MD, writing instructor, 1978–79; Boston Indian Council, Boston, MA, communications director and editor of *The Circle*, 1979–80; Charles-Merrill Co., textbook writer, 1980. Previously employed as a beet weeder in Wahpeton, ND; waitress in Wahpeton, Boston, and Syracuse, NY; psychiatric aide in a Vermont hospital; poetry teacher at prisons; lifeguard; and construction flag signaler. Has judged writing contests.

Memberships: International Writers, PEN (member of executive board, 1985–88), Authors Guild, Authors League of America.

Address: Hanover, New Hampshire.

LOVE MEDICINE (1982)

From *Love Medicine*, Holt, Rinehart and Winston, copyright ©1984 by Louise Erdrich

LIPSHA MORRISSEY

I never really done much with my life, I suppose. I never had a television. Grandma Kashpaw had one inside her apartment at the Senior Citizens, so I used to go there and watch my favorite shows. For a while she used to call me the biggest waste on the reservation and hark back to how she saved me from my own mother, who wanted to tie me in a potato sack and throw me in a slough. Sure, I was grateful to Grandma Kashpaw for saving me like that, for raising me, but gratitude gets old. After a while, stale. I had to stop thanking her. One day I told her I had paid her back in full by staying at her beck and call. I'd do anything for Grandma. She knew that. Besides, I took care of Grandpa like nobody else could, on account of what a handful he'd gotten to be.

But that was nothing. I know the tricks of mind and body inside out without ever having trained for it, because I got the touch. It's a thing you got to be born with. I got secrets in my hands that nobody ever knew to ask. Take Grandma Kashpaw with her tired veins all knotted up in her legs like clumps of blue snails. I take my fingers and I snap them on the knots. The medicine flows out of me. The touch. I run my fingers up the maps of those rivers of veins or I knock very gentle above their hearts or I make a circling motion on their stomachs, and it helps them. They feel much better. Some women pay me five dollars.

I couldn't do the touch for Grandpa, though. He was a hard nut. You know, some people fall right through the hole in their lives. It's invisible, but they come to it after time, never knowing where. There is this woman here, Lulu Lamartine, who always had a thing for Grandpa. She loved him since she was a girl and always said he was a genius. Now she says that his mind got so full it exploded.

How can I doubt that? I know the feeling when your mental power builds up too far. I always used to say that's why the Indians got drunk. Even statistically we're the smartest people on the earth. Anyhow with Grandpa I couldn't hardly believe it, because all my youth he stood out as a hero to me. When he started getting toward second childhood he went through different moods. He would stand in the woods and cry at the top of his shirt. It scared me, scared everyone, Grandma worst of all.

Yet he was so smart—do you believe it?—that he *knew* he was getting foolish.

He said so. He told me that December I failed school and come back on the train to Hoop-dance. I didn't have nowhere else to go. He picked me up there and he said it straight out: "I'm getting into my second childhood." And then he said something else I still remember: "I been chosen for it. I couldn't say no." So I figure that a man so smart all his life—tribal chairman and the star of movies and even pictured in the statehouse and on cans of snuff—would know what he's doing by saying yes. I think he was called to second childhood like anybody else gets a call for the priesthood or the army or whatever. So I really did not listen too hard when the doctor said this was some kind of disease old people got eating too much sugar. You just can't tell me

The proliferation of mothers in Erdrich's novels—absent mothers, all-too-present mothers, abusive mothers, silent mothers—reflects the Chippewa emphasis on the family as [in Gerald Vizenor's words] "the basic political and economic unit in the woodland and the primary source of personal identity." . . . Mother is not merely one's biological parent; she is all one's relations (male and female, human and animal, individual and tribal); and she is connected to the earth. Erdrich, however, is not a "traditional Chippewa," and, with one or two exceptions, neither are her characters. Having had their totem/family identities destroyed by Euroamerican domination, these characters must reformulate notions of self, family, and community.

—Hertha D. Wong, "Adoptive Mothers and Thrown-Away Children in the Novels of Louise Erdrich," in *Narrating Mothers: Theorizing Maternal Subjectivities,* **The University of Tennessee Press, 1991.**

LOUISE ERDRICH

that a man who went to Washington and gave them bureaucrats what for could lose his mind from eating too much Milky Way. No, he put second childhood on himself.

Behind those songs he sings out in the middle of Mass, and back of those stories that everybody knows by heart, Grandpa is thinking hard about life. I know the feeling. Sometimes I'll throw up a smokescreen to think behind. I'll hitch up to Winnipeg and play the Space Invaders for six hours, but all the time there and back I will be thinking some fairly deep thoughts that surprise even me, and I'm used to it. As for him, if it was just the thought there wouldn't be no problem. Smokescreen is what irritates the social structure, see, and Grandpa has done things that just distract people to the point they want to throw him in the cookie jar where they keep the mentally insane. He's far from that, I know for sure, but even Grandma had trouble keeping her patience once he started sneaking off to Lamartine's place. He's not supposed to have his candy, and Lulu feeds it to him. That's one of the reasons why he goes.

Grandma tried to get me to put the touch on Grandpa soon after he began stepping out. I didn't want to, but before Grandma started telling me again what a bad state my bare behind was in when she first took me home, I thought I should at least pretend.

I put my hands on either side of Grandpa's head. You wouldn't look at him and say he was crazy. He's a fine figure of a man, as Lamartine would say, with all his hair and half his teeth, a beak like a hawk, and cheeks like the blades of a hatchet. They put his picture on all the tourist guides to North Dakota and even copied his face for artistic paintings. I guess you could call him a monument all of himself. He started grinning when I put my hands on his templates, and I knew right then he knew how come I touched him. I knew the smokescreen was going to fall.

And I was right: just for a moment it fell.

"Let's pitch whoopee," he said across my shoulder to Grandma.

They don't use that expression much around here anymore, but for damn sure it must have meant something. It got her goat right quick.

She threw my hands off his head herself and stood in front of him, overmatching him pound for pound, and taller too, for she had a growth spurt in middle age while he had shrunk, so now the length and breadth of her surpassed him. She glared up and spoke her piece into his face about how he was off at all hours tomcatting and chasing Lamartine again and making a damn old fool of himself.

"And you got no more whoopee to pitch anymore anyhow!" she yelled at last, surprising me so my jaw just dropped, for us kids all had pretended for so long that those rustling sounds we heard from their side of the

Novels
Love Medicine, Holt, 1984; expanded edition, 1993.
The Beet Queen, Holt, 1986.
Tracks, Holt, 1988.
(With Michael Dorris) *The Crown of Columbus*, HarperCollins, 1991
The Bingo Palace, HarperCollins, 1994.

Poetry
Jacklight, Holt, 1984.
Baptism of Desire, Harper, 1989.

Nonfiction
Imagination (textbook), C. E. Merrill, 1980.

(Author of preface) Michael Dorris, *The Broken Cord: A Family's Ongoing Struggle with Fetal Alcohol Syndrome*, Harper, 1989; published as *The Broken Cord: A Father's Story*, Collins, 1990.

Other
Author of short story, "The World's Greatest Fisherman"; contributor to anthologies, including the *Norton Anthology of Poetry: Best American Short Stories of 1981–83*, 1983, and 1988; and *Prize Stories: The O. Henry Awards*, in 1985 and 1987. Contributor of stories, poems, essays, and book reviews to periodicals, including *New Yorker, New England Review, Chicago, American Indian Quarterly, Frontiers, Atlantic, Kenyon Review, North American Review, New York Times Book Review, Ms., Redbook* (with her sister Heidi, under the joint pseudonym Heidi Louise), and *Woman* (with Dorris, under the joint pseudonym Milou North).

Adaptation
The Crown of Columbus has been optioned for film production to Cinecom.

---

room at night never happened. She sure had pretended it, up till now, anyway. I saw that tears were in her eyes. And that's when I saw how much grief and love she felt for him. And it gave me a real shock to the system. You see I thought love got easier over the years so it didn't hurt so bad when it hurt, or feel so good when it felt good. I thought it smoothed out and old people hardly noticed it. I thought it curled up and died, I guess. Now I saw it rear up like a whip and lash.

She loved him. She was jealous. She mourned him like the dead.

And he just smiled into the air, trapped in the seams of his mind.

So I didn't know what to do. I was in a laundry then. They was like parents to me, the way they had took me home and reared me. I could see her point for wanting to get him back the way he was so at least she could argue with him, sleep with him, not be shamed out by Lamartine. She'd always love him. That hit me like a ton of bricks. For one whole day I felt this odd feeling that cramped my hands. When you have the touch, that's where longing gets you. I never loved like that. It made me feel all inspired to see them fight, and I wanted to go out and find a woman who I would love until one of us died or went crazy. But I'm not like that really. From time to time I heal a person all up good inside, however when it comes to the long shot I doubt that I got staying power.

And you need that, staying power, going out to love somebody. I knew this quality was not going to jump on me with no effort. So I turned my thoughts back to Grandma and Grandpa. I felt her side of it with my hands and my tangled guts, and I felt his side of it within the stretch of my mentality. He had gone out to lunch one day and never came back. He was fishing

L O U I S E   E R D R I C H

in the middle of Lake Turcot. And there was big thoughts on his line, and he kept throwing them back for even bigger ones that would explain to him, say, the meaning of how we got here and why we have to leave so soon. All in all, I could not see myself treating Grandpa with the touch, bringing him back, when the real part of him had chose to be off thinking somewhere. It was only the rest of him that stayed around causing trouble, after all, and we could handle most of it without any problem.

Besides, it was hard to argue with his reasons for doing some things. Take Holy Mass. I used to go there just every so often, when I got frustrated mostly, because even though I know the Higher Power dwells everyplace, there's something very calming about the cool greenish inside of our mission. Or so I thought, anyway. Grandpa was the one who stripped off my delusions in this matter, for it was he who busted right through what Father Upsala calls the sacred serenity of the place.

We filed in that time. Me and Grandpa. We sat down in our pews. Then the rosary got started up pre-Mass and that's when Grandpa filled up his chest and opened his mouth and belted out them words.

HAIL MARIE FULL OF GRACE.

He had a powerful set of lungs.

And he kept on like that. He did not let up. He hollered and he yelled them prayers, and I guess people was used to him by now, because they only muttered theirs and did not quit and gawk like I did. I was getting red-faced, I admit. I give him the elbow once or twice, but that wasn't nothing to him. He kept on. He shrieked to heaven and he pleaded like a movie actor and he pounded his chest like Tarzan in the Lord I Am Not Worthies. I thought he might hurt himself. Then after a while I guess I got used to it, and that's when I wondered: how come?

So afterwards I out and asked him. "How come? How come you yelled?"

"God don't hear me otherwise," said Grandpa Kashpaw.

I sweat. I broke right into a little cold sweat at my hairline because I knew this was perfectly right and for years not one damn other person had noticed it. God's been going deaf. Since the Old Testament, God's been deafening up on us. I read, see. Besides the dictionary, which I'm constantly in use of, I had this Bible once. I read it. I found there was discrepancies between then and now. It struck me. Here God used to raineth bread from clouds, smite the Phillipines, sling fire down on red-light districts where people got stabbed. He even appeared in person every once in a while. God used to pay attention, is what I'm saying.

Now there's your God in the Old Testament and there is Chippewa Gods as well. Indian Gods, good and bad, like tricky Nanabozho or the water monster, Missepeshu, who lives over in Lake Turcot. That water monster was the last God I ever heard to appear. It had a weakness for young girls and grabbed one of the Blues off her rowboat. She got to shore all right, but only after this monster had its way with her. She's an old lady now. Old Lady Blue. She's still won't let her family fish that lake.

Our Gods aren't perfect, is what I'm saying, but at least they come around. They'll do a favor if you ask them right. You don't have to yell. But you do have to know, like I said, how to ask in the right way. That makes problems, because to ask proper was an art that was lost to the Chippewas once the Catholics gained ground. Even now, I have to wonder if Higher Power turned it back, if we got to yell, or if we just don't speak its language.

I looked around me. How else could I explain what all I had seen in my short life—King smashing his fist in things, Gordie drinking himself down to the Bismarck hospitals, or Aunt June left by a white man to wander off in the snow. How else to explain the times my touch don't work, and farther back, to the oldtime Indians who was swept away in the outright germ warfare and dirty-dog killing of the whites. In those times, us Indians was so much kindlier than now.

We took them in.

Oh yes, I'm bitter as an old cutworm just thinking of how they done to us and doing still.

So Grandpa Kashpaw just opened my eyes a little there. Was there any sense relying on a God whose ears was stopped? Just like the government? I says then, right off, maybe we got nothing but ourselves. And that's not much, just personally speaking. I know I don't got the cold hard potatoes it takes to understand everything. Still, there's things I'd like to do. For instance, I'd like to help some people like my Grandpa and Grandma Kashpaw get back some happiness within the tail ends of their lives.

I told you once before I couldn't see my way clear to putting the direct touch on Grandpa's mind, and I kept my moral there, but something soon happened to make me think a little bit of mental adjustment wouldn't do him and the rest of us no harm.

It was after we saw him one afternoon in the sunshine courtyard of the Senior Citizens with Lulu Lamartine. Grandpa used to like to dig there. He had his little dandelion fork out, and he was prying up them dandelions right and left while Lamartine watched him.

"He's scratching up the dirt, all right," said Grandma, watching Lamartine watch Grandpa out the window.

Now Lamartine was about half the considerable size of Grandma, but you would never think of sizes anyway. They were different in an even more noticeable way. It was the difference between a house fixed up with paint

LOUISE **ERDRICH**

and picky fence, and a house left to weather away into the soft earth, is what I'm saying. Lamartine was jacked up, latticed, shuttered, and vinyl sided, while Grandma sagged and bulged on her slipped foundations and let her hair go the silver gray of rain-dried lumber. Right now, she eyed the Lamartine's pert flowery dress with such a look it despaired me. I knew what this could lead to with Grandma. Alterating tongue storms and rock-hard silences was hard on a man, even one who didn't notice, like Grandpa. So I went fetching him.

But he was gone when I popped through the little screen door that led out on the courtyard. There was nobody out there either, to point which way they went. Just the dandelion fork quibbling upright in the ground. That gave me an idea. I snookered over to the Lamartine's door and I listened in first, then knocked. But nobody. So I went walking through the lounges and around the card tables. Still nobody. Finally it was my touch that led me to the laundry room. I cracked the door. I went in. There they were. And he was really loving her up good, boy, and she was going hell for leather. Sheets was flapping on the lines above, and washcloths, pillowcases, shirts was also flying through the air, for they was trying to clear out a place for themselves in a high-heaped but shallow laundry cart. The washers and the dryers was all on, chock full of quarters, shaking and moaning. I couldn't hear what Grandpa and the Lamartine was billing and cooing, and they couldn't hear me.

I didn't know what to do, so I went inside and shut the door.

The Lamartine wore a big curly light-brown wig. Looked like one of them squeaky little white-people dogs. Poodles they call them. Anyway, that wig is what saved us from the worse. For I could hardly shout and tell them I was in there, no more could I try and grab him. I was trapped where I was. There was nothing I could really do but hold the door shut. I was scared of somebody else upsetting in and really getting an eyeful. Turned out though, in the heat of the clinch, as I was trying to avert my eyes you see, the Lamartine's curly wig jumped off her head. And if you ever been in the midst of something and had a big change like that occur in the someone, you can't help know how it devastates your basic urges. Not only that, but her wig was almost with a life of its own. Grandpa's eyes were bugging at the change already, and swear to God if the thing didn't rear up and pop him in the face like it was going to start something. He scrambled up, Grandpa did, and the Lamartine jumped up after him all addled looking. They just stared at each other, huffing and puffing, with quizzical expression. The surprise seemed to drive all sense completely out of Grandpa's mind.

"The letter was what started the fire," he said. "I never would have done it."

"What letter?" said the Lamartine. She was stiff-necked now, and elegant, even bald, like some alien queen. I gave her back the wig. The Lamartine replaced it on her head, and whenever I saw her after that, I couldn't help thinking of her bald, with special powers, as if from another planet.

"That was a close call," I said to Grandpa after she had left.

But I think he had already forgot the incident. He just stood there all quiet and thoughtful. You really wouldn't think he was crazy. He looked like he was just about to say something important, explaining himself. He said something, all right, but it didn't have nothing to do with anything that made sense.

He wondered where the heck he put his dandelion fork. That's when I decided about the mental adjustment.

Now what was mostly our problem was not so much that he was not all there, but that what was there of him often hankered after Lamartine. If we could put a stop to that, I thought, we might be getting someplace. But here, see, my touch was of no use. For what could I snap my fingers at to make him faithful to Grandma? Like the quality of staying power, this faithfulness was invisible. I know it's something that you got to acquire, but I never known where from. Maybe there's no rhyme or reason to it, like my getting the touch, and then again maybe it's a kind of magic.

It was Grandma Kashpaw who thought of it in the end. She knows things. Although she will not admit she has a scrap of Indian blood in her, there's no doubt in my mind she's got some Chippewa. How else would you explain the way she'll be sitting there, in front of her TV story, rocking in her armchair and suddenly she turns on me, her brown eyes hard as lake-bed flint.

"Lipsha Morrissey," she'll say. "you went out last night and got drunk."

How did she know that? I'll hardly remember it myself. Then she'll say she just had a feeling or ache in the scar of her hand or a creak in her shoulder. She is constantly being told things by little aggravations in her joints or by her household appliances. One time she told Gordie never to ride with a crazy Lamartine boy. She had seen something in the polished-up tin of her bread toaster. So he didn't. Sure enough, the time came we heard how Lyman and Henry went out of control in their car ending up in the river. Lyman swam to the top, but Henry never made it.

Thanks to Grandma's toaster, Gordie was probably spared.

Someplace in the blood Grandma Kashpaw knows things. She also remembers things, I found. She keeps things filed away. She's got a memory like them video games that don't forget your score. One reason she remembers so many details about the trouble I gave her in early life is so she can flash back her total when she needs to.

L O U I S E **E R D R I C H**

Like now. Take the love medicine. I don't know where she remembered that from. It came tumbling from her mind like an asteroid off the corner of the screen.

Of course she starts out by mentioning the time I had this accident in church and did she leave me there with wet overhalls? No she didn't. And ain't I glad? Yes I am. Now what you want now, Grandma?

But when she mentions them love medicines, I feel my back prickle at the danger. These love medicines is something of an old Chippewa specialty. No other tribe has got them down so well. But love medicines is not for the layman to handle. You don't just go out and get one without paying for it. Before you get one, even, you should go through one hell of a lot of mental condensation. You got to think it over. Choose the right one. You could really mess up your life grinding up the wrong little thing.

So anyhow, I said to Grandma I'd give this love medicine some thought. I knew the best thing was to go ask a specialist like Old Man Pillager, who lives up in a tangle of bush and never shows himself. But the truth is I was afraid of him, like everyone else. He was known for putting the twisted mouth on people, seizing up their hearts. Old Man Pillager was serious business, and I have always thought it best to steer clear of that whenever I could. That's why I took the powers in my own hands. That's why I did what I could.

I put my whole mentality to it, nothing held back. After a while I started to remember things I'd heard gossiped over.

I heard of this person once who carried a charm of seeds that looked like baby pearls. They was attached to a metal knife, which made them powerful. But I didn't know where them seeds grew. Another love charm I heard about I couldn't go along with, because how was I suppose to catch frogs in the act, which it required. Them little creatures is slippery and fast. And then the powerfullest of all, the most extreme, involved nail clips and such. I wasn't anywhere near asking Grandma to provide me all the little body bits that this last love recipe called for. I went walking around for days just trying to think up something that would work.

Well I got it. If it hadn't been the early fall of the year, I never would have got it. But I was sitting underneath a tree one day down near the school just watching people's feet go by when something tells me, look up! Look up! So I look up, and I see two honkers, Canada geese, the kind with little masks on their faces, a bird what mates for life. I see them flying right over my head naturally preparing to land in some slough on the reservation, which they certainly won't get off of alive.

It hits me, anyway. Them geese, they mate for life. And I think to myself, just what if I went out and got a pair? And just what if I fed some part—say the goose heart—of the female to Grandma and Grandpa ate the other heart? Wouldn't that work? Maybe it's all invisible, and then maybe again it's magic. Love is a stony road. We know that for sure. If it's true that the higher feelings of devotion get lodged in the heart like people say, then we'd be home free. If not, eating goose heart couldn't harm nobody anyway. I thought it was worth my effort, and Grandma Kashpaw thought so, too. She had always known a good idea when she heard one. She borrowed me Grandpa's gun.

So I went to this particular slough, maybe the exact same slough I never got thrown in by my mother, thanks to Grandma Kashpaw, and I hunched down in a good comfortable pile of rushes. I got my gun loaded up. I ate a few of these soft baloney sandwiches Grandma made me for lunch. And then I waited. The cattails blown back and forth above my head. Them stringy blue herons was spearing up their prey. The thing I know how to do best in this world, the thing I been training for all my life, is to wait. Sitting there and sitting there was no hardship on me. I got to thinking about some funny things that happened. There was this one time that Lulu Lamartine's little blue tweety bird, a paraclete, I guess you'd call it, flown up inside her dress and got lost within there. I recalled her running out into the hallway trying to yell something, shaking. She was doing a right good jig there, cutting the rug for sure, and the thing is it *never* flown out. To this day people speculate where it went. They fear she might perhaps of crushed it in her corsets. It sure hasn't ever yet been seen alive. I thought of funny things for a while, but then I used them up, and strange things that happened started weaseling their way into my mind.

I got to thinking quite naturally of the Lamartine's cousin named Wristwatch. I never knew what his real name was. They called him Wristwatch because he got his father's broken wristwatch as a young boy when his father passed on. Never in his whole life did Wristwatch take his father's watch off. He didn't care if it worked, although after a while he got sensitive when people asked what time it was, teasing him. He often put it to his ear like he was listening to the tick. But it was broken for good and forever, people said so, at least that's what they thought.

Well I saw Wristwatch smoking in his pickup one afternoon and by nine that evening he was dead.

He died sitting at the Lamartine's table, too. As she told it, Wristwatch had just eaten himself a good-size dinner and she said would he take seconds on the hot dish when he fell over to the floor. They turnt him over. He was gone. But here's the strange thing: when the Senior Citizen's orderly took the pulse he noticed that the wristwatch Wristwatch wore was now working. The moment he died the wristwatch started keeping perfect time. They buried him with the watch still ticking on his arm.

I got to thinking. What if some gravediggers dug up Wristwatch's casket in two hundred years and that watch was still going? I thought what question they would ask and it was this: Whose hand wound it?

I started shaking like a piece of grass at just the thought.

Not to get off the subject or nothing. I was still hunkered in the slough. It was passing late into the afternoon and still no honkers had touched down. Now I don't need to tell you that the waiting did not get to me, it was the chill. The rushes was very soft, but damp. I was getting cold and debating to leave, when they landed. Two geese swimming here and there as big as life, looking deep into each other's little pinhole eyes. Just the ones I was looking for. So I lifted Grandpa's gun to my shoulder and I aimed perfectly, and *blam! Blam!* I delivered two accurate shots. But the thing is, them shots missed. I couldn't hardly believe it. Whether it was that the stock had warped or the barrel got bent someways, I don't quite know, but anyway them geese flown off into the dim sky, and Lipsha Morrissey was left there in the rushes with evening fallen and his two cold hands empty. He had before him just the prospect of another day of bone-cracking chill in them rushes, and the thought of it got him depressed.

Now it isn't my style, in no way, to get depressed.

So I said to myself, Lipsha Morrissey, you're a happy S.O.B. who could be covered up with weeds by now down at the bottom of this slough, but instead you're alive to tell the tale. You might have problems in life, but you still got the touch. You got the power, Lipsha Morrissey. Can't argue that. So put your mind to it and figure out how not to be depressed.

I took my advice. I put my mind to it. But I never saw at the time how my thoughts led me astray toward a tragic outcome none could have known. I ignored all the danger, all the limits, for I was tired of sitting in the slough and my feet were numb. My face was aching. I was chilled, so I played with fire. I told myself love medicine was simple. I told myself the old superstitions was just that—strange beliefs. I told myself to take the ten dollars Mary MacDonald had paid me for putting the touch on her arthritis joint, and the other five I hadn't spent yet from winning bingo last Thursday. I told myself to go down to the Red Owl store.

And here is what I did that made the medicine backfire. I took an evil shortcut. I looked at birds that was dead and froze.

All right. So now I guess you will say, "Slap a malpractice suit on Lip-sha Morrissey."

I heard of those suits. I used to think it was a color clothing quack doctors had to wear so you could tell them from the good ones. Now I know better that it's law.

As I walked back from the Red Owl with the rock-hard, heavy turkeys, I argued to myself about malpractice. I thought of faith. I thought to myself that faith could be called belief against the odds and whether or not there's any proof. How does that sound? I thought how we might have to yell to be heard by Higher Power, but that's not saying it's not *there*. And that is faith for you. It's belief even when the goods don't deliver. Higher Power makes promises we all know they can't back up, but anybody ever go and slap an old malpractice suit on God? Or the U.S. government? No they don't. Faith might be stupid, but it gets us through. So what I'm heading at is this. I finally convinced myself that the real actual power to the love medicine was not the goose heart itself but the faith in the cure.

I didn't believe it, I knew it was wrong, but by then I had waded so far into my lie I was stuck there. And then I went one step further.

The next day, I cleaned the hearts away from the paper packages of gizzards inside the turkeys. Then I wrapped them hearts with a clean hankie and brung them both to get blessed up at the mission. I wanted to get official blessings from the priest, but when Father answered the door to the rectory, wiping his hands on a little towel, I could tell he was a busy man.

LOUISE ERDRICH

"Booshoo, Father," I said. "I got a slight request to make of you this afternoon."

"What is it? he said.

"Would you bless this package?" I held out the hankie with the hearts tied inside it.

He looked at the package, questioning it.

"It's turkey hearts," I honestly had to reply.

A look of annoyance crossed his face.

"Why don't you bring this matter over to Sister Martin," he said. "I have duties."

And so, although the blessing wouldn't be as powerful, I went over to the Sisters with the package.

I rung the bell, and they brought Sister Martin to the door. I had her as a music teacher, but I was always so shy then. I never talked out loud. Now, I had grown taller than Sister Martin. Looking down, I saw that she was not feeling up to snuff. Brown circles hung under her eyes.

"What's the matter?" she said, not noticing who I was.

"Remember me, Sister?"

She squinted up at me.

"Oh yes," she said after a moment. "I'm sorry, you're the youngest of the Kashpaws. Gordie's brother."

Her face warmed up.

"Lipsha," I said, "that's my name."

"Well, Lipsha," she said, smiling broad at me now, "what can I do for you?"

They always said she was the kindest-hearted of the Sisters up the hill, and she was. She brought me back into their own kitchen and made me take a big yellow wedge of cake and a glass of milk.

"Now tell me," she said, nodding at my package. "What have you got wrapped up so carefully in those handkerchiefs?"

Like before, I answered honestly.

"Ah," said Sister Martin. "Turkey hearts." She waited.

"I hoped you could bless them."

She waited some more, smiling with her eyes. Kindhearted though she was, I began to sweat. A person could not pull the wool down over Sister Martin. I stumbled through my mind for an explanation, quick, that wouldn't scare her off.

"They're a present," I said, "for Saint Kateri's statue."

"She's not a saint yet."

"I know," I stuttered on, "in the hopes they will crown her."

"Lipsha," she said, "I never heard of such a thing."

So I told her. "Well the truth is," I said, "it's a kind of medicine."

"For what?"

"Love."

"Oh Lipsha," she said after a moment, "you don't need any medicine. I'm sure any girl would like you exactly the way you are."

I just sat there. I felt miserable, caught in my pack of lies.

"Tell you what," she said, seeing how bad I felt, "my blessing won't make any difference anyway. But there is something you can do."

I looked up at her, hopeless.

"Just be yourself."

I looked down at my plate. I knew I wasn't much to brag about right then, and I shortly became even less. For as I walked out the door I stuck my fingers in the cup of holy water that was sacred from their touches. I put my fingers in and blessed the hearts, quick, with my own hand.

I went back to Grandma and sat down in her little kitchen at the Senior Citizens. I unwrapped them hearts on the table, and her hard agate eyes went soft. She said she wasn't even going to cook those hearts up but eat them raw so their power would go down strong as possible.

I couldn't hardly watch when she munched hers. Now that's true love. I was worried about how she would get Grandpa to eat his, but she told me she'd think of something and don't worry. So I did not. I was supposed to hide off in her bedroom while she put dinner on a plate for Grandpa and fixed up the heart so he'd eat it. I caught a glint of the plate she was making for him. She put that heart smack on a piece of lettuce like in a restaurant and then attached to it a little heap of boiled peas.

He sat down. I was listening in the next room.

She said, "Why don't you have some mash potato? So he had some mash potato. Then she gave him a little piece of boiled meat. He ate that. Then she said, "Why you didn't never touch your salad yet. See that heart? I'm feeding you it because the doctor said your blood needs building up."

I couldn't help it, at that point I peeked through a crack in the door.

LOUISE **ERDRICH**

I saw Grandpa picking at that heart on his plate with a certain look. He didn't look appetized at all, is what I'm saying. I doubted our plan was going to work. Grandma was getting worried, too. She told him one more time, loudly, that he had to eat that heart.

"Swallow it down," she said. "You'll hardly notice it."

He just looked at her straight on. The way he looked at her made me think I was going to see the smokescreen drop a second time, and sure enough it happened.

"What you want me to eat this for so bad?" he asked her uncannily.

Now Grandma knew the jig was up. She knew that he knew she was working medicine. He put his fork down. He rolled the heart around his saucer plate.

"I don't want to eat this," he said to Grandma. "It don't look good."

"Why it's fresh grade-A," she told him. "One hundred percent."

He didn't ask percent what, but his eyes took on an even more warier look.

"Just go on and try it," she said, taking the salt shaker up in her hand. She was getting annoyed. "Not tasty enough? You want me to salt it for you?' She waved the shaker over his plate.

"All right, skinny white girl!" She had got Grandpa mad. Oopsy-daisy, he popped the heart into his mouth. I was about to yawn loudly and come out of the bedroom. I was about ready for this crash of wills to be over, when I saw he was still up to his old tricks. First he rolled it into one side of his cheek, "Mmmmm," Mmmmmmm," again. Then he stuck his tongue out with the heart on it and put it back, and there was no time to react. He had pulled Grandma's leg once too far. Her goat was got. She was so mad she hopped up quick as a wink an slugged him between the shoulderblades to make him swallow.

Only thing is, he choked.

He choked real bad. A person can choke to death. You ever sit down at a restaurant table and up above you there is a list of instructions what to do if something slides down the wrong pipe? It sure makes you chew slow, that's for damn sure. When Grandpa fell off his chair better believe me that little graphic illustrated poster fled into my mind. I jumped out the bedroom. I done everything within my power that I could do to unlodge what was choking him. I squeezed underneath his ribcage. I socked him in the back. I was desperate. But here's the factor of decision: he wasn't choking on the heart alone. There was more to it than that. It was other things that choked him as well. It didn't seem like he wanted to struggle or fight. Death came and tapped his chest, so he went just like that. I'm sorry all through my body at what I done to him with that heart, and there's those who will say Lipsha Morrissey is just excusing himself off the hook by giving song and dance about how Grandpa gave up.

Maybe I can't admit what I did. My touch had gone worthless, that is true. But here is what I seen while he lay in my arms.

You hear a person's life will flash before their eyes when they're in danger. It was him in danger, not me, but it was *his* life come over me. I saw him dying, and it was like someone pulled the shade down in a room. His eyes clouded over and squeezed shut, but just before that I looked in. He was still fishing in the middle of Lake Turcot. Big thoughts was on his line and he had half a case of beer in the boat. He waved at me, grinned, and then the bobber went under.

Grandma had gone out of the room crying for help. I bunched my force up in my hands and I held him. I was so wound up I couldn't even breathe. All the moments he had spent with me, all the times he had hoisted me on his shoulders or pointed into the leaves was concentrated in that moment. Time was flashing back and forth like a pinball machine. Lights blinked and balls hopped and rubber bands chirped, until suddenly I realized the last ball had gone down the drain and there was nothing. I felt his force leaving him, flowing out of Grandpa never to return. I felt his mind weakening. The bobber going under in the lake. And I felt the touch retreat back into the darkness inside my body, from where it came.

One time, long ago, both of us were fishing together. We caught a big old snapper what started towing us around like it was a motor. "This here fishline is pretty damn good," Grandpa said. "Let's keep this turtle on and see where he takes us." So we rode along behind that turtle, watching as from time to time it surfaced. The thing was just about the size of a washtub. It took us all around the lake twice, and as it was traveling, Grandpa said something as a joke. "Lipsha," he said, "we are glad your mother didn't want you because we was always looking for a boy like you who would tow us around the lake."

"I ain't no snapper. Snappers is so stupid they stay alive when their head's chopped off," I said.

"That ain't stupidity," said Grandpa. "Their brain's just in their heart, like yours is."

When I looked up, I knew the fuse had blown between my heart and my mind and that a terrible understanding was to be given.

Grandma got back into the room and I saw her stumble. And then she went down too. It was like a house you can't hardly believe has stood so long, through years of record weather, suddenly goes down in the worst yet. It makes sense, is what I'm saying, but you still can't hardly believe it. You think a person you know has got through death and illness and being broke and living on commodity rice will get through anything. Then they fold and you see how fragile were the stones that underpinned them. You see how instantly the ground can shift you thought was solid. You see the stop signs and the yellow dividing markers of roads you traveled and all the instructions you had played according to vanish. You see how all the everyday things you counted on was just a dream you had been having by which you run your whole life. She had been over me, like a sheer overhang of rock dividing Lipsha Morrissey from outer space. And now she went underneath. It was as though the banks gave way on the shores of Lake Turcot, and where Grandpa's passing was just the bobber swallowed under by his biggest thought, her fall was the house and the rock under it sliding after, sending half the lake splashing up to the clouds.

Where there was nothing.

You play them games never knowing what you see. When I fell into the dream alongside of both of them I saw that the dominions I had defended myself from anciently was but delusions of the screen. Blips of light. And I was scot-free now, whistling through space.

I don't know how I come back. I don't know from where. They was slapping my face when I arrived back at Senior Citizens and they was oxygenating her. I saw her chest move, almost unwilling. She sighed the way she would when somebody bothered her in the middle of a row of beads she was counting. I think it irritated her to no end that they brought her back. I knew from the way she looked after they took the mask off, she was not going to forgive them disturbing her restful peace. Nor was she forgiving Lipsha Morrissey. She had been stepping out onto the road of death, she told the children later at the funeral. I asked was there any stop signs or dividing markers on that road, but she clamped her lips in a vise the way she always done when she was mad.

Which didn't bother me. I knew when things had cleared out she wouldn't have no choice. I was not going to speculate where the blame was put for Grandpa's death. We was in it together. She had slugged him between the shoulders. My touch had failed him, never to return.

All the blood children and the took-ins, like me, came home from Minneapolis and Chicago, where they had relocated years ago. They stayed with friends on the reservation or with Aurelia or slept on Grandma's floor. They were struck down with grief and bereavement to be sure, every one of them. At the funeral I sat down in the back of the church with Albertine. She had gotten all skinny and ragged haired from cramming all her years of study into two or three. She had decided that to be a nurse was not enough for her so she was going to be a doctor. But the way she was straining her mind didn't look too hopeful. Her eyes were bloodshot from driving and crying. She took my hand. From the back we watched all the children and the mourners as they hunched over their prayers, their hands stuffed full of Kleenex. It was someplace in that long sad service that my vision shifted. I began to see things different, more clear. The family kneeling down turned to rocks in a field, It struck me how strong and reliable grief was, and death. Until the end of time, death would be our rock.

So I had perspective on it all, for death gives you that. All the Kashpaw children had done various things to me in their lives—shared their folks with me, loaned me cash, beat me up in secret—and I decided, because of death, then and there I'd call it quits. If I ever saw King again, I'd shake his hand. Forgiving somebody else made the whole thing easier to bear.

Everybody saw Grandpa off into the next world. And then the Kashpaws had to get back to their jobs, which was numerous and impressive. I had a few beers with them and I went back to Grandma, who had sort of got lost in the shuffle of everybody being sad about Grandpa and glad to see one another.

Zelda had sat beside her the whole time and was sitting with her now. I wanted to talk to Grandma, say how sorry I was, that it wasn't her fault, but only mine. I would have, but Zelda gave me one of her looks of strict warning as if to say, "I'll take care of Grandma. Don't horn in on the women."

If only Zelda knew, I thought, the sad realities would change her. But of course I couldn't tell the dark truth.

It was evening, late. Grandma's light was on underneath a crack in the door. About a week had passed since we buried Grandpa. I knocked first but there wasn't no answer, so I went right in. The door was unlocked. She was there but she didn't notice me at first. Her hands were tied up in her rosary, and her gaze was fully absorbed in the easy chair opposite her, the one that had always been Grandpa's favorite. I stood there, staring with her, at the little green nubs in the cloth and plastic armrest covers and the sad little hair-tonic stain he had made on the white doily where he laid his head. For the life of me I couldn't figure what she was staring at. Thin space. Then she turned.

"He ain't gone yet," she said.

Remember that chill I luckily didn't get from waiting in the slough? I got it now. I felt it start from the very center of me, where fear hides, waiting to attack. It spiraled outward so that in minutes my fingers and teeth were shaking and clattering. I knew she told the truth. She seen Grandpa. Whether or not he had been there is not the point. She had *seen* him, and

LOUISE **ERDRICH**

that meant anybody else could see him, too. Not only that but, as is usually the case with these here ghosts, he had a certain uneasy reason to come back. And of course Grandma Kashpaw had scanned it out.

I sat down. We sat together on the couch watching his chair out of the corner of our eyes. She had found him sitting in his chair when she walked in the door.

"It's the love medicine, my Lipsha," she said. "It was stronger than we thought. He came back even after death to claim me to his side."

I was afraid. "We shouldn't have tampered with it," I said. She agreed. For a while we sat still. I don't know what she thought, but my head felt screwed on backward. I couldn't accurately consider the situation, so I told Grandma to go to bed. I would sleep on the couch keeping my eye on Grandpa's chair. Maybe he would come back and maybe he wouldn't. I guess I feared the one as much as the other, but I got to thinking, see, as I lay there in darkness, that perhaps even through my terrible mistakes some good might come. If Grandpa did come back, I thought he'd return in his right mind. I could talk with him. I could tell him it was all my fault for play-ing with power I did not understand.

Maybe he'd forgive me and rest in peace. I hoped this. I calmed myself and waited for him all night.

He fooled me though. He knew what I was waiting for, and it wasn't what he was looking to hear. Come dawn I heard a blood-splitting cry from the bedroom and I rushed in there. Grandma turnt the lights on. She was sit-ting on the edge of the bed and her face looked harsh, pinched-up gray.

"He was here, " she said. "He came and laid down next to me in bed. And he touched me."

Her heart broke down. She cried. His touch was so cold. She laid back in bed after a while, as it was morning, and I went to the couch. As I lay there, falling asleep, I suddenly felt Grandpa's presence and the barrier between us like a swollen river. I felt how I had wronged him. How awful was the place where I had sent him. Behind the wall of death, he'd watched the living eat and cry and get drunk. He was lonesome, but I understood he meant no harm.

"Go back," I said to the dark, afraid and yet full of pity. "You got to be with your own kind now," I said. I felt him retreating, like a sigh, growing less. I felt his spirit as it shrunk back through the walls, the blinds, the brick courtyard of Senior Citizens. "Look up Aunt June," I whispered as he left.

I slept late the next morning, a good hard sleep allowing the sun to rise and warm the earth. It was past noon when I awoke. There is nothing, to my mind, like a long sleep to make those hard decisions that you neglect under stress of wakefulness. Soon as I woke up that morning, I saw exactly what I'd say to Grandma. I had gotten humble in the past week, not just losing the touch but getting jolted into the understanding that would prey on me from here on out. Your life feels different on you, once you greet death and understand your heart's position. You wear your life like a garment from the mission bundle sale ever after—lightly because you realize you never paid nothing for it, cherishing because you know you won't ever come by such a bargain again. Also you have the feeling someone wore it before you and someone will after. I can't explain that, not yet, but I'm putting my mind to it.

"Grandma," I said, "I got to be honest about the love medicine."

She listened. I knew from then on she would be listening to me the way I had listened to her before. I told her about the turkey hearts and how I had them blessed. I told her what I used as love medicine was purely a fake, and then I said to her what my understanding brought me.

"Love medicine ain't what brings him back to you, Grandma. No, it's something else. He loved you over time and distance, but he went off so quick he never got the chance to tell you how he loves you, how he doesn't blame you, how he understands. It's true feeling, not no magic. No supermarket heart could have brung him back."

She looked at me. She was seeing the years and days I had no way of knowing, and she didn't believe me. I could tell this. Yet a look came on her face. It was like the look of mothers drinking sweetness from their children's eyes. It was tenderness.

"Lipsha," she said, "you was always my favorite."

She took the beads off the bedpost, where she kept them to say at night, and she told me to put out my hand. When I did this, she shut the beads inside of my fist and held them there a long minute, tight, so my hand hurt. I almost cried when she did this. I don't really know why. Tears shot up behind my eyelids, and yet it was nothing. I didn't understand, except her hand was so strong, squeezing mine.

The earth was full of life and there were dandelions growing out the window, thick as thieves, already seeded, fat as big yellow plungers. She let my hand go. I got up. "I'll go out and dig a few dandelions," I told her.

Outside, the sun was hot and heavy as a hand on my back. I felt it flow down my arms, out my fingers, arrowing through the ends of the fork into the earth. With every root I prized up there was return, as if I was kin to its secret lesson. The touch got stronger as I worked through the grassy after-

LOUISE   ERDRICH

noon. Uncurling from me like a seed out of the blackness where I was lost, the touch spread. The spiked leaves full of bitter mother's milk. A buried root. A nuisance people dig up and throw in the sun to wither. A globe of frail seeds that's indestructible.

HANAY  GEIOGAMAH

Geiogamah is known for plays in which he employs humor, realism, and idiomatic language to subvert negative stereotypes about Native Americans and to address the alienation felt by Indians in contemporary American society. Critics have consistently praised Geiogamah for his compelling characterizations, his emphasis on survival and self-knowledge, and his realistic portrayal of the social and political conditions under which Native Americans live today. Jeffrey Huntsman has stated: "Geiogamah's purpose is, first, to present and thereby preserve living Indian traditions and, next, to demonstrate the facts of Indian life in America today, unvarnished by either Indian or non-Indian romanticizers."

Essay by

RUTH ROSENBERG

Geiogamah's best-known plays, *Body Indian*, *Foghorn*, and *49*, are collected in *New Native American Drama: Three Plays*. Although these works often address such problems as alcoholism, poverty, and racism, they are considered optimistic in outlook because of their focus on the importance of developing pride, unity, and self-respect among Native Americans. For example, in *Foghorn*, Geiogamah satirizes the relationship between Natives and whites in America from colonial times to the present.

While he attacks the long history of white exploitation of Indians, he does so in a way, as stated by Kenneth Lincoln, that "purges the anguish and celebrates what it means to be alive today in Indian America." Geiogamah himself has written: "Almost all the characters in [*Foghorn*] are stereotypes pushed to the point of absurdity. The satire pro-

Kiowa playwright and director.

Born: 1945 in Oklahoma.

Education: University of Indiana, B.A., 1980.

Career: Native American Theater Ensemble (NATE), artistic director, 1972–76; Native Americans in Arts in New York City, artistic director, 1980–82; University of California, Los Angeles, taught in theater department, 1982–92; Colorado College, Colorado Springs, visiting professor of theater, 1983; American Indian Registry for the Performing Arts in Los Angeles, executive director, 1984–88; American Indian Dance Theater, conducted tours in U.S. and Europe, 1988–89; technical consultant advisor for the Wildwood Production feature film *Dark Wind,* 1989; American Indian Dance Theater, codirected the Theater's special on "Great Performances, Dance in America Series," 1989.

ceeds by playful mockery rather than bitter denunciation." In addition to writing plays, Geiogamah has served as artistic director of several art and theater organizations, including the Native American Theater Ensemble (NATE), Native Americans in Arts, and the American Indian Dance Theater.

49

From *New Native American Drama,* University of Oklahoma Press, copyright © 1980 by Hanay Geigomah

Author's Note

A 49 celebration usually begins about midnight or just after, when the more formal activities of the powwow or Indian fair or tribal celebration are over. There is a loosely structured pattern of time and movement in the formation of a 49 congregation. Forty-nines always take place at night; really good ones go on until sunrise and after. More young people are involved than older ones, and thus the scene is charged with the energy of hundreds of youths. A typical timetable for a 49 is as follows:

Midnight—gradual formation; 1 A.M.—singing and dancing begin; 2 A.M.—singing and dancing intensify, fringe activities well underway; 3 A.M.—singing still strong, dancing dropping off, fringe activities at zenith, traffic jams, first police efforts at raids; 4 A.M.—singing sporadic, fights, all important contacts made, police seriously threaten periphery of 49; 5 A.M.—singing stops, thin groupings, car activities, final effort to "snag"; 6 A.M.—sunup, stragglers, efforts to start stalled cars, diehards gradually depart the scene.

In a memorandum to the members of the Native American Theater Ensemble before beginning rehearsals for the show, I made these comments about the specialness of 49'ing:

—While taking part in a 49, young Indians are in an extremely heightened state of awareness of their "Indianness."

—They achieve, with amazing rapidity and with a minimum of friction, a group conviviality that is intertribal.

—They flirt with the dangers of police harrassment and arrest, jailing, automobile accidents, and injuries from fighting.

—They sing and dance their own versions of Indian songs with more earnestness, sensitivity, and good humor than they do at any other time (some do not sing and dance at all except during 49s).

An interesting thing happened to me as a just-beginning-to-function-artist-person: I realized the incredible pow-er of humor. Before that I had just been a Kiowa person growing up. From the humor point of view, the Kiowas have a very, very rich sense of humor, very complete, very satirical, very scatological, very screwball, loony, and yet all somehow controlled. You go around Kiowas, like you go to our fair, and you get around a bunch of Kiowas, and they're always laughing, always laughing.

—Hanay Geiogamah, in an interview in *MELUS,* Fall 1989–90.

Given the difficult circumstances that often prevent so many Indians from taking any meaningful part in tribal ceremonies, they find in the 49 not only an emotional release but also a means of expressing thoughts and attitudes difficult to articulate under less stimulating conditions.

In the play the figure of the shaman Night Walker creates the tie between the young people's past and future. He can move supernaturally between both eras and speak directly to both generations. Night Walker is probably a little disappointed that nothing more solid and serious than 49 has emerged for the young Indians, but he is always optimistic, never without hope. His movements and statements provide the text with what I would describe as a combination of restraint and release, turbulence and repose.

More than anything else I wanted the young people to be affirmative in the face of despair and unreasoning force. I had an instinct to minimize the negative and sought to do this even though much of the action is essentially negative. Let that be, I said, and let the principal focus fall on the young people's spirit, the sinews of strength that hold all of them together, that keep them going, that provide their energy.

179

HANAY GEIOGAMAH

The self-realization comes about largely through nonverbal means. Instead of using the kind of abuse ("Pigs!") that accomplishes nothing, they move smoothly to form the human barricade in the final scene as if by a shared and positive instinct. Their defiance is strong, but calm and totally controlled. They feel and know what they should do, and the power of this understanding is expressed in the body formation that is the "beautiful bird" that Night Walker sees flying.

Scene 1

A single light reveals a dance area of tightly packed earth with trees, grass, and bushes growing alongside. There are brush arbors in the background, and a roadway extends out of the area. A high embankment rises about the roadway, and more trees are in back of this. Other lights start to come up with the Ute Flute Calling Melody, which floats through the night air. The lights progressively illumine other corners of this ceremonial area, a much-used site with a long history of many tribespeople coming and going. Night Walker enters slowly, moves around the area with poise and dignity, gesturing expansively.

Night Walker:

Greetings. Hello. Good day to you.

Greetings. Hello. Good day to you.

I, Night Walker, spiritual leader of the tribe, our people, speak to all of the young people of the tribe, our people.

Will you hear my voice?

Will you hear my voice?

Hear me, Night Walker. I have a thing of very strong purpose to say to you. It is a thing of deepest concern for the tribe, our people.

I ask all of the young men and women of the tribe, our people, to come to the ceremonial circle, to our people's arbor, so that I may speak with you.

I will pray for all of you there. I will tell you of this purpose.

(now with more urgency)

The tribe, our people, need you!

The tribe, our people, need you!

(moving off now)

Thank you.

Thank you.

The flute melody fades as the lights dim out.

Scene 2

A sudden, jagged crackle of a two-way police radio breaks the calm. The lights on the set are shifting gently, magically.

PATROL VOICE 1: Unit 9? Unit 9? This is Unit 4. Do you read me?

PATROL VOICE 2: I read you, Unit 4.

PATROL VOICE 1: I'm sittin' solid three miles west, two miles north of the Apache Y.

PATROL VOICE 2: Ain't seen none yet. City says they're a-drivin' around town like ants. Hunnerds of 'em. More'n all week. Lot of 'em from out of town. It always gets kind-ee wild t'ord the end of this fair, but this year seems wilder than ever.

PATROL VOICE 1: Yep, it's perty wild. Got sixty-five of 'em in the county jail and all filled up in the city. Ever damn one of 'em's under age. Can't pay their fines. We'll get us a bunch more of 'em tonight, I betcha.

Body Indian (play; also see below), produced by American Indian Theater Ensemble, La Mama Theatre, New York City, 1972.
Foghorn (play; also see below), produced by Native American Theater Ensemble, West Berlin, West Germany, 1973.
New Native American Drama: Three Plays (includes *Body Indian*, *Foghorn*, and *49*), introduction by Jeffrey Huntsman, University of Oklahoma Press (Norman), 1980.

Also editor of *American Indian Culture and Research Journal*.

PATROL VOICE 2: I have an idee they'll be a-headin' for the old White-horse Road tonight. They claim that lil' dance ground out there's Indian property and that no law officers can trespass or arrest a Indian there.

PATROL VOICE 1: Trespass my ass. *(He laughs.)*

PATROL VOICE 2: *(with surprise)* Hey! Boy! One just went by . . . loaded down! Left front out. I'm a-following.

A spotlight locates the Balladeer. A single car headlight hits the road-way directly in a flash as lights reveal youths packed into a car, a mixed lot, obviously en route to a 49.

BALLADEER:
COME ON, DANCE 49, HONEY
COME ON, DANCE WITH ME
COME ON, DANCE 49, HONEY
COME ON, DANCE WITH ME.

TEACH YOU HOW TO SING TURTLE SONG, HONEY
SHOW YOU HOW TO DANCE WITH ME
TEACH YOU HOW TO SING TURTLE SONG, HONEY
SHOW YOU HOW TO DANCE WITH ME.

I GOT A DRUM
LET'S MAKE A SONG
I'LL SING TO YOU, HONEY
ALL NIGHT LONG.

TAKE YOU DOWN TO ANADARKO WITH ME, HONEY
TAKE YOU OUT TO TAHLEQUAH
UP TO THE OSAGE COUNTRY FOR THE POWWOWS
HONEY COME ON BLAZE WITH ME
HONEY COME ON BLAZE WITH ME.

COME ON DANCE 49, HONEY
COME ON SING WITH ME
COME ON DANCE 49, HONEY

COME ON, BE WITH ME.
(light out on Balladeer.)

YOUTH IN CAR: *(looking back)* Damn cops!

The 49 group mimes the car as they careen around the environment, the lights following their movements. The Balladeer moves about, following their progress, and begins to sing accompaniment as the police give chase with red lights flashing.

BALLADEER:
THEY DON'T KNOW WHY THOSE DAMNED PATROLS
WON'T LEAVE 'EM ALONE
HO WAY YAW HEY YEY
THEY DON'T KNOW WHY THOSE DAMNED PATROLS
WON'T LEAVE 'EM ALONE
HO WAY YAW HEY
HO WAY YAW HEY YEY EY YO!

THEY WANT TO TAKE 'EM ALL TO JAIL
HO WAY YAW HEY
HO WAY YAW HEY YEY
LOCK 'EM UP
GIVE 'EM HELL
HO WAY YAW HEY
HO WAY YAW HEY YEY EY YO.

DIS/OR/DER/LY AND DRUNK/EN/NESS
HO WAY YAW HEY
HO WAY YAW HEY YEY
THIRTY DAYS!
HO WAY YAW HEY
HO WAY
HO WAY
HO WAY YAW HEY YEY EY YO!

BUT THEY CAN ALL GO STRAIGHT TO HELL!
HO WAY YAW HEY
HO WAY YAW HEY YEY
STRAIGHT TO HELL!
HO WAY YAW HEY
HO WAY
HO WAY
HO WAY YAW HEY YEY EY YO!

The 49 group dive for cover in the underbrush to escape the police and take positions of hiding. A police car search-light scans the terrain slowly, fades out.

H A N A Y   G E I O G A M A H

Scene 3

Lights reveal Night Walker, whose body is making the motions of a journey through rugged terrain. Odd flashes of light illuminate his progress, which is being observed by masks and faces of humans and animals. The 49 group are in their hiding positions throughout the scene. Night Walker reaches a clearing, composes himself, and delivers a prayer that is directed as much to himself as to the power spirits.

NIGHT WALKER:

I heed as unto those I call.

I heed as unto those I call.

Send to me thy potent aid.

Help us, the tribe, our people, oh, holy place around.

Help us, our friends, our brothers and sisters. We heed as unto thee we call.

I come to visit with my brothers and sisters.

Will you hear my voice?

Will you hear my voice? The voice of a friend who has honor and respect deep in his heart for you?

I am the oldest man of the tribe, our people. You, my brothers and sisters, have given me this honor of life.

The masks and faces and supernatural activities become larger.

You know my voice. We sing together. You were at my birth. You know my father. You know my father's father, and you know his father. You are kind and generous to all of us, the tribe, our people.

Will I sing for you now? I will tell you a story of a bear who comes to watch the dancing of the tribe, our people. *(pause)* Some of the people say the bear is learning our songs.

I have brought food for my friends. I will make a meal for us. I will make a fire. I will spread my blankets.

He does these things.

I have tobacco with me. It is good tobacco.

I have sage that was brought to the tribe our people from a place far away from our home. I will burn it for you.

He waits, then lights the sage.

I saw a young man and a young girl of the tribe our people the other day. *(pause)* They both were smiling and happy. I looked at them for a long time. I watched them walk about. I saw in their smiles the signs of a family of wonderful hunters and weavers.

I had a feeling to speak with them, but I . . . did . . . not.

The faces move closer.

The faces of these two young ones appear before me now. I bring their smiles here for my friends to see.

I am made sad . . . by . . . these smiles. My friends!

I am the youngest man of the tribe, our people. You, my brothers and sisters have given me this honor.

Haw!

Haw!

I know.

I hope.

I pray.

He has established communication.

I dream.

I smile.

I do.

Haw!

I know the smiles.

I see.

I am the oldest man of the tribe. Haw! Haw!

The young ones' smiles are my smiles.

It is I who am smiling.

I am the girl.

I am the boy.

Geiogamah's interest does not lie in reconstructing the dear, dead, romanticized past when every phrase had a poetic sparkle and every utterance was an oration. Nor does it lie in a self-indulgent vituperation of the White Man and his forked culture, where the failures of 1978 are blamed on the slaughter of the buffalo a century before. In its political aspect Geiogamah's call is not Baraka's shout for mayhem and revolution; it is rather the alarm of Thoreau's Chanticleer (or the warning blast of a foghorn), designed to stimulate Indian people to think about their lives of quiet or confirmed desperation . . . [H]e is interested more in survival and self-knowledge than in reproach and confrontation.

—Jeffrey Huntsman, in an introduction to *New Native American Drama: Three Plays,* by Hanay Geiogamah, University of Oklahoma Press, 1980.

Yes.

They will both know that I am they.

A longer pause. A Jew's harp and Apache violin¹ are heard.

The men chiefs of the tribe, our people, do not look to me when they talk with me of the things that concern the good of the tribe, our people.

They do not tell me all that they want me to know.

When they return to the tribe, our people, after fighting with the enemies, I must talk more and more to Brother Death.

I must ask Brother Death . . . to . . . take the spirits . . . of the young men . . . who have stopped living . . . with us.

Haw! I wait.

Haw!

I see.

I see. Brother Death sees too. How long? How far?

He lights more sage, then the young people begin, with soft voices, the Sioux Medicine Chant, and sing it as a counterpoint to Night Walker's prayer.

I have come here for the young man whose smiles I see.

I have come here for the young woman, who is so pretty.

I have come here for the warrior chiefs who will not look at me.

I am the oldest man of the tribe.

I have come here as two smiles who cannot see into the darkness that I see, gathering ahead on our road.

Must Brother Death direct their eyes? *(very firmly)*

Must all life be taken from us?

My friends know.

I do not know about the smiling faces of the young man and the young woman of the tribe, our people.

I do not know how long the young people will know the smell of the sage and the cedar.

I sing. Will they sing? Many beautiful songs?

I dance. How will they know to dance?

I make pictures of color. Will they see this beauty?

I conduct the ceremonies of our journey. Which one of them will follow me to lead?

I heal my sister's child. Will they know the medicine of the tribe, our people?

I have learned the way of Brother Winter and I talk with our brothers in the grass and trees and in the sky. Will they know these friends?

I am the oldest man of the tribe, our people, and I give help to my brothers and sisters in our journey.

The answer is completed.

They will hear my voice. They will hear your voices.

They will look to me. They will look to you.

We live a very long time. They will live a very long time. I am not afraid. I will not stop walking. I will not stop singing. I will not stop dancing. I will talk to all of my friends for a very long time. We will walk through the dark that *has* passed us, the tribe, our people. A-ho! A-ho, pah-bes. A-ho.

We will live and walk together for a long time. All of us will live and walk together for a long time.

He bows deeply and remains in the position as the Sioux Medicine Chant builds, then fades to end the scene. His exit is like a disappearance.

Note

1. An Apache violin is a one-string instrument that produces a monotone similar to a running single note repeated on a violin.

DIANE  GLANCY

Glancy is known for works in which she uses realistic language and vivid imagery to address such subjects as spirituality, family ties, her identity as a mixed blood, and her relationship to the landscape of the Great Plains. She was born in Kansas City, Missouri; her mother was English and German and her father one-quarter Cherokee. Of her Native American heritage, Glancy has written: "Out of my eight great-grandparents, only one was Cherokee. How can the influence of one be as strong as seven together? Yet in my writing, as well as in my life . . . it is my Indian heritage that emerges again and again."

Essay by

SUSAN NOGUERA

While Glancy often explores issues of illiteracy, alcoholism, discrimination, colonialism, and government neglect as related to Native Americans in her poetry and prose, critics note that her works are also universally relevant because of their focus on ordinary people and everyday concerns. Her short story collection *Firesticks*, for example, includes stories about a man who wants to be a pilot despite his color-blindness, and a woman who longs for her dead husband. Known for her focus on language, Glancy also infuses her prose and poetry with Indian words and often arranges poetic lines so that their placement on the page creates verbal landscapes.

Critical reaction to Glancy's works have been positive, with reviewers praising her realistic depictions of the effects of assimilation, her thoughtful examination of cultural differences, and her emphasis on renewal and survival. Regarding poetry in particular, Glancy has stated:

"Poetry should expose effulgence. Indian poetry, especially, should promote stability, precision, hope. It should be salve for the broken race which is enriched by its bloody suffering and permanent loss of a way of life. The Indian is a barn with the loft door open to the universe. Our poetry should rise from despair. We should use our special `sight.' If our poetry is a vent for anger, it should also transcend." In addition to her writing, Glancy has worked as an artist-in-residence for the State Arts Councils of Oklahoma and Arkansas, a writer-in-residence at Tulsa's Heller Theater, and a professor of English at various universities. She was also poet laureate for the Five Civilized Tribes from 1984 to 1986.

FEMALE SEMINARY, TAHLEQUAH, INDIAN TERRITORY, 1850–1905

From *Offering*, Holycow! Press, copyright © 1988 by Diane Glancy

"Bison moved through the valley at night,
their heads above the fog."
My grandmother's voice lifted the blanket it wore and
I listened to her talk.

"The mistress of the school did not like the sound of
bison,
packed cotton in her ears we saw on the table the next
morning
curled like small horns.

When she snored,
we used pieces of her cotton cloth.
No one heard anything but what came from within
where the Great Spirit called from another world.

In dream we saw strange bison roam
and tiny sheep with cotton-wad horns.

I hear the voice of my mother once." Grandmother
went on.
"She said not to forget our ways.
She said to count my brothers.

I do not think it was her.
In the Female Seminary we learned there is no grief

Cherokee poet, short story writer, playwright, essayist, and educator.

Born: March 18, 1941, in Kansas City, Missouri.

Partnerships: Married Dwane Glancy, May 2, 1964 (marriage ended, March 31, 1983); children: David, Jennifer.

Education: University of Missouri, graduated, 1964; Central State University, M.A., 1983; University of Iowa, M.F.A., 1988.

Career: Macalester College, St. Paul, MN, assistant professor of English, beginning in 1992. Five Civilized Tribes, poet laureate, 1984–86; Oklahoma State Arts Council, artist-in-residence.

Address: Home—261 Brimhall, St. Paul, MN 55105. Office—Department of English, Macalester College, 1600 Grand, St. Paul, MN 55105.

in the next world
but my mother was as I remember her.
Maybe a rabbit spoke her breath.
Maybe someone not saved by Christ.

I do not remember how many brothers I had.

But I knew the girls in camp before we scattered.
We threw game stones at rabbits
as though we were boys
and watched limbs move in ripples of the creek.

Squirrels jumped from trees.
The holy mass of clouds prowled the sky and hid in shallows
of the stream.

We chewed mullin and Jesuit's bark.
I hear a child crying once;
the voice of an older child tried to quiet it.

It was a long time ago.
I was a small girl.

Sometimes I heard a quarrel in another camp across
the hill.

I remember a hunter looking for quail
when one of our braves with an orange strip on his face
startled him.
We giggled and were punished later,

191

D I A N E   **G L A N C Y**

went with our fathers carrying their hatchet,
wedge, and fish gig.

We pulled off our leggings to wade in the stream.

Our brothers drew bear with arrow-marks where they wanted
their arrows to go in.

But I do not know how many brothers."

My grandmother pulled the blanket around her voice until I
lost the visions she gave me and their small, curled
voices
diminished like horns.

HERE I AM
STANDING BESIDE MYSELF

From *Lone Dog's Winter Count*, West End Press, copyright © 1991 by Diane Glancy

Just look at the family album. My white mother
her sisters their husbands our cousins. Then my
father my brother & I the stuffed skin of sparrow
hawks on our heads the g'ig'ig'ig'ig'i in our
throats.

My father said his grandfather fled Indian
Territory *kuna' yeli st'di* [claw-scratch-like]
when he'd done something wrong. We were outcast
now as well as Indian. & only part of them.
Outcast of outcasts. *ju!jiji skew!* It was a
sense I had. I'm trying to find the words.

It's when I remember the taste of cornbread soaked
in squirrel-grease. The feeling we weren't but
really were. The Cherokee hymns I heard in brush-
arbors. The corn-god Jesus at festival hops.

It's when I see the moon is male. Vigilant &
traveling at night. [Now cast some beads around
the neck of your wife the sun & wrap her in weasel-
skin & darken her face so the clouds will come.]

192

Poems
Traveling On, Myrtlewood Press, 1982.
Brown Wolf Leaves the Res, and Other Poems, Blue Cloud Quarterly Press, 1984.
One Age in a Dream, illustrated by Jay Moon, Milkweed Editions, 1986.
Offering: Aliscolidodi (poems and prose), illustrated by Terry John Swabey, Holy Cow! Press, 1988.
Iron Woman, New Rivers Press, 1990.
Lone Dog's Winter Count, West End Press, 1991.

Stories
Trigger Dance, Fiction Collective Two, 1990.
Firesticks: A Collection of Stories, University of Oklahoma Press, 1993.
(Editor with C. W. Truesdale) *Two Worlds Walking: Short Stories, Essays, and Poetry by Writers With Mixed Heritages* (stories, essays, poems), New Rivers Press, 1994.

Nonfiction
Claiming Breath, University of Nebraska Press, 1992.

Other
Plays include *Segwohi*, *Weebjob*, and *Stickhorse*. Work represented in anthologies, including *I Tell You Now: Autobiographical Essays by Native American Writers*, edited by Brian Swann and Arnold Krupat, University of Nebraska Press, 1987; *The Heartlands Today*, edited by Larry Smith and Nancy Dunham, Bottom Dog Press, 1991; and *Talking Leaves*, 1991. Contributor to literary journals.

It's when I remember the raccoon turtle deer that
nibbled at my feet at night. I still hold my legs
up to myself pull my fingers insideout draw my
arms into my chest my ears & nose into my head.

REGRETFULLY

From *Trigger Dance*, Fiction Collective Two, copyright © 1990 by Diane Glancy

The cat sits with me this morning when sleep leaves like love for the man I married & lived with 19 years until love puckered, shriveled to pit & seeds of grapes & melon. This morning sleep steps away too early like a person from the room or the company of one I once wanted to stay. Now I am awake in darkness. The clunk of paper on the porch. The alimony check left under the door. The cat's legs tucked under, her head bowed as one of the manger animals.

What is it she thinks when she stares at the wall \ bookcase \ coffee mill \ water color of the Black Mesa \ gouache of an Indian blanket?

Out of the silence \ the airplane & city noise \ the bluejay's shrill bark.

The ragged edge of fire was a sawblade in our last winter together when bones crushed into fertilizer for the zinnias & marigolds. Only the hardy flowers for this climate.

You lost wife & job \ married again \ look for another job. I will stay with the child who stayed in the house with you so she could remain in the same school. Now she does not want to go with you as I did not want to go. When you leave I will move back into our territory. Pay too much rent. What choice is there?

193

D I A N E **G L A N C Y**

You say, what the shit. Child support, lawyer's fees. We are whipped before we start. I left your drunken romp in the rude leaves. I could not stay.

You are someone to whom commitment was made, in whose bed \ I slept 20 years. What do you want?

You kept the house, the furniture, savings, now they belong to you & the new wife & I am left chewing the jerky of this trail. I hear men say how they lost all they had. I am the same after divorce. My property settlement in monthly payments \ you are tired of not two years later. We jab, pinch, poke one another.

The cat sits by me this morning I cannot sleep. You are the locust she carried yesterday in her mouth, laid on the floor for me to see. It squeaked like a proud man without a job & a young wife you must satisfy or lose again.

This beast in me wants to pull off your wings, bite into your ass, butt you with my paw until you walk sideways in helpless hysteria.

You say I cause a heart attack but you bring it on yourself. The cat stares at the bookcase. Wooden spools from grandmother's sewing basket \ thread gone \ these artifacts she left \ the dark wicker \ the bright beads on the frayed lid.

& yet there are enough predators in this life. I want to live with dignity. I want a strange reverence for this failed life I feel.

Church bells in the early morning dark. The cat beside me desires nothing for the moment. Later she will prowl, bring in the tail & back legs of a small mouse \ the headless baby bird \ the cruelty with which each animal day goes by.

In the stillness I peel away the layer of years like the tight skin of grapes. Uncovering the seeds of the first years we lived together. Somehow not together the way we should be. You with your job, the children were mine. Once we went to the zoo & your anger there over nothing angered me. The memory stalks my head like corridors in the monkey house.

The books from my years in school, pictures from trips, portraits of family above the bookcase. A cow's skull I found in the grasslands of western Oklahoma, prairie weeds standing in a jar. Rocks. Some of them my father gave me before he died. We had the same habit of picking them up. A worn brick from an old street in a small Kansas town. Birds' nests. A flowered couch upon which I sit with my cat. The semé chairs.

In the trunk, where I rest my feet, a brown bear, drawings by the children, the collection of the second 20 years of my life, vacant as two cat eyes. Pointed ears \ the long tail of counsel I have given myself \ a pewter bowl from our marriage on an early May evening when we were young &

I wonder sometimes why I am drawn to words. Maybe because language is so much more than I am. Maybe words chose me because they would have such a challenge. I smile when I think of my [Cherokee] grandmother who could not write. . . . But words are not alone by themselves. They carry meaning. I must have something to say and must say it well: I want to represent life with respect. I want to write about what I feel and think what I experience and come to believe. I want to write about the dignity of the common man and the uniqueness of the ordinary moment. I want to have courage to face the wilderness within. It provides tension. And I want to have a sense of self as whole even though fragmented. It gives voice.

—Diane Glancy, in *I Tell You Now: Autobiographical Essays by Native American Writers,* University of Nebraska Press, 1987.

DIANE GLANCY

The traditional Cherokee esthetic of unified art, spirituality and nature is present throughout Ms. Glancy's latest collection of short stories, Trigger Dance. *Her pieces are bound together by a stream of nature imagery which manifests her cultural heritage and the influence of the White World on Native American life. These references to the past are never romanticized, but have a bittersweet edge that typifies tribal people's adjustment to twentieth-century society.*

—Katherine Finch, in a review of *Trigger Dance* in *San Francisco Review of Books,* Winter, 1990–91.

awkward & not prepared for a single-bottom plow on a field cankered by weeds & red clay.

I hissed & growled at you \ tore the wall between us \ left \ & know we are still bound.

It is as though I live near the dark morning you inhabit but could never enter. & I screamed at you that I have the responsibility but not the fun of marriage \ throwing off my imprisonment \ my own capture \ I stayed with you years longer than I wanted to & your sad eyes looked at me regretfully when I said I was no longer your wife.

It was too hard for me \ my father's death, your rantings, our son's surgeries, then my mother's. I couldn't always swallow my anger like the bowl of melons on the table. This vacancy you left me. I regret your neglect of me. Your early lessons of expedience & compromise. I would have learned them anyway.

The cat sighs \ her little side heave \ she stretches when I rub her back. She curls up like a withered petunia beside my newspaper & coffee. Her counsel is to stare at the bookcase & wall, the trunk of children's drawings, the basket of empty spools, the thread somewhere in old clothes hanging in secondhand stores. She pulls at the button on my robe, curls up again.

Fussing like clucking squirrels I hear in the tree, I cannot change my feelings. A distant siren. A neighbor starting his car. The squeak of the rollaway in the other room. Strata of rock on the Black Mesa slant like early rain falling on the prairie.

I watch the chimney broom \ the grapevine wreath & read the paper.

Soon the sun rises moist as the melon in my hands. The slick wet seeds spill through my fingers. I hold the soft bear in the trunk \ the baby I once rocked \ the young husband I once had.

JANET CAMPBELL  HALE

Essay by

LINDA CULLUM

Hale's work examines the social, psychological, and economic dimensions of the Native American experience. Her essays and autobiographical fiction delineate reservation life, the adverse effects of poverty and alcoholism on families, and the struggle of Native Americans to maintain a sense of identity in contemporary American society. For example, Hale's first novel, The Owl's Song, *focuses on a Native American boy who, after enduring an alcoholic father and his cousin's suicide, moves from his Idaho reservation to an urban setting where he is mistreated by his schoolmates.* The Jailing of Cecelia Capture, *which was nominated for a Pulitzer Prize, is the story of a young Native woman who is jailed for drunk driving and welfare fraud.*

Hale was raised on the Colville and Yakima Indian reservations of the Coeur d'Alene in Washington, moving frequently as her mother tried to elude her abusive, alcoholic husband. These early experiences fueled Hale's desire to become literate as she sought refuge in reading and writing: "I wrote poetry, stories, essays because of a deep personal need." Hale's marriage at sixteen resulted in divorce one year later, and these hardships—marriage, divorce, and single parenthood—figure prominently in her work. Hale received a B.A. from the University of California, Berkeley, in 1974 and attended law school at Berkeley and Gonzaga Law School in Spokane, Washington. She received an M.A. in English from the University of California, Davis, in 1984 and began a career as visiting writer and lecturer. Critics marvel at Hale's accomplishments in light of the disadvantages she experienced, and Hale herself attributes her ability

1 9 7

Coeur d'Alene novelist, poet, essayist, and autobiographer.

Born: January 11, 1947, in Riverside, California .

Partnerships: Married Harry Arthur Dudley III, July 23, 1964 (divorced, 1965); married Stephen Dinsmore Hale (a biology student and baggage clerk), August 23, 1970; children: (first marriage) Aaron Nicholas; (second marriage) Jennifer Elizabeth.

Education: Attended Institute of American Indian Arts, Santa Fe, NM; attended City College of San Francisco, 1968; University of California, Berkeley, B.A., 1974; graduate study in law at the University of California, Berkeley, and Gonzaga Law School in Spokane, WA, 1973–74; M.A. in English at University of California, Davis, 1984.

Career: Harcourt Brace Jovanovich, Inc., San Francisco, CA, editorial assistant, 1972; University of California, Berkeley, instructor in Native American studies; University of California, Davis, instructor; DQ University, Davis, CA, instructor; Western Washington University, Bellingham, WA, instructor; University of Oregon, instructor; Lummi College, Bellingham, WA, instructor.

Address: c/o Jeff Jefferson, 2885 Haxton Way, Bellingham, WA 98226.

to surmount them to her Coeur d'Alene heritage, stating: "Courage has been bred into you. It's in your blood."

RETURN TO BEAR PAW

From *Bloodlines: Odyssey of a Native Daughter,* Random House, copyright © 1993 by Janet Campbell Hale

I lived in Seattle in 1986 when Salish-Kootenay Community College (in Western Montana) invited me to do an eight-day speaking tour, sponsored by Salish-Kootenay through a grant from Montana State Council on the Humanities. I went to Montana in May 1986 on a tour that began at the National Indian Youth Conference at the University of Montana in Missoula and took me to four Indian Colleges: Salish-Kootenay, Blackfeet, Rocky Boy and Fort Belknap. I flew from Seattle to Missoula. An employee of SK [Saskatchewan] College, himself a Kootenay Indian, drove me from Missoula to the end of my tour in the eastern part of the state. I had never been to Montana before.

I

Montana was startlingly cold for May, especially compared to the mild drizzle I had just left in Seattle. I didn't bring any cold-weather clothing, no coat, no scarf, no gloves, no shoes except for the open-toed pumps I wore on the airplane. Before I went to sleep the first night, I had a sore throat.

198

When I woke, I had a bad cold that would last the length of my stay in Montana.

Montana was cold and big and desolate, full of empty, wide-open spaces, no greenery, it seemed (compared to Seattle), very few trees . . .BIG SKY COUNTRY,the license plates proclaimed. Nothing blocked the view of the sky, so it seemed to be bigger than in other places. I kept my speaking engagements, ate in roadside diners, slept in cheap motels, took liberal doses of my cold remedy and endured. Twangy country western music played everywhere in Montana, seemed to permeate the crisp mountain air. The cold weather became even colder. (Hard to believe it was really May.) From the beginning I longed to be home in Seattle.

I did not come to Montana to make a pilgrimage to the Bear Paw battleground, to close the circle. I hadn't even realized, at first, that the place where the cavalry finally caught up with the Indians led by Chief Joseph was in Montana. And I hadn't thought of my grandmother, my father's mother, who had been among those Indians, for many years.

Born when her mother was 40, Hale somehow became the family's scapegoat, ostracized by her much older sister, abused by her mixed-race mother, and beaten down by their compulsively vagabond and poverty-stricken life. Books and writing became her refuge and, ultimately, her liberation. . . . [I]n this set of eight brooding but brave essays [published as Bloodlines: Odyssey of a Native Daughter]*, she confronts the painful facts not only of her life but of the tragically difficult lives of several generations of her female relatives. . . . [S]he perceives the deep roots of her struggle for survival and achievement, and recognizes the unseverable bond that connects her to her culture.*

—**Donna Seaman, in a review of** *Bloodlines: Odyssey of a Native Daughter,* **in** *Booklist,* **May 15, 1993.**

1 9 9

But now it was impossible not to think of her, not to think of Chief Joseph and the Great Flight of 1877, for often my path and the path of those fugitive Indians would cross. Sometimes a stone or metal "state historical marker" would mark the spot where a skirmish or some other event had occurred. Sometimes my driver would point out a certain place and tell me what had happened there.

Near one small town the army had put a barricade of timber to stop the Indians. But when dark fell, the nine hundred and some Indians, including women, children, old people, with their horses and belongings, slipped

JANET CAMPBELL **HALE**

up along a narrow ledge where it didn't seem a mountain goat could go, up above the heads of the sleeping soldiers, around the white man's barricade and down the other side.

"Do you know about Chief Joseph and his war with the government?" asked my driver. I nodded yes. Sure. The government promised Chief Joseph of the Nez Percé he would be allowed to remain in his homeland, the beautiful, fertile Wallowa Valley in Oregon, but then the government took another look and changed its mind. The Wallowa Valley was good land, too good to be Indian land. They told him he would have to remove himself and his people to a seedy, rocky, arid piece of land in Idaho nobody wanted, but Joseph refused to go there. At first, I think, Joseph intended to fight a war. My father told me how it was said he went to all the tribes of the region—the Coeur d'Alene, Kalispell, Spokane, Kootenay—seeking support, but no one would join forces with him. By 1877 the Indian wars in what would become Washington, Idaho, and Oregon had been fought and lost, treaties had been signed. The great power and ruthlessness of the United States government was well understood by then. Fighting another war would be a futile endeavor. And besides, the other tribes did not get as raw a deal as Chief Joseph.

My tribe, the Coeur d'Alene (whose French name, given them in the early 1700s, means "heart of steel"), were never removed from their beautiful ancestral land, only confined to one small corner of it. What the tribes wanted now was peace. No more war. No more bloodshed. No more taking away of land. Chief Joseph and his followers were on their own.

He and his chiefs—Looking Glass, Toolhoolzote and the others—decided they would run away from the United States rather than turn themselves in to the soldiers who had hunted them since they left the Wallowa. They would run to Canada and join the Sioux chief, Sitting Bull, who had been granted political asylum there after his defeat of Custer and the 7th Cavalry at the Little Big Horn. The army, led by General Howard, was relentless in its pursuit of Chief Joseph, but not good at keeping up with Indians. For a while the 7th Cavalry, seeking revenge after once having been wiped out by the Indians, joined in the chase, but the 7th Cavalry was easily shaken. Four months after the fight began, the Indians stopped and made camp in the Little Bear Paw Mountains just thirty miles from the safety of the Canadian border, unaware that another division, commanded by General Sherman (of Civil War fame), approached from the east. There Sherman's forces found them, and the last battle began.

A Nez Percé warrior named Yellow Wolf described his feelings after the Battle at the Bear Paw had begun, but before it was over, when they all knew it could only end in defeat: "I felt the end coming. All for which we had suffered was lost. Thoughts came of the Wallowa where I grew up, of my own country when only Indians were there, of teepees along the bending river, of the blue clear lake, wide meadows with horses and cattle herds.

From the mountains and forests, voices seemed to be calling. I felt as though dreaming; not my living self . . . then, with rifle I stood forth, saying to my heart, 'Here I will die fighting for my people and for our home!'"

"That place where the last battle was fought," my driver told me, "is right near your last stop, about twenty miles or so from Fort Belknap." But it would be late by then, I thought, and I would still have a trip ahead of me, to Great Falls, where I would spend the night, then board my plane for Seattle the next morning. And it was cold and getting colder, and I wasn't feeling well.

"We could go there if you like. To the Bear Paw." My throat still felt raw.

"I don't know," I said. "Maybe. Is there anything there?"

"No. An empty field. A stone monument. Nothing."

"Maybe. Maybe I'll want to go there. I can't say yet. My grandmother was there, you know. She was with those Chief Joseph people."

"Is that so? She was Nez Percé?"

"No. How she happened to be with them had to do with a case of mistaken identity."

When I was four or five, my father told me how it was: My grandmother, a young girl of fifteen or sixteen in the summer of 1877, had been with a group of Coeur d'Alene root gatherers. As was their custom, they had gone quite a distance from Coeur d'Alene country into what used to be Nez Percé territory to dig camas roots. (Camas was dried and stored, used as winter food.) And, as was also their custom whenever they traveled away from their own home, the camas diggers—women, children, old people—had a small group of armed men watching over them as they worked. This was during the time Chief Joseph and his band hid out and evaded the soldiers who tried to find them.

One day while my grandmother and the others dug camas in an open field and warriors watched from hiding places in the hills above, the United States cavalry came riding up.

An army translator spoke in Chinook* asking the root gatherers to tell them where Chief Joseph was. They were looking for Nez Percé and believed they had found some.

One old man spoke Chinook to the translator, explaining the situation, telling him they were Coeur d'Alene root gatherers, not Nez Percé, and they knew nothing about Chief Joseph. The commander yelled in English, "Liar!" and raised his gun, aimed it at the old man, and told the translator to tell him to take him to Chief Joseph or he would kill him.

The old man said again he didn't know where Chief Joseph was; the commander shot him dead. The warriors swooped down from their hiding places firing their guns, picking off soldiers. Those few Coeur d'Alene killed

J A N E T   C A M P B E L L   **H A L E**

The Owl's Song (juvenile novel), Doubleday, 1974.

Custer Lives in Humboldt County and Other Poems (poems), Greenfield Review Press, 1978.

The Jailing of Cecelia Capture (fiction), Random House, 1985.

Bloodlines: Odyssey of a Native Daughter (autobiographical essays), Random House, 1993.

Also contributor to poetry anthologies *Whispering Wind*, edited by T. D. Allen, Doubleday, 1970, and *People of the Rainbow*, edited by Kenneth Rosen, Viking. Contributor of short fiction to journals.

a good many soldiers that day and beat the rest into retreat. They were a long way from home. They had no choice after that but to find Chief Joseph and join forces with him. That was how it happened that my grandmother, a Coeur d'Alene, was swept along with the Chief Joseph people pursued by Howard, Miles, the 7th Cavalry, and the Great Warrior himself, Sherman, running for her life for the Canadian border and the camp of Sitting Bull.

*Chinook: An Indian trade language.

II

My grandmother, the one who ran with Chief Joseph, died five years before my birth so I have no memories of my own of her. But I heard a lot about her from both my parents, from my uncle and cousins and sisters who did know her and had memories. My three sisters, who are ten, twelve, and fourteen years older than I, remember a little old woman who liked to joke, who told them Indian stories in our Native language. (She never learned English. They knew Indian as children.) How I envied them. How I wished I, too, had known her, had listened to her stories, had understood the language. I imagined her, though, when I was a child, and she became almost real to me.

My family had a photograph of her taken in old age: She is small and thin, her face very wrinkled, her eyes squint in the sun. Her long hair is white. She wears it parted in the middle and in two braids that hang in front to her waist. She is dressed Indian style.

She had a fragile appearance, but she was never fragile, they said, never. She was strong and tough, full of energy and industry, she kept busy. She made her own soap and scented it with pine needles. She went berry picking and she made Indian dishes nobody knows how to make anymore. She sewed all her own clothes. One ongoing activity of hers was the making of beautiful, useful articles: deerskin bags decorated with colored glass beads, cornhusk bags, and these, too, with intricate designs, moccasins, and infant cradle boards. She put them away and kept them sort of in the way young girls once kept a hope chest—for a day that would follow her death and funeral—the feast day when her belongings would be given away to friends and family. She wanted them to have something she made herself by which to remember her.

She was a rider of horses, too, a great rider of horses. She never gave up riding.

Way into old age she would ride, my mother told me, bareback, sometimes long distances. It was twenty miles from their home to the mission village. My grandmother preferred to ride her horse to the village on Sundays rather than go with my parents in their automobile, and she always would if weather permitted. She liked to get an early start, go to an early Mass, eat with friends and relatives, rest, attend a second Mass and visit a bit with her old cronies before heading home. In my mind's eye I can see her riding through the woods and open meadows on Sunday, all decked out in her finery—blue flower-print dress, her long-fringed maroon Spanish trade shawl, a silk scarf tied around her head, riding proud, beautiful, white-haired Indian woman, grandmother I could only know in my mind's eye, in my heart's eye.

My grandmother was a very devout Catholic, as were her parents before her. The conversion of the Coeur d'Alene was in response to an ancient prophecy that said three black ravens would come to them one day bringing the sacred word of the Creator. The ravens would only come when the people were ready to receive the new revelations. In time three Jesuit missionaries, or Black Robes, as they were called, did come, and they were welcomed and listened to. The tribe embraced Catholicism. As practiced by the Coeur d'Alene, it was a rather peculiar brand of Catholicism, and it was not at all "in place of" traditional religious beliefs, but rather an extension of them.

My father's generation, though, was of that first generation born *after* the conquest and the advent of the reservation system, the first generation of Indians to have Christianity forced upon it. The Church, for him, was an instrument of assimilation, an authority sponsored and sanctioned by the government whose primary purpose was to "civilize" the Indian and make him as much like a white man as possible. My father could recall, for instance, being beaten by a priest at mission school for speaking his own language. He, unlike his mother, was not a devout Catholic. He was, in fact, about as far from a devout Catholic as one could get.

My parents once told me (actually they were retelling each other the story, remembering it, laughing about it, after forty years of marriage) about when they were newlyweds and his mother, who had been living with him prior to his marriage, took extreme measures to get them to marry in the Catholic church.

When my father married my mother and brought her, his new part-white, English-speaking wife home, he told his mother they did not intend to marry in the Church. His mother tried to get him to change his mind, but he would not. His mother could not live with the two of them under the circumstances. She moved out—not to live with another son, as she could have, though. She pitched her tepee in the woods behind the house and lived there.

She used the same well, the same paths they used. They saw her all the time, coming and going, busy around her home. She would not speak to them, nor look at them, nor acknowledge their presence in any way. To her, they were invisible.

They continued to speak to her, to say good morning, how are you, to invite her to go for rides in their automobile, to go into town with them on a hot summer day for some ice cream. But the old lady had a heart of steel. The summer wore on in this way.

One month passed. Then two. My grandmother steadfastly continued to live in the woods in her tepee. In the end the old lady won, despite my father's feelings about the Church. Before the first frost my parents married in a Catholic ceremony, and my grandmother moved back into the house and stopped pretending they were invisible.

III

The Big Sky Country of Montana, the mountainous terrain, the grey, cold weather, the country western music, the motion of the car took me out of myself and my own petty hardships. (I had a cold, I had to eat in diners and sleep in cheap motels.) I had to speak to nine audiences in eight days (as a single mother I needed the money), though I would rather be home. I recognized these as petty concerns as we made our way across the big, big state of Montana. I saw her, my grandmother, the young girl she had been in 1877, more and more clearly. I drew closer and closer to her. She was there when they drove their ponies and cattle across a treacherous river and over two mountain ranges (they sometimes reached altitudes of ten thousand feet). Always (until that last day) they managed to keep ahead of the soldiers. In the last month they had no more cattle herds and only a few ponies.

Their food supplies ran out. Their clothes and moccasins were worn out. They became ragged, cold and hungry and could not stop to hunt or gather food or make new clothes. They wrapped their bleeding feet in rags and continued. They hurriedly buried their dead in shallow graves along the wayside. Soldiers noted scarred trees where hungry Indians had eaten bark and that they left behind a path marked by blood.

I thought of her, the devout Catholic girl she was, swept along with Nez Percé, who were never the friend of the Coeur d'Alene, whose language was not the same or even similar, whose culture was not her own.

I remembered something I heard about Chief Joseph when I was a child of eleven: he, always portrayed as "noble" in books, films, poems (in *Bury My Heart at Wounded Knee*), had actually been a mean person, a wicked man who hated women and treated them very badly.

My two best friends when I was a girl living on the Yakima Reservation were sisters and they were half Nez Percé. They and their mother were direct descendants of Chief Looking Glass. There was very bad blood between Joseph and Looking Glass (even on that last evening they disagreed). Joseph wanted to let the exhausted people stop and rest at the Bear Paw, then, refreshed, make the thirty miles into Canada in one long march the next day. Looking Glass urged that they push on, despite the belief that no soldiers were near, that they would be safe. They would not be safe, he argued, until they reached Canada. Then they could rest. But Joseph prevailed. Looking Glass, among many others, lost his life at the Bear Paw.

The grandfather of my friends was a grandson of Looking Glass. He said (and his mother, who had been there, told him) that Chief Joseph beat women and worse. On one occasion he had one of his wives put to death because he believed she had brought him bad luck at stick games.*

Whether or not it is true that Chief Joseph was a misogynist and had had a woman put to death because she brought him bad luck, I'll never know for sure. But I didn't doubt it when I heard it at age eleven, and I've read accounts of Indian chiefs of that region (of an earlier time) having wives put to death for the same reason. It could be true. At any rate the Nez Percé, to my grandmother, were strange people with different beliefs and customs. Maybe their leader held women in low regard, as the grandson of Looking Glass told me. They were not in any way *her people*. Except one: they were Indians and all Indians had in common a powerful enemy who had conquered them and would now hold them in captivity and would not tolerate any defiance.

So there she was, a young Catholic Coeur d'Alene, running for her life with Nez Percé (they left a trail marked by blood) from the United States Army (which was commanded by a man who was in fact against the reservation system, who believed Indians should all be killed off lest the government end up supporting "a race of paupers." "The only good Indian is a dead Indian" was a heartfelt sentiment in the America of 1877). And where were they going? To Canada to join the Sioux chief, Sitting Bull. And what kind of a life would she, the little girl who would be my grandmother, have were they to make good their escape? While the Nez Percé were never the friend of the Coeur d'Alene, the Sioux, still polygamous in 1877, were their bitter enemy. The literal translation of the Coeur d'Alene word for "Sioux" is "cutthroat."

The last days of the Great Flight were in September, and that year it was, as it often is, very cold in Montana, maybe as cold as the time of my

JANET CAMPBELL **HALE**

own journey. I know it snowed in the night while they camped and slept in the Little Bear Paw Mountains. I know the snow fell softly throughout the next day.

*Stick games: a form of gambling among Indians of the West and the Pacific West. Two teams face each other. Each team has a "hider," who hides a marked bone, and a "guesser," who guesses where the bone is hidden. Sometimes the game is played for high stakes.

IV

The morning of the last day of my tour I woke in the predawn hours and looked out the motel-room window and saw snow. Three or four inches of snow covered the ground, the rooftops, the cars, weighed heavily upon electrical wires. Somewhere I heard a radio: country western music at five A.M. The snow fell hard. It was time to go.

We reached Fort Belknap by noon and found my lecture there had been canceled. Classes had all been canceled, too, due to the heavy snowfall that closed the roads in the northern part of the reservation, where most of the students lived. They were snowed in. I had time now, lots of time. I had noticed a sign that said, TO THE INDIAN BATTLEGROUND. It was twenty-odd miles away. That was all. After eight days' time, all those hours of recalling what I knew about my grandmother and the Great Flight of 1877, and imagining how it must have been, after traveling all those hard Montana miles, I felt compelled to complete the journey now, to close the circle. I asked my driver if, given the snow, it would be possible to visit the Bear Paw. Would the roads be passable? Yes, he said. The roads would be fine. If not, we could turn back. But he thought it would be all right.

Those twenty-odd miles were hard ones. The wind blew and the snow drifted across the narrow winding road as we climbed higher and higher. Sometimes the road would be entirely hidden by snowdrifts.

The car was small, and I felt our vulnerability, should something go wrong. But my driver was used to bad weather and lonely stretches of country road. This probably wasn't even bad weather to him. Just a light spring snowfall.

Cattle lined up against the fence alongside the road, their white faces watching us. "It's as though they heard we were coming through," I said, "and all turned out to watch us pass."

"Maybe," he said, "they heard you were disappointed because you didn't see any buffalo in Montana and came to act as stand-ins. Actually that's what they do when they know a storm is coming."

"Why?"

"I don't know."

I sat back and watched the snow fall as we passed through this desolate area. We passed no house along the way, no filling station. We didn't even pass any other cars on the road. After what seemed like a long time my driver pulled over and stopped the car.

"Here we are," he said.

We climbed out of the car into the snow, four or five inches deep. I slipped and almost fell. My shoes, my thin high-heeled pumps, filled with snow, and snow fell on my hair and clothes and melted. I clutched my long red cardigan sweater close to me. It didn't keep me warm.

How quiet it was now that the car's engine no longer ran. No sound of wind or birds calling or human voices, only the quiet of the softly falling snow.

"There"—he indicated the mountains in the distance, barely visible through the veil of falling snow—"is Canada." Their destination.

We walked over to the monument, a bronze plate set in stone. On the plate, in relief, were two figures: one a soldier in uniform, presumably General Howard; the other an Indian, naked from the waist up, presumably Chief Joseph. Below the figures, also in relief, the words FROM WHERE THE SUN NOW STANDS I WILL FIGHT NO MORE FOREVER. The last words of Joseph's surrender speech.

"Look at this," he said, lightly touching the figure of the Indian. I touched it too. Some kind of blemishes . . . deep scratches on the figure of the Indian.

"What is this?"

"Bullet nicks," he answered. It took a moment for it to sink in, to imagine good old boys up here drinking beer and getting in a little target practice and expressing themselves. After all these years Indians aren't generally very popular in Montana. FROM WHERE THE SUN NOW STANDS, it said. I WILL FIGHT NO MORE . . . , and there were bullet-nicks, . . . FOREVER, on the bronze monument. FROM WHERE THE SUN, depicting the peace-making SUN NOW STANDS . . . , the final surrender, I WILL FIGHT . . . , after the slaughter, NO MORE. . . . They shot only at FOREVER, the Indian. Not the solider. Bullet nicks.

We stood on a rise above what I realized had to be the battleground. "There it is," he said, "down here." Yes.

The Indians had come far, had suffered such great hardships, were so tired and hungry. There would be time enough, or so they thought, to stop for the night, their last night. They knew of Howard, a good long distance away, and they knew they had completely lost the other, the 7th Cavalry. But they were not aware of a third division, which now came towards them from the

J A N E T   C A M P B E L L   **H A L E**

east. So they went down there, made their camp in the gulch beside Snake Creek. They hunted, cooked their fresh meat, ate and rested. What did that girl dream of that night as she lay sleeping? Did she dream of the beautiful Coeur d'Alene country that was her home? Did she see the faces of her father and mother? Or did she now dream of her new life in Canada?

The cavalry attacked just before dawn while the Indians still slept. The battle raged as the snow fell, hour after bloody hour, throughout most of the day. When the Battle at the Bear Paw ended, 419 Indians—88 men, 184 women and 147 children—lay dead on the frozen ground.

"Do you want to go down there?" he asked me. I said no. Not in those shoes. Not dressed as I was. I wouldn't be able to take the cold much longer. He went alone. My ears ached in the cold, and my feet felt as though they would turn to ice. I saw him brush the snow from the markers for the communal grave. He stayed there awhile, kneeling in the snow.

The cold reached my bones, yet I stood in the snow and felt myself being in that place, that scared place. I say how pitifully close lay the mountains of Canada. I felt the biting cold. I was with those people, was part of them. I felt the presence of my grandmother there as though two parts of her met each other that day: the ghost of the girl she was in 1877 (and that part of her will remain forever in that place) and the part of her that lives on in me, in inherited memories of her, in my blood and in my spirit.

At length the spell broke. I could take the cold no longer. I went back to the car, to the relative warmth and comfort there.

My driver joined me in five or ten minutes. He started the engine, breaking the silence. The tires spun in the mud, but just a bit. Then we pulled forward, made a circle and turned back onto the road, which was easier to travel going down.

The snow stopped, turned to rain. We didn't talk much the rest of the way to the highway and then to Great Falls. The day grew dim.

Chief Joseph of the Nez Percé was thirty-six years old at the time of the Battle at the Bear Paw. His surrender speech was made through an interpreter and recorded on the spot by an army clerk. It would become one of the most famous of American speeches:

> *Tell General Howard I know his heart. What he told me before I have in my heart. I am tired of fighting. Our chiefs are killed. Looking Glass is dead. Toolhoolzote is dead. The old men are all dead. It is cold and we have no blankets. The little children are freezing to death. My people, some of them, have run away to the hills and have no blankets, no food; no one knows where they are—perhaps freezing to death. I want to have time to look for my children and see how many of them I can find. Maybe I*

shall find them among the dead. Hear me, my chiefs! From where the sun now stands I will fight no more forever."

After it was all over, my grandmother would return to Coeur d'Alene country in northern Idaho. She would live through a smallpox epidemic that would wipe out most of the tribe, begun when the Coeur d'Alene people, no longer permitted to go to Montana to hunt buffalo, were given smallpox-infected army blankets.

She would marry a tall, shrewd Coeur d'Alene man, who would, as a rancher, provide very well for her and the six sons and one daughter they would have together.

She would give birth to my father in the mountains one summer day in 1892 while out picking huckleberries. She would tell him about his birth in the mountains and how she came riding down with the basket strapped to her horse on one side filled with huckleberries and the basket on the other side containing her new baby boy.

My father would go to mission school at the age of twelve, where he would learn English: to read, to write, to speak. He would become a soldier in the United States Army during World War I (though Indians would not be made citizens until 1924). He would marry and have one son. His first wife would die. He would marry my mother when he was thirty-nine years old, and they would have four daughters together.

My paternal grandmother would live to be a very old woman, and she and my three older sisters would know each other very well. She would tell them stories, speaking the old language they would understand as children but forget as adults (and I would never know).

The old woman who survived the Great Flight and the Battle at the Bear Paw and the smallpox epidemic would die peacefully in her sleep in her home in Idaho in 1941.

I would be born five years later in 1946, shortly after the end of World War II. And though I would live on that same Idaho reservation, and then on the Yakima in Washington State, I would grow up knowing only the English language. I would go to college and law school. Eventually I would become a writer. As a writer I would go back to that hard Montana country, and on a cold day in May 1986, I would, at last, return to the Bear Paw.

JOY HARJO

Essay by

JOHN SCARRY

Strongly influenced by her Muskogee Creek heritage, feminist and social con-

cerns, and her background in the arts, Harjo frequently incorporates Native

American myths, symbols, and values into her writing. Her poetry additional-

ly emphasizes the Southwest landscape and the need for remembrance and

transcendence. She asserts: "I feel strongly that I have a responsibility to all

the sources that I am: to all past and future ancestors, to my home country, to

all places that I touch down on and that are myself, to all voices, all women,

all of my tribe, all people, all earth, and beyond that to all beginnings and end-

ings. In a strange kind of sense [writing] frees me to believe in myself, to be

able to speak, to have voice, because I have to; it is my survival."

Harjo's work is largely autobiographical, informed by her love of the natural world and preoccupation with survival and the limitations of language. The search for freedom and self-actualization are considered central to her *She Had Some Horses*, which is known for its incorporation of
prayer-chants and animal imagery. Nature is also central to Harjo's prose
poetry collection, *Secrets from the Center of the World*, in which each
poem is accompanied by a photograph of the American Southwest. Her
best-known and most recent volume, *In Mad Love and War*, more overtly
is concerned with politics, tradition, remembrance, and the transformational aspects of poetry. In the first section, which relates various acts of
violence, including others' attempts to deny Harjo her heritage as well as
the murder of an Indian leader, Harjo explores the difficulties many
Native Americans face in modern American society: " . . . *we have too*

2 I I

Muskogee Creek poet, scriptwriter, editor, film-maker, and musician.

Born: May 9, 1951, in Tulsa, Oklahoma.

Children: Phil, Rainy Dawn.

Education: University of New Mexico, B.A., 1976; University of Iowa, M.F.A., 1978.

Career: Institute of American Indian Arts, Santa Fe, NM, instructor, 1978–79, 1983–85; Arizona State University, Tempe, part-time instructor in creative writing and poetry, 1980–81; University of Colorado, Boulder, assistant professor, 1985–88; University of Arizona, Tucson, associate professor, 1988–90; University of New Mexico, Albuquerque, professor, 1991–. Visiting professor of creative writing at the University of Montana, 1985. Writer and consultant for Native American Public Broadcasting Consortium, National Indian Youth Council, and National Endowment for the Arts, all 1980–83. Member of steering committee of En'owkin Centre International School of Writing.

Memberships: International PEN.

Address: Home—P.O. Box 40074, Albuquerque, NM 87196. Office—Department of English, University of New Mexico, Albuquerque, NM 87131.

---

many stories to carry on our backs like houses, we have struggled too long to let the monsters steal our sleep, sleep, go to sleep. But I never woke up. Dogs have been nipping at my heels since I learned to walk. I was taught to not dance for a rotten supper on the plates of my enemies. My mother taught me well." The second half of the book frequently emphasizes personal relationships and change.

Harjo has been consistently praised for the thematic concerns of her writings, and scholars predict that she will soon become a major figure in contemporary American poetry. They note that while Harjo's work is often set in the Southwest, emphasizes the plight of the individual, and reflects Creek values, myths, and beliefs, her oeuvre has universal relevance. Dan Bellm asserts: "Harjo's work draws from the river of Native tradition, but it also swims freely in the currents of Anglo-American verse—feminist poetry of personal/political resistance, deep-image poetry of the unconscious, 'new-narrative' explorations of story and rhythm in prose-poem form."

212

THE WOMAN HANGING FROM THE THIRTEENTH FLOOR WINDOW

From *She Had Some Horses*, Thunder's Mouth Press, copyright © 1983 by Joy Harjo

She is the woman hanging from the 13th floor
window. Her hands are pressed white against the

concrete moulding of the tene-
ment building. She
hangs from the 13th floor window
in east Chicago,
with a swirl of birds over her head.
They could
be a halo, or a storm of glass waiting to crush her.

She thinks she will be set free.
The woman hanging from the 13th
floor window
on the east side of Chicago is not
alone.
She is a woman of children, of the
baby, Carlos,
and of Margaret, and of Jimmy
who is the oldest.
She is her mother's daughter and
her father's son.
She is several pieces between the
two husbands
she has had. She is all the women
of the apartment
building who stand watching her,
watching themselves.
When she was young she ate wild
rice on scraped down
plates in warm wood rooms. It
was in the farther
north and she was the baby then.
They rocked her.

She sees Lake Michigan lapping at the shores of
herself. It is a dizzy hole of water and the rich
live in tall glass houses at the edge of it. In some
places Lake Michigan speaks softly, here, it just sputters
and butts itself against the asphalt. She sees
other buildings just like hers. She sees other

I was born in Tulsa. I'm Creek, Muskogee. We are originally from Alabama, though the Creek Confederacy covered the southeast United States. I'm related to Alexander Posey, the Creek poet; he was my father's father's mother's cousin . . . I grew up in Oklahoma until I was about sixteen, when I went to Indian boarding school in Santa Fe, New Mexico. And I've lived in New Mexico much of my life. My son was born in Tahlequah, but I moved back to New Mexico when he was 18 months old. I attended graduate school in Iowa at the Iowa Writers' Workshop—"did time" there. But Oklahoma is my home, and New Mexico is my other home. I'm a poet and a writer because I am curious about this process called living, the transformational aspects of language.

—Joy Harjo, quoted in *MELUS*, Spring 1989–1990

2 1 3

JOY HARJO

women hanging from many-floored windows
counting their lives in the palms of their hands
and in the palms of their children's hands.

She is the woman hanging from the 13th floor window
on the Indian side of town. Her belly is soft from
her children's births, her worn levis swing down below
her waist, and then her feet, and then her heart.
She is dangling.

The woman hanging from the 13th floor hears voices.
They come to her in the night when the lights have gone
dim. Sometimes they are little cats mewing and scratching
at the door, sometimes they are her grandmother's voice,
and sometimes they are gigantic men of light whispering

to her to get up, to get up, to get
up. That's when she wants
to have another child to hold onto
in the night, to be able
to fall back into dreams.

And the woman hanging from the
13th floor window
hears other voices. Some of them
scream out from below
for her to jump, they would push
her over. Others cry softly
from the sidewalks, pull their
children up like flowers and
gather
them into their arms. They would
help her, like themselves.

But she is the woman hanging
from the 13th floor window,
and she knows she is hanging by
her own fingers, her
own skin, her own thread of inde-
cision.

She thinks of Carlos, of Margaret,
of Jimmy.
She thinks of her father, and of her mother.
She thinks of all the women she has been, of all
the men. She thinks of the color of her skin, and
of Chicago streets, and of waterfalls and pines.
She thinks of moonlight nights, and of cool spring storms.
Her mind chatters like neon and northside bars.
She thinks of the 4 A.M. lonelinesses that have folded
her up like death, discordant, without logical and
beautiful conclusion. Her teeth break off at the edges.
She would speak.

The woman hangs from the 13th floor window crying for
the lost beauty of her own life. She sees the

Joy Harjo's particular poetic turf is cities, especially from the point of view of an Indian woman traveling between them. Her poems are full of planes, cars, pick-ups, borders, and white center-lines; she writes not only of the Oklahoma of her childhood and New Mexico, where she's spent many of her adult years, but of Iowa and Kansas, Calgary and East Chicago, Anchorage and New Orleans, and corrugated tunnels in airports, "a space between leaving and staying."

—Patricia Clark Smith and Paula Gunn Allen, "Earthy Relations, Carnal Knowledge: Southwestern American Indian Women Writers and Landscape," in *The Desert Is No Lady: Southwestern Landscapes in Women's Writing and Art,* **Yale University Press, 1987.**

sun falling west over the grey plane of Chicago.
She thinks she remembers listening to her own life
break loose, as she falls from the 13th floor
window on the east side of Chicago, or as she
climbs back up to claim herself again.

REMEMBER

From *She Had Some Horses*, Thunder's Mouth, copyright © 1983 by Joy Harjo.

Remember the sky that you were born under,
know each of the star's stories.
Remember the moon, know who she is. I met her
in a bar once in Iowa City.
Remember the sun's birth at dawn, that is the
strongest point of time. Remember sundown
and the giving away to night.
Remember your birth, how your mother struggled
to give you form and breath. You are evidence of
her life, and her mother's, and hers.
Remember your father. He is your life, also.
Remember the earth whose skin you are:
red earth, black earth, yellow earth, white earth
brown earth, we are earth.
Remember the plants, trees, animal life who all have their
tribes, their families, their histories, too. Talk to them,
listen to them. They are alive poems.
Remember the wind. Remember her voice. She knows the
origin of this universe. I heard her singing Kiowa war
dance songs at the corner of Fourth and Central once.
Remember that you are all people and that all people
are you.
Remember that you are this universe and that this
universe is you.
Remember that all is in motion, is growing, is you.
Remember that language comes from this.
Remember the dance that language is, that life is.
Remember.

2 1 6

Poetry
The Last Song, Puerto Del Sol Press, 1975.
What Moon Drove Me to This?, I. Reed Books, 1980.
She Had Some Horses, Thunder's Mouth, 1983.
(With Steven Strom) Secrets from the Center of the World, University of Arizona Press, 1989.

In Mad Love and War, Wesleyan University Press, 1990.

Scripts and Recordings
Origin of Apache Crown Dance (script), Silver Cloud Video, 1985.
Furious Light (recording), Watershed, 1986.
Also co-author of filmscript, *The Beginning*, Native American Broadcasting Consortium.

Other
Contributor to several literary journals, including *Conditions, Beloit Poetry Journal, River Styx, Tyuoyi*, and *Y'Bird*.

Work in Progress
A book of stories.

GRACE

From *In Mad Love and War*, Wesleyan University Press, copyright © 1990 by Joy Harjo

(For Wind and Jim Welch)

I think of Wind and her wild ways the year we had nothing to lose
and lost it anyway in the cursed country of the fox. We still talk
about that winter, how the cold froze imaginary buffalo on the stuffed
horizon of snowbanks. The haunting voices of the starved and mutilated
broke fences, crashed our thermostat dreams, and we couldn't stand it
one more time. So once again we lost a winter in stubborn memory, walked
through cheap apartment walls, skated through fields of ghosts into
a town that never wanted us, in the epic search for grace.

Like Coyote, like Rabbit, we could not contain our terror and clowned
our way through a season of false midnights. We had to swallow
that town with laughter, so it would go down easy as honey. And one
morning as the sun struggled to break ice, and our dreams had found us
with coffee and pancakes in a truck stop along Highway 80,
we found grace.

I could say grace was a woman with time on her hands, or a white
buffalo escaped from memory. But in that dingy light it was a promise
of balance. We once again understood the talk of animals, and spring
was lean and hungry with the hope of children and corn.

I would like to say, with grace, we picked ourselves up and walked
into the spring thaw. We didn't; the next season was worse. You went
home to Leech Lake to work with the tribe and I went south. And, Wind,

2 I 7

I am still crazy. I know there is something larger than the memory
of a dispossessed people. We have seen it.

AUTOBIOGRAPHY

From *In Mad Love and War*, Wesleyan University Press, copyright © 1990 by Joy Harjo

We lived next door to the bootlegger, and were lucky. The bootlegger reigned.
We were a stolen people in a stolen land. Oklahoma meant defeat. But the
sacred lands have their own plans, seep through fingers of the alcohol
spirit. Nothing can be forgotten, only left behind.

Last week I saw the river where the hickory stood; this homeland doesn't
predict a legacy of malls and hotels. Dreams aren't glass and steel but made
from the hearts of deer, the blazing eye of a circling panther. Translating
them was to understand the death count from Alabama, the destruction of
grandchildren, famine of stories. I didn't think I could stand it. My father
couldn't. He searched out his death with the vengeance of a warrior who has
been the hunted. It's in our blood.

Even at two I knew we were different. Could see through the eyes of
strangers that we were trespassers in the promised land. The Sooner State
glorified the thief. Everyone and no one was Indian. You'd best forget, claim
a white star. At three my mother told me this story:

*God decided to make people. He put the first batch in the oven, kept
them in too long. They burned. These were the black people. God put in the
next batch. They were uncooked, not done. These were the white people.
But the next batch he cooked* just *right, and these were the Indian people,
just like you.*

By then I was confused.
At five I was designated to string beads in kindergarten. At seven I knew
how to play chicken and win. And at fourteen I was drinking.

I found myself in a city in the Southwest at twenty-one, when my past came
into focus. It was near midnight. We were walking home and there he was,
curled in the snow on the sidewalk, that man from Jemez. We had all been
cheated. He hid his shame beneath a cold, downy blanket. We hid ours in
poems. We took him home, where he shivered and cried through the night

like a fighting storm, then woke in the morning, knowing nothing. Later
I would see him on the street, the same age I am now. It was my long dark
hair that cued his daughter, the chili, the songs. And I talked to him as if
he were my father, with that respect, that hunger.

I have since outlived that man from Jemez, my father and that ragged self I
chased through precarious years. But I carry them with me the same as this
body carries the heart as a drum. Yesterday there was rain traveling east to
home. A hummingbird spoke. She was a shining piece of invisible memory,
inside the raw cortex of songs. I knew then this was the Muscogee season of
forgiveness, time of new corn, the spiraling dance.

LANCE  HENSON

Lance Henson is a poet of Cheyenne heritage whose work is deeply rooted in his ancestral background. His early collections include Naming the Dark: Poems for the Cheyenne, *published in 1976, and a 1982 chapbook,* In a Dark Mist. Selected Poems, 1970–1983 *appeared in 1985, its contents culled from his previously published selections in anthologies and poetry journals. Henson's style has been described as minimalist: his poems are typically short, terse, and filled with powerful imagery. Explaining his approach in an interview in Joseph Burchac's book* Survival This Way, *Henson noted: "We are born out of a perfect state to be here. . . . I think brevity is . . . one way to acknowledge and pay homage to the Great Silence we came out of."*

Henson's subject matter is also derived from his Native American background; *Selected Poems, 1970–1983,* for example, includes an exploration of the peyote ritual, which involves ingesting hallucinogens in order to attain communion with the spirit world. Critiquing the volume for *World Literature Today,* Robert L. Berner noted that Henson's poems "are the work of a poet who knows that language is the original magic."

Another Song for America, *Henson's 1987 collection of verse, is buttressed by two poems that serve as critiques of the violence of the Native American experience at the hands of white civilization and the contemporary social and racial tensions of twentieth-century America. The first poem is taken from a death song of a Native American warrior killed in

Cheyenne poet

Born: 1944 in Oklahoma.

Partnerships: Married Pat French (marriage ended).

Education: Graduated from Oklahoma College of Liberal Arts (now University of Science and Arts of Oklahoma), Chickasha, OK; earned master's degree in creative writing at University of Tulsa, Tulsa, OK.

Career: Writer and educator. Served in the United States Marine Corps during the Vietnam war.

Memberships: Cheyenne Dog Soldier Society.

Agent: Jeanetta Calhoun, 2541 Northwest 36th St., Oklahoma City, OK 73112.

---

battle, while the closing piece is based on the incident at Kent State University in 1970, when antiwar protesters were killed by National Guard troops. Other selections return to Henson's Cheyenne heritage, such as "january song." In reviewing the volume for another issue of *World Literature Today*, Berner asserted that the poet's "great strength is his ability to create striking images which he relates to the history and wisdom of his Cheyenne forebears."

Another Distance: New and Selected Poems, published in 1991, contains sixty-three poems that are, for the most part, either no longer available in print or recently written; of the latter category, many were composed in Europe and manifest what Berner, in a *World Literature Today* review, called "the chilling awareness of exile." This volume also reflects Henson's concern for environmental issues. In his "walking at teutoburger wald," Henson describes the ancient forest now ravaged by acid rain as "a war zone." Berner notes that in this volume Henson seems to expand his view of the situation of the modern Native American, suggesting that "the old victories and defeats seem less important than the present predicament—international, ecological, basic—of the entire race in a world which continues to be threatened by social stupidity."

222 | WARRIOR NATION TRILOGY

From *A Cheyenne Sketchbook: Selected Poems 1970–1991*, Greenfield Review Press, copyright © 1985 by Lance Henson

1

from the mountains we come
lifting our voices for the beautiful
road you have given

SMOKE RISING

we are the buffalo people
we dwell in the light of our father
    sun
in the shadow of our mother earth

we are the beautiful people
we roam the great plains without
    fear
in our days the land has taught us
    oneness
we alone breathe with the rivers
we alone hear the song of the
    stones

2

oh ghost that follows me
find in me strength to know the
    wisdom
of this life

take me to the mountain of my
    grandfather
i have heard him all night
singing among the summer leaves

3

great spirit (maheo)

make me whole
i have come this day with my spirit
i am not afraid
for i have seen in vision
the white buffalo
grazing the frozen field
which grows near the full circle
of this
world

Ceremonies have a way of lifting simplicity and grace to a level of understanding that's ultimate—perception circles back: the way a child understands life, the way a mother understands life. . . and a father and a grandfather and a grandmother and, I might even be so courageous to say, the way an animal or a tree or some of the natural forces view their relationship in this grand mystery called life. . . . The ceremonies have offered me that and that has been enough and that is all I ask for. There is no greater thing one can learn than to reach out and help and to allow people to help you: to love and be loved by someone who cares enough to do that.

—Lance Henson, in an interview with Joseph Bruchac in *Survival This Way: Interviews with American Indian Poets,* 1987.

223

Poetry

Keeper of Arrows, Renaissance Press, 1972.
Naming the Dark: Poems for the Cheyenne, Point Rider's Press, 1976.
Mistah, Strawberry Press, 1978.
Buffalo Marrow on Black, Full Count Press, 1979.
A Circling Remembrance, The Blue Cloud Quarterly Press, 1982.
Selected Poems, 1970–1983, Greenfield Review Press, 1985.
Another Song for America, Point Rider's Press, 1987.

Dieser kleine Klang/This Small Sound, Institut fur Indianishe Kulturen Nordamerikas (Germany), 1987.
Tepee, Cooperativa La Parentesi/Soconos Incomindios (Italy), 1987.
Tonger Ut Stiennen/Thunder from Stones, Fryske Nasjonale Partij (Netherlands), 1987.
Le Orme del Tasso/The Badger Tracks, Soconos Incomindios (Italy), 1989.
Another Distance: New and Selected Poems, Point Rider's Press, 1991.
A Motion of Sudden Aloneness, University of Arkansas Press, 1991.
Poems for a Master Beadworker, OMBA Germany, 1991.

Other

In a Dark Mist (chapbook), Cross-Cultural Communications, 1982.
Also contributes to numerous publications, including *Wooster Review* and *Nimrod*.

BUFFALO MARROW ON BLACK

From *A Cheyenne Sketchbook: Selected Poems 1970–1991*, Greenfield Review Press, copyright © 1985 by Lance Henson

wind of sage in which the world dreams
    strike the earth where i have walked
        let my relatives hear this

scent of cedar pass tonight over the faces of the
sleeping
    world and the paths of the sick and troubled
       and weak

brother sun
    help me to be remembered among all
      growing things

sister water
    grandfather fire

     muts i mi u na
       wo is ta
       henah haneh
       henah haneh

2 2 4

SMOKE RISING

buffalo calf road woman
      buffalo woman
          this is all
              this is all

IMPRESSIONS OF THE CHEYENNE WAY

From *A Cheyenne Sketchbook: Selected Poems 1970–1991*, Greenfield Review Press, copyright © 1985 by Lance Henson

1

it is dawn
pity the names we have spoken
touch these feathers that have flown
your road

LANCE HENSON

Henson's strength is that he has remained rooted in the earth of Oklahoma, where he was born, and in the traditions of his Cheyenne forebears. His best work is informed by his awareness of those traditions and by his ability to infuse a poem with the emotional force of original Cheyenne elements. For example, in the six poems in "impressions of the peyote ritual," the peyote traditions, while retaining their original force, become an intense personal possession. Henson shows that the most vital asset of modern poets—one which many American Indian poets are particularly fortunate to possess—is the ability to retain an organic relationship to their own tradition.

—**Robert L. Berner**, in a review of *Selected Poems, 1970–1983,* in **World Literature Today,** Vol. 60, No. 3, Summer 1986.

grandfather cedar
i am picking up your ways

2

maheo walks among us
in a wind of sage the world
is dreaming

scent of water
the smoke has circled

i am looking for your face

3

our father
maheo

i send my song
the darkest sinew of my life

pity me
this night opens on my small spirit

i am alone

TOMSON HIGHWAY

Essay by

RUTH ROSENBERG

Highway is primarily known for his award-winning plays The Rez Sisters *and* Dry Lips Oughta Move to Kapuskasing, *both of which deal with life on the reservation. Born in northwest Manitoba, Highway spoke only Cree until age six when he began attending a Roman Catholic boarding school. A musical prodigy in high school, Highway studied music in Canada and England and later obtained degrees in English and music from the University of Western Ontario. After spending several years working for various Native support organizations and with Canadian writer James Reaney, Highway "started writing plays, where I put together my knowledge of Indian reality in [Canada] with classical structure, artistic language. It amounted to applying sonata form to the spiritual and mental situation of a street drunk, say, at the corner of Queen and Bathurst."*

227

The Rez Sisters and *Dry Lips*, the first two works of a proposed cycle of seven plays, are set on the fictional Wasaychigan Hill Indian reserve on Manitoulin Island, Canada. *The Rez Sisters* involves seven females, who plan to go to the world's largest bingo game in Toronto, and a male Nanabush—the Ojibway name for "The Trickster"—a Native mythological being who can assume various guises and who is a central figure in Cree culture. In contrast, *Dry Lips* revolves around a female Nanabush and seven males only referred to in *The Rez Sisters*. Although sometimes considered stronger in characterization and humor than in plot, these plays

Cree playwright and musician.

Born: December 6, 1951, in northwest Manitoba, Canada.

Education: Attended Guy Hill Indian Residential School, The Pas, Manitoba, 1957–66; Churchill High School, Winnipeg, Manitoba, graduated 1970; University of Manitoba, Faculty of Music; University of Western Ontario, B. Mus. (with honors), 1975, and B.A. in English, 1977.

Career: Worked with Canadian writer James Reaney on the plays *The Canadian Brothers* and *Wacousta*; associated with numerous Native support groups; De-ba-jeh-mu-jig Theatre Group, then located in West Bay, Ontario; Native Earth Performing Arts, Inc., Toronto, Ontario, artistic director, until 1992.

have been acclaimed for Highway's revealing portrayal of reservation life and for his examination of the cultural, religious, environmental, and societal issues confronting Natives in a contemporary, urban-oriented world.

Critics note, however, that the spiritual insights and ultimately hopeful messages revealed in these works have universal implications. As the then artistic director of the Native Earth Performing Arts, Inc., Highway stated: "Native culture is beautiful, Native mythology is beautiful and powerful, [and these] are very relevant, increasingly so, as time goes on. At a time in our history, as a community of human beings, when the world is about to get quite literally destroyed, and all life forms have a very good chance of being completely obliterated—at a crucial time like this, Native people have a major statement to make about the kind of profound change that has to come about in order for the disaster to be averted. From that perspective alone I think it is important that we put out Native works of literature, Native works of theatre."

THE REZ SISTERS

Fifth House, copyright © 1988 by Tomson Highway

A Note on Nanabush

The dream world of North American Indian mythology is inhabited by the most fantastic creatures, beings, and events. Foremost among these beings is the "Trickster," as pivotal and important a figure in the Native world as Christ is in the realm of Christian mythology. "Weesageechak" in Cree, "Nanabush" in Ojibway, "Raven" in others, "Coyote" in still others, this Trickster goes by many names and many guises. In fact, he can assume any guise he chooses. Essentially a comic, clownish sort of character, he teaches us about the nature and the meaning of existence on the planet Earth; he straddles the consciousness of man and that of God, the Great Spirit.

Some say that "Nanabush" left this continent when the whiteman came. We believe he is still here among us—albeit a little the worse for wear and tear—having assumed other guises. Without him—and without the spiritual health of this figure—the core of Indian culture would be gone forever.

Cast of Characters

Pelajia Patchnose, 53

Philomena Moosetail, 49, sister of Pelajia

Marie-Adele Starblanket, 39, half-sister of Pelajia & Philomena

Annie Cook, 36, sister of Marie-Adele & half-sister of the other two

Emily Dictionary, 32, sister of Annie & ditto

Veronique St. Pierre, 45, sister-in-law of all the above

Zhaboonigan Peterson, 24, mentally disabled adopted daughter of Veronique

Nanabush—who plays the Seagull (the dancer in white feathers), the Nighthawk (the dancer in dark feathers), and the Bingo Master.

Time: Late summer, 1986

Place: The Wasaychigan Hill Indian Reserve, Manitoulin Island, Ontario. (Note: "Wasaychigan" means "window" in Ojibway.)

Act One

It is mid-morning of a beautiful late August day on the Wasaychigan Hill Indian Reserve, Manitoulin Island, Ontario. Pelajia Patchnose is alone on the roof of her house, nailing shingles on. She wears faded blue denim men's cover-alls and a baseball cap to shade her eyes from the sun. A brightly-colored square cushion belonging to her sister, Philomena Moosetail, rests on the roof beside her. The ladder to the roof is off-stage.

PELAJIA: Philomena. I wanna go to Toronto.

PHILOMENA: *From offstage.* Oh, go on.

PELAJIA: Sure as I'm sitting away up here on the roof of this old house. I kind of like it up here, though. From here, I can see half of Manitoulin Island on a clear day. I can see the chimneys, the tops of apple trees, the garbage heap behind Bid Joey's dumpy little house. I can see the seagulls circling over Marie-Adele Starblanket's white picket fence. Boats on the North Channel I wish I was on, sailing away somewhere. The mill at Espanola, a hundred miles away . . . and that's with just a bit of squinting. See? If I had binoculars, I could see the superstack in Sudbury. And if I were Super-woman, I could see the CN Tower in Toronto. Ah, but I'm just plain old Pela-jia Rosella Patchnose and I'm here in plain, dusty, boring old Wasaychigan Hill . . . Wasy . . . waiting . . . waiting . . . nailing shining shingles with my trusty silver hammer on the roof of Pelajia Rosella Patchnose's little two-bedroom welfare house. Philomena. I wanna go to Toronto.

> *Philomena Moosetail comes up the ladder to the roof with one shingle and obviously hating it. She is very well-dressed, with a skirt, nylons, even heels, completely impractical for the roof.*

PHILOMENA: Oh, go on.

PELAJIA: I'm tired, Philomena, tired of this place. There's days I wanna leave so bad.

PHILOMENA: But you were born here. All your poop's on this reserve.

PELAJIA: Oh, go on.

PHILOMENA: You'll never leave.

PELAJIA: Yes, I will. When I'm old.

PHILOMENA: You're old right now.

PELAJIA: I got a good 30 years to go . . .

PHILOMENA: . . . and you're gonna live every one of them right here beside me . . .

PELAJIA: . . . maybe 40 . . .

PHILOMENA: . . . here in Wasy.

> *Tickles Pelajia on the breasts.*

Chiga-chiga-chiga.

PELAJIA: *Yelps and slaps Philomena's hand away.*

Oh, go on. It's not like it used to be.

PHILOMENA: Oh, go on. People change, places change, time changes things. You expect to be young and gorgeous forever?

PELAJIA: See? I told you I'm not old.

PHILOMENA: Oh, go on. You.

PELAJIA: "Oh, go on. You." You bug me like hell when you say that.

PHILOMENA: You say it, too. And don't give me none of this "I don't like this place. I'm tired of it." This place is too much inside your blood. You can't get rid of it. And it can't get rid of you.

PELAJIA: Four thirty this morning, I was woken by . . .

PHILOMENA: Here we go again.

PELAJIA: . . . Andrew Starblanket and his brother, Matthew. Drunk. Again. Or sounded like . . .

PHILOMENA: Nothing better to do.

PELAJIA: . . . fighting over some girl. Heard what sounded like a baseball bat landing on somebody's back. My lawn looks like the shits this morning.

PHILOMENA: Well, I like it here. Myself, I'm gonna go to every bingo and I'm gonna hit every jackpot between here and Espanola and I'm gonna buy me that toilet I'm dreaming about at night . . . big and wide and very white . . .

PELAJIA: Aw-ni-gi-naw-ee-dick. [1]

PHILOMENA: I'm good at bingo.

PELAJIA: So what! And the old stories, the old language. Almost all gone . . . was a time Nanabush and Windigo and everyone here could rattle away in Indian fast as Bingo Betty could lay her bingo chips down on a hot night.

PHILOMENA: Pelajia Rosella Patchnose. The sun's gonna drive you crazy.

And she descends the ladder.

PELAJIA: Everyone here's crazy. No jobs. Nothing to do but drink and screw each other's wives and husbands and forget about our Nanabush.

From offstage Philomena screams. She fell down the ladder.

Philomena!

As she looks over the edge of the roof.

What are you doing down there?

PHILOMENA: What do you think? I fell.

PELAJIA: Bring me some of them nails while you're down there.

PHILOMENA: *Whining and still from offstage, from behind the house.* You think I can race up and down this ladder? You think I got wings?

PELAJIA: You gotta wear pants when you're doing a man's job. See? You got your skirt ripped on a nail and now you can see your thighs. People gonna think you just came from Big Joey's house.

PHILOMENA: *She comes up the ladder in a state of disarray.* Let them think what they want. That old cow Gazelle Nataways . . . always acting like

The Rez Sisters (two-act play), first produced at National Canadian Centre, Toronto, Ontario, 1986; published by Fifth House, 1988.
Aria (monologues), produced at Makka Kleist Annex Theatre, Toronto, Ontario, 1987.

Dry Lips Oughta Move to Kapuskasing (play), first produced at Theatre Passe Muraille, Toronto, Ontario, 1989; published by Fifth House, 1989.
(With Rene Highway and Bill Merasty) *The Sage, the Dancer, and the Fool* (play), first produced at National

Canadian Centre, Toronto, Ontario, 1989.

Also collaborated with Rene Highway on the multimedia dance production *New Song . . . New Dance*, 1987–88.

she thinks she's still a spring chicken. She's got them legs of hers wrapped around Big Joey day and night . . .

PELAJIA: Philomena. Park your tongue. My old man has to go the hundred miles to Espanola just to get a job. My boys. Gone to Toronto. Only place educated Indian boys can find decent jobs these days. And here I sit all brokenhearted.

PHILOMENA: Paid a dime and only farted.

PELAJIA: Look at you. You got dirt all over your backside.

Turning her attention to the road in front of her house and standing up for the first and only time.

And dirt road! Years now that old chief's been making speeches about getting paved roads "for my people" and still we got dirt roads all over.

PHILOMENA: Oh, go on.

PELAJIA: When I win me that jackpot next time we play bingo in Espanola . . .

PHILOMENA: *Examining her torn skirt, her general state of disarray, and fretting over it.* Look at this! Will you look at this! Ohhh!

PELAJIA: . . . I'm gonna put that old chief to shame and build me a nice paved road right here in front of my house. Jet black. Shiny. Make my lawn look real nice.

PHILOMENA: My rib-cage!

PELAJIA: And if that old chief don't wanna make paved roads for all my sisters around here . . .

PHILOMENA: There's something rattling around inside me!

PELAJIA: . . . I'm packing my bags and moving to Toronto.

Sits down again.

PHILOMENA: Oh, go on.

She spies Annie Cook's approach a distance up the hill.

Why, I do believe that cloud of dust over there is Annie Cook racing down the hill, Pelajia.

PELAJIA: Philomena. I wanna go to Toronto.

PHILOMENA: She's walking mighty fast. Must be excited about something.

PELAJIA: Never seen Annie Cook walk slow since the day she finally lost Eugene to Marie-Adele at the church 19 years ago. And even then she was walking a little too fast for a girl who was supposed to be broken-heart. . . *Stopping just in time and laughing.* . . . heart-broken.

Annie Cook pops up the top of the ladder to the roof.

ANNIE: *All cheery and fast and perky.* Halloooo! Whatchyou doing up here?

PELAJIA: There's room for only so much weight up here before we go crashing into my kitchen, so what do you want?

ANNIE: Just popped up to say hi.

PELAJIA: And see what we're doing?

ANNIE: Well . . .

PELAJIA: Couldn't you see what we're doing from up where you were?

ANNIE: *Confidentially, to Philomena.* Is it true Gazelle Nataways won the bingo last night?

PHILOMENA: Annie Cook, first you say you're gonna come with me and then you don't even bother showing up. If you were sitting beside me at that bingo table last night you would have seen Gazelle Nataways win the big pot again with your own two eyes.

ANNIE: Emily Dictionary and I went to Little Current to listen to Fritz the Katz.

PELAJIA: What in God's name kind of a band might that be?

ANNIE: Country rock. My favorite. Fritz the Katz is from Toronto.

PELAJIA: Fritzy . . . ritzy . . . Philomena! Say something.

PHILOMENA: My record player is in Espanola getting fixed.

ANNIE: That's nice.

PHILOMENA: Good.

ANNIE: Is it true Gazelle Nataways plans to spend her bingo money to go to Toronto with . . . with Big Joey?

PHILOMENA: Who wants to know? Emily Dictionary?

233

TOMSON HIGHWAY

ANNIE: I guess so.

PELAJIA: That Gazelle Nataways gonna leave all her babies behind and let them starve to death?

ANNIE: I guess so. I don't know. I'm asking you.

PELAJIA AND PHILOMENA: We don't know.

ANNIE: I'm on my way to Marie-Adele's to pick her up.

PELAJIA: Why? Where you gonna put her down?

Pelajia and Philomena laugh.

ANNIE: I mean, we're going to the store together. To the post office. We're going to pick up a parcel. They say there's a parcel for me. They say it's shaped like a record. And they say it's from Sudbury. So it must be from my daughter, Ellen . . .

PELAJIA AND PHILOMENA: . . . "who lives with this white guy in Sudbury" . . .

ANNIE: How did you know?

PHILOMENA: Everybody knows.

ANNIE: His name is Ray<u>mond</u>. Not <u>Ray</u>mond. But Ray<u>mond</u>. Like in Bon Bon.

Philomena tries out "bon bon" to herself.

He's French.

PELAJIA: Oh?

ANNIE: Garage mechanic. He fixes cars. And you know, talking about Frenchmen, that old priest is holding another bingo next week and when I win . . .

To Philomena.

Are you going?

PELAJIA: Does a bear shit in the woods?

2 3 4 ANNIE: . . . when I win, I'm going to Espanola and play the bingo there. Emily Dictionary says that Fire Minklater can give us a ride in her new car. She got it through Ray<u>mond</u>'s garage. The bingo in Espanola is bigger. And it's better. And I'll win. And then I'll go to Sudbury, where the bingos are even bigger and better. And then I can visit my daughter, Ellen . . .

PELAJIA: . . . "who lives with this white guy in Sudbury" . . .

ANNIE: . . . and go shopping in the record stores and go to the hotel and drink beer quietly—not noisy and crazy like here—and listen to the live bands. It will be so much fun. I hope Emily Dictionary can come with me.

PHILOMENA: It's true. I've been thinking . . .

PELAJIA: You don't say.

PHILOMENA: It's true. The bingos here are getting kind of boring . . .

ANNIE: That old priest is too slow and sometimes he gets the numbers all mixed up and the pot's not big enough.

PHILOMENA: And I don't like the way he calls the numbers. *Nasally.* B 12, O 64.

ANNIE: When Little Girl Manitowabi won last month . . .

PHILOMENA: She won just enough to take a taxi back to Buzwah.

ANNIE: That's all.

Both Annie and Philomena pause to give a quick sigh of yearning.

PHILOMENA: Annie Cook, I want that big pot.

ANNIE: We all want big pots.

PELAJIA: Start a revolution!

PHILOMENA AND ANNIE: Yes!

Highway is perhaps the first Canadian member of the international tradition of accomplished writers who work in their second language. . . . The fact that Highway's first language is Cree contributes to his unusual dramatic style. As Highway points out, Cree differs from English in three obvious ways. First, he says, "[it] is hilarious. When you talk Cree, you laugh constantly." Second, it is visceral, in the sense that bodily functions are discussed openly and casually. Finally, words in Cree have no gender. The impact of these three qualities on Highway's plays goes beyond language to their mythopoetic core. . . .

—Denis W. Johnston, "Lines and Circles: The 'Rez' Plays of Tomson Highway," in *Canadian Literature,* Spring–Summer 1990.

ANNIE: All us Wasy women. We'll march up the hill, burn the church hall down, scare the priest to death, and then we'll march all the way to Espanola, where the bingos are bigger and better . . .

PHILOMENA: We'll hold big placards!

ANNIE: They'll say: "Wasy women want bigger bingo!"

PELAJIA: And one will say: "Annie Cook Wants Big Pot!"

PHILOMENA: . . . and the numbers at those bingos in Espanola go faster and the pots get bigger by the week. Oh, Pelajia Patchnose, I'm getting excited just thinking about it!

ANNIE: I'm going.

PELAJIA: You are, are you?

ANNIE: Yes. I'm going. I'm running out of time. I'm going to Marie-Adele's house and then we'll walk to the store together to pick up the parcel—I'm sure there'll be a letter in it, and Marie-Adele is expecting mail, too—and we'll see if Emily Dictionary is working today and we'll ask her if Fire Minklater has her new car yet so we can go to Espanola for that big pot.

She begins to descend the ladder.

PELAJIA: Well, you don't have much to do today, do you?

ANNIE: Well. Toodle-oo!

And she pops down the ladder and is gone.

PELAJIA: Not bad for someone who was in such a hurry to get her parcel. She talks faster than she walks.

Noticing how dejected and abandoned Philomena looks, she holds up her hammer.

Bingo money. Top quality. $24.95.

PHILOMENA: It's true. Bingo here in Wasy are getting smaller and smaller all the time. Especially now when the value of the dollar is getting lesser and lesser. In the old days, when Bingo Betty was still alive and walking these dirt roads, she'd come to every single bingo and she'd sit there like the Queen of Tonga, big and huge like a roast beef, smack-dab in the middle of the bingo hall. One night, I remember, she brought two young cousins from the city—two young women, dressed real fancy, like they were going to Sunday church—and Bingo Betty made them sit one on her left, with her three little bingo cards, and one on her right, with her three little ones. And Bingo Betty herself sat in the middle with 27 cards. Twenty seven cards! Amazing.

Pelajia starts to descend the ladder, and Philomena, getting excited, steps closer and closer to the edge of the roof.

And those were the days when they still used bingo chips, not these dabbers like nowadays, and everyone came with a little margarine container full of these bingo chips. When the game began and they started calling out the numbers, Bingo Betty was all set, like a horse at the race-track in Sudbury, you could practically see the foam sizzling and bubbling between her teeth. Bingo Betty! Bingo Betty with her beady little darting eyes, sharp as needles, and her roly-poly jiggledy-piggledy arms with their stubby little claws would go: chiga-chiga-chiga-chiga-chiga-chiga arms flying across the table smooth as angel's wings chiga-chiga-chiga-chiga-chiga-chiga-woosh! Cousin on the left chiga- chiga, cousin on the right chiga, chiga-eeee!

She narrowly misses falling off the roof and cries out in terror.

PELAJIA: Philomena!

PHILOMENA: *Scrambling on hands and knees to Pelajia, and coming to rest in this languorous pose, takes a moment to regain her composure and catch her breath.* And you know, to this very day, they say that on certain nights at the bingo here in Wasy, they say you can see Bingo Betty's ghost, like a mist, hovering in the air above the bingo tables, playing bingo like it's never been played before. Or since.

PELAJIA: Amazing! She should have gone to Toronto.

Black-out.

The same day, same time, in Wasaychigan Hill. Marie-Adele Starblanket is standing alone outside her house, in her yard, by her 14-post white picket fence. Her house is down the hill from Pelajia Patchnose's, close to the lake. A seagull watches her from a distance away. He is the dancer in white feathers.

Through this whole section, Nanabush (i.e. Nanabush in the guise of the seagull), Marie-Adele, and Zhaboonigan play "games" with each other. Only she and Zaboonigan Peterson can see the spirit inside the bird and can sort of (though not quite) recognize him for who he is. A doll belonging to a little girl lies on the porch floor. Marie-Adele throws little stones at the seagull.

MARIE-ADELE: Awus! Wee-chee-gis. Ka-tha pu-g'wun-ta oo-ta pee-wee-sta-ta-gu-mik-si. Awus! Neee. U- wi-nuk oo-ma kee-tha ee-tee-thi-mi-soo-yin holy spirit chee? Awus! Hey, maw ma-a oop-mee tay-si-thow u-wu seagull bird. I-goo-ta poo-goo ta-poo. Nu-gu-na-wa-pa-mik. Nu-gu-na-wa-pa-mik.

NANABUSH: As-tum.

MARIE-ADELE: Neee. Moo-tha ni-gus-kee-tan tu-pi-mi-tha-an. Moo-tha oo-ta-ta-gwu-na n'tay-yan. Chees-kwa. *Pause.* Ma-ti poo-ni-mee-see i-goo-ta wee-chi-gi-seagull bird come shit on my fence one more time and you and anybody else look like you cook like stew on my stove. Awus! [2]

Veronique St. Pierre "passes by" with her adopted daughter Zhaboonigan Peterson.

VERONIQUE: Talking to the birds again, Marie-Adele Starblanket?

MARIE-ADELE: Aha. Veronique St. Pierre. How are you today?

VERONIQUE: Black Lady Halked's sister-in-law Fire Minklater, Fire Minklater's husband, just bought Fire Minklater a car in Sudbury.

MARIE-ADELE: New?

VERONIQUE: Used. They say he bought if from some Frenchman, some garage. Cray-<u>on</u>.

MARIE-ADELE: Ray<u>mond</u>.

VERONIQUE: These Frenchmen are forever selling us their used cars. And I'm sure that's why Black Lady Halked has been baring those big yellow teeth of hers, smiling all over the reserve recently. She looks like a hound about to pounce on a mouse, she smiles so hard when she smiles. I'd like to see her smile after plastic surgery. Anyway. At the bingo last night she was hinting that it wouldn't be too long before she would be able to go to the bingo in Espanola more frequently. Unfortunately, a new game started and you know how Black Lady Halked has to concentrate when she plays bingo—her forehead looks like corduroy, she concentrates so hard—so I didn't get a chance to ask her what she meant. So. Fire Minklater has a used car. Imagine! Maybe I can make friends with her again. NO! I wouldn't be caught dead inside her car. Not even if she had a brand-new Cadillac. How are your children? All 14 of them.

238

MARIE-ADELE: Okay, I guess.

VERONIQUE: Imagine. And all from one father. Anyway. Who will take care of them after you . . . ahem . . . I mean . . . when you go to the hospital?

MARIE-ADELE: Eugene.

ZHABOONIGAN: Is he gentle?

MARIE-ADELE: Baby-cakes. How are you?

ZHABOONIGAN: Fine.

Giggles.

VERONIQUE: She's fine. She went berry-picking yesterday with the children.

ZHABOONIGAN: Where's Nicky?

MARIE-ADELE: Nicky's down at the beach.

ZHABOONIGAN: Why?

MARIE-ADELE: Taking care of Rose-Marie.

ZHABOONIGAN: Oh.

MARIE-ADELE: Yup.

ZHABOONIGAN: Me and Nicky, ever lots of blueberries.

MARIE-ADELE: Me and Nicky picked lots of blueberries.

ZHABOONIGAN: I didn't see you there.

MARIE-ADELE: When?

ZHABOONIGAN: Before today.

MARIE-ADELE: How come Nicky didn't come home with any?

ZHABOONIGAN: Why?

Marie-Adele shrugs. Zhaboonigan imitates this, and then pretends she is stuffing her mouth with berries.

MARIE-ADELE: Aw, yous went and made pigs of yourselves.

2 3 9

ZHABOONIGAN: Nicky's the pig.

MARIE-ADELE: Neee.

ZHABOONIGAN: Are you going away far?

MARIE-ADELE: I'm not going far.

ZHABOONIGAN: Oh. Are you pretty?

Marie-Adele, embarrassed for a moment, smiles and Zhaboonigan smiles, too.

MARIE-ADELE: You're pretty, too.

Zhaboonigan tugs at Marie-Adele's shoelaces.

Oh, Zhaboonigan. Now you have to tie it up. I can't bend too far cuz I get tired.

Zhaboonigan tries to tie the shoelaces with great difficulty. When she finds she can't she throws her arms up and screams.

ZHABOONIGAN: Dirty trick! Dirty trick!

She bites her hand and hurts herself.

MARIE-ADELE: Now, don't get mad.

VERONIQUE: Stop it. Stop it right now.

ZHABOONIGAN: No! No!

MARIE-ADELE: Zha. Zha. Listen. Listen.

ZHABOONIGAN: Stop it! Stop it right now!

MARIE-ADELE: Come on Zha. You and I can name the koo-koos-suk. [3] All 14 of them.

ZHABOONIGAN: Okay. Here we go.

Marie-Adele leads Zhaboonigan over to the picket fence and Veronique follows them.

ZHABOONIGAN: *To Veronique.* No.

Veronique retreats, obviously hurt.

MARIE-ADELE: *Taking Zhaboonigan's hand and counting on the 14 posts of her white picket fence.* Simon, Andrew, Matthew, Janie, Nicky, Ricky, Ben, Mark, Ron, Don, John, Tom, Pete, and Rose-Marie. There.

Underneath Marie-Adele's voice, Zhaboonigan has been counting.

ZHABOONIGAN: One, two, three, four, five, six, seven, eight, nine, ten, eleven, twelve, thirteen, fourteen.

Giggles.

MARIE-ADELE: Ever good counter you, Zhaboonigan.

ZHABOONIGAN: Yup.

VERONIQUE: This reserve, sometimes I get so sick of it. They laugh at me behind my back, I just know it. They laugh at me and Pierre St. Pierre because we don't have any children of our own. "Imagine, they say, she's on her second husband already and she still can't have children!" They laugh at Zhaboonigan Peterson because she's crazy, that's what they call her. They can't even take care of their own people, they'd rather laugh at them. I'm the only person who would take Zhaboonigan after her parents died in that horrible car crash near Manitowaning on Saturday November 12, 1964 may they rest in peace. *She makes a quick sign of the cross without skipping a beat.* I'm the only one around here who is kind enough. And they laugh at me. Oh, I wish I had a new stove, Marie-Adele. My stove is so old and broken down, only two elements work anymore and my oven is starting to talk back at me.

MARIE-ADELE: Get it fixed.

VERONIQUE: You know that Pierre St. Pierre never has any money. He drinks it all up.

She sighs longingly.

Some day! Anyway. Zhaboonigan here wanted to go for a swim so I thought I'd walk her down—drop by and see how you and the children are doing—it will do my weak heart good, I was saying to myself.

MARIE-ADELE: Awus!

As she throws a pebble at the seagull on the stone, Veronique, for a second, thinks it's her Marie-Adele is shooing away. There is a brief silence broken after awhile by Zhaboonigan's little giggle.

VERONIQUE: Anyway. I was walking down by that Big Joey's shameless little shack just this morning when guess who pokes her nose out the window but Gazelle Nataways—the nerve of that woman. I couldn't see inside but I'm sure she was only half-dressed, her hairdo was all mixed up and she said to me: "Did you know, Veronique St. Pierre, that Little Girl Manitowabi told me her daughter, June Bug McLeod, just got back from the hospital in Sudbury where she had her tubes tied and told her that THE BIGGEST BINGO IN THE WORLD is coming to Toronto?"

MARIE-ADELE: When?

VERONIQUE: I just about had a heart attack.

MARIE-ADELE: When?

VERONIQUE: But I said to Gazelle anyway: Is there such a thing as a BIGGEST BINGO IN THE WORLD? And she said: Yes. And she should know about these things because she spends all her waking and sleeping hours just banging about in bed with the biggest thing on Manitoulin Island, I almost said.

MARIE-ADELE: This bingo. When?

VERONIQUE: She didn't know. And now that I think of it, I don't know whether to believe her. After all, who should believe a woman who wrestles around with dirt like Big Joey all night long leaving her poor babies to starve to death in her empty kitchen? But if it's true, Marie- Adele, if it's true that

241

THE BIGGEST BINGO IN THE WORLD is coming to Toronto, I'm going and I want you to come with me.

MARIE-ADELE: Well . . .

VERONIQUE: I want you to come shopping with me and help me choose my new stove after I win.

MARIE-ADELE: Hang on . . .

VERONIQUE: They have good stoves in Toronto.

MARIE-ADELE: Let's find out for sure. Then we start making plans.

VERONIQUE: Maybe we should go back and ask that Gazelle Nataways about this. If she's sure.

MARIE-ADELE: Maybe we should go and ask June Bug McLeod herself.

VERONIQUE: We can't walk to Buzwah and I'm too old to hitch-hike.

MARIE-ADELE: There's Eugene's van. He'll be home by six.

VERONIQUE: I want to find out NOW. But what if people see us standing at Big Joey's door?

MARIE-ADELE: What do you mean? We just knock on the door, march right in, ask the bitch, and march right out again.

VERONIQUE: Zhaboonigan dear, wait for me over there.

She waits until Zhaboonigan is safely out of earshot and then leans over to Marie-Adele in a conspiratorial whisper.

Anyway. You must know, Marie-Adele, that there's all kinds of women who come streaming out of that house at all hours of the day and night. I might be considered one of them. You know your youngest sister, Emily Dictionary, was seen staggering out of that house in the dead of night two nights ago?

MARIE-ADELE: Veronique St. Pierre, what Emily Dictionary does is Emily's business.

Annie Cook enters, walking fast and comes to a screeching halt.

ANNIE: Hallooooo! Whatchyou doin'?

VERONIQUE: *Giving Annie the baleful eye.* How are you?

ANNIE: High as a kite. Just kidding. Hi, Zha.

ZHABOONIGAN: Hi.

Giggles. She runs toward Marie-Adele, bumping into Annie en route.

ANNIE: Hey, Marie-Adele.

ZHABOONIGAN: Marie-Adele. How's your cancer?

Giggles and scurries off laughing.

VERONIQUE: Shkanah, Zhaboonigan, sna-ma-bah . . . [4]

MARIE-ADELE: Come on, before the post office closes for lunch.

VERONIQUE: You didn't tell me you were going to the store.

ANNIE: Well, we are.

To Marie-Adele.

Hey, is Simon in? I'm sure he's got my Ricky Skaggs album. You know the one that goes *Sings.* "Honeee!"

Calling into the house.

Yoo-hoo, Simon!

MARIE-ADELE: He's in Espanola with Eugene.

VERONIQUE: Expecting mail, Annie Cook?

ANNIE: A parcel from my daughter, Ellen, who lives with this guy in Sudbury . . .

VERONIQUE: So I've heard.

ANNIE: And my sister here is expecting a letter, too.

VERONIQUE: From whom?

ANNIE: From the doctor, about her next check-up.

VERONIQUE: When?

MARIE-ADELE: We don't know when. Or where. Annie, let's go.

ANNIE: They say it's shaped like a record.

VERONIQUE: Maybe there'll be news in that parcel about THE BIGGEST BINGO IN THE WORLD!

Shouts toward the lake, in a state of great excitement.

Zhaboonigan! Zhaboonigan! We're going to the store!

ANNIE: THE BIGGEST BINGO IN THE WORLD?

VERONIQUE: In Toronto. Soon. Imagine! Gazelle Nataways told me. She heard about it from Little Girl Manitowabi over in Buzwah who heard about it from her daughter June Bug McLeod who just got back from the hospital in Sudbury where she had her tubes tied I just about had a heart attack!

ANNIE: Toronto?

MARIE-ADELE: We gotta find out for sure.

ANNIE: Right.

243

MARIE-ADELE: We could go to Big Joey's and ask Gazelle Nataways except Veronique St. Pierre's too scared of Gazelle.

VERONIQUE: I am not.

ANNIE: You are too.

MARIE-ADELE: We could wait and borrow Eugene's van . . .

VERONIQUE: I am not.

ANNIE: . . . drive over to Buzwah . . .

MARIE-ADELE: . . . and ask June Bug McLeod . . .

ANNIE: . . . but wait a minute! . . .

MARIE-ADELE AND ANNIE: Maybe there IS news in that parcel about this BIGGEST BINGO IN THE WORLD!

MARIE-ADELE: Come on.

VERONIQUE: *Shouting toward the lake.* Zhaboonigan! Zhaboonigan!

ANNIE: And here I was so excited about the next little bingo that old priest is holding next week. Toronto! Oh, I hope it's true!

VERONIQUE: Zhaboonigan! Zhaboonigan! Zhaboonigan! Dammit! We're going to the store!

Notes

1. Oh, go on. (Ojibway)

2. MARIE-ADELE: Go away! You stinking thing. Don't coming messing around here for nothing. Go away! Neee. Who the hell do you think you are, the Holy Spirit? Go away! Hey, but he won't fly away, this seagull bird. He just sits there. And watches me. Watches me.

NANABUSH: Come.

MARIE-ADELE: Neee. I can't fly away. I have no wings. Yet. *Pause.* Will you stop shitting all over the place you stinking seagull bird etc. (Cree).

(Note: "Neee" is a very common Cree expression with the approximate meaning of "Oh you.")

3. The little pigs. (Cree).

4. Shush, Zhaboonigan, don't say that. (Ojibway)

LINDA  HOGAN

Essay by

PHYLLIS

"PICTURESTONE"

NOAH

Linda Hogan has played a prominent role in the development of contemporary Native American poetry, particularly in its relationship to environmental and antinuclear issues. She has stated that her father and grandparents imbued her with a strong appreciation for Native American legends and the art of storytelling; the Oklahoma landscape, as well as her Chickasaw heritage, provided her with an equally strong belief in the sacredness of the earth and all its inhabitants.

Hogan began publishing poetry in 1975, and issued her first collection, a chapbook entitled *Calling Myself Home*, in 1979. Like much of her later work, these poems are grounded in her familial and tribal history and written in simple, graceful language that relates both personal and universal revelations. In 1981 Hogan published the verse collection *Daughters, I Love You*, an indictment of nuclear proliferation, and produced her play, *A Piece of Moon*, which garnered the Five Civilized Tribes Museum Award for drama. Subsequent publications include several volumes of poetry and short stories, as well as a mystery novel entitled *Mean Spirit*, which portrays the illegal reclamation of oil-rich Osage reservation land by the U.S. government during the 1920s.

Regarded as an accomplished writer, Hogan deftly combines her activist leanings with lyrical fiction and poetry. Throughout her work Hogan has championed nature, tribal life, and the traditions of Native Americans. Most critics agree that her spiritual attitude toward the natural world and her confrontational attitude toward all forces detrimental to the human spirit raise the impact of her work above the ordinary.

2 4 5

Chickasaw poet, short story writer, novelist, play-wright, and essayist.

Born: July 16, 1947, in Denver, Colorado.

Partnerships: married Pat Hogan (divorced); chil-dren: Sandra Dawn Protector, Tanya Thunder Horse.

Education: University of Colorado at Boulder, M.A., 1978.

Career: University of Colorado, Boulder, instructor in creative writing, fiction, and Native American lit-erature, 1977–79; Colorado Women's College, Col-orado Springs, instructor in creative writing and English, 1979; Rocky Mountain Women's Institute, University of Denver, Denver, CO, associate in pro-gram, 1979–80; poet-in-schools for states of Col-orado and Oklahoma, 1980–84; workshop facilitator in creative writing and creativity, Arvada Center for the Performing Arts Womanschool Network,

1981–84; Colorado College Institutes, Colorado Springs, assistant professor of English in TRIBES program, 1982–84; University of Minnesota—Twin Cities, Minneapolis, associate professor of American and American Indian studies, 1984–89; University of Colorado, Boulder, associate professor of English, 1989–. Has also worked variously as a nurse's aide, dental assistant, waitress, homemaker, secretary, administrator, teacher's aide, library clerk, freelance writer, and researcher; member of board of directors of Denver Indian Center, 1979; organizer of Col-orado Cultural Congress. Volunteer worker at Min-nesota Wildlife Rehabilitation Clinic.

Memberships: National American Studies Program, National Council of Teachers of English, Modern Language Association of America.

Address: P.O. Box 141, Idledale, CO 80453.

Hogan's admirers have perceived the political nature of her writing as not merely insightful and relevant, but absolutely central to her function as an honest and enlightened social commentator.

HERITAGE

From *Red Clay*, Greenfield Review Press, copyright © 1991 by Linda Hogan

From my mother, the antique mirror
where I watch my face take on her lines.
She left me the smell of baking bread
to warm fine hairs in my nostrils,
she left the large white breasts that weigh down
my body.

From my father I take his brown eyes,
the plague of locusts that leveled our crops,
they flew in formation like buzzards.

From my uncle the whittled wood
that rattles like bones

2 4 6

and is white
and smells like all our old houses
that are no longer there. He was the man
who sang old chants to me, the words
my father was told not to remember.

From my grandfather who never spoke
I learned to fear silence.
I learned to kill a snake
when begging for rain.

And grandmother, blue-eyed woman
whose skin was brown,
she used snuff.
When her coffee can full of black saliva
spilled on me

LINDA **HOGAN**

it was like the brown cloud of grasshoppers
that leveled her fields.
It was the brown stain
that covered my white shirt.
That sweet black liquid like the food
she chewed up and spit into my father's mouth
when he was an infant.

It was the brown earth of Oklahoma
stained with oil.
She said tobacco would purge your body of poisons.
It has more medicine than stones and knives
against your enemies.
That tobacco is the dark night that covers me.

She said it is wise to eat the flesh of deer
so you will be swift and travel over many miles.
She told me how our tribe has always followed a stick
that pointed west
that pointed east.
From my family I have learned the secrets
of never having a home.

CROW

From *Red Clay*, Greenfield Review Press, copyright © 1991 by Linda Hogan

Even though she always has peppermint in her apron pockets, nobody much visits Grandma anymore. Once in a while my brother, Buster, stops by to pick me up and we go out to the flats to see her. Or someone who has moved away returns to town on their summer vacation to look over their old homeplace, trying to pick up the lost pieces of their lives, wanting stories about their kin. They stop by to ask my grandmother where old so-and-so has gone. More often than not, she directs them to the cemetery, peppermint candy in their hands.

"That bag goes out to the car." I point at the brown paper sack. Buster moves the coleus plants and the clay sheep that has grass sprouting from its back like green wool. He snoops in the bag. "The cookies are in the cupboard," I tell him.

He opens the cupboard and rummages around for the Oreos. I have just enamelled the kitchen and the cabinet doors stick. "Leave them open," I say to

Buster. I inspect the kitchen before leaving for Grandma's. It passes my scrutiny, the clean blue paint and the new tablecloth I made of white strawberry-print cotton.

We pack up Buster's Chevy with my clothes, the groceries, my dog Teddy, and the radio I bought for Grandma. We drive past the Drunkard Brethren Church. There are some people, perhaps the choir, standing outside in dark robes. I think we look pretty flashy, passing by in the gold Chevrolet with shining chrome, and the bumper stickers saying *Indian Affairs are the Best,* and *Pilgrim, Go Home.* I sit very straight with my eyelids lowered even though inside my body I am exhilarated, enjoying this ride in my brother's car. We drive past the stand of scrub oak and then turn off the paved road into the silence that exists between towns. The crows fly up off the road, cursing at us. Since his wife isn't along, Buster accelerates and lets the car go almost as fast as it will, "tying on the tachs." We speed along. "I clocked her at one ten," he says. He slows down by the cornfields, and paces himself on out through the flatlands where Grandma lives. It has been raining and everything is moist and bright, the outlines of the buildings cleaner than usual.

When we pull off the road at Grandma's I stay in the car a few minutes to look at the morning glories she had planted. They are blooming, the blue flowers on a vined arch over the old front door. The Heaven Blue circles nod in the ozone-smelling breeze.

Teddy is anxious to get out and go searching for moles. He whines and paces across the back seat. "Let that damn dog out," Buster says, but he opens the door before I can turn around and get to it. Teddy runs out barking, his tail pulling him sideways with joy. Grandma hears. She comes to the door and stands waiting in the shade, surrounded by the morning glories on her front steps. She already has her hand in her apron pocket, ready to lure us with peppermint, when Teddy turns and circles back viciously, barking at

Poetry is a large spiritual undertaking. . . . I have learned that to be spiritually conscious means to undertake a journey that is often a political one, a vision of equality and freedom. It is often to resist, to be a person who has not cooperated in giving up the Self or in joining up with the world that has denied us our full lives and rights. . . . It is a paradox in the contemporary world that in our desire for peace we must willingly give ourselves to struggle. When once the spiritual people could advocate the path of least resistance, now the road to peace is often a path of resistance.

—Linda Hogan, in *I Tell You Now: Autobiographical Essays by Native American Writers,* University of Nebraska Press, 1987.

249

Novel
Mean Spirit, Atheneum, 1990.

Poetry
Calling Myself Home, Greenfield Review Press, 1979.
Daughters, I Love You, Loretto Heights Women's Research Center, 1981.
Eclipse, American Indian Studies Center, University of California, Los Angeles, 1983.
Seeing through the Sun, University of Massachusetts Press, 1985.
Savings, Coffee House Press, 1988.
Red Clay: Poems and Stories, Greenfield Review Press, 1991.

The Book of Medicines, Coffee House Press, 1993.

Stories
That Horse, Pueblo of Acoma Press, 1985.
(Editor with Carol Buechal and Judith McDaniel) *The Stories We Hold Secret: Tales of Women's Spiritual Development*, Greenfield Review Press, 1986.
The Big Woman, Firebrand Press, 1987.

Other
A Piece of Moon (three-act play), first produced in Stillwater, OK, at Okla-

homa State University, October, 1981.
Also author of screenplays *Mean Spirit* and *Aunt Moon*, 1986. Contributor to *What Moves Me Brings Me to Myself*, edited by Lynda Koolish, Indiana University Press. Guest editor of *Frontiers Failures of Love*; essays on human-animal relations.

Work In Progress
A book of poems, tentatively entitled *Hands*; a novel, *The Failures of Love*.

a car that has pulled up silently behind us. I didn't hear the limousine drive up and now Teddy is all around it, barking and raging at the waxed, shining dark metal of the car, and at its tires that remain miraculously clean, even driving through the mud.

"Theodore!" I yell out his proper name, reserved for reprimands and orders. Teddy continues to bark, his golden tail down between his short Dingo legs, his claws digging into the wet red clay. The chauffeur ignores him and goes around stiffly to open the back car door.

Grandma is taking it all in, looking proud and pompous. She respects money but she hates those people who have it. All money is dirty, she has said. It all started with the Rockefellers and their ilk. Now she remains standing very straight and tall, her hand still in the blue-flowered pocket, while a woman is let out of the car and begins walking across the chicken yard. The white woman's shoes are expensive. They are rich beige leather and I feel tense watching her heels dig into the clay soil and the chicken droppings. The muddy clay tries to suck the woman down. The chickens make a path for her, scurrying off and clucking. A copper hen that has been roosting in a tree falls out and screeches, runs off muddy, waddling.

250

I recognize the lady. She stopped in once for a meal at the Hamburger Heaven where Buster used to work. She was out of place and the customers and employees all stared at her. She made them uneasy and they alternately talked too much and too loud, or they were silent. When the order was ready, Buster took several plates around the room and stopped at the woman's table, flustered. He was overly serious in his discomfort, his face tense. Like an accusation, he said, "You're the hamburger." Laughter floated up into the entire room.

I step out close to hear the conversation between Grandma and the woman. Grandma's jaw is tight like trouble is in the air. While they talk, I pull a stamen from a morning glory and suck it.

"I'd like to buy two dozen eggs," says the beige shoe lady, opening her pocketbook and releasing the odor of French perfume and money.

"We're all out of eggs." Grandma still has her hand in her pocket. She avoids looking at the woman's face. She looks past her at the horizon. It is the way she looks through city people, or people with money, as though they aren't there.

I'll take a bag of feed then." The woman is thin and wispy. Her hair falls forward as she opens her wallet. The bills are neatly ordered. I can't help but notice Grandmas eyes on them.

"Haven't had any feed delivered from the co-op as late," says Grandma, nonchalantly. Grandma is the local distributor of feed grain and Watkins products, including the cherry-flavored drink mix. She keeps an entire room neatly stocked with bags of grains and bottles of vanilla, aspirin, vitamins, and linament. And she sells eggs. It is how she supports all those chickens, she claims.

Grandma offers the woman a mint, but the woman refuses and grows huffy. "Perhaps the diet type," I hear Buster say under his breath and I'm sure the woman overheard him because she is clearly put out, and says to Grandma, "Why don't you close all the way down or put a sign out?"

"I'm fixing to once you leave." I can feel a smile under Grandma's words even though her face has no expression and her eyes are blank, staring off into Kansas or some other distant state. The woman doesn't know she is being made fun of, and she wants something else, I can tell. She wants to help Grandma out, to be good to the less fortunate, or something. It is often that way with the rich. But it seems to me that there are some barriers in life that can't be passed through by good deeds or money. Like the time I found a five dollar bill picking it up. It was a fire in my pocket. On the way home I saw a man going through the trash, collecting cans to cash in. I took out the bill and handed it to him. I said I just found it and maybe it was his. He took it, but there was a dreadful and shameful look on his face and I knew then that everyone ought to stay in their own place, wherever that may be, without trespassing on other people's lives. Maybe money just goes where it wants and leaves the rest of us alone.

But Grandma will not be shamed, even though the house looks dilapidated in contrast to the woman and her car. Grandma is proud enough still to plant the flowers and water them with the blue plastic pitcher.

The woman returns to the limousine and they drive away. If it weren't for the recent rain, the car would have covered the morning glories in a cloud of dust. I wonder what it is that made the chauffeur so anxious to leave.

LINDA HOGAN

"Last week she wanted to buy the house,"Grandma says, and takes out two lint-covered peppermint kisses and gives one each to me and Buster.

"This old place?" Buster has no tact. I give him one of my looks which he has said could kill, but he goes on talking. "How much did she offer you? You should have taken it." His cheek is swollen with peppermint. "You are probably sitting on an oil well."

But Grandma loves her home and will never leave it as long as she lives.

Now and then, she is in a bad mood and this is going to be one of those times. Her eyes are sullen. I remind myself of her better moments. Out loud I say to Buster, "Remember the day we took Grandma to town? When she was in such a good humor that she went up to that tall policeman and asked, 'Do you know where any trouble is?'"

Buster's smile begins on the left side of his face, but Grandma ignores what I say. She hands me the egg basket. "Sis, why don't you go out and gather up the eggs?"

Teddy is overjoyed to go with me, looking in the corners of the barn, the storage shed, under old tires on the ground. I find a few eggs in new places, in a batch of damp grass, under the morning glories. Teddy runs in circles and the crows fly up around us. They remind me of stories, like how Old Crow Raven used to be white, white snowy feathers, marble white beak and claws, until one day he got too sure of himself and offered to go to an island of fire and bring back a coal for the two-legged, unwinged people. As he descended to the island, following the orange flames and black smoke billowing up from a hollow tree, he was overcome with the heat and blinded by a thick dark cloud of smoke. Disoriented, he flew straight into the flames and was scorched. That is the reason, people say, why the crows are black. Grandma's theory is that the bird went for the wrong reasons. He didn't really care about the people at all. He just wanted to prove his worth.

When I go inside and set the eggs on the table, Grandma is on one of her lectures about how people are just like blackbirds except they are paling. "Money is turning everybody to white," she says. "All the Indians are going white. Oh, I suppose they still care about their little ones and go to church on Sunday, but all they've got their minds on is the almighty dollar." She stops abruptly while I recount the eggs. There are thirty-one of them, and what with yesterday's eggs around the house, she could have sold the woman four dozen or so. She fixes her gaze on me and the whites around her dark pupils startle me. Even the eggs seem to wobble on the unlevel table. "How come you never come to visit me anymore? I have a hundred grandchildren and no one ever comes out here." It's no use arguing, so I don't answer.

"They're all trying to make a buck, Grandma," Buster says.

Most of the time Grandma doesn't have anyone to talk to and she gets lonely. All of my cousins have been breaking away like spiders, going to cities, to California, marrying and moving. That's why I brought her the radio.

"I don't want to hear anything about money or bucks." Her jaw is tight. She looks straight at Buster.

I turn on the water in the sink and the sound of it running drowns out Grandma's voice. She is still talking about all the Indians out here acting like white people, and about how no one comes to see her. "Those men bullying their sons," she says. "They shoot the birds right out of the air. And money, I wouldn't touch that stuff if you paid me to." And then she notices the radio and becomes quiet. "What's this?"

I dry my hands and plug it in. "I brought it for you. I thought you might like some music." I turn the station selector. Buster says, "You can talk to *that* thing all you want."

I put it on a gospel station, because that is her favorite music. But it's only a man talking and he has a bad voice. *I know my mother went to heaven, harumph, and I had a brother who died and I know he went to heaven.* The man clears his throat. *One by one, we uh, proceed, our candles lighted. We, you, you, I, I think that maybe some of those Europeans haven't reached the heights of Christianity, harumph, that we have, but maybe we have really gone below them and maybe we have, uh, wronged them.*

Buster imitates a rooster, his fists in his armpits. "Bock, Bock," he says. I give him a dirty look.

"Don't you make fun," Grandma says, "The first time I ever heard a radio, don't you know, was Coolidge's inaugural address."

And she starts in again, right over the voice of the radio, about how no one comes to talk to her and how we don't even call her on the telephone. Buster gets angry. He says she's getting senile and he walks out the door and slams it. Grandma and I are silent because he walked out stiff and angry, and the radio says, *"I got saved from the sermons you preach, uh, that's what he said, and from the sermons on your pages in the mail."*

I'm still thinking about going to heaven with a candle, but I hear Buster outside, scurrying around. I look out the window but can't tell what he's doing.

When he returns, he is carrying a crow and tracking in red mud. "How did you catch that?" I ask. Its eyes are wild but it is beautiful with black feathers shining like silk and velvet. I go closer to look at it. "Can I touch it?" I put my hand over the bird. "Is it hurt?"

Buster pulls back and looks me in the eye. His look scares me. He is too intense and his eyes are darker than usual. He takes hold of the wing. "Don't," I say, but he grabs that glorious coal-colored wing and twists it.

L I N D A   **H O G A N**

"Buster!" I yell at him and the crow cries out too.

He throws it down on the floor. I'm too afraid to move. "Now, don't say no one comes to see you. The damn crow won't leave. You can tell him all you want how nobody comes to see you." Buster stalks out and we hear the car engine start. I am standing, still unable to move, looking at the bird turning circles on the floor, and beginning to cry. "Oh, Grandma, how could Buster be so awful?" I go down to pick up the injured bird, but it tries to get away. I don't blame it. There's no reason to be trusting. Grandma is sad too, but she just sits at the table and I know we are both thinking of Buster's cruelty and we are women together for the first time.

I turn off the radio and I am thinking of all the poor earthly creatures.

There is a cardboard box in the Watkins room so I go in to get it for the bird and notice that the room is full of the feed Grandma refused to sell the beige shoe lady.

Grandma has already broken a stick and is fitting it to the bird's wing. It is quiet in her hands. I strip off a piece of red calico cotton from her quilting cloth. She takes it in her wrinkled hand and wraps the smooth wing.

"I hate him," I say. "He's always been mean." But Grandma doesn't say anything. She is busy with the crow and has placed it in the box on a nest of paper towels.

"I guess that's what happens to people who think about money all the time," she says. "They forget about the rest of life. They pay no mind to the hurts of each other or the animals. But the Bible teaches me not to judge them." Still, she says nothing else about money or visitors.

The crow listens when Grandma talks. For several days it has been nodding its head at her and following her with its eyes. It listens to the gospel radio, too. "That crow is a heartbreaker," she says. "Just look at him." I hope it isn't true. It is a lovely bird and sometimes it cries out weakly. It has warm black wings and eyes made of stolen corn. I am not a crow reverencer, but I swear that one night I heard it talking to Grandma and it was saying that no one comes to visit.

Grandma is telling it a story about the crows. "They were people and used to speak our tongues," she tells it. It listens. It is raining outside and the rain is hitting the windows. The earth is full of red puddles and they are moving. Somewhere outside, a door is slamming open and closed in the wind.

"You'd like that rain water," she tells the crow. "Make your feathers soft."

Though I am mad at Buster, I can see that he was right. This bird and Grandma are becoming friends. She feeds it grain and corn. It rides on her shoulder and is the color her hair used to be. Crow pulls at the strands of her gray hair. It is like Grandma has shed a skin. She is new and soft, a candle-light inside her.

"Bird bones heal pretty fast," she tells me. "Not like ours."

"Can we listen to something besides gospel for a while?" I ask her. She ignores the question so I go into the bedroom to read a magazine and take a nap. The phone rings and I hear grandmother talking and then the radio goes off and the front door opens and closes. I get up and go out into the kitchen but it is silent, except for the bird picking at the cardboard box.

For a moment I consider putting him out in the rain, splint and all, he looks so forlorn. But Grandma would never forgive me. I ask him, "Have you heard that money is evil?"

Teddy is barking at the front door. It's Buster. Even the dog is unkind to him, growling back in his throat. Buster wants to see if we need anything or if I am ready to go home. I don't speak to him and he sits down on the sofa to read the paper. I stay in the kitchen with Crow.

A house without its tenant is a strange place. I notice for the first time that without Grandma's presence, the house smells of Vicks and old wool. Her things look strange and messy, even the doilies on the couch and end tables are soiled. The walls are sweating and the plaster is stained. I can see Buster sitting on the sofa reading the paper and I decide to tell him I think he is beyond forgiveness.

"Leave me alone." He stands up. His pants ride low and he puts his hands in his pockets and pushes the pants down lower. It is a gesture of intim-idation. "She's got company, hasn't she? And maybe that crow will teach her how to behave." He says he is bringing a cage and I say a cage is no place for a wild bird that longs to be outside in the free air. We are about to get into it when Grandma returns. She is crying. "I ought to kill myself," she says.

We grow quiet and both look down at the floor. I have never seen her cry except at funerals, and I sneak glances up at her now and then while she is crying, until she tells me, "Quit gawking. I just lost all my money."

"Your money?" I am struck stupid. I am surprised. I know she never believed in banks and I thought she didn't believe much in money either. I didn't know she had any. I worry about how much she lost. By her tears, I can tell it wasn't just the egg money.

"I hid it in the umbrella because I was scared of robbers, and I lost it in the rain. When I went back looking for it, it wasn't there." She checks inside the wet umbrella, opening and closing it as if she couldn't believe its absence, running her hand around the spokes. "I forgot I hid it there. I just plain forgot," she wails. "I used to keep it in the cupboard until I heard about the burglars."

L I N D A **H O G A N**

Hogan's poetry is dedicated to "gentle women" and her children, and the work looks to reconciliations for the survival of family, community, and the natural world. Her personal visions of Indian continuance come inseparable from contemporary politics and the scars of history. Hogan's voice spans tribes and traditional lands, racial and sexual schisms, Native and mainstream separations, natural expressions of "the people" and the more specialized tongues of contemporary poetry.

—**Kenneth Lincoln, in a foreword to** *Eclipse,* **University of California, 1983.**

There is a circle of water around her on the floor and her face is broken, but she takes two pieces of peppermint from her pocket and absently hands one to each of us, that old habit overpowering grief. "I think I should have sold that woman the eggs."

She has a lot of sorrow bending her back. "I walked up the road as fast as I could, but it was already gone."

She became as quiet as the air between towns. I turn on the radio and it sounds like a funeral with We Shall Gather at the River. Grandma picks up Crow and he seems to leap right to her chest and balance there on one of the old ivory buttons. She reaches into her left pocket and takes out grains of corn.

Grandma's shoes are ruined. She puts them on the stove to dry but they are already curling upward at the toes and the leather soles are coming apart.

"How's your kids, Buster?"

"Pretty good," but he looks glum. He's probably worried about his lost inheritance.

"How's Flora?"

Buster has his ready-made answers. "Well," he drawls, "by the time I met her I knew what happiness was." I chime in, mocking, "But it was too late to do anything about it." I finish the sentence with him. Grandma looks at me, startled, and is silent a moment, and then she begins to laugh.

256

There's nothing else to do, so I get up. "Grandma, you want some eggs?" I turn on the stove. "I'll cook up some eggs and cornmeal pancakes." I wonder how much money she had hidden away.

"I'm all out of molasses," she says. "Plum out."

"Buster will go to the store and get some. Won't you Buster?"

"In this rain?" But he looks at me and I look stern. "Oh sure, yeah, I'll be right back." And he carefully folds the paper and picks up his keys and goes to the door. He is swallowed up by the blowing torrents of water.

I take Grandma's shoes off the stove and put them by the back door.

"Edna fell down the stairs last night," Grandma says, an explanation of where she has been. "Broke her hip."

"How is she?"

"I didn't get to see her. Because of the money. Maybe Buster will take me."

I put some batter in the pan and it sizzles. Crow chatters back at it and it sounds like he is saying how hard it is to be old. I want to put my hand on Grandma's shoulder, but I don't. Instead I go to the window and look out. Crow's lovers or cousins are bathing in the puddles of rain water, washing under their wings and shaking their feathers. I think even though his body is so much like the night sky, he is doomed to live another life. I figure he's going to stay here with Grandma to make up for his past mistakes. I think Grandma is right about almost everything. I feel lonely, I go over and touch her. She clasps my hand tightly and then lets go and pats it. "Your pancakes are burning," she says.

CROSSINGS

From *The Book of Medicines*, Coffee House Press, copyright © 1993 by Linda Hogan

There is a place at the center of earth
where one ocean dissolves inside the other
in a black and holy love;
It's why the whales of one sea
know songs of the other,
why one thing becomes something else
and sand falls down the hourglass
into another time.

Once I saw a fetal whale
on a block of shining ice.
Not yet whale, it still wore the shadow
of a human face, and fingers
that had grown before the taking
back and turning into fin.
It was a child from the curving world
of water turned square,
cold, small.

Sometimes the longing in me
comes from when I remember
the terrain of crossed beginnings
when whales lived on land
and we stepped out of water
to enter our lives in air.

Sometimes it's from the spilled cup of a child
who passed through all the elements
into the human fold,
but when I turned him over
I saw that he did not want to live
in air. He'd barely lost
the trace of gill slits
and already he was a member of the clan of crossings.
Like tides of water,
he wanted to turn back.

I spoke across elements
as he was leaving
and told him, Go.
It was like the wild horses
that night when fog lifted.
They were swimming across the river.
Dark was that water,
darker still the horses,
and then they were gone.

BASIL H. JOHNSTON

A prolific author, Johnston is predominantly concerned with the preservation of his native Ojibway culture. Through retellings of ancient legends and stories, he relates the traditions of Ojibway people with humor and dignity. Johnston was born on the Parry Island Indian Reserve in Ontario, Canada, and received his elementary school education on the Cape Croker Indian Reserve. His experiences at the Spanish Indian Residential School, a boarding school run by the Jesuit order, were the basis for his autobiographical work Indian School Days.

After studying at Loyola College in Montreal in the 1950s and receiving his high school assistant's certificate from the Ontario College of Education in 1962, Johnston joined the Royal Ontario Museum in Toronto in the 1960s to develop a series of Native American history courses. This experience reinforced his interest in Native American mythology, and in 1976 he published *Ojibway Heritage*. His focus on Ojibway tradition and storytelling is also evident in *Tales the Elders Told: Ojibway Legends*, which collects traditional Ojibway tales in English, and *Ojibway Ceremonies*, which relates the relationship between Ojibway rituals and mythology. His most popular book, *Moose Meat & Wild Rice*, is a collection of twenty-two short stories that depict modern Native American life on a fictional reserve, Moose Meat Point.

Critics have praised Johnston's gentle satire of both Native Americans and whites, yet some reviewers have asserted that Johnston's characters are stereotypical and therefore offensive to Native Americans. In response, Johnston and other Ojibway scholars point to the limitations of

Ojibway ethnologist, nonfiction writer, essayist, short story writer, autobiographer, and educator.

Born: July 13, 1929, in Parry Island, Ontario, Canada.

Partnerships: Married Lucie Bella Desroches, July 29, 1959; children: Miriam Gladys, Elizabeth Louise, Geoffrey Lawrence.

Education: Loyola College, Montreal, Quebec, graduated (cum laude), 1954; Ontario College of Education, secondary school teaching certificate, 1962.

Career: History teacher in secondary school, Toronto, Ontario, 1962–69; Royal Ontario Museum, Toronto, lecturer in North, Central, and South American history, 1969–72, member of ethnology department, 1972–. Night school teacher of English, 1965–70; lecturer in Indian culture. Vice-president of Canadian Indian Centre of Toronto, 1963–69; secretary of Indian consultations with Canadian Government, 1968; committee member of Indian Hall of Fame, 1968–70.

Memberships: Indian Eskimo Association, Toronto Indian Club (president, 1957, member of executive committee, 1965–68); Union of Ontario Indians.

Address: Home—253 Ashlar Rd., Richmond Hill, Ontario, Canada. Office—Royal Ontario Museum, 100 Queens Park, Toronto, Ontario, Canada.

translation as a justification for his characterizations. His interest in language, especially the preservation and instruction of his mother tongue, has additionally led to the production of *Ojibway Language Course Outline* and *Ojibway Language Lexicon for Beginners*. Written for the Ministry of Indian and Northern Affairs, both texts are considered vital to the education of students of Ojibway. Johnston's accurate and loving portrayals of customs and ceremonies, his humorous characters, his attention to language, and his desire to preserve his Native heritage for modern readers and students constitutes, as S. Penny Petrone asserts, "an impressive testimony to the richness and diversity of the cultural heritage of Canada's Ojibway people."

SENTENCED TO SPANISH

From *Indian School Days*, Key Porter, copyright © 1988 by Basil Johnston

2 6 0

Most of the 135 inmates of Spanish, ranging in age from four to sixteen, with the occasional seventeen-year-old, came from broken homes; some were orphans, having lost one or both parents; others were committed to the institution as punishment for some misdemeanor; and a few were enrolled by their parents in order to receive some education and training.

The reason for and the mode of my own committal were typical. My parents had separated, and, following the break-up, Mother, my four sisters and I lived with my grandmother for a while.

But unknown to either my mother or my grandmother, the Indian agent and the priest had conferred—with nothing but our welfare in mind, of course—and decided that not even the combined efforts of Grandmother and Mother were enough to look after five children and that they ought to be relieved of two of their burdens.

The decision must have been relayed to Mother, for she told me that I would soon be going on a short trip. So ecstatic was I at the prospect of going abroad that I immediately made preparations and grew more impatient with each passing day. My sister Gladys was to have accompanied me, but two days before departure, much to her dismay and discomfort, she succeeded in getting contaminated by poison ivy.

It is in the hope that the heritage of the Ojibway speaking peoples and their Algonkin brothers and sisters will be a little better understood that this book was written, though it represents but a small portion of the total fund of unwritten tradition. It is one way of perpetuating and enhancing the bequest of our fore-fathers as it is a means of sharing that gift with those whose culture and heritage may be very different but who wish to enlarge their understanding.

—From the author's preface to *Ojibway Heritage.*

On the fateful day, Grandmother and Mother wept as they scrubbed and polished and clothed me in the finest second-hand clothing that they had been able to scrounge at the bazaar. I could not understand why they did not share my pleasure at my good fortune. I tried reassuring them with their own assurances that I would return shortly, but it made little difference. There was something final in their tears and caresses that was lost on me at that moment. Anxious to leave, I waited outside for the car and chauffeur.

He eventually came around the corner dragging a cloud of dust behind him on the dirt road. I waited at the door and loudly announced his arrival. I jammed my cap on, ready to leave forthwith.

Mr. F. Tuffnel did not come in as invited; instead he stood at the doorway, glowering through his rimless glasses and pursing his mouth as if afraid to open it lest he be contaminated.

Mr. Tuffnel unstitched his lips after looking at me and rasped, "Well! Where's the other one?"

"She's sick," Mother replied in her best English. "Got poison ivy, her . . . in bed."

"You sure?" the agent asked, peering inside.

2 6 1

BASIL H. JOHNSTON

"Yeah, you wanna see?" Mother countered. "You don't believe me, you?"

The agent flinched, perhaps not wanting to catch poison ivy. "Well, gotta take two at least," he said, showing that dispensing pills at the agency wasn't his only skill; he could also count. "How about her?" he rasped, pointing at Marilyn, my four-year-old sister, who came running into the house to find out what was going on. "She can go; old enough . . . and that'll make two!" Once more he demonstrated that he could count.

Mother and Grandmother were both appalled. "No! She's too young," they wailed. "She can't go to school yet, she's only four. No!"

But the agent knew how to handle Indians, especially Indian women. "Well! If you don't want her to go, we'll take the whole family. Now! Get her ready. Hurry up!"

Mother and Grandmother whimpered as they washed and clothed my sister.

"Hurry up or we'll miss the ferry!" Mr. Tuffnel urged, looking at his watch and down the road.

When my sister was ready, Mr. Tuffnel placed us in the back seat of his car. We made the ferry at Tobermory in ample time. On board the *Normac,* the agent put us on chairs in the cabin with the order, "Don't you move." By this time, I was getting frightened, not only of the man but of my circumstances as well. Moreover, I was getting downright uncomfortable.

Nature would not leave me alone, and I went in search of the "poop house," which fortunately was just around the corner. But before I got there, I was collared by the agent.

"Where do you think you're going? Didn't I tell you not to move?" And I was shoved and pushed back to my chair. "Now! Don't you move. Do you understand?" The agent wagged a finger in front of my nose for emphasis before he withdrew. Though I could not see him I was certain that he kept an eye on us through narrow crevices from below, above and behind.

Worse, the passengers who were sitting in the cabin began regarding my sister and me as if we were fugitives or dangerous felons. I now began desperately to wish that I had not come on this journey. What my sister's thoughts were I do not know; she just sat and stared ahead.

At this moment of desolation an old man, or so he seemed to me, asked if we wanted anything. I told him that I wanted to go to the toilet and that my sister wanted a drink. Now, I don't know if she did want anything, but I nevertheless spoke on her behalf.

The old man went around the corner and reappeared with the agent, who looked dour.

Legends and Stories
Moose Meat & Wild Rice (stories), McClelland & Stewart, 1978; published as *Ojibway Tales*, University of Nebraska Press, 1993.
Tales the Elders Told: Ojibway Legends (legends), Royal Ontario Museum, 1981.
Tales of the Anishinaubae: Ojibway Legends (legends), University of Toronto Press, 1994.

Young Adult
How the Birds Got Their Colours, Kids Can Press, 1978.
By Canoe and Moccasins, Waapoone Publishing, 1986.

Nonfiction
Ojibway Heritage, Columbia University Press, 1976.
Ojibway Language Course Outline, Ministry of Indian and Northern Affairs (Ottawa), 1978.
Ojibway Language Lexicon for Beginners, Ministry of Indian and Northern Affairs (Ottawa), 1978.
Ojibway Ceremonies, McClelland & Stewart, 1982.
Indian School Days (autobiography), Key Porter, 1988.
Work represented in anthologies, including *Flowers of the Wild*, edited by Ziles Zichman and James Hodgins, Oxford University Press (Toronto),

1982; *First People, First Voices*, edited by Penny Petrone, University of Toronto Press, 1983; and *Contexts: Anthology Three*, edited by Clayton Graves, Thomas Nelson, 1984. Contributor to periodicals, including *Toronto Native Times*, *Ontario Indian*, *Whetstone*, *Sweetgrass*, *Canadian Fiction*, and *Native American Prose and Poetry*.

Work in Progress
Book tentatively called *The Manitous: The Spiritual World of the Ojibway*, scheduled for publication in the United States by Harper Collins and Key Porter in Canada, 1995.

"Okay! You can go to the toilet," he said in a tone that suggested he would have preferred not to let me go; and to make sure that I did not make a getaway, the agent took my arm and conducted me to the lavatory. At the doorway he warned me: "Don't try anything funny!"

Such was my alarm that I could not relieve myself properly; I was certain the squint-eyed agent was peering at me. Finished, I went out, only to be accosted by my captor at the door for escort back to my seat. "Don't move; I'll be watching you," were his words as he slithered around the corner.

The old man came back with two bottles of pop, which my sister and I drank with relish.

"Where'd you get that? Where'd you get those? Where'd you get the money?" Sharp and biting the questions. I almost dropped my pop. It was a good thing that Sis did not understand English, otherwise she would have cried, I'm sure.

"I bought them," the old man said, coming forward and standing beside us. "Anything wrong with that?" he asked pugnaciously.

The agent's lips quivered while some of the ruddiness receded from his face. Gone was the firmness of tone with which he had addressed my mother and grandmother; instead, his voice weakened till it resembled a bleat. "They are my charges. I'm responsible for them. I have to watch . . . because . . . you never know what these two may do."

"What did they do? What can they do? Where are you taking them?" the man demanded.

2 6 3

B A S I L   H .   **J O H N S T O N**

"I . . . I . . . I'm taking them to Spanish . . . a . . . it's a school for bad kids," the agent stammered.

"I know the school," the old man said. "The kids up there are not a bad bunch; in fact, they're a good bunch of kids, so don't give me any baloney about bad kids. Let me look after these two for a while—you don't know how."

The agent slunk out of the cabin under the accusatory stares and whispers of the passengers.

With the old man as our guardian, Sis and I had a pleasant voyage, promenading on the decks and sightseeing while gobbling ice cream, sipping pop and eating chocolate bars. But the agent was in the background lurking—or so it seemed—behind lifeboats and smokestacks or underneath stairwells.

The next thing I remember with clarity was our arrival in the late afternoon at the schools. After my sister was deposited at St. Joseph's, I did not see her for another six weeks. As for me . . . I was driven to St. Peter Claver's school. No sooner did the car stop at the south-west corner of the school than the boys—all of them, it seemed—assembled on the veranda and around the agent's car. Many more had their noses pressed against the school's windows, which were barred by strong-meshed screens bolted to the bricks with heavy-duty eyebolts.

All the boys were dressed alike in beige corduroy riding breeches, beige shirts, grey woollen socks and black leather work boots; all were dark and dirty, their heads shaved bald. Every one of them stared and grinned.

Through this crowd a priest made his way to the car. The agent told him who I was and where I came from. "I'm Father Book!" he said. "Come with me."

With fear and misgiving I followed the priest to the third floor, where he ordered me to shed my clothing. He handed me a bar of carbolic soap and shoved me into a shower. "Scrub. Scrub hard." The shower hissed and then stopped. The curtain opened. Father Book (it was really Father Buck, but because of his German accent I first heard it as "Book") poured some vile-smelling substance on my head that smelled like turpentine and gasoline and coal oil combined. "Wash! Wash good!" The shower resumed. I washed good!

When I emerged from this purge, Father Buck gave me a small green bag with my uniform inside and a pair of work boots. After I had dressed, my guide led me to the dormitory where he assigned me a bed in the junior section. It smelled of piss.

"You are number forty-three," he informed me, prodding me downstairs, so that I stumbled on the metal-topped risers and almost fell. In the recreation hall a large crowd of boys waited, curious to know who the newest inmate might be.

With the command "Outside! Outside!" Father Buck dispersed the boys, who, on their way out, yelled, "German! German! Johnsh [Ojibway for Nose]!"

"Here!" Father Buck growled, shoving me toward a thirteen-year-old boy armed with a pair of clippers.

"Numudubin [Sit down]!" the Indian boy said, pointing to the bench he had dragged out. "Aneesh abi-ondjibauyin [Where are you from]?"

"Nayausheenagameeng [Cape Croker]."

"That's where I'm from," he chirped, flitting from behind to the front of me and examining me from nose to eyeball. "Yeaaaah! I remember you. Geee! I didn't recognize you!" and he laughed as he clipped my hair, which fell in chunks to the floor.

Cheered a little, I looked at him more closely, but I could not recall ever having seen him before.

"What's your name?" I asked him.

"Euge! Eugene! Eugene Keeshig!" he warbled, looking at me from side to side.

"Come on, Keeshig! Hurry up! What's the hold-up?" Father Buck inquired from the doorway.

"Awright, Father." Euge's visage darkened as every muscle stiffened. Almost involuntarily he clenched his fists till his knuckles whitened. "Don' hurry me up. Take my time if I wan' to. No white man's gonna make me hurry . . . this guy's hair is tough, like wires." Euge was defiant, born ready to fight and capable. As bears the badger, so did Father Buck leave Keeshig alone.

"No pries' ain' gonna boss me aroun'," Euge declared, looking at the door as if he were about to run after Father Buck. Then just as quickly as he'd flared up, he calmed down and his expression brightened. "You're my cousin. My Grandma Christine and your Grandma Rosa are sisters." He chatted on, clipping and snipping and shearing. "You know who else is here?"

Johnston is, first and foremost, a storyteller in the tradition of his ancestors. His style is remarkable for its linguistic exuberance, dramatic flair, and energetic affirmation of life. His works constitute an impressive testimony to the richness and diversity of the cultural heritage of Canada's Ojibway people. They also reveal Johnston's ability to nurture, renew, and share it with native and nonnative readers alike.

—Penny Petrone, in *Dictionary of Literary Biography*, Vol. 60, Gale Research Inc., 1987.

BASIL H. JOHNSTON

"No."

"There's Charlie Shoot."

"Yeah?" So that's where my old hunting buddy had disappeared to, just as Miss Burke had predicted—probably for the hunting episode.

"An' there's Hector." I wondered what he was in for.

"That's four of us from the Cape," Euge said. "I better cut your hair 'fore that pries' come back. Never know what he's gonna do. Might hit you with a bat or a strap." Euge clipped and sheared.

Father Buck came back. "You finished?"

"Yeah! I'm finished," Euge replied, his tone and manner surly and disrespectful.

"Come here!" Father Buck said, beckoning with his forefinger. He led me outside toward the north-east corner of the building, where a group of boys about my age were busy shelling peas. He made me sit down on a bench and shoved a bushel of peas in front of me. "Shell these peas! Fast. These are the Canadiens. You are on their team." Father left.

I did not like the Canadiens. I would have preferred to be a Ranger, but I didn't have any choice; moreover, it made no difference.

None of my teammates introduced himself to me; each was too preoccupied with shelling peas; cursing and heaping damnation on all peas. For my part, I was too engrossed with other thoughts—how long I would be in the accursed institution; when I would get home. The more I thought about home and my little sister in "the other place," the more lonesome I became. I guess my thoughts must have slowed my rate of shelling peas, which displeased the teammate next to me. He thumped me between my shoulder blades. "Hurry up! The Maple Leafs an' the Rangers an' the Black Hawks is ahead of us."

Not caring about the Leafs or Rangers or Black Hawks, I promptly belted my teammate in the beak, and the fight was on. But I had the advantage, for when I biffed my teammate, he fell backwards off the bench. I immediately leaped on him, fists flailing; in the assault, we knocked over a couple of bushel baskets of peas.

There were yelps and shouts of, "Come on, Simon [Martin]! Get up! Give it to him!" No one was cheering for me, and that made me angrier. I pummelled Simon even harder until his nose was bloody.

"What means this?" the gruff voice of Father Buck inquired. I felt myself lifted by the collar.

"He started it. He hit me first; he hit me for nothin'," I hastily explained.

266

"He was jus' sittin' there; he wasn' doin' no work, and the Rangers an' the Leafs an' the Hawks was beatin' us. It was his fault. I jis' tol' ' im to hurry up," Simon countered through puffed lips.

"Aha! You like fights, no? But no like work?" Father Buck smirked. "Then you shell Simon's peas, too . . . no? And no supper until all peas finished. Come on, boys; get back to work."

Through tears I looked into the grinning faces of all the Canadiens, Black Hawks, Rangers and Maple Leafs. No doubt the enemy were happy at the dissension within the ranks of the Canadiens. I sat down with my bushel of peas and Simon's half bushel.

While I was shelling peas, Simon came back and shook a fist in my face, threatening, "I'll get you after." The other Canadiens heartily endorsed Simon's intentions with, "Yeah, Simon, get him good. He don' fight fair. He hit you when you wasn' ready. He's a coward!"

Fortunately for me, Euge came back. He sat down with me, cursed the peas with me and helped me shell them. He told the Canadiens who I was and that I was his cousin. The Canadiens were impressed. "Holy Moses, he can fight," they murmured in admiration. With Euge as my protector, I was safe from Simon . . . for a while. But I had thereafter to fight my own battles.

Such was my induction to St. Peter Claver's school. Originally, the Indian residential school had been situated in Wikwemikong on Manitoulin Island, but the building had burned down in 1913 or 1914 and a new school had been constructed in Spanish, Ontario, at the mouth of and on the banks of the Spanish River.

The school itself was located about a mile from Highway 17 and from the town. It was owned, operated and managed by the Jesuits. Across the dirt road was St. Joseph's, a girls' residential school run by a non-accredited order known as the Daughters of Mary.

St. Peter Claver's was more than a school; it was an institution. The main building, a three-storied structure, contained dormitories, classrooms, a study hall, a recreation hall, dining rooms, several lavatories, chapels, a kitchen, a scullery, a pantry, a refrigerated area, corridors, offices, a cloistered area, a laundry room, an infirmary, a bakery and a tailor shop. In the cellar were huge furnaces surrounded by cords of wood, sacks of potatoes, beans and other produce, coal, paint, pipes, boards and other supplies. Near the school were clustered a windmill, a power house and a shoe shop. Close to the river were a mill and storage shed where wheat, corn and anything else that could be milled were milled. There was also an immense barn that sheltered a herd of cows, several teams of horses, a bull of immense carnality for the greater joy of the cows, a dairy operation and, of course, tons of hay and straw and assorted feeds and equipment. Between the barn and the mill were a blacksmith shop, a piggery and a sheepery. In the north-west corner of the complex was the chicken coop, which harboured four hundred chickens and one forlorn and harried rooster. Between the buildings was a playground, bare and hardpacked from years of baseball games and running feet. Fenced off from the playground and stretching from mill to school was the Garden of McLaren (Brother McLaren) yielding tomatoes, cucumbers and boundless temptations. At the wharf were tethered the Garnier, a thirty-foot cruiser-like vessel; the Iron Boat, a former lifeboat, now an all-purpose vessel; the Red Bug, an open-topped rowboat-styled ark used for transporting cattle, boys and girls, and cordwood or heavy equipment under tow by either the Garnier or the Iron Boat; a scow; and several punts. In addition, there were nearly a thousand acres of land in Spanish and in Walford.

The entire institution was as nearly self-sufficient as the mid-north would allow. Under the guidance of priests and brothers, between 130 and 135 boys, with the exception of the four- and five-year-olds, ploughed, seeded and harvested potatoes, beans and other produce; milled the wheat and corn and baked the bread; forged the shoes and shod the horses; mixed the paints and painted the buildings; measured planks and repaired floors; cut the hides and made shoes; cut the bolts of textiles and tailored shirts and pants and pyjamas; fed and tended cows, horses, sheep and swine and even slaughtered them; and swept, dusted and polished floors and furniture. There was little in the entire institution that was not done by the inmates.

For our shelter, food, clothing and education the government doled out forty cents per student per day. Hockey sticks, ball, hats and coats came from donors.

St. Peter Claver's existed for two reasons. One was to train Indian youth for some vocation: tailoring, milling, blacksmithing, shoemaking, tinsmithing, painting, carpentry, baking, cooking, plumbing, welding, gardening, sheep and swine herding, animal husbandry and poultry care. Alas, while there were some accomplished chicken farmers and shoemakers, no graduate went into business; the trades for which we had been trained were rendered obsolete by new technology. The school's other purpose was to foster religious vocations by frequent prayer and adoration. But all the prayers, masses, novenas and benedictions could not overcome the natural resistance of most boys to a career in holy orders. The school produced neither tradesmen nor priests.

MAURICE  KENNY

Born in Watertown, New York, in 1929, Kenny has been a leading figure in the renaissance of Native American poetry since the 1970s. Although his works derive their subject matter primarily from Iroquois traditions and history, he has also written knowledgeably and sympathetically about other groups of Native Americans. His poem "I Am the Sun: A Lakota Chant," for instance, is based on a Lakota Ghost Dance song and was inspired by the 1973 Wounded Knee confrontation in South Dakota.

Kenny's works typically focus on the links between humanity and nature as well as the spiritual forces of renewal and creation. Comparing him to Walt Whitman and William Carlos Williams, critics have praised Kenny's ability to create a world in which humankind and nature are fused and have noted his adept use of oral traditions and such symbolic images as the strawberry, which possesses spiritual power in Mohawk culture.

Kenny has also written poetry about historical incidents involving confrontations between Mohawks and Europeans. *Blackrobe: Isaac Jogues, b. March 11, 1607, d. October 18, 1646,* for instance, centers on the brief career of Isaac Jogues, a Jesuit missionary whom the Mohawks killed in 1646; commentators have praised the work's balanced treatment of French and Native American characters and articulate presentation of the Mohawks' myth-oriented worldview. As Robert Berner has stated: "Kenny's most successful efforts derive from his greatest strength as a poet, his ability to let his theme emerge out of his Mohawk context."

269

Mohawk poet, short story writer, and playwright.

Born: August 16, 1929, in Watertown, New York.

Education: Attended Butler University, Indianapolis, IN; St. Lawrence University, Canton, NY; and New York University.

Career: Writer. Associate professor at Paul Smith's College, Paul Smith's, NY; University of Victoria, British Columbia, Canada; and North Country Community College, Saranac Lake, NY. Visiting professor at University of Oklahoma, Norman. Visiting poet, Lehigh University, 1987. Coordinator of the Robert Louis Stevenson Annual Writers Conference, 1987 and 1988. Has given lectures and read-ings throughout the country, including New York, Minneapolis, and California. Panelist for CAPS (New York state) and Educational Testing Service Arts Recognition and Talent Search, Princeton, NJ. Board member, WCFE-TV, 1989–91. Coeditor of *Contact/II*; publisher of Strawberry Press; advisory editor of *S.A.I.L.*, *Akwesasne Notes*, *Akwekon*, and *Time Capsule*.

Memberships: PEN, Coordinating Council of Literary Magazines (member of board of directors, 1980–86), New York Foundation of the Arts (member of board of governors, 1990–).

Address: Box 1029, Saranac Lake, NY 12983.

LEGACY

From *Between Two Rivers: Selected Poems 1956–1984*, White Pine Press, copyright © 1987 by Maurice Kenny

my face is grass
    color of April rain;
arms, legs are the limbs
    of birch, cedar;
my thoughts are winds
    which blow;
pictures in my mind
    are the climb uphill
    to dream in the sun;
    hawk feathers, and quills
    of porcupine running
    the edge of the stream
    which reflects stories
    of my many mornings
    and the dark faces of night
    mingled with victories
    of dawn and tomorrow;
corn of the fields and squash...
    the daughters of my mother
    who collect honey

2 7 0

S M O K E   R I S I N G

and all the fruits;
meadow and sky are the end of my day
    the stretch of my night
    yet the birth of my dust;
my wind is the breath of a fawn
    the cry of the cub
    the trot of the wolf
    whose print covers
    the tracks of my feet;
my word, my word,
    loaned
legacy, the obligation I hand
    to the blood of my flesh
    the sinew of the loins
to hold to the sun
    and the moon

271

MAURICE KENNY

Poetry

Dead Letters Sent, and Other Poems, Troubador Press, 1958.

With Love to Lesbia, Aardvark Press, 1959.

North: Poems of Home, Blue Cloud Quarterly Press, 1977.

Dancing Back Strong the Nation, introduction by Paula Gunn Allen and illustrations by Rokwaho (Daniel Thompson), Blue Cloud Quarterly Press, 1979.

I Am the Sun: A Lakota Chant, White Pine Press, 1979.

Only as Far as Brooklyn, introduction by Kirby Congdon, Good Gay Poets, 1979.

Blackrobe: Isaac Jogues, b. March 11, 1607, d. October 18, 1646, French translation by Huguette Lapierre, North Country Community College Press, 1982; bilingual edition, Chauncey Press, 1987.

The Mama Poems, White Pine Press, 1984.

Between Two Rivers: Selected Poems 1956–1984, White Pine Press, 1987.

Greyhounding This America: Poems and Dialog, foreword by William M. Kunstler, Heidelberg Graphics, 1988.

Selections, edited and translated by A. Vaschenku, Korky Institute (Russia), 1988.

Tekonwatonti: Molly Brant (1735–1795); Poems of War, White Pine Press, 1992.

Other

Kneading the Blood, drawings by Peter Jemison, Strawberry Press, 1981.

Boston Tea Party, Soup, 1982.

The Smell of Slaughter, Blue Cloud Quarterly Press, 1982.

Is Summer This Bear, Chauncey Press, 1985.

Rain and Other Fictions (stories and drama), Blue Cloud Quarterly Press, 1985; expanded edition, White Pine Press, 1990.

Humors and/or Not So Humorous, Swift Kick Press, 1987.

(Editor and author of introduction) *Wounds beneath the Flesh,* White Pine Press, 1987.

The Short and the Long of It, University of Arkansas Press, 1990.

Last Mornings in Brooklyn (chapbook), Renegade, 1991.

Roman Nose and Other Essays (essays), Howe Brothers, 1991.

On Second Thought: A Compilation of Work, University of Oklahoma Press, in press.

Has also composed poetry for television programs, including *Today in New York,* NBC, 1984; and *Poems, Poets, and Song,* CBS, 1990; and for videos and radio programs. Consulting editor for *New Voices from the Longhouse: An Anthology of Contemporary Iroquois Writing,* edited by Joseph Bruchac, Greenfield Review Press, 1989; author of introduction, *Interpreting the Indian,* University of Oklahoma Press, 1991. Contributor to anthologies, including *Native American Writing,* Greenfield Review Press, 1982, *Harper's Book of Twentieth Century Native American Poetry,* Harper, 1987, and *American Book Award Anthology,* Norton, 1991. Contributor to periodicals, including the *New York Times,* *Small Press Review,* *American Indian Quarterly,* *Saturday Review,* and *Beloit Poetry Journal.*

Work in Progress

What's in a Song (tentative title), short fiction

Loons and Other Peoples: Essays

Angry Rain: A Brief Autobiography

Strangers at the Doors, short fiction

Ceremonies in Summer and Winter, poems

Black-eyed Susan (tentative title), poems

---

which direct the river
that carries my song
and the beat of the drum
to the fires of the village
which endures.

272

THEY TELL ME I AM LOST

From *Between Two Rivers: Selected Poems 1956–1984,* White Pine Press, copyright © 1987 by Maurice Kenny

For Lance Henson

my feet are elms, roots in the earth
my heart is the hawk

my thought the arrow that rides
    the wind across the valley
my spirit eats with eagles on the
    mountain crag
      and clashes with the thunder
the grass is the breath of my flesh
    and the deer is the bone of my
      child
my toes dance on the drum
    in the light of the eyes of the
      old turtle

my chant is the wind
my chant is the muskrat
my chant is the seed
my chant is the tadpole
my chant is the grandfather
    and his many grandchildren
    sired in the frost of March
    and the summer noon of
      brown August
my chant is the field that turns
    with the sun
      and feeds the mice
      and the bear red berries and
        honey
my chant is the river
    that quenches the thirst of the
      sun
my chant is the woman who bore me
    and my blood and my flesh of tomorrow
my chant is the herb that heals
    and the moon that moves the tide
    and the wind that cleans the earth
      of old bones singing in the morning dust
my chant is the rabbit, skunk, heron
my chant is the red willow, the clay
    and the great pine that bulges the woods
    and the axe that fells the birch
    and the hand that breaks the corn from the stalk

I think [Native American themes are] always there. Okay, there's that old bromide that if you're Indian you're going to write Indian. Not necessarily true. That's hogwash, quite frankly. The themes were there because that's what I grew up with. I didn't know there was anything different from that. It was already in my work when I was thirteen, when I was seventeen and heavily influenced by [Walt] Whitman. He was one of the poets I read a great deal. It didn't come out of Whitman, but his being a singer naturally appealed to me. The poems I was writing at that time which were in natural speech, natural rhythm, reflected my Indian background.

—**Maurice Kenny, in** *Survival This Way: Interviews with American Indian Poets,* **1987.**

2 7 3

M A U R I C E   K E N N Y

and waters the squash and catches stars
my chant is a blessing to the trout, beaver
    and a blessing to the young pheasant
        that warms my winter
my chant is the wolf in the dark
my chant is the crow flying against the sun
my chant is the sun
    sleeping on the back of the grass
        in marriage
my chant is the sun
    while there is sun I cannot be lost
my chant is the quaking of the earth
    angry and bold

although I hide in the thick forest
    or the deep pool of the slow river
    though I hide in a shack, a prison
    though I hide in a word, a law
    though I hide in a glass of beer
        or high on steel girders over the city
        or in the slums of that city
    though I hide in a mallard feather
        or the petals of the milkwort
        or a story told by my father

though there are eyes that do not see me
    and ears that do not hear my drum
    or hands that do not feel my wind
    and tongues which do not taste my blood

I am the shadow on the field
    the rain on the rock
    the snow on the wind
    the footprint on the water
    the vetch on the grave
I am the sweat on the boy
    the smile on the woman
    the paint on the man
I am the singer of songs
    and the hunter of fox

274

SMOKE RISING

I am the glare on the sun
    the frost on the fruit
    the notch on the cedar
I am the foot on the golden snake
I am the foot on the silver snake
I am the tongue of the wind
    and the nourishment of grubs
I am the claw and the hoof and the shell
I am the stalk and the bloom and the pollen
I am the boulder on the rim of the hill
I am the sun and the moon
    the light and the dark
I am the shadow on the field

I am the string, the bow and the arrow

275

MAURICE KENNY

THOMAS KING

Essay by

JASON GALLMAN

Of Greek and German as well as Cherokee Indian descent, Thomas King has had to study the Native traditions and cultures that predominate in his works. Regarding how his identity affects his writing, King told Jace Weaver of Publishers Weekly *that "in some ways, I'm this Native writer who's out there in the middle, not of nowhere, but I don't have strong tribal affiliations. My responsibilities are to the story and to the people from whom I get some of the stories. Other than that, I feel rather free to ask some of the really nasty questions that other writers may not want to ask. . . . One of the questions that's important to ask is, 'Who is an Indian? How do we get this idea of Indianness?'" Described as a "Native American Kurt Vonnegut" by Weaver, and compared to a "darkly funny" Mark Twain by Malcolm Jones, Jr., in* Newsweek, *King's storytelling technique has been praised by readers and reviewers alike.*

2 7 7

King's first novel, *Medicine River*, utilizes the strategy of comedy to imply subtle but serious commentary on the continuing domination of Native American Indians and their culture by the white world. At the center of a meandering narrative, which critics have praised for its humorous vignettes and unusual characters, is half-Blackfoot Indian, Will, who makes his living as a photographer, and who is still searching for his identity. In a series of connected stories, King interweaves traditional native cultural values with the modern lives of the characters, many of whom

When someone says, "are you a Native writer?," I take it as a description of me, and who I am, and not my work particularly. So, what they're saying is, "you are a Native who writes." And that is a perfectly good description for me. But if they ask me, "are you a Native writer?" and what they mean is, "are you a writer who happens to be Native who only writes about Native things?," that's a poor description because I write about non-Native material too.

—**Thomas King, in** *Contemporary Challenges: Conversations with Canadian Native Authors*, **edited by Hartmut Lutz, Fifth House, 1991.**

live on the reservation. Will's family and friends—especially the trickster Harlan Bigbear—provide much of the insight and commentary in the novel. M. T. Kelly in a *Globe and Mail* review, declared "it isn't too much of an assumption to see that, below his high tops and basketball sweater, his easy banter and wit, Will does believe in native cultural values, values that are reflected in the culture today." Likewise describing *Medicine River* as much more than a charming tale, Jack Butler in *New York Times Book Review* praised the narrative's "many subtleties" in countering Indian stereotypes, and remarked: "This most satisfying novel ends as it should, not in a clash of cymbals, but with the brushes laid quietly against the drums for a beat or so after the music ends." Kelly's *Globe and Mail* review concluded: "For all its sly parodies . . . its oral structure, its sadness and rushing hilarity, *Medicine River* is a very human book."

Similarly, *Green Grass, Running Water*, King's next novel, features characters in often comical situations where the underlying theme is a serious attempt to define and balance the Indian identity against the surrounding white culture. The title alludes to the standard phrasing of Indian treaties that the land will be theirs "as long as the grass is green and the water runs." Central to the novel, ironically, is a dam which threatens to stop the water and dry up the grass. Uncle Eli, who refuses to move out of the way for construction of the dam, singlehandedly halts the progress, while four mystical elderly Indians, named Hawkeye, Ishmael, Robinson Crusoe and Lone Ranger, escape from a mental hospital and appear determined to restore the natural balance of the environment. Woven throughout the narrative is a talking coyote who tells a creation myth. Malcolm Jones, Jr. lauds the work in *Newsweek*: "Successfully mixing realism and myth, comedy and tragedy (and any writer who can bring off a talking coyote has to be called successful), King has produced a novel that defies all our expectations about what Native American fiction

2 7 8

Cherokee novelist, short story writer, editor, scriptwriter and author of children's books.

Born: 1943.

Partnerships: Married second wife, Helen Hoy; children: three.

Education: Graduated from Chico State College (now California State University, Chico); received Ph.D. from University of Utah.

Career: Novelist and editor. Instructor at University of Lethbridge, Alberta, Canada, beginning in 1980; professor at University of Minnesota. King has also worked as a photojournalist.

Address: St. Paul, MN.

Agent: Denise Bukowski, Bukowski Agency, 182 Avenue Rd., Suite 3, Toronto M5R 2J1, Ontario.

should be. It is a first-class work of art." "I think of myself as a serious writer," King told Jones. "Tragedy is my topic. Comedy is my strategy."

MEDICINE RIVER

Viking Penguin, copyright © 1989 by Thomas King

Chapter Six

I was standing under the basket trying to catch my breath when Raymond Little Buffalo split Frankie's head open. The two of them were going after a rebound. Frankie dove for the ball, and Ray jumped on top of him, cocked his arm and threw an elbow into Frankie's face.

Ray was all apologies. He got a towel and told Frankie to hold it against his head. He even drove Frankie to the emergency room and waited while they put fifteen stitches in the gash above Frankie's eye. The whole time Ray stood around telling jokes, offering encouragements and rubbing his elbow as though it hurt.

"Ray used to be a regular," Harlen told me. "Then he got that job in Calgary. Big oil company. Should have seen the car they gave him. And all those credit cards. Ray took me to lunch once. You know, it cost sixty-five dollars. And the soup was cold. You believe that, Will? Ray said that's the way they do it."

I tried to stay out of Ray's way. On the court, he was unpredictable. He'd slap you on the back and tell you what a great move you had made to get by him. The next time he'd put a knee in your thigh or try to catch you in the face with the back of his head.

279

"Should have seen him, Will, skinny and fast. He got a little fat sitting at that desk in Calgary."

Most of the time, I got to guard Ray. He wasn't fast any more, but you had to be careful when everyone got crowded in the paint.

"People who start off skinny," Harlen told me, "have a tough time being fat because they haven't had time to develop the muscle to carry the extra weight."

Ray still had some good moves, and I generally played off him out of range of his head and elbows and took the rebounds off his missed shots as they came my way.

"People may think you're a little heavy, Will. But you been like that all your life so you got the muscle to manage it."

Off the court, Ray was as friendly as a puppy. Watching him sitting around after practice at Tino's Pizza, laughing, drinking beer, telling the boys about the time he wasn't looking and caught a basketball with his face or the time he had to sleep on the floor in a motel in Medicine Hat because Floyd was in the only bed with two women and how one of the women rolled off the bed in the middle of the night and landed on top of him, you'd never know this was the same Raymond Little Buffalo who forty-five minutes earlier had tried to put you in the hospital.

Harlen, who could always find allowances lying around, said that Ray was still angry about losing that job. "Oil bust put a lot of people out of work. Ray's working for Canada Packers in town now. Must have been hard to give up that Lincoln." Along with allowances, Harlen always had a pocketful of suggestions. "Maybe you could talk him into coming out and playing regular, Will. Ray likes you. Basketball is a great way to forget your problems."

I never said a word to Ray about that. He'd come out about once or twice a month and play, and that was plenty.

I suppose if you don't like someone, you're willing to go looking for faults that most people wouldn't ever see. For instance, Floyd smoked, but I liked Floyd, so I never said much. Ray smoked too, and whenever he'd light up, even if he was clear across the table from me, I'd snort and cough and wave my hand around.

Most of the boys bragged on themselves from time to time: the games they had won with last-minute shots, the women they had slept with, the times they had outrun the cops, the amount of beer they could drink before they passed out. We'd all laugh as though we believed every story. But with Ray it was different. Anything you had done, Ray had done it before and had done it better. If Floyd had a story about a woman with large breasts, Ray would have a story about another woman with huge breasts. If Elwood told about the time the cops threw him in jail in Browning and someone in the drunk tank stole his new sneakers, Ray would have a story about the time he was in jail in Penticton and someone stole all his clothes, and when he woke up the next morning, he was bare-assed naked.

Whenever Ray would start in on one of his stories, I'd snort and cough and wave my hand around.

The stories that Ray liked to tell best were the ones where he won basketball games with incredible last-second shots. Harlen didn't help.

"I remember that alright," Harlen would say. "You were a great player, Ray. Should come back out. Look at Will. Will wasn't too good when he started, but look at him now."

"Ain't no Clyde Whiteman."

"That's for sure. But he's got a pretty good hook."

"Ain't no Clyde Whiteman."

I can remember exactly when it started. I was flying back to Toronto. I hate flying, and whenever the plane hit a bump, I'd grab the seat in front of me. There was an older woman sitting across the aisle.

"I have a son who hates to fly, too," she told me. "And when he flies, he gets just like you. And then, sometimes, he throws up."

I laughed and told her I didn't think I'd throw up, and we started to talk. She told me about her husband, Morris, and her children. Her daughter was a doctor in Victoria, and her son was a dancer in Winnipeg. I told her I had a brother who was an artist. And then she asked me what my father did.

Maybe it was the way she asked the question, smiling, expecting that I had a father and that what he did was worth talking about. Like Morris.

"My father is a senior engineer with Petro-Canada."

"That's wonderful," said the woman. "Morris teaches at the university. English. You must be very proud of your father."

"He's gone a lot of the time. Engineers have to travel around."

"I'm sure he thinks about you and your brother all the time." And she took a plastic folder from her purse and stretched it out on her lap. There was Morris and Laura and William and Pooch the cat.

Ray got himself elected to the Native Friendship Centre board. He was popular, and it didn't hurt that he had had all that executive experience in Calgary. We didn't see him at practice for about two months after that, but when he did come out, he was driving a brand-new Lincoln.

281

THOMAS KING

"Didn't know the centre paid that well," said Floyd.

"Didn't know the centre paid at all," said Ray.

"No wonder you ain't been playing with us," said Elwood. "Been too busy collecting bottles and cans from behind the American."

Ray was all smiles. "Once you drive one of these babies," he said, "you can never go back to Fords or Chevys." Ray opened all four doors and turned on the stereo. "You can't buy a home system that sounds any better. Put your head in there. What you smell is leather."

It was a nice car if you liked that kind of thing.

"The salesman is still picking horse shit off his shoes. Poor bastard didn't know what hit him." Ray put his arm around my shoulder and gestured with his chin towards the car. "You still driving that truck?"

Ray said he'd drive the boys over for pizza. Harlen was going to ride with me, but Ray insisted that there was enough room. "You can ride shotgun," he told Harlen. "You can pick the first tape, too. We'll meet you over there, Will."

I had to stop for gas, and when I got to the pizza parlour, Ray's car wasn't in the parking lot. I sat in my truck and waited for half an hour, and then I went home.

I mean, I wasn't a kid. I was at least twenty-five when I told that woman on the plane that my father was a senior engineer. And there was no reason to do that. I didn't miss him. I didn't even think about him. I had never known the man.

So, I began to invent him.

"My father's a pilot. He flies the big jets for Air Canada.

"Dad's in stocks and bonds.

"He's a career diplomat.

"He's a photographer.

"He's a doctor.

"He's a lawyer."

He was never a rodeo cowboy, and out of consideration for Morris, he was never a university professor either.

Sometimes I'd sit in my apartment and try to think up new professions for my father. And then I'd tell myself to quit fooling around. I'd laugh at myself, shake my head in disgust, promise that I'd stop the whole stupid business. What if I got caught? What if someone back home heard about my father being a rich opal miner in Australia?

(Editor with Cheryl Dawnan Calver and Helen Hoy) *The Native in Literature*, illustrated by Jay Belmore, ECW Press, 1987.
Medicine River, Viking Penguin, 1990.

All My Relations: An Anthology of Contemporary Canadian Native Fiction, University of Oklahoma Press, 1992.
A Coyote Columbus Story, Groundwood, 1992.

Green Grass, Running Water, Houghton Mifflin, 1993.

Ray stopped practising with the team altogether, which was okay with me. Instead he started going to the American Hotel. The American was the local Indian bar, a tall, skinny, brick building wedged in by a surplus clothing store on one side and by an old wood-floored Kresge's on the other. The two floors above the bar were rooms that no one ever rented overnight.

The place had a lot of character. The original owner had been something of a collector, and the walls were hung with Indian artifacts from the 1920s. Before he died, he told Harlen that he had been offered almost a million for his Indian stuff by some big museum back east, but he had told the museum people to piss off, he was going to give it all back to the Indians.

The new owner, a businessman from Edmonton whom no one had ever seen, left everything the same. Tony Balonca ran the place, and most of us thought he owned it, until the night he got a little drunk and told Floyd that if the bar were his, he'd take down the beads and feathers and the rest of the shit and put up a big mural of the Italian coast. Harlen said he'd take the stuff away for Tony, no charge, but Tony said no, the owner liked the quaintness. When Tony said quaint, he curled his lips so you could see his teeth.

I didn't go to the American much, and I wasn't particularly interested in what was happening to Ray. But Harlen's theory on information was that the more you had, the more you knew, which made good sense as far as it went.

"Will, did you hear about Ray?"

"They repossess his Lincoln?"

"His Lincoln? Why would they do that? Where did you hear that, Will?"

Ray had come up with a plan to raise money. The Friendship Centre was always needing money for their community programs, and there wasn't much in yard sales and car washes. Ray's plan was to produce a calendar that featured prominent Indian people of Canada and maybe a few from the States and sell it to companies in Calgary and Edmonton.

"Ray says there are hundreds of businesses that give away calendars every year. You know, Will, like the banks or the auto-supply stores. A lot of those businesses are always saying how much they appreciate Indian people. Ray figures you can sell the calendars in blocks of, say, five hundred for the small businesses, one thousand for the medium-sized companies and two thousand for the oil companies and the government. What do you think, Will?"

"Beats another bake sale."

"That's the spirit, Will. Ray wants you to do the photography work. I told Ray what a great photographer you are, and he said, sure, might as well give the business to one of our own people. He's got a lot of respect for you, Will."

I told Harlen it wouldn't be cheap, that that kind of photography with colour separations and everything was going to be expensive. And then there would be printing costs.

"Not to worry, Will. Ray figures we can maybe get a grant to pay for most of the costs. That way there won't be any risk. Louise is going to do the accounting, and Elwood has a friend in Winnipeg who owns a press."

"Am I doing this for costs?"

"No, Will. Ray said that was bad business. He said to make sure you add in for your time."

"What's Ray going to do?"

"He's going to be in charge. Ray's got the brains for this kind of thing. We're driving over to Calgary next week to talk with the oil companies. Figure while we're in the city, we can look at basketball uniforms, too."

"Uniforms?"

"Sure. Big John said some of the money could go to the team. There might even be enough for new shoes and socks and stuff like that."

Ray stopped by the studio the following week. He wanted cost estimates on the photography work. He was dressed in a good-looking dark blue suit, and he didn't waste any time on words.

"Could mean a lot of money for the centre. We need a top-quality product. The big companies don't buy second-rate stuff. You know what I mean?"

I said that I did, and I said I'd get an estimate to him the first of the week. His Lincoln was parked on Third. I could see it through the window.

The cost was over five thousand dollars, and with my time, it came to almost six thousand. Ray came by with a folder with twelve photographs in it, dropped it on my desk, and said, "Do it."

Three months later, we had our calendar, and it looked good. The first print run was ten thousand. The second run was twenty thousand, and according to Harlen, they were all gone in two months.

"Ray's a great salesman, Will. Thirty thousand calendars. Do you know how much profit that means for the centre?"

"No idea."

"Oh," said Harlen. "Neither do I. I was hoping you knew how these things work."

I only told strangers, but there was always the chance that something would get back to my mother or to James.

"My father is a television producer.

"My father is an investment consultant.

"My father is physicist.

"My father is a computer designer."

I ran out of interesting professions fast, and instead of trying to top each new career I created for him, I began to imagine long and elaborate stories that I could tell again and again, adding to them as I went along.

THOMAS **KING**

Within Native communities, there's a desire to maintain a balance, to make things right if they're wrong—not to make everything good, but to maintain a balance. The old Indians [in my book] recognize that they haven't taken such good care of the world. Things went wrong—as things will. It's like having too many people on a teeter-tooter and never having the right balance. You try for it, and the important thing is that attempt.

—Thomas King, in an interview with Jace Weaver in *Publishers Weekly*, March 8, 1993.

It was best on airplanes, where everyone was a stranger. The conversation helped to take my mind off the fact we were in the air. I even began to look forward to the next opportunity to talk about my father and slowly, over the months and years, he began to take on a particular shape, a distinctive sound.

He was a tall man with a low, pleasant voice. I imagined him best as a free-lance journalist who roamed the world taking his own pictures and writing his stories. He had a slight limp, the result of his plane coming down in the Yucatan. (He was a pilot, too.) Most of his stories were about oppressed people, and he wrote about them with grace and wit. His stories had been published all over, but he generally wrote under pseudonyms because he was a shy man. You've probably read some of his pieces in *Saturday Night, Time,* or *Newsweek,* I told the people I met, and you didn't even know it.

Most of all, I liked to point out, he loved his family, and I was always getting postcards and letters with pictures of him standing against some famous place or helping women and children take sacks of rice off the back of trucks.

There was the time in New Zealand when he spent four months around Rotorura living with a group of Maoris. He had taken over five hundred pictures for *National Geographic* and had written a superb piece on traditional and contemporary Maori life, how the two flowed into each other, how the culture continued to maintain itself in spite of the inroads that technology had made. Two days before he was to leave, a delegation of the elders came by the house where he was staying and told him that they had talked and would prefer that he didn't put their pictures in a magazine. That evening the village had a feast, and after everyone had eaten, my father took the story he had worked on for four months and all the film and placed them on the fire.

That was my dad.

Then, for my twenty-seventh birthday, my mother sent me a white shirt and a photograph.

2 8 6

By the end of the month, things were getting a little thin, and I kept hoping for the cheque to arrive. I could have called the Friendship Centre, but I didn't want to appear anxious. By the time the fifteenth rolled around, I was closer to desperate.

"Hi" I said. "It's Will. This Martha?"

"Yep."

"You know, I was just looking over my records, and I don't think I ever received a cheque for the calendar project. Have those cheques gone out yet?"

"Yep."

"Well, did my cheque go out?"

"You have to ask Ray."

"It was that bill I dropped off about a month ago."

"Ray took all that stuff. Said he was going to take care of it."

I couldn't bring myself to call Ray and ask him about my money, so I called Harlen.

"Sure, Will," said Harlen. "I can do that. Must have been a mix-up with the cheques. Could still be in the mail. Ray'll be real embarrassed."

Harlen didn't call back that day, and he didn't call back the next day either. When he did call, he told me that he had been right, that Ray was real embarrassed.

"Ray paid all the bills. But he said he didn't see your bill in the folder Martha gave him. Said he paid everyone. What was left over went to the centre."

"I can send him another bill."

"No need to do that, Will. Ray said we could just take what you're owed out of what the centre got."

"That's fine with me."

"Boy, Ray was real embarrassed. How much was your bill?"

"Almost six thousand dollars."

"That much, huh?"

"How much did the centre get?"

"Three hundred and forty dollars. Look like we're going to have to wait on the uniforms.

THOMAS KING

The photograph was of my father. He was leaning against a fence with four other men. He had on a pair of jeans, a work shirt and a hat that was pulled down over much of his face. There was a short letter from my mother with the photograph that said, "Happy birthday. Found this picture. Third from the right. That's him." And she signed it "love" like she always did. That was it. He had a cigarette hanging from his mouth. My mother had drawn a circle around him with an arrow pointing at the side of his head.

I had to take a loan out with the bank. Harlen spent the next two weeks apologizing for Ray.

"He feels awful, Will. Blames himself for what happened."

"What happened to all the money the centre was going to make?"

"Expenses, Will. The expenses took a lot of the profit."

"Yeah, but we sold, what, thirty thousand calendars?"

"Not quite that many in the end."

"How many?"

"Don't know. Ray said it wasn't as good as it might have been. Ray had to put in five thousand dollars of his own money."

"Ray lost five thousand dollars on the calendar?"

"Not exactly."

"So, how much did he lose?"

I ran into Ray about a month later in the American. I had just finished work, and it was hot, and a cold beer sounded good. Ray was sitting at a table near the back. Harlen was with him.

Ray had on his suit. He looked clean and neat sitting in the chair. "Sorry to hear you had to take out a loan," he said. "Harlen and me figure that as soon as the money starts to come in next year, you'll get paid first with interest. Damn, but I wish I knew what happened to that bill."

I guess I wasn't smiling when I sat down. "Expenses will sure eat into the profits quick."

Ray wasn't smiling either. "They sure will."

Ray ordered another pitcher, and I sat there staring at him until he disappeared in the smoke and the noise of the evening.

My mother normally sent me a shirt for my birthday. She sent shirts at Christmas, too. Generally, they were used, shirts she had found at yard sales. Sometimes they were new. New or used, she would wash them, iron them, and pin them up in a neat rectangle. She didn't make a distinction between new and used. There were clean shirts and dirty shirts, and that was it. She never missed my birthday.

She had pinned the photograph to the shirt pocket. "That's him," the letter said, as if knowing was an important thing for me to have.

LEE  MARACLE

Maracle is a Native Canadian writer whose works reflect her antipathy toward sexism, racism, and white cultural domination. She grew up in a poor neighborhood in North Vancouver, dropped out of school, and later became part of the hippie subculture. During subsequent years, she drifted from western California to Toronto, at times involved in drugs, and eventually found work as a political activist.

Throughout her adult life, Maracle has remained active in the Native struggle against racism and economic oppression. Her first book, *Bobbi Lee: Indian Rebel,* is an autobiography in which she describes the experience of growing up as a member of an oppressed minority population. In 1988 she published *I Am Woman,* a collection of poetry and prose that reflects her adult struggle for liberation from prejudice, both as a woman and as a Native North American. *Sojourner's Truth* is a collection of stories in which she consciously works to integrate European literary styles and Native oral storytelling forms.

291

In her novels, *Sundogs* and *Ravensong,* Maracle examines her female protagonists' attempts to confront the cultural rifts between Native and white society and the resulting problems of individual identity. Critics have acknowledged Maracle's works as having "vitality" and a sense of immediacy and emotional intensity reflective of her spiritual approach to life and writing. In explaining her Native perspective on thought and creativity, Maracle has said, " . . . you harness all your energy, physical, spiritual, emotional, and intellectual, and you retreat into solitude to work out the nature of your particular solidarity with creation."

Métis autobiographer, poet, short story writer, and novelist.

Born: In 1950; raised in Vancouver, British Columbia, Canada.

Partnerships: Married, husband's name Dennis; children: Tania, Columpa.

Education: Attended Simon Fraser University.

Career: Writer, public speaker, and political activist. En'Owkin Center, Penticton, British Columbia, teacher.

Memberships: Red Power Movement and Liberation Support Movement.

Address: 223 Conklin, Penticton, British Columbia, Canada, V2A ZT1.

Early Rebellion

From *Bobbi Lee: Indian Rebel*, Women's Press, copyright © 1990 by Lee Maracle

I barely managed to pass grade eight—more by chance than merit or hard work. Then in the summer our old man got a Veteran's Land Act loan (or mortgage) and we built a brand new house. We cultivated a half-acre of land nearby and planted a garden in the small orchard that was there. We girls helped dig and transfer soil, but after that all we did was tend the orchard and harvest the cherries and other fruit. It was nice then, especially during the summer.

After the house was built, dad started working for a fishing company. I got a job as a live in baby-sitter for a family in South Vancouver and mom had just finished a year at nurses' training school and was saving for the next. We were counting on help from the old man, but he didn't contribute much. Can't blame him a lot, though. The company he worked for never paid their workers till the end of the fishing season.

About three weeks before school was about to begin again, mom phoned and asked if I could loan them five dollars; they'd been living on potatoes and spinach from the garden for over a week. I went home on Sunday and gave them forty dollars—most of my savings. When school started I didn't have enough money to pay for book rentals. I had registered at the Argyle Secondary School, but now was too poor to go. I wasn't really upset; school hadn't left me with many fond memories, so it was fine to think of never going back.

Eventually, however, Welfare stepped in and paid the school fees for all of us. Mom felt ashamed to accept their money, and was very angry with dad because of it. They had a big fight and she yelled at him, "If you're workin' why is it you can't feed the kids and pay their school fees?" After the fight, dad left us and lived most of the time on his boat—just coming back to

292

visit us at Christmas time. He was much different than mom; taking welfare didn't bother him a bit anymore. He was a quiet man . . . never talked very much. The only time I really enjoyed him was when he got a little drunk and would sing and play his guitar. Then he was full of jokes and laughs. After the fishing season was over, in 1963, dad started working for MacMillan-Bloedel up at Powell River. He would come home every couple of weeks or so, give mom some money, and head back to work.

It is inevitable, Europeans, that you should find yourself reading my work. If you do not find yourself spoken to, it is not because I intend rudeness—you just don't concern me now.

—From I Am Woman, a book of prose and poetry written expressly for Native people.

In the beginning I was one of the top students at Argyle Secondary, getting all A's and B's during the first semester. I did it more or less to prove something to myself. Kids used to say I was dumb, but I knew that I wasn't. Not caring isn't being dumb—I knew I was intelligent and could get the grades if I tried. After about half a year, however, I soured on school again. I had few friends and found the work boring. So I just about stopped going, missing 72 days of classes during the school year.

Earlier someone told me that if I joined the track team I could get out of some classes and detentions—which was the way they punished us when we played hooky. So I decided to run track and won my first race against the Kensington team. Then I went on to compete in the Vancouver Area School District Games, which involved 52 schools. I entered the 440, 880 and mile senior women's races. When I won all three I was really surprised; I hadn't competed much before then and had no idea how I'd do against good competition. It was a great feeling to win, and it qualified me for the B.C. Championships, which were held at Brockton Oval in Stanley Park. I entered four races, coming in third in the 220 and first in the quarter, 880 and mile. At 14 I'd become the B.C. champion in women's distance races.

Soon, however, I started having real trouble with my back; it was from a roller skating accident I'd had a year earlier. I saw a doctor and he put me on heat treatments and other kinds of physiotherapy. But it didn't work; I still had backaches all the time and was forced to give up track. I was really getting sick of school at the time, anyway.

293

Sometimes I played hooky for one or two weeks at a time. Mom didn't find out about it until later. She was back at nurses' training school and all I had to do was keep the house clean. So one day I put a baby-sitting ad in the newspaper and soon, instead of going to school some days, I began baby-sitting for various people. Then in January, I got a job in the evening at a restaurant where my brother was working. This only lasted a month or so, however,

LEE MARACLE

[Maracle] says her book [I Am Woman] "addresses the Native people in desperate circumstances, who need to recover the broken threads of their lives." To write her book, she gathered stories, scribbled on paper napkins and brown bags, stories which she says come from "the people of my passion." She resisted publishing for a long time because she could not commit the "voices of the unheard" to paper or to "squeeze one's loved ones so small." All the voices carry the same theme: "Racism is for us, not an ideology in the abstract, but a very real and practical part of our lives. The pain, the effect, the shame are all real."

—Agnes Grant, in *Native Writers and Canadian Writing*, edited by W. H. New, UBC Press, 1990.

as the Labour Relations Board found out that I wasn't sixteen yet and told the manager he couldn't employ me in any capacity.

When summer came I turned fifteen and started baby-sitting for the Martin family. They didn't live far from us, so I stayed at home nights and took the bus back and forth to their house. Mrs. Martin paid my bus fare plus five dollars a day. She had two kids—a boy about three and a girl, Elissa, who was eighteen months old and had epilepsy. She would be okay, then suddenly become paralysed. They took her to all sorts of doctors even the Mayo Clinic in New York, but no one could figure her out or help. I had to walk around with her because sometimes she would become paralysed and fall on her face. It was a hard job and I really felt sorry for the kid and her mother.

During this time, some guy kept coming to the Martin's apartment and knocking at the door. I never answered or opened the door. Then one day I saw him molesting the little girl down the street. I called the police and they caught him. Turned out he had already raped and murdered two young girls twelve and thirteen, the Rainee sisters. It used to scare me to think about it—and about how close I came several times to opening the Martin's door.

294   Not long after this, my brother and I started to steal things, small things, but we kept at it. We'd take cartons and boxes of cigarettes from big stores and sell them for two-bits a pack. Soon we'd become typical delinquents. I wasn't giving money to mom anymore, just using it for my own pleasures. I didn't care about the others; I was just for myself, nothing else mattered. I also started smoking, but not around mom—who didn't know. I began with just a couple of cigarettes a day, but quickly went up to around a pack as my stealing increased. I often baby-sat at night, or would go downtown to the nightclubs. I was still only fifteen, but looked much older than my age.

Poetry and Stories
I Am Woman, Write-On Press, 1988.
Sojourner's Truth, Press Gang, 1990.

Novels
Sundogs, Theytus, 1992.
Ravensong, Press Gang, 1993.

Other
Bobbi Lee: Indian Rebel (autobiography), Liberation Support Movement Press, 1975; expanded version, Women's Press, 1990.

Work represented in anthologies. Contributor to magazines.

I remember the first time I got drunk. It was down at the Pacific National Exhibition (PNE) Playland with my sister, Toni. She was twenty-one and bought a "mickey" of whiskey for me . . . it didn't bother her that I was only fifteen. In fact, she didn't have moral qualms about anything. I went into one of the bathrooms and drank it all down. Next thing I remember I was out of the PNE down near some sawmill. I was running along, holding a big bottle of beer, and some guys were chasing after me. I guess I'd stolen if from them and was pouring it out as I ran, laughing as they yelled. I somehow lost them—or they just stopped coming, seeing the beer spilling over the ground—and went into a store and bought a coke. I didn't drink it, just spilled it on the counter. Then I went out and was really feeling good. There was still some beer left in the bottle I was carrying and I drank it down.

The guys who'd been chasing me spotted me again, but I lost them and finally wound up back at the PNE. I decided not to pay my way in twice and climbed up and over the fence. A watchman saw me. He caught up with me and took me into a little house. I was really mad. A couple of watchmen had arrived and they were sticking my head under the watertap, putting their fingers down my throat and making me walk around. I kept shouting abuses and swearing, calling them assholes, sons-of-bitches, and so forth. The watchman was about forty and really seemed to be concerned about me. I hadn't realized how late it was when I climbed the fence—it was about 4 a.m.—and had no idea the PNE was closed. When he took me outside for air and a walk about, I somehow got away from him, climbed back over the fence and ran away. The policemen had been sitting in their patrol car.

295

Finally, as I was walking across the bridge, some neighbours picked me up. I didn't say anything, but they could see I'd been drinking and was in trouble. I was soaking wet, though it hadn't been raining. To make sure, they asked if I was the Lee girl. (I must have really looked something else.) I said "Yes," and they drove me home. It was five in the morning when I climbed into bed. Mom didn't say anything, though I knew she heard me coming in.

It was about four months later when I told mom I wanted to go to a dance in town. She got angry and told me not to go . . . it wasn't a place

L E E   M A R A C L E

for young girls. I was set on going anyway and while she was in the kitchen, I snuck out the window and went into town. When I came home it was late and I crawled right into bed. Mom wasn't sleeping, however. She came into my room, dragged me out of bed by the hair and gave me a good beating. My sister Joyce was crying and Joan kept asking mom to stop. But she was furious: just kept pulling me around the room by my hair and screaming at me. I thought she was going crazy. She kept yellin' "Cut it out! Smarten up!"

296

I didn't get along with my mother after that incident . . . practically broke off relations with her altogether. And I kept going out whenever I wanted, not even telling her I was leaving, or where I was going. Sometimes I'd stay away for a couple of days and not even call. I hung around mostly with Toni, then later with a cousin from Deep Cove who was sixteen. We met a group of guys and I started going around with one of them; a great big guy named Rich. Then I went around with Nigel for a while. I was like that: fickle, intense, always on the move.

School had practically dropped out of sight: I rarely went and when I did was always getting into trouble. Several times they threatened to expel me, but mom kept calling up and talking them out of it, saying I had problems but would settle down soon . . . things like that. By this time, mom was a practical nurse; she'd worked hard and completed her schooling. I kept telling her I'd be good, promising to go to school regularly and so forth. But then I'd fall back into my old habits. My brother Roger was doing the same thing—in fact, he was worse than I was, attending only about half his classes. Somehow, I barely managed to pass Grade Ten.

It was a really bad time for me. There was this one teacher who was always getting on me about my playing hooky and just being a "visitor" to his classes. Then one morning I was late, my back was aching, and he came on with the same stuff, saying, "Ah, here's Bobbi, our visitor" . . . Well, for some reason, I just flipped out; something snapped in my head and I started crying and throwing desks around. I even threw one at the teacher and turned over his table. In a few minutes some teachers came in and grabbed hold of me, dragging me down to the nurses' station where I was given a bunch of tranquilizers. They sent me home after I'd calmed down.

For the next week or so I just stayed home, crying all the time and not wanting to do anything. Finally, my mom decided to take me into the hospital for a check-up. They put me in a psychiatric wing of Lion's Gate Hospital in North Van for three weeks of forced rest. The doctors told me I'd had a nervous breakdown and, with a little rest, would soon be all right. I was pretty upset about being put in a psychiatric ward and was very uncooperative at first. They had all these little programs for the patients and I refused to participate in any of them. A girl down the hall was also uncooperative and my first afternoon in the hospital she tried to escape. They caught her sneaking down the stairs and she fought like a wild cat with the nurses. They finally calmed her down with some injections and the next morning she was sent off to Riverview Mental Hospital.

One of the first year nurses, who'd known my brother in school, said they'd send me off to Riverview too if I didn't start cooperating. This scared me a bit so I decided to start playing their stupid games. On the third morning I went to what they called occupational classes. They had us crushing egg shells and I started complaining, saying, "What good is crushing these egg shells? That won't get us jobs anywhere!" I was warned again by the young nurse: "If you keep complaining like that," she said, "they'll probably send you to Riverview for three months. You'd better play it cool so you can get out of here and go home soon." It took me almost a week, but finally I decided to do everything they asked or wanted without question or complaint. The tranquilizers they gave me four times a day helped; I was dozing or spaced out most of the time and was given sleeping pills at night.

I saw a psychiatrist three times while I was at Lion's Gate and, despite the fact that he kept telling me I'd just had a nervous breakdown—which was very common—I was pretty disturbed by the whole experience. I didn't think I was crazy and resented being kept in the psychiatric ward. Anyway, after three weeks they sent me home with a prescription for tranquilizers which I was supposed to take regularly and get renewed every three months. I was also supposed to see this psychiatrist they set up appointments for me with. I rarely took the tranquilizers and never went to see the psychiatrist. At home I just tried to forget the whole thing. I started school again, switching from the Sciences to the Humanities and taking English, French and Drama.

I did pretty good in Drama, because I liked it, but did poorly in everything else. Acting helped me overcome my shyness and get outside myself. It helped me a lot. I stared talking to people and making friends. One was Donna Wooten, a girl who was very similar to me. Her father was very mean, always beating up on her. She told me he didn't like Indians, and neither did the rest of her family. Her brother would sometimes come up to us and make like he was a TV Indian doin' a little dance and saying "Hoo, hoo, hoo." And that was pretty typical. Sometimes we'd make friends with white kids, then they'd tell us after a while to stop coming over because their parents didn't want Indians around the place. I remember going to this girl's house—she was my first friend at school and very nice—and when her mother saw me she blew her stack. Right in front of me she said: "What do you think you're doing bringing this Indian into the Lynn residence? Don't you know we don't want Indians here!" The poor girl started crying—just didn't know what to do or say. Guess she never knew that her folks were like that. You know, like when you're eleven and watch TV stuff about cowboys and Indians you just don't associate that racist crap with your own existence or with your parents' attitudes; it's just exciting and something to do after dinner. Well, after that experience I thought a lot about just taking that sort of thing—letting it just happen to me without doing anything. I started being a bit arrogant and found that the more cocky I was, the more racism came out . . . and I was glad when it did because I didn't like phoniness. I like people to be sincere, not the usual phoney and paternalism. Anyway, Donna Wooten was different from the other whites I knew—except for Glenn Hampton, who was also a friend of mine for a very long time. (I think he's a mechanic now somewhere in Vancouver, though I never see him anymore.) Donna and I were real close. She was raised in Quathiasca Cove right next to the Indian Reserve and, in fact, seemed very much like an Indian herself. We stuck together despite her parents' protest and the trouble it caused with the other white kids at Arglye and in the neighbourhood. She'd say that in Quathiasca all her friends were Indians anyway—so what? But at Quathiasca there were no white kids to be friends with.

I remember noticing around this time, when I was fourteen or fifteen, that my sister Joyce was really different than me. She got along with everybody very well, but I thought she was a "yes girl"' always saying "Oh, yes, you're much smarter than me. Yes, of course. Yes, yes." And always walking like she was ashamed, around white guys. It seemed to me she just accepted being a second-class citizen, kept her place and naturally, there was no friction. But I couldn't do it—or didn't want to. I fought all the time to maintain some dignity, refusing to accept any racist crap or be a "yes girl." I figured myself to be a fairly intelligent person; more intelligent than most, in fact, I thought white kids didn't know what the hell was going on. The liberal whites with their racist hangups made me sick. It was really ugly. Because I am Métis and light skinned, whites were sometimes confused. It happened fairly regularly that one would come up to me and ask "No offense, but are you Indian?" I would always reply, saying "Yes I am . . . but, no offense, are you white?" This happened a lot at school and sometimes all hell broke loose. It got to be that I was ostracized by all the white kids except Donna and Glenn. And because I wouldn't kowtow, bow and scrape or be their scapegoat, I got into a lot of fights and was beaten up more than any kid I knew.

JOHN JOSEPH ▌ MATHEWS

Essay by

JOHN E. LITTLE

Best known for the novel Sundown, *Mathews is highly regarded for his sensitive depictions of Native Americans who feel alienated from both their tribal heritage and American society. He is additionally remembered for his nonfiction works, in which he documented Osage history and culture, the settlement of Oklahoma by whites, and the impact this had on the region's Native Americans. While only one-eighth Osage, Mathews had strong ties to the Osage nation: his great-grandfather, William Shirley Williams, was a missionary and "mountain man" fur trader who translated the Bible into the Osage language, and Mathews's family lived on an Indian reservation where his father managed the local bank and ran a trading post. Mathews frequently "passed" for white and attended white schools, but he could speak Osage and, through frequent contact with full bloods, was well-acquainted with Osage traditions. In addition to his literary efforts to document tribal culture, Mathews was elected to the Osage Tribal Council in 1934. An active spokesperson, he also frequently represented the tribe in Washington, D.C., and helped the Osage attain the rights to natural gas and oil deposits found on their lands.*

3 0 1

Incorporating events from Mathews's life, *Sundown* is set in the early part of the twentieth century and centers around Challenge Windzer, an Osage

"I didn't presume that I would come out of the blackjacks with the banner of truth flying, [but that] . . . I might find some connections between man's artificial ornamentation and the useless ornamentations among the creatures in my little corner of the earth. . . ."

—from **Talking to the Moon**

of mixed descent. Due to his education at the state university, his father's political activism, and the growing white population, Chal becomes increasingly familiar with the ways of white America and embarrassed by his tribe's customs. After his father's death and a brief stint as a pilot during World War I, the protagonist finds himself alone and alienated from both Osage and white society. Mathews's nonfiction works similarly focus on his heritage and the history of his people and home state. *Wah'Kon-Tah: The Osage and the White Man's Road*, in part the biography of Laban J. Miles, Indian agent to the Osage nation, focuses on the tribe's interaction with the United States federal government when the Oklahoma territories were being settled. History is also central to *Life and Death of an Oilman: The Career of E. W. Marland*, the biography of the first governor of Oklahoma, and to the lengthy *The Osages: Children of the Middle Waters*, which provides an overview of Osage traditions and beliefs as well as events which strongly affected the tribe. Relating Mathews's experiences in the Blackjack Hills of Oklahoma, *Talking to the Moon* likewise emphasizes Osage culture, delineating Mathews's attempts to commune with the natural world and achieve greater spiritual harmony.

Mathews's literary stature rests largely on *Sundown*, and scholars frequently credit him as being one of the first Native Americans to write fiction about Native Americans. Critics praise *Sundown* for its realism and argue that Mathews's objective treatment of the mixed blood has universal relevance. His nonfiction works, often considered evocative sociological and anthropological tracts about the Osage, have also been praised for their inherent literary qualities. *Talking to the Moon*, for example, has been favorably compared to Henry David Thoreau's *Walden* (1854) and John Muir's *My First Summer in the Sierras* (1911).

SUNDOWN

XIV

Chal didn't know what to do with himself. He flung himself into an overstuffed chair and sat with his legs apart, then arose and walked to the

Osage novelist, biographer, historian, and auto-biographer.

Born: November 16, 1895, in Pawhuska, Oklahoma.

Died: 1979.

Partnerships: Married Elizabeth Palmour, April 5, 1945; children: Virginia H., John H.

Education: University of Oklahoma, B.A. 1920; Oxford University, B.A., 1923; summer study at University of Sewanee, 1915, University of Geneva, 1923. *Career:* Realtor in Los Angeles, CA, and Pasadena, CA, 1926–28; rancher, and writer since 1928. Member of Osage Tribal Council, 1934–42, and Oklahoma State Board of Education, 1935.

Memberships: Order of Daedalians, American Legion, Phi Beta Kappa.

Address: Home—Blackjacks, Pawhuska, OK 74056. Office—P.O. Box 1247, Pawhuska, OK 74056.

Agent: Robert T. Center, 240 East 76th St., New York, NY 10021.

window with a cigarette hanging from his lips. The cars were parked along the curbing across the street, and there were some parked in front of his father's house. Those cars parked there annoyed him. People didn't care whether they parked their cars in front of your drive or not. He believed that his mother ought to sell this property for business, though. They were too close to the heart of town—no wonder people parked their cars in front of the house. He believed they ought to sell this lot and buy one on the hill, where all the best people were building; build a big house on the hill.

He heard his mother moving about in the next room and the fact that they lived down in the valley in an old house seemed to be an injury, and he felt in his annoyance that his mother had something to do with it. That his mother was injuring him intentionally. He frowned as he watched the cars pass up and down along the street. His mother's soft tread continued. He wished his mother would go out more in society—go out with the society people of the town. He never saw her name among the select people who gave dinners at the new country club on the hill across the creek. He wished his mother would go out more and for pete's sake, say something—talk like other women. She just sat, and when she did talk you could tell she didn't talk English very well. She didn't talk like other people, but like the books she read. He thought it was a wonder that she had ever stashed her blankets, shrouding and leggings, but even yet when she had to go outside the house into the yard on a cold day, she threw her blanket over her shoulders instead of a coat. Threw that loud Indian blanket over her nice blue dress with the lace down the front.

He turned away from the window and sat down again in the over-stuffed chair, and threw his leg over the arm. He wished he had something to do—some business, but there wasn't anything for him to do. He couldn't get a job. No one would give a job to an Indian. Certainly he wouldn't have any chance to run for a county office, 'cause the voters always said that an

3 0 3

J O H N   J O S E P H   **M A T H E W S**

Indian had too much money and didn't need the job. But anyway, he felt that he could get more respect if he had a job or was in some business for himself. He knew in his heart, however, that he wouldn't go into business or get a job if he had a chance. There seemed to be another dignity somewhere that would be hurt if he worked. Then he had a thought that made him smile: he guessed he must have two dignities, one tellin' him to do something, and one tellin' him not to do anything.

He paced the floor for a few minutes, then went into his room. He uncorked a bottle of corn whisky which had little specks swimming about in it. He looked at the door; he didn't want his mother to see him. Funny how it was now—he had to hide his whisky, and he could remember when the *Rock and Rye* used to stand on the front room table with glasses about. Of course it was against the law to get it then, but everybody had it and no one seemed to think anything about it. But now you had to hide whisky and go out into the country to drink it , and everybody thought it was smart to drink.

He turned the bottle up and took a big swallow. He went back into the other room, paced up and down the floor for a while, then went back and took another drink. He knew that it would be several days or perhaps a week before he could sober up, but he didn't care—there wasn't anything else to do anyway.

He went back to the chair in the front room. He felt warmed and contented as he sat there, and he certainly wasn't the young man who had doubted himself a few minutes ago. He felt quite important now. Suddenly he felt sentimental about the dance out at the village the other day, and he made up his mind that he would dance next time. He pictured himself in breech clout and moccasins, as the most graceful dancer in the Roundhouse. Suddenly he felt very important. He was so full of the dream that he went to the window and looked out, then began to day-dream that he was dancing alone at the Roundhouse, the drum-beats became faster and louder, and the spectators suddenly became horrified when they realized that Chal was doing a death dance. He saw Blo's face among the spectators. He saw both horror and admiration in her eyes, and he danced faster, thrilled with the idea that she would be very sorry when the end of the dance came and he killed himself as a sacrifice.

He had never heard of anything like this, but his fume-exhilarated brain was indulging in fantastic acrobatics. As he stood there looking out, he saw only the pictures in his day-dream, and he was experiencing a bitter-sweet happiness, which grew to the extent that he suddenly came back to realization, so sweet and intense was the thrill.

He turned from the window, went back into his room, put the bottle in his hip pocket, then went out to the garage to get his red roadster. He suddenly decided he would go out to the village and see Sun-on-His-

Wings. He drove very fast, causing the dust to rise in a cloud which floated out over the fields.

There were no more lodges in the village now. In their places were houses; some small, and some rather large ones, and behind each house a lot for horses. Many of the houses had drying racks for meat, and open structures covered with boughs around them.

Chal drew up in front of Sun-on-His-Wings' house and called a slovenly negro to him. The negro said that Sun-on-His-Wings was out to the old man's. Chal looked at him, then said, "You mean out to his father's? You mean out to Chief Watching Eagle's ranch?" Chal didn't like to hear the older men referred to with disrespect, and it was particularly distasteful to him today. He sat looking at the negro as his motor purred, and he said, "Looks like you'd have more respect for a chief, at least—I don't wantta hear you call him 'the old man' any more." Fear came into the negro's face. "Yes suh," he said. Chal's sense of injury became almost intense. "You know you're treated better when you work for an Indian than when you work for white men in town—why don't you appreciate it?" The negro had become quite frightened, and he said, "Yes suh, Mistuh Chal, Ah know 'at—Ah sho knows 'at." Chal felt better as he drove away.

As he sped along he thought of that black man's face and he realized how very funny it was. He smiled, but his emotion of humor was intensified by the fumes in his brain and he lost control of it and laughed out. There was something in him which magnified the humor inspired by that fear on the negro's face. He could control the ridiculous urge to laugh for a moment, but it kept returning.

The old men of his people always said that the Great Mysteries had sent the Black Rears to their people to make them laugh and forget their troubles. They came with the white man who brought trouble; they said the Black Rears had come for that reason; to make them laugh and forget those troubles which the white man had brought to them. They said the Black Rears came from the South; from the direction of Good.

There was activity around Watching Eagle's ranch. The women were cutting up meat and they had erected a sweatlodge just east of the conical Peyote church. Chal stopped on the hill overlooking the houses and took another drink from the bottle.

The main house was a large one and built on top of a standstone hill, and it was surrounded by the smaller houses and the Peyote church stood apart. Most of the older Indians, those who were influenced very slightly by that which they called the Great Frenzy, lived their daily lives as the fathers had lived, dressing in their leggings, blankets and bandeau. The only change being that they now lived in houses with modern conveniences; radios, telephones, bathrooms and modern furniture. They were now Peyote wor-

305

Wah'Kon-Tah: The Osage and the White Man's Road, University of Oklahoma Press, 1932.
Sundown, Longmans, Green, 1934.
Talking to the Moon, University of Chicago Press, 1945.

Life and Death of an Oilman: The Career of E. W. Marland, University of Oklahoma Press, 1951.
The Osages: Children of the Middle Waters, University of Oklahoma Press, 1961.

Also contributed articles to the *Philadelphia Ledger* and *The Sooner Magazine*, a publication of the University of Oklahoma Alumni Association.

shipers, which was a mixture of the old religion, Christianity, and the new belief in passivity and retribution.

Chal drove up among the houses and stopped under a tree. They were glad to see him. Bird Feather, the wife of Sun-on-His-Wings, looked at her neat shoes when he spoke to her. Sun-on-His-Wings wore citizen's clothes, as did all the younger men present. The older men lay in the shade of the trees in their native blankets.

Sun-on-His-Wings waved his hand to where the meat for the feast was being prepared. "You will eat with us," and he smiled. "But you must wait until tomorrow—we gonna have sweatlodge tonight." The last drink had warmed Chal considerably. He smiled at Wings and said, "I'll stay with you tonight." He didn't want Sun-on-His-Wings to know that he had been drinking.

"All right, you do not believe in Peyote—but tonight you will go to sweatlodge with me. Purty soon now, when sun sets."

They walked toward one of the small houses, went in and began stripping off their clothes. Chal was buoyed up by his drinking and he believed he wanted to see the Peyote ceremony. Sun-on-His-Wings pointed to a blanket, and Chal threw it over his shoulders, then followed his friend out of the house. They walked slowly toward the sweatlodge.

The lodge was made of cedar saplings, stripped and peeled. They were stuck in the ground in a circle, then bent over and the upper ends were tied together by rawhide. This framework was covered with canvas in place of skins. On one side of the entrance were four buckets of water, two hot and two cold, and on the other side was a small pile of limestones and a pile of wood. Near this a fire was burning, and some of the limestones were being heated there, while two attendants stood watching the fire. The fire had been lighted by Watching Eagle with the sparks from two flints.

Chal and Sun-on-His-Wings entered at the east entrance. The lodge was steaming from the hot limestones piled in a pyramid in the center of the room, over which attendants poured water. Chal cast his blanket to one side, following every movement of Sun-on-His-Wings, and they sat down together.

There were several other naked figures in the lodge, sitting in a circle, but no one looked up; they seemed to be thinking profoundly, with their heads bowed. The sweat dripped from their foreheads and rolled down their bodies, dripping from their fingertips.

Near the center of the lodge was a small kettle sitting over a fire. An attendant came in with a quart cup full of buckeye root and poured it into the hot water in the kettle. He stirred the mixture a few moments, then filled two cups and handed them to the left around the circle. Each man supped as much as he wanted, then passed the cup to his neighbor. Chal noticed that Sun-on-His-Wings chewed some of the root as well, but he only drank of the liquid.

He wanted to see everything that was going on, but he felt that he might be ill-mannered if he watched too closely, so he kept his head bowed like the rest, but covertly watching the Road Man who sat at the west end of the lodge. On each side of the Road Man sat an old man—the Fire Chief and another old counselor.

As Chal sat, the sweat began to ooze out all over him, and he had to keep his hand to his forehead most of the time, but when he noticed the others let the sweat fall, he did likewise. Then a terrific pain came into his stomach; it seemed that many little live things stirred there. He could scarcely keep from groaning softly, and he looked up with an expression of silent appeal to the motionless, bowed figures in the darkening lodge, but they were unaware of his pain. Sweat came faster as the pain became more acute, and he knew he must get out of the lodge very soon; must get out and rid himself of that terrible working in his stomach that was like many live things attempting to roll themselves into balls.

Just at the moment when he thought he could bear it no longer, Sun-on-His-Wings looked over at him. His face was covered with sweat drops. Sun-on-His-Wings then spoke to the Road Man and asked permission to go out. He got up, threw his blanket around him, and started for the door. Chal followed his example quickly. Outside, a little way from the lodge, they turned their faces to the north, the direction of Evil, and emptied their stomachs. Sun-on-His-Wings smiled, "That is the evil that has come into your body," he said.

They accepted the dipper of warm water handed to them by the attendant. Chal's blanket stuck to him and made him want to take it off, as they stood for a moment longer facing the north. As they stood there, Chal saw Runs With Cow come out of the lodge. He turned to the north, but seemed to be having trouble. An attendant, seeing this trouble, brought him the wing feather of a crow, which he used as an aid by tickling his throat.

They went back into the lodge and Chal felt suddenly quite well, and pleasantly weak, but his head was clear. They took off their blankets and took their places again in the broken circle.

JOHN JOSEPH **MATHEWS**

Oxford-educated John Joseph Mathews, great-grandson of an Osage woman and a missionary who translated the Bible into the Osage language, has written a sympathetic history of his great-grandmother's tribe [in The Osages: Children of the Middle Water]. *Likening his task to the reconstruction of a dinosaur from many scattered fragments, he has fitted together ingeniously the Indians' oral traditions and the writings of explorers, traders, travelers, missionaries, government officials and ethnologists, making allowances for white men's fragmentary knowledge, and the prejudices and special pleadings which impeded their understanding of Osage life and values.*

—John C. Ewers, "Tribal Tribute," in *The New York Times Book Review,* September 24, 1961.

One by one the worshipers asked permission, got up and passed outside, then returned to resume their attitude of bowed prayer. A dipper of cold water was passed around the circle, and it seemed to Chal that the water went to the very bottom of the stomach.

It seemed that they sat there for several hours, and it seemed odd to Chal that he could sit thus, silently and without moving. He was fascinated and calmed. There was a complete absence of urges, and his thoughts were light and left no impressions; like sycamore leaves dropping to the surface of calm water, not even making concentric ripples, but riding away on the imperceptible current; riding on into eternity.

He thought he heard a sound, but he didn't look up. Then he was sure, and he sat many minutes listening to the intermittent sobbing. He heard a movement, and he felt compelled to look up then. White Deer rose from his place and went over to the Road Man, who was sitting at the west end of a line running east and west through the circle. He was weeping as he sat down by the Road Man. He picked up a cigarette paper and slowly filled it with the ground-up, dried sumac, which had been prepared in a little box for that purpose. He rolled the cigarette slowly as he wept. He lit it and handed it to Watching Eagle, who was the Road Man.

308

The little fire under the buckeye kettle made their faces the color of dawn. Watching Eagle placed the cigarette in his mouth, and the smoke rose like a thread to the top of the lodge. Watching Eagle took several puffs from the cigarette then waited.

White Deer said, "Road Man, my heart is heavy. Evil surrounds my heart." He made a motion, rubbing his body downward, passing his hands over his thighs, then he continued, "This evil which surrounds my heart is like mud that clogs the hoof of a horse when it has rained for many days. Many times I have cried, and this evil around my heart comes out my eyes, and I say it is gone, this evil, but again it comes. I close my heart and keep what is good there, but hate comes into my heart like the frost comes on the inside walls of a closed lodge. My heart is cold and I say I ought to kill these white men who shot my son, Running Elk."

Chal felt a slight shock at the name of his friend. So they knew who was killing those Big Hills one by one. He listened intently.

White Deer continued, "They have put this dynamite into house of my cousin, those same white men. Sometime I say I shall go to agent and tell him this. Sometime I say I shall go to sheriff and tell him this. I don't know what to do. Thoughts pull at my shirt like little children and I do not know which one to follow; I do not know which direction is good road."

There was a long silence and the prayer smoke climbed to the top of the lodge in the heavy, steamy air. Watching Eagle looked straight ahead, then he spoke softly, and slowly, using many words of which Chal had to guess the meaning: "My son, this evil in your body comes out now from your body. This evil in your heart comes out through your eyes. This evil cannot stay in your body forever.

"Long time ago there was one road and People could follow that road. They said, 'There is only one road. We can see this road. There are no other roads.' Now it seems that road is gone, and white man has brought many roads. But that road is still there. That road is still there, but there are many other roads too. There is white man's road, and there is road which comes off from forks. The bad road which no white man follows—the road which many of the People follow, thinking it is the white man's road. People who follow this road say they are as the white man, but this is not white man's road. People who follow this road say that road of Indian is bad now. But they are not Indians any more, these People who follow that road.

"The road of our People is dim now like buffalo trail across prairie. We cannot follow this road with our feet now, but we can see this road with our eyes, and our hearts will go along this road forever. Even if our bodies are carried by our feet on this road that is not Indian road. There are few of us whose eyes can see old road of our People, I believe."

The attendants came no more to pour water on the hot limestones, and the worshipers had stopped sweating. White Deer stopped crying and remained motionless. The silence that came over the lodge rang in Chal's ears. He wasn't aware of how long the silence lasted, but he was happy and contented, sitting there. Soon he became detached from this covered lodge, and he began dreaming.

There was nothing about him but the gray-blue bowl of the sky and the prairie. He was walking along a twisted trail that lay crazily, like a lost

JOHN JOSEPH **MATHEWS**

lariat rope, across the prairie. He began running and held out his arms, then suddenly he was flying. He would be lifted on an uprising current from the hot prairie, then would drop into a pocket, and he felt that he couldn't get his breath. He began to fear that he might fall, but just as he thought he might hit a hill and be crushed, he would rise on a current and be lifted to dizzy heights. But he couldn't get down. When he folded his arms, he would drop like a plummet, then when he opened his arms, he would catch and sail off, rising suddenly on an upward current with the intense fear that he should never come down again.

His dream was broken. Someone moved, but nothing followed, so he sat listening to the silence. He wondered what the others were thinking about. He knew they were thinking and praying, and he felt that he ought to be very fervent about something too. He decided he would ask Sun-on-His-Wings later what you were supposed to think about during the long silences in the sweatlodge.

He began to think again about White Deer and Running Elk. He was impressed by White Deer's story about the white men in the Big Hill country, and their killing of Running Elk. He wondered if White Deer imagined this or if white men were really killing the Big Hills for some purpose. He had been absent when Running Elk was killed, and when he heard of his death he was very glad that he was not at home because he knew that the relatives would have asked him to help paint Running Elk's face for the last ride to the Happy Hunting Ground. Now he was sorry that he had not been present.

He recalled instances of their boyhood together; the twinkle in Running Elk's eyes and his dare-devilish escapades. Chal had always thought that Running Elk had been born too late; that he might have been a great warrior in the old days. He remembered that he was ever in trouble and had gradually become a drunkard and a dope addict, and believed that he was being a white man. Chal thought of the times when he walked the streets in a queer dream, and of the times he had visited him at the jail or the hospital. Some of his dreams had been very funny, but they hadn't been funny to Running Elk, as he told them to Chal from a hospital bed or from a jail cot.

He often told Chal the story of the fat white man who followed him. He said that he would wake up in the night and that fat white man, completely naked and glistening, would stand at the door of his room with a spear in his hand. One time at the hospital that fat white man had appeared and Running Elk said he was so frightened that he jumped out of bed and ran down the hall, down the stairs, and into the basement, and hid behind the furnace until the nurses and the attendants had made the fat man go away. He told Chal that the white man's belly shook like jelly when he ran; that that naked white man shook like a woman.

Chal had laughed at these stories when Running Elk told them to him with a very serious expression, but tonight as he thought of them he was

3 1 0

SMOKE RISING

very sorry that he had laughed. As he sat there he was sorry that he had avoided Running Elk. His thoughts were cut short by the voice of Watching Eagle, who had begun to talk to White Deer again.

"Your son and those People who have been killed by these white men, followed that road which they thought was white man's road. Your son married white woman. You have children of your son, but they are not your children. They can never have a name among their people. They have no people. Your son drank white man's whiskey. He stuck his arm many times with that thing which brings bad dreams to white man. Take this son out of your mind. Take these children who are not your grandchildren out of your mind. Let this evil flow out of your heart through your eyes. Let this evil flow out of your body in sweat. Think no more of these things. These white men who kill these people will be punished. You are Indian. Here are graves of your grandfathers. You came out of this earth here. The life of this earth here comes out of ground into your feet and flows all over your body. You are part of this earth here like trees, like rabbit, like birds. Our people built their lodges here. That which came out of the ground into their feet and over their bodies into their hands, they put into making of their lodges. They made songs out of that which came out of ground into their bodies. Those lodges were good and beautiful. Those songs were good and beautiful. Thoughts which they had were good because they came out of ground here. That ground is their mother.

"White man came out of ground across that sea. His thoughts are good across that sea. His houses are beautiful across that sea, I believe. He came out of earth across that sea, and his songs are beautiful there. But he did not come out of earth here. His houses are ugly here because they did not come out of this earth, and his songs and those things which he thinks, those things which he talks, are ugly here too. They did not come out of earth here. He killed our brothers because they were not his brothers.

"We can do nothing. But we are Indian, we are not white men. We live in white man's houses now, and our feet go along another road, but our hearts are on road that is dim.

"White man's god. He came from across that sea too. Every Sunday he comes back. Maybe he is good god. I do not know this thing. Maybe he is same god everywhere. I do not know about this thing. This Jesus brings dreams that are good, and they said that this Jesus knew how to die. He comes back every Sunday, they say. But I do not know about this thing. It is Wahkon; it is spirit mystery. We are only men."

There was another long silence and Chal began to be cramped. All this seemed to be as a dream to him and he wondered if time were actually going on outside in the night. He wondered what time it was. Then far off down the creek he heard a rooster crow, and he thought it must be about three o'clock.

J O H N   J O S E P H   **M A T H E W S**

Watching Eagle moved slightly as though to ease his position and White Deer took his place in the circle. Then Watching Eagle began again:

"We are clean now. Evil has flowed out of our hearts and evil has flowed out of our bodies. Soap and water will make outside clean, but evil may stay on inside. I cannot say what you shall do. You are men like me. It is better if your sons marry among our people. We have no time for troubles, and we must not make troubles. We must keep all of these things out of our minds. We must have time to keep our place on earth. If we have many troubles we cannot fight to keep our place on earth. We cannot stay here all time. Our children must keep our place on earth. If we think all time of these troublous things, we will not have time to think of other things. We will not have time to keep our place on earth. Everything that comes out of earth here must fight to keep its place on earth. That is good, because that way it will always be strong. We cannot fight white man, but we are Indian; we cannot be white men. We must use our time to fight our troubles. To fight that evil which comes on inside of us.

"We must to within our hearts. Let northeast wind blow upon us. Let southwest wind blow upon us and find what is in our souls. Let that sadness around our hearts; that sadness which becomes evil, break and flow out through our eyes."

A heaviness came over Chal and he felt very sleepy. He scarcely heard the last words uttered by Watching Eagle, and the abrupt ending wakened him. He wondered what would happen now, though his drowsiness made him indifferent, and he felt that he should like to go to sleep.

He must have dozed off. There was a movement in the lodge, and the Road Man was standing before White Deer. He put the palms of his hands on White Deer's forehead, then made a motion of passing his hands over White Deer's body. He placed the palms of his hands on his own forehead, then passed them down over his body, then he went back and sat down. The Fire Chief rose and left the lodge, then one by one the worshipers left, Chal following close behind his friend. Last of all to come from the lodge was Watching Eagle, the Road Man. He stood in the line facing the east with the rest of them. They stood there in the dawnlight, silently facing the east. They stood for many minutes, then the sun appeared on the horizon. They all placed their hands on their foreheads, then extended them to the sun, and brought them back to their foreheads. They stretched their hands to the sun again, and this time brought them back to their chests, then out again and then back to their stomachs. Then they moved their hands down over their bodies, over their thighs, as though laving themselves with the rays of the sun. Chal watched Watching Eagle very closely and copied every movement he made.

The worshipers then turned to the west and faced the Peyote church, holding their hands out toward the church. After they had held their hands out thus for a moment, they brought them back to their bodies, and made a movement as though laving themselves.

After this ceremony, they went back into the lodge, picked up their blankets, and dispersed. Chal drew his blanket closely around him as the morning air was quite cool. He followed Sun-on-His-Wings back to the little house. Sun-on-His-Wings threw his blanket down, went into a little room, and stepped under a shower of cold water, then came out smiling very amiably. When Chal came out from under the shower, he felt a keenness that he had not felt for days; an exhilaration that made everything interesting. He looked around for a towel, but he noticed that Sun-on-His-Wings was allowing himself to dry without the aid of a towel, so he didn't say anything.

As they stood in the little room, Sun-on-His-Wings seemed to be enjoying himself hugely. He said, "Chal, maybe you will think about church now. I am goin' to church today, but you can't go—you do not belong. You better go to sleep, and after while we will have feast." Chal could smell the meat broiling, and he became very hungry.

He watched Sun-on-His-Wings walk toward the main ranch house with the end of this blanket trailing. He knew he was going there to put on fresh clothes; he didn't want to touch the clothes he had taken off before the ceremony of the sweatlodge. Chal felt in his clothes and found his cigarettes, lit one and lay down on the only bed in the room. Despite his hunger and drowsiness, he was still moved by the happiness of the night, and he wanted to lie there and recapitulate. But he was too sleepy, and he was soon sound asleep. His hand slipped off the bed, and the cigarette fell to the floor, when the morning breezes, the awakening breath of the summer morning, played delicately with the blue smoke.

313

D'ARCY  MCNICKLE

Considered by many critics to be among the founders of modern Native American literature and ethnohistory, McNickle was widely recognized for his scholarly works on Native American history and anthropology and as an expert on government policy concerning Native Americans. His two novels The Surrounded *and* Wind from an Enemy Sky *have also been praised as masterful depictions of the conflict between white and American Indian cultures.*

Born in St. Ignatius, Montana, McNickle was a mixed blood of Cree ancestry who was adopted into the Salish-Kootenai Flathead tribe. He became one of the most highly educated Native Americans of his generation, attending the University of Montana, Oxford University in England, and the University of Grenoble in France. After working in New York City and Washington, D.C., as a writer for several years, he accepted a position with the United States Bureau of Indian Affairs in 1936, where he strove to improve relations between the United States government and American Indian communities and to shape official policies favorable to Native Americans. He was eventually promoted to executive director of American Indian Development, a position he held until 1952 when he accepted a post as a professor of anthropology at the University of Saskatchewan.

McNickle was praised for such nonfiction works as *Indians and Other Americans: Two Ways of Life Meet,* which explores the varied causes of negative relations between whites and Indians. Also among his groundbreaking works of ethnohistory and anthropology are *The Indian*

Flathead writer, historian, and activist.

Born: January 18, 1904, in St. Ignatius, Montana.

Died: December 1977.

Partnerships: Married Roma Kaufman (an editor), September 13, 1939; children: Antoinette, Kathleen.

Education: Attended University of Montana, 1925–25, Oxford University, 1925–26, and University of Grenoble, 1931.

Career: Editorial work in New York, NY, 1926–35; Federal Writers Project, Washington, D.C., staff writer, 1935–36; Bureau of Indian Affairs, Washington, D.C., 1936–52, began as assistant to commissioner, became field representative and director of tribal relations; American Indian Development, Inc., Boulder, CO., director, 1952–66; University of Saskatchewan, Saskatoon, professor of anthropology, 1966–71; Newberry Library, Chicago, Ill., program director, Center for American Indian History, beginning 1972. Member of Colorado State Advisory Committee, U.S. Commission on Civil Rights.

Memberships: American Anthropological Association (fellow), Society for Applied Anthropology, Current Anthropology (associate).

Address: Home—4824 Guadalupe Trail N.W., Albuquerque, NM 87107. Office—Center for American Indian History, Newberry Library, 60 West Walton St., Chicago, IL 60610.

Tribes of the United States: Ethnic and Cultural Survival (later published as *Native American Tribalism: Indian Survivals and Renewals*) and *They Came Here First: The Epic of the American Indian.* Characterized by tragedy and fatalism, McNickle's acclaimed novels *The Surrounded* and *Wind from an Enemy Sky* portray the destruction resulting from such conflicts as the European concept of property ownership versus the Indian belief in sacred land, and American individualism versus the importance of tribalism in Native cultures.

THE SURROUNDED

University of New Mexico Press, copyright © 1936 by D'Arcy McNickle

316 | **Chapter One**

Archilde Leon had been away from his father's ranch for nearly a year, yet when he left the stage road and began the half-mile walk to the house he did not hurry. When he emerged from behind a clump of thornbush and cottonwood and caught his first glimpse of the cluster of buildings before him, he looked once, and that was all.

He avoided the front of the big house, where his father would most likely be sitting, and made for the dirt-roofed log cabin which occupied lower ground, down toward the creek. Two dogs, one yellow and one black and white, leaped and howled, but they were the only ones to meet him.

He walked past the big house, which was his father's, and went to the cabin, his mother's. There she was, as he knew she would be, sitting in the shade. If she heard him she did not look up at once. But she was a little deaf and a little blind—perhaps she had not sensed his approach. He let the heavy suitcase slip from his sweating hand.

Then she looked up. A sigh escaped here and a quick smile multiplied the many fine lines in her wrinkled brown face.

Here he was, the best of her sons, and the youngest, home again after a year—but would he stay? She had only a faint idea of where he had been; the world out that way was so unlike Sniél-emen; she had even less of an idea of what he did when he went away. But never mind. Here he was again. She smiled quickly, a little at a distance; she did not wish to embarrass him with her attention.

"So you have come back," she said.

"Yes, I am here." He turned his suitcase over on its side for a seat.

"Where have you been this time?"

"To Portland. That's where the stinking water is."

She let the word echo in her ears, saying nothing herself, but it had no meaning. If he had said he had been toward the mouth of the Snpoilshi (Columbia) River, she would have known what he meant. But Portland! Her red-rimmed eyes gazed toward the timber which came down to the far bank of the creek. Two boys were splashing in the water down there.

"You have been gone a long time."

"I had a job. I played my fiddle in a show house. I can always get a job now any time I go away."

She looked at him quickly, taking him in. He wore a blue suit and a white shirt and his tan shoes were new and polished. So he could go away any time now? He did not have to be fed at home?

"They paid me this money. Look!" She barely glanced at the offered money. It was all strange, she could not make it into a picture. An Indian boy, she thought, belonged with his people.

They sat in silence for some time. It was useless to speak of fiddle-playing, and for a while Archilde could think of nothing that was not equally useless. When you came home to your Indian mother you had to remember that it was a different world. Anyhow you had not come to show your money and talk about yourself. There would be fishing, riding, climbing a mountainside—those things you wanted to do one more time. Why talk of fiddle-playing?

317

The heat of the afternoon lingered. The three horses in the pasture below the house were bothered by the flies. They had been in the timber across the creek since midday and had come out only a short while before. As they ate, they moved along, stopping now and then to rub their muzzles on their forelegs or to kick themselves under the belly.

His gaze returned to his mother. How did she look after a year? No different. He had not expected her to look any different. Her eyes, which were getting weaker each year, were watery slits in the brown skin. She wore a handkerchief around her head and her calico dress was long and full and held in at the waist by a beaded belt. Her buckskin moccasins gave off a pungent odor of smoke. Nothing was any different. He knew it without looking. He had not come all the way from Portland to these mountains in Montana to satisfy himself on that score.

"No one fishes when you are away. My bones groan so loud when I walk the fish stay under their rocks."

It seemed impossible that no one cared to fish. The creek was full of swift, cunning trout. He got excited just thinking about it. Tomorrow he would cut himself a pole and try it.

The old lady was saying something else. "I will have some people here. We will make a feast and my friends will see you again."

That was something he had forgotten to include in his visit—the old lady and her feasts! You gorged yourself on meat until you felt sick, and a lot of old people told tiresome stories. He frowned. He ought to refuse. He had not come for a feast. She ought to be told that. But it was a small matter. His mother was old. It was a small matter.

"How is everybody?" He had begun to smoke a cigarette which he took ready rolled out of a package.

The question made the old lady sigh. Eheu! It was bad!

"Louis stole some horses last week. I think no one knows it yet. He's in the mountains."

"He'll go to pen if they find him."

"He'll go to hell!"

Already he was hearing the old stories—quarreling, stealing, fighting. His brothers knew nothing else. And his mother knew nothing but the fear of hell, for herself and for her sons.

A small girl, his niece, came to the corner of the cabin. Her hair was braided, with white strings tied to the end of each braid. She was bashful and kept her chin on her breast.

"Gran'pa wants to see you," she announced when she was still a dozen paces away.

The Surrounded (fiction), Dodd, 1936.
They Came Here First: The Epic of the American Indian, Lippincott, 1949.
Runner in the Sun: A Story of Indian Maize (fiction), Winston, 1954.
(With Harold E. Fey) *Indians and Other Americans: Two Ways of Life Meet*, Harper, 1959.

The Indian Tribes of the United States: Ethnic and Cultural Survival, Oxford University Press, 1962.
Indian Man: A Life of Oliver La Farge, Indiana University Press, 1971.
Wind from an Enemy Sky, Harper, 1978.

Contributor to *Encyclopaedia Britannica*. Member of editorial advisory board, *Handbook of North American Indians*, beginning 1971.

She looked at him but hugged the cabin wall.

Archilde got to his feet and stretched himself. He looked toward the mountains in the east, and then upward to the fleckless sky. Nowhere in the world, he imagined, was there a sky of such depth and freshness. He wanted never to forget it, wherever he might be in times to come. Yes, wherever he might be!

Down by the creek his two nephews were standing uncertainly and watching the house. They had just seen Archilde. Thier shouts died away and they went behind the bush to dress.

As Archilde picked up his suitcase and walked toward the house he realized of a sudden that he dreaded meeting his father, Max Leon, the Spaniard. That dread was something which went back a long time, and Archilde, who was growing into a man now, was disturbed by it. It ought not to be.

His father had just awakened from his afternoon nap and was sitting on the front porch, his gray hair tousled and matted. Every afternoon on awakening he drank a whisky eggnog. A half-empty glass stood on the table at his elbow. He stretched out his hand.

It was a thin, bony hand. Archilde looked down at it with some surprise. This was his father's hand.

"Sit down, my *son!*" With what sarcasm he could utter that word! "Agnes said you were here. Where have you been this time?" His voice was deep and its least variation gave strong emphasis to his words. He handled his voice like a whip.

"In Portland."

"Portland, I suppose, is a busy city. They make you work to live. And what did you do? I see you have good clothes."

"I played in an orchestra."

"Yes? What do you play—the accordion, or mouth-harp?"

"The fiddle."

"Really? I've never heard you. You never play for your people at home."

Archilde sat down then and looked at his Spanish father. He was of middle size and build, of stocky limbs. His face sagged into pouches and under the stubble of gray whiskers the skin looked oily. He had a high fore-head and a long nose. It was not a weak face, and not a commonplace one. What was it in that face that could so dominate one who was no longer a child? Archilde gazed steadily at his father and tried not to show his irritation.

"Some day you must play for me," his father was saying.

"I have no fiddle now. I gave it to a friend."

"In a card game, perhaps?" There was a slight smile.

"No, it was a present."

"But don't you play cards?"

"No."

"What kind of Indian are you, then?"

Archilde shrugged his shoulders. His confidence was failing him. It was just as it had always been in recent years; after a few more thrusts from Max he would be helpless before him. He had thought it would never hap-pen again.

"You haven't many answers. But tell me this, have you any money after working, as you say?"

Archilde showed his money. He wanted to refuse, out of defiance, but he showed the money.

"You better let me put it in the bank for you."

"No. I'll keep it."

"So! You have learned nothing! You will blow your money on a good time and then go on living off me!"

It was more than Archilde could stand. He had to speak out in anger and so confess his helplessness.

"I didn't come to live off you, God damn it! I came to see my mother, not you, and in a few days I'm going again. Keep your stinking money!" He knew it was the answer of a child.

Old Leon laughed. "I see you're getting a good opinion of yourself." He said it insultingly, and yet his eyes looked closely at the boy. At least he had not slunk away like a whipped dog.

320

A horseman appeared in the lane, riding swiftly, a cloud of dust hanging like a plume in the still air. The rider, a rancher from the flat-lands of the valley, tied his horse and entered the front gate.

"You're riding fast on a hot day," Max called out. "Come up in the shade!"

"That's fine grain you got down by the road. On the flat we're burned out."

"So I 've heard. No doubt you're thirsty. Here, Agnes! Bring water to Emile Pariseau!"

Agnes, his daughter, kept his house. Her full-blood husband had had his head kicked in by a horse, and Max, though he spoke pro-fanely of her husband, brought her and her three children to live with him. She appeared on the porch with a pail of water and a long-handled dipper.

Max scowled. "Where's the pitcher? You're not bringing water to an Indian!"

The rancher was good-natured. "I never drink out of a pitcher—this is all right." Seeing Archilde standing off to one side Pariseau spoke to him.

"How long you been away, Arsheel?"

When the question was answered another was asked. "Have you seen your brother Louis?" The rancher avoided Max's eyes.

"No. I've just come."

"Are you looking for Louis?" Max asked. "God knows where he is, Pariseau. I probably know less about my family than you do."

"That's what I come to see you about."

McNickle, in his works, identified the concept of individual transferable title to the land as the "prime source of misunderstanding" between whites and Indians. McNickle thought that Indians understood land payment as a gift and perhaps as a rental fee for land use, but that probably even late in the 19th century, Indians could not conceive of private land ownership. [In Indians & Other Americans] *McNickle elo-quently states the difference between the white transmutation of land to money and the Native American view: "One cannot grow a tree on a pile of money, or cause water to gush from it; one can only spend it and then one is homeless."*

—Franco Meli, "D'Arcy McNickle: The Indian War That Never Ends, or the Incredible Survival of Tribalism," in *Revue Francaise d'Etudes Americaines,* November 1988.

321

D ' A R C Y   M C N I C K L E

Archilde went inside. He had waited to be dismissed but Max appeared to ignore him.

Pariseau stopped to roll a cigarette, saying nothing meanwhile. When he had finished he looked up.

"What I come to tell you is this. Louis stole some horses from me. We got the goods on him. Somebody seen him with the horses."

Max's face went cold. "What's that got to do with me?"

"Well, we used to be neighbors—I wanted to tell you. If we catch him it'll have to go hard. There's too damn much horse stealing by these young fellows—"

"Good!" Max cut in on him. "Send 'em up to pen, hang 'em—but what's it got to do with me?"

"Well, I dunno. I just thought I'd tell you. Then you could tell him to lay low—or you could maybe tell me where to find him. His mother's relations are everywhere. Don't ask me."

In a little while the rancher rode away, having heard Max Leon curse his sons up one side and down the other, as they say.

He sat motionless for several minutes, watching the rider disappear behind a cloud of dust. His eyes had been alert before the rancher came; now they looked dull. He was slow and heavy in getting to his feet. His legs were slightly bowed from many years of riding. He walked toward his wife's cabin.

She was sitting as Archilde had left her an hour before. The shadow of the cabin had lengthened. Max stopped and looked down at his Indian wife. When he talked to her he had to use her tongue, since if he tried to use English, which she knew perfectly, she would pretend not to understand. He had tried to overcome here obstinacy by never talking to her. That was some years ago. He had not been able to keep it up, there were occasions when he had to speak, and in the end he had decided that it was better to get an answer than to fight an endless battle. So he spoke her Salish.

"Where's Louis?"

"How should I know!"

"Have you heard about him?"

"I hear nothing. My sons are scattered."

"He stole some horses."

She was silent, gesturing slightly with her hand.

"A friend has come to warn me. He said the police would hang him. If you know where he is tell me."

"I know nothing. My sons are afraid to come here."

"I'll send a rider to warn him."

A silence.

He had been married for forty years to this woman, she had borne him eleven children, and he had come no closer to her than that. She would not tell him what he knew she knew. She did not trust him. That was something to make a man reflect on the meaning and purpose of his life.

He spat and walked away. He entered his house through the kitchen. It was as well furnished as any white man's house. A stove with nickel trimmings, a linoleum covering on the floor, a white enameled kitchen cabinet against the wall, a well-stocked pantry—no white man with a white woman for wife had more.

Agnes sat on the floor by the window peeling potatoes. Max took a drink from the water bucket.

"Where's Louis?" he asked as he stood drinking.

"Perhaps in town. I don't know."

He stood there for a moment on the point of asking another question, but scowled and walked away. To Archilde, who was drinking coffee at the kitchen table, he motioned to follow him to the porch.

"What does your mother say about Louis?"

Archilde appeared to reflect. "His name wasn't mentioned. Did Pariseau want him?"

"He's been stealing horses. You didn't know about that, eh?"

Archilde didn't know.

Max was wrathful, his face deeply colored. "So! You're going to be like the rest! Lying to me already and you're not home for an hour! I'm telling you this for Louis' good. If they catch him they'll hang him! Tell the old lady yourself, if you won't take my word. I'll save his damn neck; I'll do that much. Understand?"

Archilde started to walk away.

"Don't let her know I talked to you about this."

That was how matters always stood in Max Leon's family. There was always this distrust, this warfare.

N. SCOTT MOMADAY

Widely recognized as one of the most successful contemporary Native American literary figures, N. Scott Momaday, also known as Tsoai-talee ("Rock Tree Boy"), has garnered critical acclaim for his focus on Kiowa traditions, customs, and beliefs, and the role of Amerindians in contemporary society. Often addressing the nature and origins of myths, Momaday's writings are largely influenced by Native oral traditions. He is of Kiowa, white, and Cherokee descent and first gained critical attention with The Journey of Tai-me, *a nonfiction account of Kiowa folktales and myths, particularly those concerning the Kiowa* tai-me, *a medicine bundle or doll used in the Kiowa sun dance. Thematically, much of the volume is also included in the autobiography,* The Way to Rainy Mountain, *which has occasionally been classified as a novel. Divided into three sections—"The Setting Out," "The Going On," and "The Closing In"—*The Way to Rainy Mountain *spans 300 years of Kiowa history, relating and at times reimagining sacred myths, tribal customs, the "Golden Age" of the Kiowas, and the encroachment of white settlers onto tribal lands in the 1800s. However, rather than merely focusing on tribal history as he did in* The Journey of Tai-me, *Momaday employs several voices and combines ethnography with personal reminiscences to depict his family's participation in tribal customs.*

Essay by

JOANN DE FILIPPO

325

I'm not concerned to define or delineate American Indian experience, except to myself and for my own purposes. But I am very concerned to understand as much as I can about myth making. . . . I regard what I'm doing as an inquiry into the nature of myth making.

—N. Scott Momaday, in an interview with Louis Owens, in *This Is About Vision: Interviews with Southwestern Writers*, 1990.

The 1976 autobiography, *The Names: A Memoir*, similarly incorporates family and tribal history, detailing the importance of naming and self-identity as well as Momaday's evolving understanding of language, imagination, and the creative process. Aspects of *The Journey of Tai-me* and *The Way to Rainy Mountain* are additionally present in *House Made of Dawn*, for which Momaday earned the 1969 Pulitzer Prize for Fiction. The novel concerns Abel, a young Native man searching for a sense of identity in white and tribal society. Following his return to the reservation after serving in World War II, *House Made of Dawn* relates the events leading up to Abel's incarceration in prison for murder, his attempt to become integrated into white society in Los Angeles upon his release, his relationship with various whites and Native Americans, and eventually a second attempt to rejoin his home community. Incorporating a circular structure, Native storytelling techniques, and biblical allusions, the novel emphasizes historical attempts to convert Native Americans to Christianity and the alienating effects of assimilation on tribal members. *House Made of Dawn* is also known for its fragmented, stream-of-consciousness narrative style, its inclusion of multiple voices, and its use of flashbacks, all of which have earned Momaday favorable comparisons with American novelist William Faulkner. Momaday's second novel, *The Ancient Child*, likewise concerns a Kiowa man alienated from his heritage.

Momaday is additionally known for the verse collections *Angle of Geese, and Other Poems* and *The Gourd Dancer*. Oral traditions and Kiowa customs are central to these volumes, which feature prose poems, syllabic verse, and Native chants, and often focus on philosophical issues regarding identity, death, knowledge, and the need for perspective. His most recent collection, *In the Presence of the Sun: Stories and Poems, 1961–1991*, contains short stories, which delineate the history of Kiowa shields, and a sequence of poems concerning the legendary outlaw Billy the Kid. A seminal figure in the American literary canon, Momaday is frequently studied worldwide by Natives and non-Natives alike. In assessing Momaday's career, Howard Meredith has observed: "Momaday relates to the reader his figures' lives in language, 'and of the awful risk involved.' On one level he prepares his readers for the risk of experiencing another plane of existence, one that can be realized through acceptance of the oneness of past, pre-

326

Kiowa novelist, poet, autobiographer, nonfiction writer, editor, and artist.

Born: February 27, 1934, in Lawton, Oklahoma.

Partnerships: Married Gaye Mangold, September 5, 1959; married Regina Heitzer, July 21, 1978; children: (first marriage) Cael, Jill, Brit (all daughters); (second marriage) Lore (daughter).

Education: Attended Augusta Military Academy; University of New Mexico, A.B., 1958; Stanford University, M.A., 1960, Ph.D., 1963.

Career: University of California, Santa Barbara, assistant professor, 1963–65, associate professor of English, 1968–69; University of California, Berkeley, associate professor of English and comparative litera-ture, 1969–73; Stanford University, Stanford, CA, professor of English, 1973–82; University of Arizona, Tucson, professor of English, 1982–. Artist; has exhibited his drawings and paintings in galleries. Museum of American Indian, Heye Foundation, New York City, trustee, 1978–. Consultant, National Endowment for the Humanities and National Endowment for the Arts, 1970–.

Memberships: Modern Language Association of America, American Studies Association, Gourd Dance Society of the Kiowa Tribe.

Address: Home—1041 West Roller Coaster Rd., Tucson, AZ 85704. Office—Department of English, University of Arizona, Tucson, AZ.

sent, and future in accord with spatial terms. Momaday provides for the defiance of renewal. He points the way to mental sanctuary. He brings American readers to a new sense of maturity through the use of the traditions of America. He asks readers to imagine themselves, but always in relationship to the American earth and sky."

THE WAY TO RAINY MOUNTAIN

University of New Mexico Press, copyright © 1969 by N. Scott Momaday

Introduction

A single knoll rises out of the plain in Oklahoma, north and west of the Wichita Range. For my people, the Kiowas, it is an old landmark, and they gave it the name Rainy Mountain. The hardest weather in the world is there. Winter brings blizzards, hot tornadic winds arise in the spring, and in summer the prairie is an anvil's edge. The grass turns brittle and brown, and it cracks beneath your feet. There are green belts along the rivers and creeks, linear groves of hickory and pecan, willow and witch hazel. At a distance in July or August the steaming foliage seems almost to writhe in fire. Great green and yellow grasshoppers are everywhere in the tall grass, popping up like corn to sting the flesh, and tortoises crawl about on the red earth, going nowhere in the plenty of time. Loneliness is an aspect of the land. All things

327

N .   S C O T T   **M O M A D A Y**

in the plain are isolate; there is no confusion of objects in the eye, but *one* hill or *one* tree or *one* man. To look upon that landscape in the early morning, with the sun at your back, is to lose the sense of proportion. Your imagination comes to life, and this, you think, is where Creation was begun.

I returned to Rainy Mountain in July. My grandmother had died in the spring, and I wanted to be at her grave. She had lived to be very old and at last infirm. Her only living daughter was with her when she died, and I was told that in death her face was that of a child.

I like to think of her as a child. When she was born, the Kiowas were living the last great moment of their history. For more than a hundred years they had controlled the open range from the Smoky Hill River to the Red, from the headwaters of the Canadian to the fork of the Arkansas and Cimarron. In alliance with the Comanches, they had ruled the whole of the southern Plains. War was their sacred business, and they were among the finest horsemen the world has ever known. But warfare for the Kiowas was preeminently a matter of disposition rather than of survival, and they never understood the grim, unrelenting advance of the U.S. Cavalry. When at last, divided and ill-provisioned, they were driven onto the Staked Plains in the cold rains of autumn, they fell into panic. In Palo Duro Canyon they abandoned their crucial stores to pillage and had nothing then but their lives. In order to save themselves, they surrendered to the soldiers at Fort Sill and were imprisoned in the old stone corral that now stands as a military museum. My grandmother was spared the humiliation of those high gray walls by eight or ten years, but she must have known from birth the affliction of defeat, the dark brooding of old warriors.

Her name was Aho, and she belonged to the last culture to evolve in North America. Her forebears came down from the high country in western Montana nearly three centuries ago. They were a mountain people, a mysterious tribe of hunters whose language has never been positively classified in any major group. In the late seventeenth century they began a long migration to the south and east. It was a journey toward the dawn, and it led to a golden age. Along the way the Kiowas were befriended by the Crows, who gave them the culture and religion of the Plains. They acquired horses, and their ancient nomadic spirit was suddenly free of the ground. They acquired Tai-me, the sacred Sun Dance doll, from that moment the object and symbol of their worship, and so shared in the divinity of the sun. Not least, they acquired the sense of destiny, therefore courage and pride. When they entered upon the southern Plains they had been transformed. No longer were they slaves to the simple necessity of survival; they were a lordly and dangerous society of fighters and thieves, hunters and priests of the sun. According to their origin myth, they entered the world through a hollow log. From one point of view, their migration was the fruit of an old prophecy, for indeed they emerged from a sunless world.

Novels

House Made of Dawn, Harper, 1968.
The Ancient Child, Doubleday, 1989.

Poetry

Angle of Geese, and Other Poems, David Godine, 1974.
The Gourd Dancer, illustrated by the author, Harper, 1976.
In the Presence of the Sun: A Gathering of Shields, Rydal Press, 1992.
In the Presence of the Sun: Stories and Poems, 1961–1991, St. Martin's Press, 1992; contains *In the Presence of the Sun: A Gathering of Shields*.

Other

(Editor) The Complete Poems of Frederick Goddard Tuckerman, University Press, 1965.
The Journey of Tai-me (retold Kiowa folktales), with original etchings by Bruce S. McCurdy, limited edition, University of California, 1967.

Nonfiction

The Way to Rainy Mountain (autobiography), illustrated by father, Alfred Momaday, University of New Mexico Press, 1969.
Colorado: Summer, Fall, Winter, Spring, illustrated with photographs by David Muench, Rand McNally, 1973.
The Names: A Memoir (autobiography), Harper, 1976.
Also author of film script of Frank Water's novel, *The Man Who Killed the Deer*. Contributor of articles and poems to periodicals; a frequent reviewer on Indian subjects for *New York Times Book Review*.

Although my grandmother lived out her long life in the shadow of Rainy Mountain, the immense landscape of the continental interior lay like memory in her blood. She could tell of the Crows, whom she had never seen, and of the Black Hills, where she had never been. I wanted to see in reality what she had seen more perfectly in the mind's eye, and traveled fifteen hundred miles to begin my pilgrimage.

Yellowstone, it seemed to me, was the top of the world, a region of deep lakes and dark timber, canyons and waterfalls. But, beautiful as it is, one might have the sense of confinement there. The skyline in all directions is close at hand, the high wall of the woods and deep cleavages of shade. There is a perfect freedom in the mountains, but it belongs to the eagle and the elk, the badger and the bear. The Kiowas reckoned their stature by the distance they could see, and they were bent and blind in the wilderness.

Descending eastward, the highland meadows are a stairway to the plain. In July the inland slope of the Rockies is luxuriant with flax and buckwheat, stonecrop and larkspur. The earth unfolds and the limit of the land recedes. Clusters of trees, and animals grazing far in the distance, cause the vision to reach away and wonder to build upon the mind. The sun follows a longer course in the day, and the sky is immense beyond all comparison. The great billowing clouds that sail upon it are shadows that move upon the grain like water, dividing light. Farther down, in the land of the Crows and Blackfeet, the plain is yellow. Sweet clover takes hold of the hills and bends upon itself to cover and seal the soil. There the Kiowas paused on their way; they had come to the place where they must change their lives. The sun is at home on the plains. Precisely there does it have the certain character of a god. When the Kiowas came to the land of the Crows, they could see the

329

dark lees of the hills at dawn across the Bighorn River, the profusion of light on the grain shelves, the oldest deity ranging after the solstices. Not yet would they veer southward to the caldron of the land that lay below; they must wean their blood from the northern winter and hold the mountains a while longer in their view. They bore Tai-me in procession to the east.

A dark mist lay over the Black Hills, and the land was like iron. At the top of a ridge I caught sight of Devil's Tower upthrust against the gray sky as if in the birth of time the core of the earth had broken through its crust and the motion of the world was begun. There are things in nature that engender an awful quiet in the heart of man; Devil's Tower is one of them. Two centuries ago, because they could not do otherwise, the Kiowas made a legend at the base of the rock. My grandmother said:

Eight children were there at play, seven sisters and their brother. Suddenly the boy was struck dumb; he trembled and began to run upon his hands and feet. His fingers became claws, and his body was covered with fur. Directly there was a bear where the boy had been. The sisters were terrified; they ran, and the bear after them. They came to the stump of a great tree, and the tree spoke to them. It bade them climb upon it, and as they did so it began to rise into the air. The bear came to kill them, but they were just beyond its reach. It reared against the tree and scored the bark all around with its claws. The seven sisters were borne into the sky, and they became the stars of the Big Dipper.

From that moment, and so long as the legend lives, the Kiowas have kinsmen in the night sky. Whatever they were in the mountains, they could be no more. However tenuous their well-being, however much they had suffered and would suffer again, they had found a way out of the wilderness.

My grandmother had a reverence for the sun, a holy regard that now is all but gone out of mankind. There was a wariness in her, and an ancient awe. She was a Christian in her later years, but she had come a long way about, and she never forgot her birthright. As a child she had been to the Sun Dances; she had taken part in those annual rites, and by them she had learned the restoration of her people in the presence of Tai-me. She was about seven when the last Kiowa Sun Dance was held in 1887 on the Washita River above Rainy Mountain Creek. The buffalo were gone. In order to consummate the ancient sacrifice—to impale the head of a buffalo bull upon the medicine tree—a delegation of old men journeyed into Texas, there to beg and barter for an animal from the Goodnight herd. She was ten when the Kiowas came together for the last time as a living Sun Dance culture. They could find no buffalo; they had to hang an old hide from the sacred tree. Before the dance could begin, a company of soldiers rode out from Fort Sill under orders to disperse the tribe. Forbidden without cause the essential act of their faith, having seen the wild herds slaughtered and left to rot upon the ground, the Kiowas backed away forever from the medicine tree. That was July 20, 1890, at the

330

great bend of the Washita. My grandmother was there. Without bitterness, and for as long as she lived, she bore a vision of deicide.

Now that I can have her only in memory, I see my grandmother in the several postures that were peculiar to her: standing at the wood stove on a winter morning and turning meat in a great iron skillet; sitting at the south window, bent above her beadwork, and afterwards, when her vision failed, looking down for a long time into the fold of her hands; going out upon a cane, very slowly as she did when the weight of age came upon her; praying. I remember her most often at prayer. She made long, rambling prayers out of suffering and hope, having seen many things. I was never sure that I had the right to hear, so exclusive were they of all mere custom and company. The last time I saw her she prayed standing by the side of her bed at night, naked to the waist, the light of a kerosene lamp moving upon her dark skin. Her long, black hair, always drawn and braided in the day, lay upon her shoulders and against her breasts like a shawl. I do not speak Kiowa, and I never understood her prayers, but there was something inherently sad in the sound, some merest hesitation upon the syllables of sorrow. She began in a high and descending pitch, exhausting her breath to silence; then again and again—and always the same intensity of effort, of something that is, and is not, like urgency in the human voice. Transported so in the dancing light among the shadows of her room, she seemed beyond the reach of time. But that was illusion; I think I knew then that I should not see her again.

Houses are like sentinels in the plain, old keepers of the weather watch. There, in a very little while, wood takes on the appearance of great age. All colors wear soon away in the wind and rain, and then the wood is burned gray and the grain appears and the nails turn red with rust. The windowpanes are black and opaque; you imagine there is nothing within, and indeed there are many ghosts, bones given up to the land. They stand here and there against the sky, and you approach them for a longer time than you expect. They belong in the distance; it is their domain.

N. Scott Momaday marks a decisive line of demarcation in the cultural tradition of the Kiowa people. In doing so, he has struck a responsive chord among the other diverse peoples of North America. He is a collector of the ancient traditions that circulated orally among the Kiowa people and others of the American Southwest. With him begins a literary tradition of those prose narratives which previously had circulated almost exclusively within specific tribal contexts.

—Howard Meredith, "N. Scott Momaday: A Man of Words," in *World Literature Today,* Summer 1990.

N . S C O T T   M O M A D A Y

Once there was a lot of sound in my grandmother's house, a lot of coming and going, feasting and talk. The summers there were full of excitement and reunion. The Kiowas are a summer people; they abide the cold and keep to themselves, but when the season turns and the land becomes warm and vital they cannot hold still; an old love of going returns upon them. The aged visitors who came to my grandmother's house when I was a child were made of lean and leather, and they bore themselves upright. They wore great black hats and bright ample shirts that shook in the wind. They rubbed fat upon their hair and wound their braids with strips of colored cloth. Some of them painted their faces and carried the scars of old and cherished enmities. They were an old council of warlords, come to remind and be reminded of who they were. Their wives and daughters served them well. The women might indulge themselves; gossip was at once the mark and compensation of their servitude. They made loud and elaborate talk among themselves, full of jest and gesture, fright and false alarm. They went abroad in fringed and flowered shawls, bright beadwork and German silver. They were at home in the kitchen, and they prepared meals that were banquets.

There were frequent prayer meetings, and great nocturnal feasts. When I was a child I played with my cousins outside, where the lamplight fell upon the ground and the singing of the old people rose up around us and carried away into the darkness. There were a lot of good things to eat, a lot of laughter and surprise. And afterwards, when the quiet returned, I lay down with my grandmother and could hear the frogs away by the river and feel the motion of the air.

Now there is a funeral silence in the rooms, the endless wake of some final word. The walls have closed in upon my grandmother's house. When I returned to it in mourning, I saw for the first time in my life how small it was. It was late at night, and there was a white moon, nearly full. I sat for a long time on the stone steps by the kitchen door. From there I could see out across the land; I could see the long row of trees by the creek, the low light upon the rolling plains, and the stars of the Big Dipper. Once I looked at the moon and caught sight of a strange thing. A cricket had perched upon the handrail, only a few inches away from me. My line of vision was such that the creature filled the moon like a fossil. It had gone there, I thought, to live and die, for there, of all places, was its small definition made whole and eternal. A warm wind rose up and purled like the longing within me.

The next morning I awoke at dawn and went out on the dirt road to Rainy Mountain. It was already hot, and the grasshoppers began to fill the air. Still, it was early in the morning, and the birds sang out of the shadows. The long yellow grass on the mountain shone in the bright light, and a scissortail hied above the land. There, where it ought to be, at the end of a long and legendary way, was my grandmother's grave. Here and there on the

dark stones were ancestral names. Looking back once, I saw the mountain and came away.

XIII

If an arrow is well made, it will have tooth marks upon it. That is how you know. The Kiowas made fine arrows and straightened them in their teeth. Then they drew them to the bow to see if they were straight. Once there was a man and his wife. They were alone at night in their tipi. By the light of the fire the man was making arrows. After a while he caught sight of something. There was a small opening in the tipi where two hides were sewn together. Someone was there on the outside, looking in. The man went on with his work, but he said to his wife: "Someone is standing outside. Do not be afraid. Let us talk easily, as of ordinary things." He took up an arrow and straightened it in his teeth; then, as it was right for him to do, he drew it to the bow and took aim, first in this direction and then in that. And all the while he was talking, as if to his wife. But this is how he spoke: "I know that

N . S C O T T **M O M A D A Y**

you are there on the outside, for I can feel your eyes upon me. If you are a Kiowa, you will understand what I am saying, and you will speak your name." But there was no answer, and the man went on in the same way, pointing the arrow all around. At last his aim fell upon the place where his enemy stood, and he let go of the string. The arrow went straight to the enemy's heart.

The old men were the best arrowmakers, for they could bring time and patience to their craft. The young men—the fighters and hunters—were willing to pay a high price for arrows that were well made.

When my father was a boy, an old man used to come to Mammedaty's house and pay his respects. He was a lean old man in braids and was impressive in his age and bearing. His name was Cheney, and he was an arrowmaker. Every morning, my father tells me, Cheney would paint his wrinkled face, go out, and pray aloud to the rising sun. In my mind I can see that man as if he were there now. I like to watch him as he makes his prayer. I know where he stands and where his voice goes on the rolling grasses and where the sun comes up on the land. There, at dawn, you can feel the silence. It is cold and clear and deep like water. It takes hold of you and will not let you go.

DANIEL DAVID MOSES

Moses is best known for works in which he combines Native Canadian concerns with such universal themes as spirituality, self-identity, and human relationships. His poetry and plays are frequently infused with powerful imagery, wry humor, and a profound sense of the interconnectedness between humanity and the natural world. Moses initially gained recognition for his plays while earning his master's degree in fine arts at the University of British Columbia, where he won the Creative Writing department's 1977 prize for playwriting. In his best-known play, Coyote City, which focuses on a young girl who is searching for her dead lover, Moses interweaves myth and reality and incorporates elements of the Nez Percé legend of Coyote the Trickster.

Moses has also achieved critical success as a poet. *Delicate Bodies*, his first poetry collection, is considered his most personal work. In this volume he draws upon his upbringing on the Six Nations Reservation near Brantford, Ontario, to depict the beauty of nature, the peacefulness of rural life, and his relationship with his grandparents. These themes are also central to his second collection of verse, *The White Line*.

335

Throughout his career Moses has been praised for his intelligence and thoughtfulness in exploring spiritual concerns, his original use of imagistic language, and his inclusion of Native oral traditions in his works. Penny Petrone has called him "one of the best of Canada's young native writers," while Maggie Helwig has stated that he "writes in a world

Delaware playwright, poet, short story writer, and editor.

Born: February 18, 1952, in Ohsweken, Ontario, Canada.

Education: York University, B.A. (with honors); University of British Columbia, M.F.A.

Career: Poet and playwright; has also served as the director of the Association for Native Development in the Performing and Visual Arts and of Native Earth Performing Arts, Inc.

Memberships: Playwrights Canada, Writers Union of Canada, League of Canadian Poets, Association of Canadian Television and Radio Artists.

Address: 1 Browning Ave., Apt. 4, Toronto, Ontario, Canada M4K 1V6.

in which everything is not only possessed of consciousness, but seems engaged in thoughtful consideration of itself." In addition to his creative works, Moses has served as president of the Association for Native Development in the Performing and Visual Arts, as director of Native Earth Performing Arts, Inc., and as coeditor of an anthology of Native Canadian literature.

GRANDMOTHER OF THE GLACIER

From *The White Line*, Fifth House, copyright © 1990 by Daniel David Moses

The icefield she had in her head started
sliding the instant she died. *Was murdered*
would be more precise—would also explain
how her corpse became this high and open

ravine. But who's got the wit to split words
when that ice is coming at us? The world
can't ever again be that room we sat
in a circle in—the mainland rain hard

on a window as we listened to her
trying to explain about words. *Winter,*
she grinned. *That's the constant thought behind all
our words. In Canada we never can*

forget the edge on the wind. But the edge
on a knife cut in, cutting off more than

336

her words. So now it's hard to
　remember
how that edge and this cold
　thought grinding down

out of her head ever seemed
　separate.
Now they're a mouth that bites off
　and chews and
it's getting so close that breath
　flakes like snow.
So we go mute too—that mouth
　edge so red

that words drop from our own lips
　like stones. None
is as finished as those of hers that
　fell
into our hands. But the stars now
　are shards
of ice—they too are cutting in.
　There's no

time for her method—to split and
　polish
words against our own skin. Is that
　how hers
got so coarse she could embrace
　and contain
not only the stars but the rest of
　this freeze?

Her body's been swallowed. Ours may be next.
But even though we throw them in, her words
keep surfacing. May ours too be heard from
again—edging some terminal moraine.

I guess just for practical concerns I'd like to call myself a Native writer. I use this example all the time, but I heard an interview on national radio with a 19-year-old Cree man, who at that point was an ex-alcoholic, -drug addict, -street prostitute, and he told the interviewer, "Well, as I was growing up, it was the only choice we had, to be on the streets!" And I think it's really important for people to know that I'm a Native person, and that there are other choices in life, that being a writer is not something only mainstream people do. When I go into the centre of myself, the labels of "Native," or "writer," or "male," are not there!

—Daniel David Moses in *Contemporary Challenges: Conversations with Canadian Native Authors,* ed. Hartmut Lutz, Fifth House, 1991.

3 3 7

BEARWALK

From *The White Line*, Fifth House Publishers, copyright © 1990 by Daniel David Moses

At night I stroll behind my eyes,
trying to avoid the bears.
Now they're invisible in the snow,

I've got to take care not to sweat,
not to let them know I know they're there,
what they are, dangerous.

If I'm ambushed I pretend
the bear's an igloo; walk up and push
my head into its maw

Poetry
Delicate Bodies, Blewointmentpress, 1980.
The White Line, Fifth House, 1990.

Plays
Coyote City, produced in Toronto, Ontario, by Native Earth Performing Arts, May, 1988, Williams-Wallace, 1990.

Big Buck City, workshopped in Toronto, Ontario, at Theatre Passe Muraille, June, 1988.
The Dreaming Beauty, published in *Impulse*, Vol. 15, No. 3, 1989.

Other
(Coeditor) *An Anthology of Canadian Native Literature in English*, Oxford, 1992.

Work represented in anthologies, including *The Last Blewointment Anthology*, Blewointmentpress, 1986; *First Person Plural*, Black Moss, 1988; and *Harper's Anthology of Native American Twentieth Century Verse*, Harper, 1990.

and comment on the reek.
Make a bear question the repute
of its jaws and it's spiritless.

Point at its mouth and say
A star! Is it Christmas?
and it's done with. I've tripped on

bones of bears who'd bitten
their own hearts out. Once they're extinct
I'll never wake up dead.

THE LINE

From *The White Line*, Fifth House Publishers, copyright © 1990 by Daniel David Moses

This is not the poem, this line
I'm feeding you. And the thought
that this line is not the poem
is not it either. Instead
the thought of what this line is
not is the weight that sinks it
in. And though this image of
that thought as a weight is quite
a neat figure of speech, you
know what it's not—though it did
this time let the line smoothly
arc to this spot, and now lets

3 3 9

D A N I E L   D A V I D   **M O S E S**

Moses' voice is firm and assured, but oddly hard to define, combining a loose colloquial sprawl and a pared-down tenseness, an on-and-off leaning towards traditional fixed forms and rhyme patterns, a mythic imagination and an everyday chattiness. He writes in a world in which everything is not only possessed of consciousness, but seems engaged in thoughtful consideration of itself. . . . Moses clearly draws some of the character of his writing from the oral literature of the Native peoples of Canada, though there is little explicit use of traditional Native stories. Rather, it is his merging of the daily and the sacred that he inherits, his sense of the thoughtful world—and his irreverence, as well.

—Maggie Helwig, "Seasons of the Sacred," in *Books in Canada,* May 1991.

it reach down to one other,
one further rhyme—the music
of which almost does measure
up, the way it keeps the line
stirring through the dampening
air. Oh, you know you can hear
the lure in that. As you know
you've known from the start the
  self
referring this line's doing
was a hood—a sharp, twisted
bit of wit that made you look
and see how clear it is no
part of this line or its gear
could be the poem. Still it cast
and kept the line reeling out
till now at least the hook's on
to itself and about to
tie this line I'm feeding you
up with a knot. Referring
to itself has got the line
and us nowhere. So clever's
not what the poem is about
either. We're left hanging there
while something like a snout starts
nudging at your ear, nibbling
near my mouth—and it's likely
it's the poem about to take
the bait. From the inside ought
to be a great way to learn

what the poem is. And we'll use
this line when the poem's drawn it
taut and fine as breath to tell
what we know, where we are and
where we'll go—unless the line
breaks. How would it feel, knowing,
at last, what the poem really
is, to lack the line to speak?

3 4 0

DUANE  NIATUM

Duane Niatum mentions painters of the impressionist and post-impression-ist schools and music among early influences on his writing. "The act of poetry is very much like the act of the painter; it must involve the entire per-son, all the senses working in unity to give form and substance to the mys-tery of life and creation."

Essay by

RUTH ROSENBERG

In an autobiographical essay, "Traveling the Road That Once Was You," Niatum writes, "Now married to the Muse over thiry years I have come to the conclusion that much of my writing deals with the conflict between faith and despair, and the many ways in which the imagination searches for a synthesis, the path that breaks free of that snare. . . ."

He continues, "the power to change, the strength to see beyond the limitations of ordinary consciousness is not diminished by the forces of reality, what we as writers see before us, if we are humbled and grateful for the special gift the Muse offers us, that is, that we are forever being altered by the surprises of language. I personally appreciate that without these word wings my deck of selves would snap apart in the wind like four crow cackles. Always a willing servant of the language, I seek a life beyond mere existence, where art is the song of landscape and spirit, and the process is balanced and reflected in the sonar colors and echoes of the heart."

Niatum's works have been translated into Dutch, Italian, Macedon-ian, Russian, Danish, Spanish, German, Polish, French, Icelandic, and Frisian.

341

Klallam poet, short story writer, and playwright.

Born: February 13, 1938, in Seattle, Washington.

Education: University of Washington, Seattle, B.A., 1970; Johns Hopkins University, M.A., 1972.

Career: Poet and freelance editor. Johns Hopkins University, Baltimore, MD, instructor in American and European literature writing seminars, 1971–72; editor, Native American Authors Program, Harper & Row Publishers, Inc., 1973–74; Immaculate High School, Seattle, WA, English and literature teacher, 1974–75; Seattle Arts Commission, Seattle, worked with elderly in artist-in-the-city program, 1977–78. Visiting instructor at University of Washington, Evergreen State College, Eastern Washington University, and Seattle Central Community College; teaching curriculum developer, College of Education, University of Washington. Has worked as an assistant librarian for over three years in libraries at University of Washington and New York Historical Society. Has read his poetry and fiction at over forty colleges and universities and at art festivals throughout the United States and Europe, including Portland Poetry Festival, Anacortes Arts Festival, Portland State University, Phoenix Indian High School, University of California, Berkeley, and University of South Dakota; invitational reading, Library of Congress, 1976; member of poet-in-schools programs in Arizona, New Mexico, Oregon, and Washington. Judged poetry contest for Washington Poets Association, 1975, and for King County Arts Commission, Seattle, Wash.

Address: 939 N. 101 St., #202 Seattle, WA., 98133.

AFTER THE DEATH
OF AN ELDER KLALLAM

From *Drawings of the Song Animals*, Holy Cow! Press, copyright © 1991 by Duane Niatum

I

Great-uncle Joe sat with a bottle of beer
in one hand and a steaming mussel in the other,
chanting under the Moon of Dry Grass,
the story of Kwatee, the Changer.
His grandchildren and his brother's huddled,
awed by his heavy-cedared frame and shadow,
painted in the sand by the fire.
When his laughter cracked with the pine logs
that smelled of kelp and seaweed, we saw
the Thunderbird surface before the whale.

Twelve years have passed the Hadlock flats
since I last saw his fishnets hanging
through winter across the common stream.
What blizzard afternoon was it

342

he pantomimed the gait of the
   black elk
who was only seen by the Trickster;
and the Chinook salmon held in a
   net,
and because of his copper eyes
   and flapping
defiance, he threw it back into the
   sea?
Oh when did the magic of a whale
   hunt
darken to nothing more than wish?

I can still hear his obscene shouts
   to the crows
the morning he slipped on a crab
   shell mound,
almost failing to toss feast bones
to the Herring People.

The main focus of my art, whether poem or short story, seems to be an attempt to illuminate the inner life of the artist—to turn into images and metaphors the constant battles waged within the psyche and its occasional moments of bliss. This struggle covers and gives substance and shape to my canvas and sets the stage for revealing the central theme: the quest for the meaning of survival and loss.

—**Duane Niatum, in an essay in** *I Tell You Now: Autobiographical Essays by Native American Writers,* **edited by Brian Swann and Arnold Krupat, University of Nebraska Press, 1987.**

II

Today, serviceberry and nettle hide his home
and my grandfather's that was across the road.
And the driftwood animals he carved
for the entrance to Old Pasty's longhouse
mirror the rainbow spirits of his grandchildren.

So what are we to make of the blue spruce
without you, grand-uncle? Who else
besides your brother and sister, father and mother,
saw the forest breathe when the red-breasted
woodpecker was silent? How long before
the Hadlock village of Old Patsy and Lach-ka-nim
vanished like the sands under a wave
did you and your family break apart?
Was it when your father's father and family
were forced to leave Hadlock Bay
to live on the Skokomish reservation,
the reservation the family kept escaping?

3 4 3

D U A N E   N I A T U M

Drawings of the Song Animals *is the perfect invitation to "Dance . . . into the burning words" with one of America's finest poets. Those already familiar with his work will find the selections characteristic of Niatum's range of voice. Those who have not yet read Duane Niatum will find this volume a painting of song in colors that should not be missed.*

—Richard K. Waters, in *American Indian Culture and Research Journal*

Or was it your son Michael's death,
your brother Francis'?

Now my generation lies stripped to our hides,
charred saplings, the youngest roots
in the soil of many seasons.

III

In the wind of audible branches I return
the song of the yew tree shield,
as my great-uncle did when the sea called
him back to live with oyster and starfish,
soothe the hunger of cod and crab.
When he waved to us for the last celebration
in the amber silence, the salmon
were weaving through the dark rapids
of sapphire to spawn in Chimacum Creek.

On visiting Seabeck, his birthplace
and my grandfather's, where in his youth
he drummed the green moon to rise,
the clan of the dead, the totem fishermen
and singers, closed my eyes to the blood's pulse.

IV

Brother to chickadee and wolf,
raven and kingfisher, deer and cougar,
rain soaked and restless,
I hold to the ground of these cedarmen,
the earth shifting and sliding beneath my feet,
continue digging for the dream wheel
of my great-uncle, Joseph, elder to Thunderbird,
hawk, and sparrow.

Poetry

(Under name Duane McGinnis) *After the Death of an Elder Klallam*, Baleen Press, 1970.

A Cycle for the Woman in the Field (chapbook, illustrated by Jane Berniker), Laughing Man Press, 1973.

Taos Pueblo and Other Poems (chapbook, illustrated by Wendy Rose), Greenfield Review Press, 1973.

Ascending Red Cedar Moon, Harper, 1974.

Digging Out the Roots, Harper, 1977.

Turning to the Rhythms of Her Song (chapbook), Jawbone Press, 1977.

Songs for the Harvester of Dreams, University of Washington Press, 1981.

Pieces, (chapbook) Strawberry Press, 1981.

Drawings of the Song Animals: New and Selected Poems, Holy Cow! Press, 1991.

Contributor to Anthologies

An American Indian Anthology, [South Dakota], 1971.

From the Belly of the Shark, edited by Walter Lowenfels, Random House, 1973.

Voices from Wah'Kon-Tah: Contemporary Poetry of Native Americans, International Publishers, 1974.

American Indian Prose and Poetry: We Wait in the Darkness, edited by Gloria Levitas, Frank Robert Vivelo, and Jacqueline Vivelo, Capricorn Books, 1974.

The Uses of Poetry, edited by Agnes Stein, Holt, 1975.

Giant Talk: An Anthology of Third World Writings, edited by Quincy Troupe and Rainer Schulte, Vintage Book, 1975.

The First Skin around Us: Contemporary American Tribal Poetry, Territorial Press, 1976.

Good Company: Poets at Michigan, edited by Jeanne Rockwell, Noon Rock Press, 1977.

Digte, edited by Vagn Lundbye, Borgens Forlag (Valby, Denmark), 1977.

The Remembered Earth: An Anthology of Contemporary Native American Literature, edited by Geary Hobson, Red Earth Press, 1978.

Arrangement in Literature, Scott, Foresman, 1979.

This Song Remembers: Self-Portraits of Native Americans in the Arts, edited by Jane B. Katz, Houghton, 1980.

Songs from Turtle Island, edited by Joseph Bruchac III, Sovremennost Press/Macedonian Review (Macedonia), 1982.

A Nation Within, edited by Ralph Salisbury, Outrigger Publishers (Hamilton, New Zealand), 1983.

Earth Power Coming: Short Fiction in Native American Literature, edited by Simon J. Ortiz, Navajo Comunity College Press, 1983.

Wounds beneath the Flesh, edited by Maurice Kenny, Blue Cloud Quarterly Press, 1983.

Songs from This Earth on Turtle's Back, edited by Bruchac, Greenfield Review Press, 1983.

Words in the Blood, edited by Jamake Highwater, New American Library, 1984.

Coyote Was Here, edited by Bo Schoeler, Seklos Publishers (Aarhus, Denmark), 1984.

I Stand in Good Relation to the Earth, Raduga Publishers (Moscow), 1984.

Editor

Carriers of the Dream Wheel, Harper, 1975.

Harper's Book of Twentieth Century Native American Poetry, Harper, 1988.

Other

"Breathless" (experimental verse drama), first performed at University of Washington, Seattle, WA, 1968.

To Bridge the Dream (story chapbook), A Press, 1978.

Raven and the Fear of Growing White, Bridge Press, 1983.

Contributor of poems, short stories, and essays to over one hundred newspapers and magazines in the United States, Canada, and Europe. Guest editor of *Pacific Search*, 1975, *Niagara*, 1976, and *Western Edge*, 1978.

APOLOGY

From *Drawings of the Song Animals*, Holy Cow! Press, copyright © 1991 by Duane Niatum

3 4 5

But a man cannot learn heroism from another,
he owes the world some death of his own invention.
   "Dying Away" / William Meredith

Great Uncle Joe,
can you hear me keen?
My temples now as salt and pepper as yours,
I am a weed in the wind by the side of your house.

I still awaken in the night
to the moment you said, *don't,*
when my eyes rolled and snagged.
You knew I had no choice but to follow
my mind pulling me so close to the elder
in the next bed that my breath was his,
and his mine. Trapped in the tide

of confusion I fought for the courage
that would keep my knees from knocking
against your bed, my head from spinning
out the door. You then told of how
your own youth snapped nerve by nerve.

Later, you admitted that your neighbor
had died that morning. No, you
did not shake your head in loathing.

S M O K E   R I S I N G

Instead, you spoke in the way of your ancestors,

the Klallams, Swinomish, and Snohomish,
that it was good I had turned from him
whose owl had torn a hole in the window.

Great Uncle Joe,
can you hear me keen?
I am a weed in the light of your totem,
the hawk, because your face was free of scorn;

a weed uprooted with shame
over two decades after your death,
yet loyal to your path, my grandfather's,
and your sister's who gave me
your father's name, why, I don't know.
Cedar man, I bury my youth on your land;
its red earth shields my song
woven into the years for you

and the body of rock on Old Patsy's mound,
for mine, chanting to be near yours,
when I am the elder in the next bed.

ROUND DANCE

From *Drawings of the Song Animals*, Holy Cow! Press, copyright © 1991 by Duane Niatum

Sweet woman, come dance with me,
let's touch earth's center, so no one's a stranger,
I welcome you on this Klallam path
as the flicker does whose tapping beak
is as moon-inlaid as the cedar bark.
O step with me round the fire,
enter the circle the blood sparks,
        the heart unearthes.

Please sway and linger like the soil's thistles,
the yellow leaf's season, the flattened shadows.
O yes, our drums were carved by the sea,
its mother foam and Thunderbird.

347

DUANE NIATUM

Like the blue wind among blue willow,
the surf unites harvest dreams to stars,
deep currents, snipe and coot, starfish and black bass,
        footprints ingrained.

Fox woman, come dance with me,
let's find earth's beach, unravel yourself and tide,
let grass burn ocher, your hands be blue camas,
we'll turn as mischievous as Raven stealing light.
O I am best welcoming a friend.
So let's mingle with guest and ancestor,
Duckabush river and tamahnous, release the abalone
  yearnings, the eyeless flights.

SIMON  ORTIZ

Simon J. Ortiz, an Acoma Pueblo Indian, is regarded as one of the finest Native American poets and short story writers. In his works, Ortiz uses straightforward and fluid language reminiscent of the Indian oral tradition to depict Native American life—the struggles, sufferings, triumphs, and pains of everyday existence—and thus reflect on the universal human experience. Critics have noted that his writings are informed by an optimistic hope for the rebirth and ultimate survival of both man and nature.

Essay by

JOANN DI FILIPPO

Known primarily for his poetry, Ortiz published his first major collection, *Going for the Rain*, in 1976. The poems in this work share a cyclical structure—moving from birth, to a departure from one's origins, to a rebirth—and are reminiscent of a Pueblo rain song. Ortiz explained this similarity in a prologue to the collection, as cited by Willard Gingerich in *Southwest Review:* "A man makes his prayers; he sings his songs. He considers all that is important to him, his home, children, his language, and self that he is. . . . A man leaves; he encounters all manner of things. . . . His traveling is a prayer as well, and he must keep on. A man returns, and even the returning has moments of despair and tragedy. But there is beauty and there is joy."

Ortiz begins *Going for the Rain* by reciting the creation myth of the Acoma people, then summons the mythological Coyote, who appears throughout the collection in a number of roles–as western rascal, wise Acoma grandfather, and Coyote Lady. The poet then alights in present-day America in "Albuquerque Back Again, 12/6/74," in which he describes how he touches the mountains for sustenance before facing "the

349

traffic / and ordinary insanity / of people going places / they might not actually know / the destinations of." Ortiz becomes tangled in this muddled environment and realizes that humanity has fallen because man has forgotten his origins. In "Fragment" and "The Poems I Have Lost," Ortiz draws a parallel between the fragments of man's broken spirit and the old bones of Indian lore. Man can rebuild his splintered self by remembering and retelling these old stories, which contain the keys to understanding the world. One must return to his origins in order to survive, for as Ortiz writes, "Neon is weak. / Concrete will soon return / to desert." Critics praised *Going for the Rain* for its unaffected and meaningful verse. The collection is "a work of both artistic and political inevitability and innocence," Gingerich asserted in *Southwest Review*, "not folkloric innocence, but clairvoyant sophistication that sees the continual rebirth of spirit in all materialism."

One year later Ortiz published *A Good Journey,* a poetry collection that focuses on the past and present Acoma way of life. These poems frequently tell stories of ordinary occurrences—such as excursions into large cities, the growth of children, the birth of a daughter, the cooking of stew—and exemplify Ortiz's conviction that Indian experiences are common to all people. "Ortiz believes that the [events] he captures in his poems . . . have to do with the true nature of all of us," acknowledged Robert L. Berner in *World Literature Today.* *A Good Journey* also reveals the poet's compassion for all of creation, as evidenced in "For Our Brothers: Blue Jay, Gold Finch, Flicker, Squirrel," a collection of elegies written for the numerous defenseless animals that have been killed by motorists. A Good Journey received favorable reviews from critics, including Geary Hobson who, in a *Western American Literature* critique, judged it "a remarkably substantial book of poems."

Fight Back: For the Sake of the People, for the Sake of the Land, Ortiz's 1980 poetry and prose collection, revolves around the Pueblos, Navahos, and whites of New Mexico's "Uranium Belt." Marking the three- hundredth anniversary of the successful Pueblo revolt against the Spanish, the poems in *Fight Back* depict the everyday joys and sorrows of the mining people and express Ortiz's theme of interlaced destinies: America cannot ignore the Indian, for the fate of the Indian—his subjugation, exploitation, and confinement—will inevitably become the fate of all people. "No More Sacrifices," the most celebrated piece in the work, conveys this belief, as quoted in fiction international: "If the survival and quality of the life of Indian peoples is not assured, then no one else's life is, because those same economic, social, and political forces which destroy them will surely destroy others."

In 1981 Ortiz published *From Sand Creek: Rising in This Heart Which Is Our America,* a collection set in a Colorado veteran's hospital in which the poet was once a patient. A Vietnam-era veteran, Ortiz parallels the 1864 massacre of 133 Indian women and children at Sand Creek with the Vietnam war and its massacres. The poems in this volume contain stories of broken spirits, young and old, providing universal insight into the alienation of human beings from their native soil. However, in one of the poems in *From Sand Creek*, Ortiz articulates his unceasing hope for a productive and harmonious relationship between man and man and between man and the land, as cited by Harold Jaffe in the *Nation*: "The future will not be mad with loss and waste though / the memory will be there; eyes will become kind / and deep, and the bones of this nation will mend." Jaffe commented that "the cumulative impression [of this collection] is, admirably, not of gloom and despair, but of a renewed faith in the prospect of relationship with the land and solidarity among the dispossessed."

Ortiz's stories are collected in his 1978 *Howbah Indians* and his 1983 *Fightin'*. Deemed "poignantly elegant" by Karl Kroeber in *Western American Literature*, the works in *Howbah Indians* impart profound lessons from everyday experiences. In one story a young widow leaves her hometown to find work and in another a family tries to cope with the father's crippling war injury. The stories in *Fightin'* revolve around the theme of survival and express Ortiz's belief in the interconnectedness between the Indian and the entire American nation. "To Change in a Good Way," the most critically acclaimed work in the collection, concerns "the passage of non-Indian characters across that brief yet vast and persistent mythic gap in American history between Indian and non-Indian," explained Gingerich in fiction international. "To Change in a Good Way" revolves around the bond between a Laguna Indian couple and an uprooted Oklahoma couple. When Bill, the migrant father, learns that his younger brother has been killed in Vietnam, he receives strength from the ancient Indian knowledge of his fellow mining friends Pete and Mary, who offer him corn, medicine, and prayer sticks, according to ritual. Although Bill is at first unsure of what to do, he decides to place the husk in an empty mine shaft. Then he speaks to his dead sibling, as cited in fiction international: "I got this here Indian thing, feathers and sticks . . . and Pete and Mary said to do this because it's important even if we're Okies and not Indians who do this. . . . Pete said he didn't know exactly all the right Indian things to do anymore but somehow I believe they're more righter than we've ever been led to believe. And now I'm trying too."

In 1991 Ortiz published two more poetry collections, *Woven Stone* and *After and Before the Lightning*, which Ortiz told *Contemporary Authors* "refers to the Great Plains, where I lived in 1985 and 1986. The awesomeness of the prairie, the winter, the struggle to maintain dignity and livelihood in the harsh natural and sociopolitical climate of South Dakota, the vision possible through day-to-day awareness are the focus of the book." These two volumes augment Ortiz's role as spokesperson for all

Acoma Pueblo poet, short story writer, essayist, author of children's books, and editor. **Born:** May 27, 1941, at Pueblo of Acoma, near Albuquerque, New Mexico.

Partnerships: Married Marlene Foster, 1981 (divorced, 1984); children: Raho, Rainy, Sara.

Education: Attended University of New Mexico, beginning 1966; University of Iowa, M.F.A., 1969.

Career: Worked in uranium mines and processing plants near Grants Ambrosia Lake, NM; San Diego State University, San Diego, CA, teacher of creative writing and American Indian literature, 1974; University of New Mexico, Albuquerque, NM, teacher of creative writing and American Indian literature; Sinte Gleska College, Rosebud, SD, teacher of creative writing and American Indian literature. Pueblo of Acoma, lieutenant governor; Pueblo of Acoma Press, consulting editor, beginning 1982. Also worked as a journalist, public relations director, and newspaper editor.

Native American people, for Ortiz "knows the spiritual geography and the secret histories of power, struggle, exploitation, deceit, promise and survival which cycles of conquest and desert have taught the peoples of this region," Gingerich claimed in fiction international. However, Ortiz's works extend further than the peoples of his own region. "I . . . [write] for the words that are sacred because they come from a community of people and all life," Ortiz said, as quoted in the *New York Times Book Review.* And his concern is not only for his homeland and its vitality, but for all, as cited in *Southwest Review:* "What I want is a full life / for my son, / for myself, / for my Mother, / the Earth."

TRAVELS IN THE SOUTH

From *Woven Stone*, University of Arizona Press, copyright © 1992 by Simon J. Ortiz

East Texas

When I left the Alabama–Coushatta people,
it was early morning.
They had treated me kindly, given me food,
spoken me words of welcome, and thanked me.
I touched them, their hands, and promised
I would be back.

When I passed by the Huntsville State Pen
I told the Indian prisoners what the people said
and thanked them and felt very humble.
The sun was rising then.

3 5 2

When I got to Dallas I did not
      want to be there.
I went to see the BIA Relocation
      man.
He told me, "I don't know how
      many Indians
there are in Dallas; they come
      every week."
I talked with Ray, a Navajo; he
      didn't have a job,
was looking, and he was a welder.
I saw an Apache woman crying for
      her lost life.

When it was evening of the next
      day,
I stopped at a lake called Caddo.
I asked a park ranger, "Who was
      Caddo?"
And he said it used to be some
      Indian tribe.

I met two Black women fishing at
      the lake.
I sat by them; they were good to
      be with.
They were about seventy years old
      and laughed,
and for the first and only time in
      my life
I cut a terrapin's head off because,
as the women said, "They won't let go until sundown."

When it was after sundown in East Texas, I prayed
for strength and the Caddo and the Black women
and my young son at home and Dallas and when
it would be the morning, the Sun.

2. The Creek Nation East of the Mississippi

Once, in a story, I wrote that Indians are everywhere.

I guess all my perceptions and expressions do go back to what I was born into and what I was developed through, that is, the original experience. That is really what I know. That is, that I was born of the Acoma people, and that my name comes from them. My mother and my father were the most immediate teachers. The elders of my clan were the stuff of life, so to speak, in every way, personal and social. My formation with regards to language was the dzehni niyah of the Acoma people: "the way they spoke," the way they thought and felt, the way they perceived. So the writing cannot help but be fundamental. I can only be who I am as an Acoma person.

—Simon Ortiz, in *Winged Words: American Indian Writers Speak,* by Laura Coltelli, University of Nebraska Press, 1990.

353

Simon Ortiz is, for one thing, unabashedly political, but his criticism of America is not that it has failed, but as Chesterton remarked of Christianity, it has yet to be really tried. What is wanting is the commitment and the humility that will give birth to hope. Much of this sense of his location can be traced to his attitude toward tribal tradition, which he sees as offering a set of values and beliefs alternative to and legitimately competing with those of the Anglo-American. The viability of those traditions is something Ortiz reinforces in almost every poem or story, by adopting a distinctly "oral" voice, directly addressing the reader, catching the local pronunciation, casting his work into narrative.

—Andrew Wiget, in his *Simon Ortiz,* Boise State University,

Goddamn right.

In Pensacola, Florida, some hot-
    dog stand
operator told me about Chief
    McGee.

"I'm looking for Indians," I said.
"I know Chief Alvin McGee," he
    said.
I bought a hotdog and a beer.
"He lives near Atmore, Alabama,
cross the tracks, drive by the
    school,
over the freeway to Atlanta, about
    a mile.
He lives at the second house on
    the right."

I called from a payphone in Atmore.
Mr. McGee told me to come on
    over.
I found his home right away,
And he came out when I stopped
    in his yard.
He had a big smile on his face.
I'd seen his face before in the his-
    tory books
when they bothered to put Creeks
    in them.

He told me about Osceola.
"He was born in this county," Chief McGee said.
He showed me his garden and fields.
"I have seventy acres," he said.
"We used to have our own school,
but they took that away from us.
There ain't much they don't try to take."

We watched the news on TV.
It was election time in Alabama,

354

Poetry

Going for the Rain, Harper, 1976.
A Good Journey, Turtle Island, 1977.
Fight Back: For the Sake of the People, For the Sake of the Land (poems and prose), University of New Mexico Press, 1980.
From Sand Creek: Rising in This Heart Which Is Our America, Thunder's Mouth Press, 1981.
A Poem Is a Journey, Pternandon, 1981.
Woven Stone, University of Arizona Press, 1991.

Short Stories

Howbah Indians, Blue Moon, 1978.
Fightin': New and Selected Short Stories, Thunder's Mouth Press, 1983.

Juvenile

The People Shall Continue, illustrated by Sharol Graves, Children's Book Press, 1978.
Blue and Red, Pueblo of Acoma Press, 1982.
The Importance of Childhood, Pueblo of Acoma Press, 1982.

Editor

(Editor with Rudolfo A. Anaya) Ceremony of Brotherhood, 1680–1980, Academia (NM), 1981.
Earth Power Coming: Short Stories in Native American Literature, Navajo Community College Press, 1983.

Other

Naked in the Wind, Quetzal-Vihio, 1971.

Song, Poetry, Language: Expression and Perception (essays), Navajo Community College Press, 1978.
After and Before the Lightning, University of Arizona Press, 1994.

Contributor to *Chaco Canyon: A Center and Its World*, edited by Mary Peck, Museum of New Mexico Press, 1994. Work represented in anthologies, including *Columbus and Beyond: Views From Native Americans*, edited by Paula Gunn Allen, Southwest Parks and Monuments Association, 1992. Contributor of poems to magazines.

George Wallace against something.
People kept coming over to his house,
wanting the Chief's support. "Wallace is the one."
"Brewer is our man." They kept that up all night.
The next morning the election was on,
but I left right after breakfast.

Chief Alvin McGee put his arms around me
and blessed me. I remembered by grandfather,
the mountains, the land from where I came,
and I thanked him for his home, "Keep together,
please don't worry about Wallace, don't worry."

3. Crossing the Georgia Border into Florida

I worried about my hair, kept my car locked.
They'd look at me, lean, white, nervous,
their lips moving, making wordless gestures.

My hair is past my ears.
My Grandfather wore it like that.
He used to wear a hat, a gray one,
with grease stains on it.

355

SIMON ORTIZ

The people called him Tall One
because he was tall for an Acoma.

I had a hard time in Atlanta;
I thought it was because
I did not have a suit and tie.
I had to stay at the Dinkler Plaza,
a classy joint, for an Indian meeting.
The desk clerk didn't believe it
when I walked up, requested a room,
towel rolled up under my arm,
a couple books, and my black bag of poems.
I had to tell him who I really wasn't.
He charged me twenty dollars for a room,
and I figured I'm sure glad
that I'm not a Black man,
and I was sure happy to leave Atlanta.

A few miles from the Florida line,
I picked some flowers beside the highway
and put them with the sage I got in Arizona.
After the Florida line, I went to a State Park,
paid two-fifty, and the park ranger told me,
"This place is noted for the Indians
that don't live here anymore."
He didn't know who they used to be.

When I got to my campsite
and lay on the ground,
a squirrel came by and looked at me.
I moved my eyes. He moved his head.
"Brother," I said.
A red bird came, hopped.
"Brother, how are you?" I asked.
I took some bread, white, and kind of stale,
and scattered some crumbs before them.
They didn't take the crumbs,
and I didn't blame them.

RELOCATION

From *Woven Stone*, University of Arizona Press, copyright © 1992 by Simon J. Ortiz

Don't talk me no words.
Don't frighten me
for I am in the blinding city.
The lights,
the cars,
the deadened glares
    tear my heart
    and close my mind.

Who questions my pain,
the tight knot of anger
in my breast?

I swallow hard and often
and taste my spit
and it does not taste good.
Who questions my mind?

I came here because I was tired;
the BIA taught me to cleanse myself,
daily to keep a careful account of my time.
Efficiency was learned in catechism;
the nuns spelled me God in white.
And I came here to feed myself—
corn, potatoes, chili, and mutton
did not nourish me they said.

So I agreed to move.
I see me walking in sleep
down streets, down streets gray with cement
and glaring glass and oily wind,
armed with a pint of wine,
I cheated my children to buy.
I am ashamed.
I am tired.
I am hungry.
I speak words.

SIMON ORTIZ

I am lonely for hills.
I am lonely for myself.

IT WAS THAT INDIAN

From *Woven Stone*, University of Arizona Press, copyright © 1992 by Simon J. Ortiz

358 | Martinez
from over by Bluewater
was the one who discovered uranium
west of Grants.
That's what they said.
He brought that green stone
into town one afternoon in 1953,
said he found it by the railroad tracks
over by Haystack Butte.

Tourist magazines did a couple spreads
on him, photographed him in kodak color,
and the Chamber of Commerce celebrated
that Navajo man,
forgot for the time being
that the brothers
from Aacqu east of Grants
had killed that state patrolman,
and never mind also
that the city had a jail full of Indians.
The city fathers named
a city park after him
and some even wanted to put up a statue
of Martinez but others said
that was going too far for just an Indian
even if he was the one who started that area
into a boom.

Well, later on,
when some folks began to complain
about chemical poisons flowing into the streams
from the processing mills, carwrecks on Highway 53,
lack of housing in Grants,
cave-ins at Section 33,
non-union support,
high cost of living,
and uranium radiation causing cancer,
they—the Chamber of Commerce—pointed out
that it was Martinez
that Navajo Indian from over by Bluewater
who discovered uranium,
it says so in this here brochure,
he found that green stone over by Haystack
out behind his hogan;
it was that Indian who started that boom.

359

LOUIS  OWENS

*Of mixed Native and Irish American heritage, Owens has published critical studies of John Steinbeck's fiction, two novels reflective of his own Native culture—*Wolfsong *and* The Sharpest Sight—*and a study of Native American novels. His work is represented in numerous anthologies, and he is a contributor of articles and reviews to such periodicals as* Northeast Indian Quarterly, Arizona Quarterly, American Indian Quarterly, *and* USA Today.

Owens's critical works on Steinbeck, *John Steinbeck's Re-Vision of America* and *The Grapes of Wrath: Trouble in the Promised Land*, have earned praise for providing balanced, accurate, and readable analyses of Steinbeck's principal themes and the importance of place in his works. Critics also laud Owens's insightful commentary about Steinbeck's apparently condescending attitude toward Native Americans.

Owens's own fiction has often been described as postmodern because of the author's use of intertextual narrative structures, wordplay, and elements of magical realism. In these works Owens explores such themes as good versus evil, humankind's destruction of the natural world, and conflicting beliefs and values between white and Native cultures. Owens has commented, "I write, in part, to explore my own identity as a mixed-blood American of Choctaw, Cherokee, and Irish-American heritage. And I write to explore the dilemmas of all mixed-bloods in America. And I write to illuminate our relationships with the natural world. And I write because it is the greatest pleasure." In addition to writing, Owens has taught at numerous universities and has won awards from the National Endowment for the Humanities and the National Endowment for the Arts.

Choctaw/Cherokee critic, novelist, educator, and nonfiction writer.

Born: July 18, 1948, in Lompoc, California.

Partnerships: Married, wife's name Polly (an auditor), April 12, 1975; children: Elizabeth, Alexandra.

Education: University of California, Santa Barbara, B.A., 1971, M.A., 1974; University of California, Davis, Ph.D., 1981.

Career: University of Pisa, Pisa, Italy, Fulbright lecturer in American literature, 1980–81; University of California, Davis, visiting lecturer in English, 1981–82; California State University, Northridge, assistant professor of English, 1982–84; University of New Mexico, Albuquerque, assistant professor, 1984–86, associate professor of English, 1986–89, Presidential Lecturer, 1986–88, director of creative writing, 1984–88; University of California, Santa Cruz, professor of literature, 1989–. Southwestern Indian Polytechnic Institute, member of advisory board, 1987–89. Member of national committee, Native American Literature Award, 1989–, and Native American Prose Award, 1990–; Native American International Prize in Literature, member of governing board, 1991–; National Medal of Arts, nominator, 1991. Member of editorial board, *Steinbeck Quarterly*, 1982–, and *New America*, 1985–88; associate editor, *American Literary Realism*, 1986–88; co-editor, *American Literary Scholarship: An Annual*, 1989–. U.S. Forest Service, worked as trail worker, firefighter, and wilderness ranger. *Memberships:* Modern Language Association of America. *Address:* Home—176 Maple Way, Boulder Creek, CA 95006. Office—Department of General Literature, Porter College, University of California, Santa Cruz, Santa Cruz, CA 95064. *Agent:* Bob Dattila, 6861 Los Altos Pl., Los Angeles, CA 90068.

THE SHARPEST SIGHT

Copyright © 1992 by the University of Oklahoma Press

Four

It was still gray, with the sycamore branches black against Pine Mountain, when Cole McCurtain came out that morning, past the shed and empty chicken coop, past the fifty-seven Chevy up on blocks and the row of black walnut trees. At the riverbank he stopped and turned toward the mountain three miles away, where a hidden sun was sending splinters of light down through the digger pines and oaks and probably the stones of the old graveyard. On the other side of the little, isolated mountain was the hospital, built into a curve of the river.

He heard the screen door of the house slam, and then a spaniel-mix dog went scuttering past him toward the river, the dog's orange back just a flash as it vanished into the thick brush of the bank downstream from the house. Cole watched the dog disappear and shook his head. He was a good dog, but too fast for a rabbit dog. A good rabbit dog shouldn't get too close to the rabbit, but Zeke damned near caught them every time, so that often as not they would light out for the next county instead of making a circle like they were supposed to. You can't train a dog not to be too fast, he thought, remembering

362

his brother's words. You can't train a brother not to be too—whatever—he added, watching the red brush of Zeke's tail vanish.

"Yea, though I walk through the valley of the shadow of death." In magic marker on the back of the jacket, blocky letters the way a kid would write it. Attis had sent the jacket back early along with the only letter he'd written over there, talking about coming home and about walking shadows and jungles that had three levels. "Don't let the bastards get you," Attis had written. "Don't let these motherfuckers get you, too."

It can be said of the protagonists in American Indian fiction that they suffer from alienation in the Marxist sense, for the self from which they are alienated is, in fact, shown to be potentially coherent and dependent upon a continuing and coherent cultural identity.

—**Howard Meredith, in a review of *Other Destinies: Understanding the American Indian Novel,* in *World Literature Today,*Summer 1993.**

He stood on the bank and watched the thick, brown water move past, clots of yellow foam and trash in the troughs of waves. After a couple of weeks the river would go down, sinking into the sand so that only scattered pools were left, with a little clear stream at the heart of the sand. And when the pools dried up you would see coon tracks pressed into the sand around the tails and bones of big fish. And then even the little stream would disappear and the river would exist only beneath the surface once again.

He followed the line of cottonwoods and brush that marked the riverbank, stretching a barbed-wire fence to step through into a barren alfalfa field that fronted the river. "I shall fear no evil, for I am. . . . " That was on the back of the jacket, too. "I am a half-breed, like my father," he thought as he looked down the bank for signs of Zeke. "Actually," he said aloud to the river, pronouncing his words precisely, "I am a three-eighths breed, since my mother is a quarter Cherokee like just about everybody who ever lived in Oklahoma." He gestured toward a cottonwood with the rifle. "Well, you see, the fact is she's really three-eighths Cherokee, since her mother was three-quarters and born in the Nation and had my mother when she was thirteen and not even five feet tall. So I guess that makes me a seven-sixteenths-breed—almost a half-breed like my father. Let's say I'm nearly a half-breed, whatever that means. Hoey McCurtain knows, but what I know from books in school and those old TV movies is that a half-breed can't be trusted, is a killer, a betrayer, a breed." He smiled as he finished the speech; it had become a litany, something he told himself frequently almost like a ceremony, always the same words and rhythm. " . . . the meanest motherfucker in the valley." He wore the jacket when he hunted the river, and he recited his identity when he wore the jacket. "I shall fear no evil," he thought, "for I am."

3 6 3

His father knew who he was—Hoey McCurtain, Choctaw form Missis-sippi, with chiefs in his family, or so he often said after a few beers. Cole had read about Choctaws, and sometimes he thought that it was just as likely his ancestors had been bone-pickers, growing their fingernails long for their task down there in Mississippi where he remembered air like water and water like earth. Boxing the bones and putting them away, as Attis had been put away in the state hospital. His father was dark, with broad shoulders and burnt-rust skin, black hair, and brown eyes except for the milky one where the carburetor had exploded in his face. Attis, too, was dark, but he, Cole McCurtain, was taller, thinner, lighter than they—from the Cherokee and Irish blood, he thought—an almost half-breed with green eyes made "slan-ty" from the epicanthic fold Indians often had. "It's hard to tell who you are in this family," Attis had once said. "Only thing for sure, there's some nuts blood somewhere in the ancestry." That even before he'd gone to Vietnam and come back.

In the fall, the rabbits stirred the leaves when they ran, breaking from one bright clump of brush to thrash across the leaves and disappear into an identical clump unless he used the twenty-two. The sky climbed high on fall mornings, and the crunch of leaves and small limbs was sharp on the air then, like breaking bird wings. Now, however, the winter leaves were a dead weight upon the earth, and the brush along the bank was sodden and still. The broken sky lay near to the ground.

When Zeke flushed the first rabbit, Cole was thinking about the Mekong Delta, trying to imagine a place he'd never seen, and when the dog yapped after the cottontail he watched the two of them until they vanished into another island of cottonwoods and brush along the bank. Then he wait-ed, listening to a flicker knocking against a dead tree close by, sounding as if it would take the whole tree down, the hammering nailing him to the cold morning. The patch of ground he stood on was hard with frost beneath the alfalfa stubble, and he could feel now the vibration of the river coming through his legs. He shifted the cold gun to his left hand and wedged the fin-gers of his right hand under his left armpit. In a few seconds the feeling came back and so did the rabbit.

A cottontail, its big white ass held high, the rabbit crawled like a cat out of a pile of brush twenty feet away. Then it sat back on its haunches and sniffed the cold air. The brown fur was sleek, and the ears twitched a little while the nose worked, but Cole was upbreeze so the rabbit couldn't smell anything except Zeke, wherever Zeke was.

Watching the rabbit, he remembered his mother's Cherokee stories about rabbits. Cherokee rabbits were smart. They lived by tricks in a world of words and had a good time doing it. He raised the rifle and aimed the notched sight at a spot just below the rabbit's ear. "Time for a trick," he whispered to the rabbit. He pulled back the hammer and shouted.

At the shout, the cottontail leaped and spun and disappeared into the brush it had appeared from, and then he saw Zeke sitting fifty feet further up the riverbank, watching.

"That'll ruin a good dog."

He turned to see his father standing a few feet away, his hands in the pockets of his old, red-plaid wool coat, the collar turned up around his thick neck so that the face was framed between black collar and black John Deere baseball cap.

"You go letting a dog down that way too often, you're going to break his spirit, even a old turdeater like that." He spat a stream of tobacco juice and shook his head.

"How come you didn't shoot? You practicing for big game, bear maybe?"

As he started to answer, Cole felt Zeke's nose against his hand where the rifle dangled at his side. He swung the long barrel of the gun away, uncocked it, and pushed the safety on. When he looked again at his father, Hoey McCurtain had shifted his head a little to one side to take advantage of the good eye. His father was the only person Cole knew wo would pour gasoline in a carburetor to get a motor started and then look to see if the carburetor was flooded so that it would blow up right in his face. Not that he could think of his father as stupid. Hoey McCurtain was one of the smartest men Cole had ever met, in some ways.

A red-tailed hawk settled on a tall tree a few hundred yards downstream. Cole saw that his father's hair had grown down past his ears and over the edges of his collar. Surprised that he hadn't noticed that before, he wondered if maybe Hoey McCurtain was going to start braiding his hair, though he didn't think that Choctaws braided their hair. He could ask his father. And then he thought about his father's question. He didn't know how to explain because it was the first time that he'd realized he didn't shoot anymore, that he hadn't shot for a long time. He tried to think back to a time when he had hunted for something more real than whatever it was he'd come to be hunting for now, and his memory ran up against the fact of Attis.

"Time flies when you're having a good time," their mother used to say when he and Attis were kids and thought it was too early to come in from whatever it was they were doing—playing stretch with pocketknives or knocking little birds out of trees with beebee guns.

"What's the matter, your tongue froze up?" Hoey McCurtain shifted the lump in his cheek and spat again.

Cole looked again at his father's longer hair. Hoey seemed to be more and more Indian every day, and the more Indian he became the stranger he seemed, as if he were trying to make himself into something Cole couldn't

Novels

Wolfsong, West End Press, 1991.
The Sharpest Sight, University of Oklahoma Press, 1992.

Criticism

(Co-author) *American Indian Novelists: An Annotated Critical Biography*, Garland Publishing, 1985.
John Steinbeck's Re-Vision of America, University of Georgia Press, 1985.

The Grapes of Wrath: Trouble in the Promised Land, G. K. Hall, 1989.
Other Destinies: Understanding the American Indian Novel, University of Oklahoma Press, 1992.
Work represented in anthologies, including *Narrative Chance: Postmodern Discourse on Native American Literatures*, University of New Mexico Press, 1989; *Rediscovering Steinbeck: Revisionist Views of His Art, Politics,*

and Intellect, edited by Cliff Lewis and Carroll Britch, Edwin Mellen Press, 1989; and *Writing the American Classics*, edited by James Barbour and Tom Quirk, University of North Carolina Press, 1990. Contributor of more than a hundred articles and reviews to periodicals, including *Northeast Indian Quarterly, Arizona Quarterly, San Jose Studies, American Indian Quarterly,* and *USA Today.*

even imagine, something as impossible as the Mekong Delta, or the Mississippi swamp he had disappeared into every night when Cole was five and six. Lately, Hoey had been doing more reading, and he had begun complaining about what a bastard Thomas Jefferson had been. For a long time he had always been after Andrew Jackson, a rednecked sonofabitch, but recently he'd taken to throwing in Jefferson, claiming Jefferson had thought up trading posts as a way to get Indian land without shooting Indians, just get them in debt and take the land in payment. Now Jefferson was a phony blue-blood sonofabitch. "The father of our country, hah!" he'd snort, maybe confusing Jefferson with Washington, Cole thought.

Since he'd taken up reading about it, his father seemed to be getting angrier and angrier about what a raw deal the Choctaws had gotten in Mississippi. Before it had turned too cold, Mundo Morales—his brother's friend—had been in the habit of coming over, and the two of them would sit behind the house drinking Pabst Blue-Ribbon and complaining about what a raw deal their ancestors had gotten, Mundo pointing out how Moraleses had once owned the whole county, and Hoey McCurtain topping that with how the Choctaws had once owned all of Mississippi and Louisiana and more. "But I thought Indians never really *owned* land," Mundo would counter. With their black hair and skin the color of old blood, Mundo Morales and Hoey McCurtain looked quite a bit alike. The difference, Cole had thought when he watched them together, was that Mundo was the law and Hoey McCurtain the outlaw. Attis, out there in the hospital, was so far beyond both law and outlaw that he couldn't be defined.

"Indians don't yell 'bang' when they go after meat," Hoey said, hunching his shoulders deeper into the coat and looking off down the river.

Cole shrugged. "Which Indians? You told us there were more than three hundred tribes. Maybe some of them yell bang. Besides, maybe it was the Irish," he said, thinking that after all he was more Irish than anything else, one-sixteenth more, and Irish were supposed to talk a lot. Then he

3 6 6

thought again of Mundo Morales and his father, wishing that he could feel like something the way they did, Indian or Irish or something. "You are what you think you are," Hoey McCurtain had once told him. Hoey McCurtain thought he was Choctaw, not just Indian but Choctaw.

"Irish my ass," he said. "Come on, let's get some breakfast before we go to work."

Cole reached down to scratch Zeke's spaniel ear, feeling that he'd let the dog down—Attis's dog—and surprised to realize that he had been hunting without shooting for a long time without knowing it, or without thinking about it, which amounted to the same thing. He could feel the river at his back as he followed his father toward the house.

In the kitchen Hoey fried venison and eggs, splashing grease up over the eggs to make the edges lacy and brown. Cole poured coffee for both of them and then stood nursing his cup and looking at a framed photograph on the dining-room wall. It was a picture of his mother, before he or Attis was born, when she'd been young and beautiful in Oklahoma. Her hair fell in thick, black waves, and her Cherokee blood was obvious in the fine edges of her cheekbones and the black pupils in her narrow eyes. He contrasted the photograph with the picture he carried in his mind. In that picture, she looked tired, more tired than it seemed a person could be, and Cole wondered how a woman with only one husband and two kids could get that way. Maybe from the disease that had finally consumed her while her oldest son was at war. Maybe from being married for twenty years to Hoey McCurtain, a California Choctaw living in a made-up

Louis Owens enunciates the character of "the American Indian novel" from a dualistic point of view in Other Destinies: Understanding the American Indian Novel. *From this perspective, authority and ethnicity loom as difficult issues. Owens treats these issues in terms of political themes and cross-cultural communication, indicating that "Native American writing represents an attempt to recover identity and authenticity. . . ." Owens views the cross-cultural concerns and the elemental differences of tradition and ideology, relying in large part upon the theory of Mikhail Bakhtin, the Russian philosopher and literary critic, emphasizing, "Bakhtin's contention that in the dialogic process context is crucial to understanding would seem self-evident."*

—Howard Meredith, in *World Literature Today,* Summer 1993.

3 6 7

world who was busy creating himself out of books and made-up memories so that it was plain he was leaving the rest of them behind. As if, Cole thought, you could really choose what you were going to be instead of just being what it was you had to be. The woman in the photograph had been what she could not avoid being.

"Put some coffee in the thermos," his father said as he slid two of the creamy brown eggs onto a plate and forked a piece of meat next to them and then repeated the action. He'd taken off the heavy coat and now stood in the kitchen doorway, holding a plate toward Cole with one hand while scratching his belly with the other.

Cole picked up his plate and said, "Thank you," and he remembered his mother's smile at such times. She would reach out to put a hand on his shoulder, a gesture it seemed one of them was always making back then, as if practicing for a day when they'd all be affectionate or something. Then she would turn back toward the stove, one of those old stoves that had gas burners but looked like a woodburner. It was probably an antique, he thought.

"That old stove's probably an antique," he said as his father carried his own plate toward the dining-room table. "It's probably worth some money." His father looked at him like he was crazy.

After breakfast they drove through town out toward the fence they were building in the hills near Morro Bay. The town of Amarga was awake, with the ranchers and grain farmers coming in early to get first crack at the hardware store and feed-supply. They'd buy their supplies, and then they'd sit around coffee for two hours at Hong's Cafe talking about hard lives. The town wasn't much, with a bowling alley, a supermarket, half-a-dozen bare-ass stores of one kind or another and the same number of bars. Even after ten years it wasn't a town Cole could feel much about one way or another.

They drove by the county sheriff's substation, and through the dirty front window Cole could see Mundo Morales fooling around with his cof-feepot.

"Mundo's in early," Hoey said. "He don't have to be there till later." They were silent for a moment and then Hoey added, "I guess he don't want to go back to being a janitor at the high school. I heard Bill Martin say that now Mundo's not cleaning toilets he's going to clean up this shitty town. Bill Martin thought that was funny."

In front of Hong's, Louise Vogler, the high-school coach's wife, was getting out of her station wagon. Cole looked at her short skirt and long legs as she rose from the seat and shut the car door, realizing for the first time that the coach's wife wasn't much older than he was. How old was she, he wondered, twenty-five or six? With her husband sleeping and eating football during the fall, she sort of rattled around the town at loose ends, often getting up early to sit alone in the cafe in the middle of all those ranchers, as if just feeling men nearby was better than nothing. Her straight hair, turned up at the shoulders, and the skirt that rode up past her thigh gave Cole a terrible feeling of loneliness.

They drove the rest of the way in silence. The narrow road snaking over the coast range was empty except for the pickup they rattled along in, and Cole looked down at the live-oak and brush-choked creek a hundred feet below the road and remembered the black trout they had caught there. Squirming through the tunnel of creekbrush to drift a worm into the dark ripples below the little falls, he and Attis taking turns at each hole. The four-pound monofilament would drift unweighted from their cut-down fiberglass poles over the falls into the gently boiling pools, and then there would be a faint tug and a shiver on the line that tingled all the way up your arm, and you would pull a small dark tumult of shadow six or seven inches long out of the black water. It had always been cool and hidden down there, and they'd crawl and fish for miles down the creek where it fell toward the coast and feel that they were the only ones to ever fish the blackest pools.

It was still cold when Hoey parked the truck. They got out and walked up to the last post they'd driven, pulling on leather gloves as they walked. From the post a gold string ran up the hill. Cole went to an oak that dragged its branches close to the ground and pulled out the two-handled pipe they used as a post-pounder, and wordlessly they began again, driving the red metal poles into the shaley ground.

As his father drove the first post, Cole glanced at two clouds that hovered over the coast range a couple of miles to the west. Below them he could hear a car whining up the grade from Amarga. When he looked back, his father was pulling on the top of the post to see if it was firmly in the ground. He heard his father's satisfied grunt and was once again struck with how much pleasure such little things gave Hoey McCurtain, while the bigger things, like history, seemed to torment him.

369

For two hours they pounded the posts in a line up the ridge, and then Hoey tossed the driver into the tall grass. "Let's take a break," he said, "before hitting those corner posts."

Cole nodded and followed his father's eyes to the cirrus building up over the mountains. Then they went to sit near the thermos. While his father poured the coffee, Cole hunched into the fatigue jacket and looked around the hillside. Under the trees, the leaves and dead oats were still gray with frost.

"Sleepy?" With the question, his father reached a chipped mug toward him.

He took the cup with both hands and shook his head. "I was thinking about when we used to go deer hunting out near Creston," he said.

"I went out there in August. I asked you to come."

Again, Cole shook his head. "I was thinking about before."

Hoey McCurtain glanced at the sun finally rising through jagged clouds over the eastern ridge, pale and distant the way the sun was in winter. "You want to go see him?" As he spoke his eyes remained focused on the oak-covered ridge. "It's about time."

"Yeah." Cole held the coffee to his lips, testing the hot edge of the cup with his tongue.

They sipped the coffee in silence for a few minutes until Hoey stripped the husks from an oat head and let them drop from his hand and then said, "This all used to be Chumash country, you know." He looked from east to west, seeing the thickening clouds lying along the coastal ridge. "Everything you see. And now there ain't no Chumash here at all, and we're here." He swirled the dregs of coffee in the thermos cap and tossed the grounds into the grass. "It's funny. Back there in Mississippi there ain't hardly any Choctaws left, compared to the ones in Oklahoma. Except Uncle Luther and a few others, mostly all them over on that new reservation near Philadelphia. And out there in Oklahoma are all them tribes that used to be somewhere else. Us Indians are a mixed-up bunch. It's like somebody took a big stick and stirred us all up." He stripped another head from a dead oat stalk and let the husks drop from his hand. "You know, I read about some tribes, like the Navajo and them others in Arizona and New Mexico, the Hopi and some others, that's still living where they always lived. Some of them people live in houses a thousand years old, maybe ten thousand. You imagine how that must feel?"

When Cole didn't reply, Hoey was silent for a few minutes, sipping the coffee. Finally he said, still looking toward the distance, "What you plan to do about the draft?"

Cole shrugged and looked more deeply into the mug of coffee.

"They'll come and get you the way they did that Jorgenson kid," his father said. "You don't owe this sonofabitchin government nothing."

Cole stood up and pulled on one of his gloves and then took it off again and shook bits of gravel out of the fingers. "I remember what you told Attis," he said. Then he walked to the pile of railroad ties they'd brought up

370

for corner posts and started to move them around as though he were looking for something.

"No snakes this time of year," Hoey McCurtain said loudly as he, too, rose and pulled his gloves on. As he walked toward the ties, he added, "You don't owe the bastards nothing. They made Pushmataha a brigadier general, a goddamned general, him thinking that now it would be okay, now they'd all get to stay in Mississippi. They give him a gold medal in Washington after the Choctaws won the Battle of New Orleans for them. And then that rednecked sonofabitch Jackson sent in the troops to steal the land and cattle and slaves and everything else and move them all to Oklahoma, except it wasn't Oklahoma yet and he didn't know nothing about oil. My folks—your folks—didn't go. Hid out in the woods and starved and didn't end up with diddlysquat. Jackson said fuck the supreme court and marched all them Indian war heroes straight to Oklahoma. And Pushmataha, one of the greatest leaders the world ever saw, didn't end up with a pot to piss in. That's what you owe those bastards."

Cole had stopped with the post-hole digger on his shoulder and was looking back, wondering how much his father said was true. Had he read all those things, or did he just make up the facts he needed? "You were a paratrooper in the war," he said, thinking about the induction notice that had lain in his drawer for a week already. At first he had planned to enlist, to follow Attis, but then he got his brother's letter from Da Nang. "Do anything you have to," Attis had written. "Shoot your big toe off, cut your nuts off, but don't let them bring you here. You know what they do with Indians? They put us on point. The stupid bastards think Indians can see at night, that we don't make any noise, that kind of shit. It doesn't matter if you're a halfbreed or full or whatever. They call you chief and put you out in the fucking jungle at night. We're killing kids here, Cole, little kids and old women and anything that fucking moves."

"That's because I was stupid," Hoey said. "I thought I had to be a warrior, just like all the other Indians that died in white men's wars. I didn't know a goddamned thing." He pulled off the black cap and ran a hand through his thick, graying hair. "You know, Indians've had the highest enlistment rates in every war, way higher than whites or colored people. They been making Indians do their fighting ever since they first got here. The French and English did it in Mississippi, making Choctaws fight Chickasaws and Creeks and then finally making Choctaws fight each other. Did I ever tell you about Red Shoe?"

Cole turned away, stabbing the post-hole digger into the ground and levering up the loose dirt. Over his shoulder, he said, "I'm not an Indian. I'm mostly white."

Hoey McCurtain set the thermos back under the tree and carried a long steel bar to where his son was working.

"That don't matter. You're a mixed-blood and that's Indian, It's what you think you are that matters. You can't tell me you'd rather be white than Indian? Hell, a hundred years ago you couldn'tve testified in a court in this state because you got Indian blood. D'you know that? Indian people lost everything, even those rich Cherokees back in Georgia, because all some white trash drifter had to do was have a phony bill of sale. The Indian couldn't testify in court, so the white just got everything automatically. You know they tried to give the Choctaws part of Mexico when they drew up that Indian Territory?" he said. "They didn't even goddamned well know where the rivers ran. Pushmataha had to set them straight—and called Jackson a liar right to his face. You want to be white?"

Cole lifted the digger out of the ground, and his father stabbed the bar down hard several times to break up the shale, and then Cole lifted the broken rock out with the digger.

"What do you call that soul-catcher thing you told me about?"

Hoey McCurtain looked hard at his son for a moment. Finally he said, "Soul-eater, you mean. Some Choctaws call it *nalusachito*. Why?"

"Just curious." He jabbed the post-hole digger into the hole and came up with nothing, so Hoey McCurtain started in again with the bar, breaking the rock and trying to remember what he'd told his son about the soul-eater, what some called soul-catcher.

On the warming hillside above them a ground squirrel whistled at the shadow of a hawk, and they both turned to watch the bird settle into the canopy of an oak.

"Ask Attis what he thinks about the draft," Hoey McCurtain said abruptly as Cole returned to work with the post-hole digger.

Cole straightened and placed a hand on the small of his back. He looked directly at his father for the first time that morning. "You want me to ask my brother what he thinks about something?" He looked away and listened as several crows spotted the hawk and began hurling insults. "Attis enlisted," he said. He thought about his brother, before and after the war. For nineteen years he'd known Attis better than he'd known himself, and then after just one year he hadn't known him at all.

"They're going to draft you pretty damned soon," his father said, and Cole could hear something in Hoey McCurtain's voice. "You could go to Mississippi. Uncle Luther would hide you."

Cole looked up in surprise. Strangely, he'd found himself thinking about the old man lately, his father's uncle whom he hadn't seen since they'd moved to California when he was eight. It was the first time in years he'd thought about the solitary old uncle who'd raised his father, and now he recalled, too, the tar-paper sharecropper's shack where they'd lived close

to the river. Daddy longlegs had crawled across the dark ceiling like delicate upside-down men on stilts, and an odor of things rotting had hung over everything. He remembered the bitter smell of the mud along the river and the acrid smell of the carbide lamps when his father would get ready to go hunting at night with Uncle Luther. And he remembered how Uncle Luther would appear like one of the swamp ghosts people talked about, beckoning his father out into the night.

"There ain't nobody going to dig you out of that Yazoo country," his father said, taking a plug of tobacco out of his jacket pocket and biting off a chew.

Suddenly Cole could feel and smell the place he hadn't seen in so many years—the deep river full of dangerous hidden things, a snake or a swirl or a shadow in the water that would disappear so fast you wondered if you'd really seen anything. It was a full-time, above-ground river as different from the Salinas as anything could be. And Uncle Luther had been short and as solid as the pecan tree in the yard, with long, stringy hair, dark as night under the big hat that hid his face, as if he, too, could have been one of the hidden things from the river. "Uncle Luther is Indian," Attis had explained

LOUIS OWENS

back then. "That's why he only shows up at night and don't never talk. Indians are funny."

Cole had understood then that Indians came from tangled swamps to stand in front of one's porch and silently call one's father out into the night. The old man had frightened him deep down, and when he'd lie in the shack at night and hear the yowl of a hound or the sound of a rifle somewhere down toward the river or on the other side, he'd think of his father and Uncle Luther killing things in the dark. Across the river the thickest swamps boomed and cracked all night, and he thought of the two of them as lights trailing one another in the darkness. Sometimes he still thought of his father that way.

"I'll think about it," he said, puzzled by his attraction to the idea.

"Don't think too long." Hoey finished tamping a corner post. "I could drive you up to Frisco and you could fly to Jackson. There used to be a bus from Jackson to Waltersville."

Cole thought about his brother alone in a room in the hospital, and then he imagined his father alone in the house by the river. Back there in Mississippi, the old man was probably alone, too.

"Ought to start raining pretty soon," Hoey said, and Cole saw his father watching the clouds building up over the coast range. "It's damned near winter already."

374

CARTER  REVARD

Carter Revard, also known as Nompehwahthe, was born in Pawhuska, Oklahoma, and raised by his stepfather on the Osage reservation. Revard and his twin sister were exposed to both Osage and Ponca culture within a large extended family. His cousin, Carter Camp, was spokesperson during the 1973 takeover at Wounded Knee, South Dakota, and a former head of the American Indian Movement (AIM). After attending the University of Tulsa, Revard went to England as a Rhodes scholar to study at Oxford University in 1952. In 1959 he obtained a doctorate in English from Yale, after which he became a professor of English literature and language specializing in medieval literature. Revard has also been a Gourd Dancer, participating in the sacred traditional dance of the southern Plains Indians.

Essay by

RUTH ROSENBERG

3 7 5

In his poetry Revard blends traditional Native images with contemporary issues and uses various verse forms and multiple voices. Robert L. Berner, in a review of *Cowboys and Indians, Christmas Shopping,* has stated: "[Revard's] merging of the Anglo-Saxon form both with a tribal sense of the purpose of poetry and with his own vision is remarkable." Believing that poetry "matters like hell" to Native Americans, Blacks, and other minorities, Revard has stated: "You can hear in the poetry of American Indian writers a genuine felt concern for what is going on. . . . I know the same ego stuff gets hold of all of us, but I feel there's more genuine concern for the human condition and people who I know are suffering things

Osage poet, short story writer, and essayist.

Born: March 25, 1931, in Pawhuska, Oklahoma.

Partnerships: Married in 1956; children: four.

Education: University of Tulsa, B.A., 1952; Oxford University, M.A., 1959; Yale University, Ph.D., 1959.

Career: Amherst College, Amherst, MA, began as instructor, became assistant professor, 1956–61; Washington University, St. Louis, MO, began as assistant professor, became associate professor, 1961–77, profes-

sor of English literature and language, 1977–. Missouri Academy of Sciences, visiting linguist, 1965–67; System Development Corporation, consultant to lexicography project, 1966–67, associate resident scientist, 1967–68.

Memberships: Modern Language Association, American Indian Center of St. Louis (board member).

Address: Home—6638 Pershing Ave., St. Louis, MO 63130. Office—Department of English, Washington University, St. Louis, MO 63130.

among these groups. The stories have got to come back, the sound stuff, the rhyme, all of that, more of it and better."

AN EAGLE NATION

From *An Eagle Nation,* University of Arizona Press, copyright © 1993 by Carter Revard

For the Camp/Jump brigades

You see, I remember this little Ponca woman
who turned her back to the wall and placed her palms
up over her shoulders flat on the wall
and bent over backwards and walked her hands down the wall
and placed them flat on the floor behind her back—that's
how limber she was, Aunt Jewell,
when I was a boy.
And FAST! you wouldn't BELIEVE how she could sprint:
when an Osage couple married, they would ask Aunt Jewell
to run for the horses for them.
Now she's the eldest in her clan, but still the fastest
to bring the right word, Ponca or English, sacred or
profane, whatever's needed to survive she brings it, sometimes in
a wheelchair, since her heart
alarms the doctors now and then.
So one bright day we loaded
the wheelchair, and ourselves, and lots of chicken

3 7 6

barbecued and picnic stuff
into our cars and zoomed away
from Ponca City and White Eagle, *Southward Ho!*
To the Zoo, we said, the Oke City Zoo—we'd picnic there!
Grandchildren, see, they love the zoo,
and has she got GRANDchildren? well, maybe
one of her children knows how many, the rest of us
stopped counting years ago, so there were quite a few
with serious thoughts of chicken barbecue and we all rolled in
to the Zoo and parked, and we walked, and scrambled, and rolled,
we scuttled and sprinted, we used up all the verbs
in English, she'd have to get those Ponca words
to tell you how we made our way,
but somehow we ALL of us got in, and found
the picnic tables, and we feasted there and laughed
until it was time to inspect the premises, to see just what
the children of Columbus had prepared for us.
Snow leopards and black jaguars, seals and dolphins, monkeys and
baboons, the elephants and tigers looked away
thinking of Africa, of Rome, oceans, dinnertime, whatever—
and as for us, we went in all directions,
grandchildren rolled and bounced like marbles up and down
the curving asphalt ways, played hide and seek, called me to look
at camels maybe. And then we were all
getting tired and trying to reassemble, when Casey
came striding back to where we were wheeling Aunt Jewell
and said "Mom,
there's this eagle over here you should see,"
and we could tell it mattered. So we wheeled along
to this cage set off to itself with a bald eagle sitting,
eyes closed and statue-still,
on the higher perch inside, and there was a couple
standing up next to the cage and trying
to get its attention.
A nice white couple, youngish, the man
neatly mustached and balding, the woman
white-bloused and blondish: the man clapped hands
and clicked his tongue and squeaked, and whistled. The eagle
was motionless. Casey wheeled Aunt Jewell
a little to the side. The man stopped making noises.

C A R T E R   **R E V A R D**

I think, if we're lucky, we'll have writers come along who know the mythical dimensions and are very, very honest, fiercely, unflinchingly, almost meanly vivid about the tough parts of Indian life and will not neglect either dimension. Which really means I'd like to see American Indian writing be a standard for this country. I'd really like to see this country judged by its Indian people as a civilization and brought into the dock and given its good and bad marks. Until you do that you don't have an epic, and I'd like to see the Indian people do the epic for this part of the earth. It may not be just one person, it may be a bunch of people. That's what I'm looking for.

—Carter Revard, in an interview with Joseph Bruchac in *Survival This Way: Interviews with American Indian Poets*, 1987.

He and the woman looked at each
    other, then at us, and
        looked away.
There was a placard on the cage's
    side that said:
*This bald eagle was found
    wounded, and*
*although its life was saved, it will
    never fly again,*
so it is given this cage to itself.
Please do not feed him.
Aunt Jewell, from her wheelchair,
    spoke in Ponca to him,
so quietly that I could hardly hear
the sentences she spoke.
Since I know only
a few words of Ponca, I can't be
    sure
what she said or asked, but I
    caught the word
Kahgay:
Brother, she said.
The eagle opened his eyes and
    turned his head.
She said something else. He partly
    opened his beak
and crouched and looked head-on
    toward her,
and made a low shrill sound.
The white couple were kind of
    dazed, and so was I.

378

I knew she was saying good things for us.
I knew he'd pass them on.
She talked a little more, apologizing
for all of us, I think.
She put one hand up to her eyes and closed them for a while
till Casey handed her a handkerchief,
and she wiped her eyes.
"I guess we're 'bout ready to go now," Aunt Jewell said,
so we wheeled along back to the car, and we gathered all

the clan and climbed aboard
and drove from the Zoo downtown to where
the huge *Red Earth* powwow was going on, because
her grandson Wesley, Mikasi, was dancing there.
We hadn't thought Aunt Jewell's heart
was up to Zoo and Powwow in one day, but as usual she
knew better. They CHARGED ADMISSION, and that really
outraged my Ponca folks, for whom
a powwow should be free. Worse than that,
the contest DANCERS had to pay a fee.
"That's not our way," Aunt Jewell said.
But once inside we found our way,
wheelchair and all, up to the higher tiers,
where we and thousands of Indian people looked down
to the huge Arena floor where twelve drums
thundered and fourteen hundred dancers spun and eddied round,
and dancing in his wolfskin there
was Mikasi where Casey pointed, and we saw
his Grampa Paul Roughface gliding
with that eagle's calm he has,
and I saw how happy Casey and Mike were then
that their eldest son was dancing down there, and I felt
what the drum did for Aunt Jewell's heart and ours, and she told us
of seventy years ago when she was a little girl and her folks
would load the wagons up there in White Eagle and go
and ford the Arkansas into the Osage country and drive all day
and camp at night on the prairie and then drive on
to the Grayhorse Osage Dances, or those in Pawhuska even.
I remembered how Uncle Woody Camp had told me
of going to the Osage dances later and seeing her
for the first time and asking:
"Who IS that beautiful Ponca girl over there?"
and someone said,
"Oh that's McDonald's girl,"
and they met that way.
And he and Uncle Dwain would tell
of the covered wagon in which they rode,
my Irish and Scotch-Irish mother's folks, from Missouri out
to the Kansas wheat harvest, and then on down
to the Osage Reservation in Oklahoma, where mules were needed,

C A R T E R **R E V A R D**

and our grandfather hauled the bricks to build
the oil-boom Agency town of Pawhuska, where the million-dollar
lease sales, and the Osage Dances, were held.
So I was thinking how the eagles soared,
in their long migration flights, over all these places,
how they looked down on the wagons moving
westward from Missouri, eastward from Ponca lands
to meet in Pawhuska, how all the circles
had brought us into this Oklahoma time and what
had passed between cage and wheelchair before
we mounted up to view on this huge alien floor the long-ago drum
in its swirling rainbow of feathers and
bells and moccasins lifting up here
the songs and prayers from long before cars or wagons,
and how it all has changed and the ways are strange but
the voices still
are singing, the drum-heart
still beating here, so whatever the placards on
their iron cages may have to say, we the people,
as Aunt Jewell and Sun Dancers say,
are an EAGLE NATION, now.

CLOSE ENCOUNTERS

From *An Eagle Nation*, University of Arizona Press, copyright © 1993 by Carter Revard

1

We of the Osage Nation have come,
as the Naming Ceremony says,
down from the stars.
We sent ahead
our messengers to learn
how to make our bodies,
to make ourselves a nation,
find power to live, to go on,
to move as the sun rises and never fails
to cross the sky into the west
and go down in beauty into the night,
joining the stars once more

Poetry

My Right Hand Don't Leave Me No More, Eedin, 1970.
Ponca War Dancers, Point Rider's Press, 1980.
Cowboys and Indians, Christmas Shopping, Point Rider's Press, 1992.
An Eagle Nation, Volume 24 of the Sun Tracks series, University of Arizona Press, 1993.
Contributor to the poetry collections *Voices of the Rainbow*, edited by Kenneth Rosen, Viking, 1975, and *The Remembered Earth*, Red Earth Press, 1978; the essay "Decipherment of the Four-Letter Word in a Medieval Manuscript" appeared in the May, 1977, issue of *Verbatim*; the short story "Report to the Nation: Claiming Europe" appeared in *Earth Power Coming: Short Fiction in Native American Literature*, edited by Simon J. Ortiz, Navajo Community College Press, 1983. Has also published in such journals as *Epoch*, *Nimrod*, and *Greenfield Review*.

Work in Progress

"A book on Middle English literature in social context; essays on Native American literature and American culture for a volume tentatively titled *American Values: Repossessing Europe*; new poems for a collection called *American Riddles: Unzipping Angels*."

to move serenely across the skies
and rise again at dawn, letting
the two great shafts of light beside the sun
become white eagle plumes in the hair
of children as we give their names.

When we came down, our messengers
encountered beings
who let us take their bodies
with which we live into the peaceful days;
we met the Thunder, and the Mountain Lion,
the Red Bird, and the Cedar Tree,
Black Bear, and Golden Eagle.
As eagles, we came down,
and on the red oak tops
we rested, shaking loose with our weight
great showers of acorns, seeds
for new oaks, and our daily bread.

The leaves were light and dancing and
we saw, through the trees,
the sun caught
among leaves moving
around its light; it was
the leaves, we saw,
those light beings, who raised
as they danced the heavy

3 8 1

CARTER **REVARD**

oak-trunks out of earth,
who gathered the wind and
   sunlight,
the dew and morning into
   timbered
lodges for the sun and stars.

And so of course, we sang:
Nothing's lighter than leaves, we
   sang,
ghost-dancing on the oak tree as
   the spirit moves,
and nothing heavier than the great
sun-wombing red oaks which their
   dancing
in time has raised up from this
   earth where we
came down as eagles.
It will not end, we sang,
in time our leaves of paper will
be dancing lightly, making a
   nation of
the sun and other stars.

2

Coming down to Las Vegas as
a passenger on Frontier Airlines is
a myth of another color. At the
   Stardust Inn deep
within that city of dice and vice and Warhead Testing,
I was to give a paper
to the Rocky Mountain Modern Language Association
on Trickster Tales.
I gave it, and
I got out solvent, astonished,
and all but stellified
on wings of flame, like Elijah
or Geoffrey Chaucer in *The House of Fame*, up
up into the stars above Lake Mead, and I looked down
into its twinkling heaven

and thought back to the many-splendored
neon and krypton lights of Las Vegas
that throbbed with the great lake's power;
I remembered the dead rapids and waterfalls
drowned in Glen Canyon and Lake Mead,
thought of those bodies of
water, swollen so huge that earth itself
quivers with constant
small tremors from them—
and there looking up at me with
his Las Vegas eyeball was the Trickster Monster,
flashing with lightning from his
serpents of copper lifted up on crossbars—
but then I remembered how
among the streaked and painted bluffs that surround
Las Vegas I saw the October dawn come streaked

383

CARTER **REVARD**

and painted down from the eastern skies to brighten
the walk from my Travelodge over the street
to a vacant lot under
its desert willows
where lived a wren, some vivid orange flowers
papery on thornleaved stems hugging the sand,
and one empty billfold
with its credit cards spread around a sole
identity card that pictured
a security guard from San Diego,
the naval base there.
I turned the billfold in
to the motel clerk, the wren
pleaded innocent and flew away like me,
and when I got the orange flower
back to St. Louis and put it in
a glass of water, it turned the water
to pungent amber and wilted as if
I'd killed it with kindness.
—That Trickster, he always carries
lost identity cards and desert flowers
and finds himself
surrounded by dawn.

And so I sang
how the white sails of Columbus, of
Cortez and the Pilgrims brought
this krypton iris here and made
the desert bloom,
how they raised
the great light-sculptured houses
of cards and dice on sand;
I sang how
the rainbow ghosts of waterfalls
are pulsed into the sockets of
Las Vegas light flashing in crimson green
gold and violet its humongous word,
VACANCY,
VACANCY,
up to the dancing stars.

SMOKE RISING

WENDY  ROSE

Essay by

HELEN JASKOSKI

Frequently examining the alienation of the halfbreed in both white and Native cultures, Rose is highly regarded for verse which details her search for tribal and personal identity. Born in California, Rose had a lonely childhood and was raised in an environment which de-emphasized her Native roots: her mother, who was of Miwok descent, refused to acknowledge her Amerindian ancestry, and Rose's white peers were often forbidden to play with her. Although her father, an artist, was a full-blood Hopi, Rose was denied full access to the tribe since Hopi membership is matrilinearly determined.

After a turbulent adolescence—she was heavily involved in drugs and dropped out of high school—Rose began to write poetry. She credits much of her success as a writer and artist to these early experiences and her subsequent search for identity as a Native American in urban, white society. For example, in such poems as "The well-intentioned question," from the Pulitzer Prize–nominee *Lost Copper*, she documents her feelings of marginalization and her desire to be part of the Native community: "My Indian name listens / / for footsteps / stopping short of my door / then leaving forever." Her experiences in academia—which, she argues, views Native writings as a fad and not a serious source of literature—were first captured in *Academic Squaw: Report to the World from the Ivory Tower*. In *The Halfbreed Chronicles and Other Poems*, written while she was studying anthropology as an undergraduate at the University of California, Berkeley, Rose's focus on the marginalized mixed blood Amerindian was expanded to include other minorities. She has stated: "[My] point is that, in an important way, the way I grew up is symptomatic of something

There is a great deal of stereotyping of Indian poetry (and Indian art in general); we may be seen as "nature children" tapping some great earth-nerve and producing poems like pulses. But all art is that way; not just Indian art. There is also the concrete, the abstract, the analytical, the mystical—all components and levels of human understanding and expression. And those qualities stereotypically Indian also exist. The deferential treatment accorded to Indians in artistic and academic settings is just as destructive, ultimately, as out-and-out racism. It is startling to find your book of poems in an anthropology section of a bookstore instead of in the poetry section. . . .

—Wendy Rose, in *Something about the Author,* Vol. 12, Gale Research, 1977.

much larger than Indian-white relations. History and circumstance have made halfbreeds of all of us."

Critics note that much of Rose's work employs elements of Native American songs and chants; is infused with overtones of pain, anger, and bitterness; and is preoccupied with spirituality, communion with the natural world, and the encroachment of white culture on Native society. Kenneth Lincoln has observed: "Wendy Rose writes with a contrary's come-and-go, the 'backwards-forwards' clowning that steeled northern plains warriors, men and women, in a world of inversions. It is also Old Man Coyote's instinct for survival on the edges of village and wilderness. Rose dares reality with Trickster's nip-and-tuck, playing the serious game of life-and-death. She is a poet who barks and scudders for cover, who won't keep quiet or give in to oppression. She battles for native rights with a brave's honest sense of ambivalence toward the cost of life, without forsaking an artist's sensitivity. Hers is an old Lakota formula for a visionary leader, a sacred 'word sender'." Rose has also achieved critical acclaim for her work as an artist and illustrator.

386

JULIA

From *The Halfbreed Chronicles and Other Poems,* West End Press, copyright © 1985 by Wendy Rose

(Julia Pastrana was a mid-19th century singer and dancer in the circus who was billed as "The Ugliest Woman in the World," or sometimes, "The Lion Lady." She was a Mexican Indian who had been born with facial defor-

SMOKE RISING

Hopi and Miwok poet, artist, educator, anthropologist, and nonfiction writer.

Born: Bronwen Elizabeth Edwards on May 7, 1948, in Oakland, California.

Partnerships: Married Arthur Murata, March 11, 1976.

Education: Attended Cabrillo College and Contra Costa College; University of California, Berkeley, B.A., 1976, M.A., 1978.

Career: Writer and speaker, 1967–. Lowie Museum of Anthropology, University of California, Berkeley, manager of museum bookstore, beginning 1974; instructor in Native American and ethnic studies, University of California, Berkeley, 1979–83, California State University, Fresno, 1983–84, Fresno City College, 1984–. Visual artist with occasional exhibits and shows around the country; designer of postcards, posters, tee-shirts, and bookbags, usually in connection with Native American organizations. Member of board of directors, Coordinating Council of Literary Magazines, 1979–.

Memberships: Modern Language Association of America (member of commission on language and literature of America), PEN, American Anthropological Association, American Association for the Advancement of Science, American Indian Movement, Association for the Study of American Indian Literatures, National Association for Ethnic Studies, Native American Writers Association, United Native Americans, Southwestern Anthropological Association, Society for California Archaeology, Native Americans of Contra Costa County (member of community council), Kroeber Anthropological Society, Society for Creative Anachronism, Poets and Writers, Elves, Gnomes, and Little Mens' Marching and Chowder Society.

Address: 3182 E. Palo Alto, Fresno, CA 93710.

---

mities and with long hair growing from all over her body, including her face. In an effort to maintain control over her professional life, her manager persuaded her to marry him and she expressed her belief that he was actually in love with her. She bore him a son who lived for only six hours and had inherited his mother's physical appearance. She died three days later. Her husband, unwilling to forfeit his financial investment, had Julia and her infant boy stuffed, mounted and put on display in a case made of wood and glass. As recently as 1975, Julia Pastrana and her little baby were exhibited in Europe and in the United States.)

Tell me it was just a dream,
my husband, a clever trick
made by some tin-faced village god
or ghost coyote, to frighten me
with his claim that our marriage is made
of malice and money.
Oh tell me again
how you admire my hands,
how my jasmine tea is rich and strong,
my singing sweet, my eyes so dark

387

W E N D Y   R O S E

Rose lives as a marginal woman on the lines between races, cultures, and languages. She is "foreign and familiar at once," the poet confesses, suffering and surviving on the limits of city and country. She stands her ground, however, in trenches of racial alienation, where mixed-bloods can exist neither Indian nor non-Indian, both and none. . . . Rose and other Indian women, born "breeds," decide to fight for their Indianness and to write about that choice. Like Indian meal leached from California buckeye on the Sierra slopes, acrid and poisonous until processed, Wendy Rose's art tempers the native sting in a daily staple. She nurtures herself on her own struggle.

—Kenneth Lincoln, "Finding the Loss," in *Parnassus: Poetry in Review,* Vol. 10, No. 1, 1982.

3 8 8

like black moss, gray as jungle fog
soaking green the tallest tree tops.
I was frail
as the breaking dry branches
of my winter sand canyons,
standing so still as if
to stand forever.

Oh such a small room!
No bigger than my elbows outstretched

you would lose yourself
        swimming
man into fish
as you mapped the pond
you would own.
That was not all.
The room grew cold
as if to joke
with these warm days;
the curtains blew out
and fell back
against the moon-painted sill.

I rose from my bed like a spirit
and, not a spirit at all, floated
        slowly
to my great glass oval
to see myself reflected
as the burnished bronze woman
skin smooth and tender
I know myself to be
in the dark
above the confusion
of French perfumes
and I was there in the mirror
and I was not.

I had become hard
as the temple stones
of O'tomi, hair grown over my
        ancient face

Poetry

Hopi Roadrunner Dancing, Greenfield Review Press, 1973.

Long Division: A Tribal History, Strawberry Press, 1976; second edition, 1980.

Academic Squaw: Report to the World from the Ivory Tower, Blue Cloud Press, 1977.

Poetry of the American Indian Series: Wendy Rose, American Visual Communications Bank, 1978.

Builder Kachina: A Home-Going Cycle, Blue Cloud Press, 1979.

Lost Copper, Malki Museum Press, 1980.

What Happened When the Hopi Hit New York, Contact/II Press, 1981.

The Halfbreed Chronicles and Other Poems, West End Press, 1985.

Going to War with All My Relations: New and Selected Poems, Entrada Press, 1993.

Bone Dance: New and Selected Poems, 1965–1993, University of Arizona Press, 1994.

Other

Aboriginal Tattooing in California (history), Archaeological Research Facility, University of California, 1979.

Contributor to anthologies, including (under pseudonym Chiron Khanshendel) *Speaking for Ourselves*, edited by Barbara Bradshaw and Lillian Faderman, Scott, Foresman, 1969, second edition (under name Wendy Rose), 1975; (under pseudonym Chiron Khanshendel) *Literature of the American Indian*, edited by Thomas E. Sanders and Walter W. Peek, Glencoe, 1974; (under pseudonym Chiron Khanshendel) *From the Belly of the Shark*, edited by Walter Lowenfels, Random House, 1974; *Time to Greez: Incantations from the Third World*, edited by Janice Mirikitani and others, Glide Press, 1975; *Carriers of the Dream Wheel*, edited by Duane Niatum, Harper, 1975; *Contemporary California Women Poets*, edited by McDowell, Merlin Press, 1977; *Reaping*, edited by Rudge, Cocono, 1977; *I Am the Fire of Time*, edited by Jane B. Katz, Dutton, 1977; *The Next World*, edited by Joseph Bruchac, Crossing Press, 1978; *Networks*, edited by Simone, Vortex Graphics, 1979; *The Third Woman*, edited by Dexter Fisher, Houghton, 1979; *In Her Own Image: The Lives and Works of Women Artists*, edited by Ingrid Wendt, Feminist Press, 1980; *The South Corner of Time*, edited by Larry Evers, Suntracks Press, 1980; *This Song Remembers*, edited by Jane B. Katz, Houghton, 1980. *Anthology of Magazine Verse*, edited by Pater, Monitor Book, in press. *The Fire of Finding: Women Poets of the World*, Macmillan, in press.

Also illustrator of numerous books and journals. Contributor of articles and poems to periodicals, including *Many Smokes*, *Early American*, *Contra Costa Advocate*, *Journal of California Anthropology*, *San Francisco Bay Guardian*, and *Janus*.

Work in Progress

Unheard Voices: A Multi-Genre Annotated Bibliography of Books by American Indian and Inuit Authors, for Serif Series of bibliographies, Kent State University.

---

and just as tall as my head.
A small room from which to sing
open the doors
with my cold graceful mouth,
my rigid lips, my silences
dead as yesterday,
cruel as the children
and cold as the coins
that glitter
in your pink fist.

And another magic
in the cold
of that small room:
in my arms
or standing near me
on a tall table

389

W E N D Y   R O S E

by my right side:
a tiny doll
that looked
like me.

Oh my husband
tell me again
this is only a dream
I wake from warm
and today is still today,
summer sun and quick rain;
tell me, husband, how you love me
for my self one more time.
It scares me so
to be with child,
lioness
with cub.

LESLIE MARMON  SILKO

Leslie Marmon Silko first received substantial critical attention in 1977 with her novel Ceremony, *which tells of a half-breed war veteran's struggle for sanity after returning home from World War II. The veteran, Tayo, has difficulties adjusting to civilian life on a New Mexico Indian reservation. He is haunted by his violent actions during the war and by the memory of his brother's death in the same conflict. Deranged and withdrawn, Tayo initially wastes away on the reservation while his fellow Indian veterans drink excessively and rail against racism.*

Essay by

ANNETTE VAN DYKE

After futilely exploring Navajo rituals in an attempt to discover some sense of identity, Tayo befriends a wise old half-breed, Betonie, who counsels him on the value of ceremony. Betonie teaches Tayo that ceremony is not merely formal ritual but a means of conducting one's life. With the old man's guidance, Tayo learns that humanity and the cosmos are aspects of one vast entity, and that ceremony is the means to harmony within that entity.

3 9 1

With its depiction of life on the Indian reservation and its exploration of philosophical issues, *Ceremony* established Silko as an important artist from the American Indian community. Charles R. Larson, writing in the *Washington Post Book World*, called Ceremony a novel "powerfully conceived" and attributed much of the book's success to Silko's incorporation of Indian elements. "Tayo's experiences may suggest that Ceremony falls nicely within the realm of American fiction about World War II," Larson wrote. "Yet Silko's novel is also strongly rooted within the author's own tribal background and that is what I find especially valuable here."

The great struggle is to make whatever language you have really speak for you. Here are the givens; you only have this and this; this is what you are trying to describe; these are the persons you are trying to describe this to; we don't want them to just see it and hear it; we want them to be it and know it. This is language and you deal in it. That's the most intriguing thing of all. We have to use language in order to define language. I'm getting more and more humbled, to the point where I think it's a wonder we can express the most simple desire in our given tongue, clearly. And sometimes I wonder if we can even hope for that.

—From *Winged Words: American Indian Writers Speak,* by Laura Coltelli, University of Nebraska Press, 1990.

Some critics considered *Ceremony* a powerful confirmation of cosmic order. Elaine Jahner, who reviewed the novel for *Prairie Schooner,* wrote that the book "is about the power of timeless, primal forms of seeing and knowing and relating to all of life." She observed that the Indian custom of communal storytelling provided the novel with both theme and structure and added that Tayo eventually "perceives something of his responsibilities in shaping the story of what human beings mean to each other."

After the publication of *Ceremony* in 1977, Silko received greater recognition for her earlier short stories. Among her most noteworthy stories were "Lullaby," "Yellow Woman," and "Tony's Story." "Lullaby" is an old woman's recollection of how her children were once taken away for education and how they returned to a culture that no longer seemed familiar or comfortable. Writing in the *Southwest Review,* Edith Blicksilver called "Lullaby" Silko's "version of the Native American's present-day reality." "Yellow Woman" concerns a Navajo woman who is abducted by a cattle ranger whom she suspects to be the embodiment of a spirit. In *MELUS,* A. LaVonne Ruoff wrote that "'Yellow Woman' is based on traditional abduction tales, [but] it is more than a modernized version." Ruoff attributed the difference to Silko's emphasis on "the character's confusion about what is real and what is not." "Tony's Story" is about an Indian who kills a vicious policeman. In *MELUS,* Ruoff noted Silko's ability to equate the murder with the Pueblo exorcism ritual. "Tony's Story," Ruoff declared, "deals with the return to Indian ritual as a means of coping with external forces."

Some of Silko's stories were included in the anthology *The Man to Send Rainclouds,* which derives its title from Silko's humorous tale of con-

392

Laguna Pueblo novelist, poet, short story writer, and nonfiction writer.

Born: 1948 in Albuquerque, New Mexico.

Children: Two sons.

Education: University of New Mexico, received B.A. (with honors), 1969.

Career: Associated with University of New Mexico, Albuquerque; professor of English at University of Arizona, Tucson, 1978–has also taught at Navaho Community College, Tsaile, AZ; writer.

Address: Home—8000 West Camireo del Cerro, Tucson, AZ 85705. Office—Department of English, University of Arizona, Tucson, AZ 85721.

---

flict between a Catholic priest and Pueblo Indians during an Indian funeral. Silko also included some of her early stories in her 1981 collection *Storyteller*, which features her poetry as well. In the *New York Times Book Review*, N. Scott Momaday called *Storyteller* "a rich, many-faceted book." Momaday acknowledged Silko's interests in ritual and the Indian storytelling tradition and her ability to portray characters and situations. "At her best," Momaday contended, "Leslie Silko is very good indeed. She has a sharp sense of the way in which the profound and the mundane often run together." James Polk gave similar praise in *Saturday Review* when he wrote that Silko's "perceptions are accurate, and her style reflects the breadth, the texture, the mortality of her subjects."

Silko's other writings include *Laguna Woman*, a 1974 poetry collection, and *With the Delicacy and Strength of Lace*, a collection of correspondence between Silko and poet James Wright, who died of cancer in 1980. In addition, Silko has been honored with a Pushcart Prize and an award from the prestigious MacArthur Foundation. The latter award—$176,000—was particularly appreciated by Silko, who produced most of her work while also working as an English professor. Acknowledging her cash prize, she told *Time* that she was now "a little less beholden to the everyday world."

CEREMONY

393

He knew the holy men had their ways during the dry spells. People said they climbed the trails to the mountaintops to look west and southwest and to call the clouds and thunder. They studied the night skies from the mountaintops and listened to the winds at dawn. When they came back down they would tell the people it was time to dance for rain. Josiah never told him much about praying, except that it should be something he felt inside himself. So that last summer, before the war, he got up before dawn and rode the bay mare south to the spring in the narrow canyon. The water oozed out from the dark orange sandstone at the base of the long mesa. He waited for the sun to come over the hills. He tied the mare to a juniper tree at the mouth of the canyon, and walked up the narrow trail, with the cliffs closer on both sides as he walked farther into the canyon. The canyon was full of shadows when he reached the pool. He had picked flowers along the path, flowers with yellow long petals the color of the sunlight. He shook the pollen from them gently and sprinkled it over the water; he laid the blossoms beside the pool and waited. He heard the water, flowing into the pool, drop by drop from the big crack in the side of the cliff. The things he did seemed right, as he imagined with his heart the rituals the cloud priests performed during a drought. Here the dust and heat began to recede; the short grass and stunted corn seemed distant.

The air smelled damp and it was cool even after the sun got high enough to shine into the canyon. The dark orange sandstone formation held springs like this one, all along the base of the sandstone where wind and erosion had cut narrow canyons into the rock. These springs came from deep within the earth, and the people relied upon them even when the sky was barren and the winds were hot and dusty.

The spider came out first. She drank from the edge of the pool, careful to keep the delicate eggs sacs on her abdomen out of the water. She retraced her path, leaving faint crisscrossing patterns in the fine yellow sand. He remembered stories about her. She waited in certain locations for people to come to her for help. She alone had known how to outsmart the malicious mountain Ka't'sina who imprisoned the rain clouds in the northwest room of his magical house. Spider Woman had told Sun Man how to win the storm clouds back from the Gambler so they would be free again to bring rain and snow to the people. He knew what white people thought about the stories. In school the science teacher had explained what superstition was, and then held the science textbook up for the class to see the true source of explanations. He had studied those books, and he had no reasons to believe the stories any more. The science books explained the causes and effects. But old Grandma always used to say, "Back in time immemorial, things were different, the animals could talk to human beings and many magical things still happened." He never lost the feeling he had in his chest when she spoke those words, as she did each time she told them stories; and he still felt it was true, despite all they had taught him in school—that long long ago things *had* been different, and human beings could understand what the animals said, and once the Gambler had trapped the storm clouds on his mountaintop.

When the shadows were gone, and the cliff rock began to get warm, the frogs came out from their sleeping places in small cracks and niches in the cliff above the pool. They were the color of the moss near the spring, and their backs were spotted the color of wet sand. They moved slowly into the sun, blinking their big eyes. He watched them dive into the pool, one by one, with a graceful quiet sound. They swam across the pool to the sunny edge and sat there looking at him, snapping at the tiny insects that swarmed in the shade and grass around the pool. He smiled. They were the rain's children. He had seen it happen many times after a rainstorm. In dried up ponds and in the dry arroyo sands, even as the rain was still falling, they came popping up through the ground, with wet sand still on their backs. Josiah said they could stay buried in the dry sand for many years, waiting for the rain to come again.

Dragonflies came and hovered over the pool. They were all colors of blue—powdery sky blue, dark night blue, shimmering with almost black iridescent light, and mountain blue. There were stories about the dragonflies too. He turned. Everywhere he looked, he saw a world made of stories, the long ago, time immemorial stories, as old Grandma called them. It was a world alive, always changing and moving; and if you knew where to look, you could see it, sometimes almost imperceptible, like the motion of the stars across the sky.

The horse was dozing under the tree. Her left hind foot was flexed and resting on the toe, the way horses did when they had to stand in one place for a long time. He rode slowly through the groves of dry sunflower stalks left over from better years, and it was then he saw a bright green hummingbird shimmering above the dry sandy ground, flying higher and higher until it was only a bright speck. Then it was gone. But it left something with him; as long as the hummingbird had not abandoned the land, somewhere there were still flowers, and they could all go on.

The next day he watched the clouds gather on the west horizon; by the next morning the sky was full of low dark rain clouds. They loaded the shovels and hoes into the back of the truck and went to the fields. While they waited, they pulled weeds around the chili plants and shoveled dirt around the low places in the rows of corn where the water might be lost. When they stopped to eat the bread and tamales Auntie had packed for them, they could hear a low rumble of thunder in the distance, from the direction of Tse-pi'na, Mount Taylor. The wind came up from the west, smelling cool like wet clay. Then he could see the rain. It was spinning out of the thunderclouds like gray spider webs and tangling against the foothills of the mountain. They joined the other people who had fields there, by the main ditch, and nobody went back to work after lunch. They stood around, smiling and joking, keeping an eye on the clouds overhead while they waited. As the first big drops began to splatter down on the leaves of the corn plants, making loud rattling sounds, Josiah motioned for Tayo to walk to the truck with him. The rain made a steady thumping sound on the cab of the truck. Josiah wrote in the little spiral notebook he carried in his shirt pocket; he tore out the blue-lined page and folded it carefully.

L E S L I E   M A R M O N   **S I L K O**

Novels

Ceremony (novel), Viking Penguin, 1977.

Almanac of the Dead (novel), Simon & Schuster, 1991.

Poetry

Laguna Woman (poems), Greenfield Review Press, 1974.

Storyteller (poems and short stories), Seaver Books, 1981.

Other

(With James A. Wright) *With the Delicacy and Strength of Lace: Letters between Leslie Marmon Silko and James Wright* (letters), Graywolf Press, 1986. *Yellow Woman* (nonfiction), edited and introduced by Melody Graulich, Rutgers University Press, 1993.

Work represented in anthologies, including *The Man to Send Rainclouds*, Viking, 1974. Contributor to periodicals, including *New York Times Book Review*.

Work in Progress

A screenplay for public television; a novel.

"Can you take this note to her? I told her I would come this afternoon and drive her to Grants, but now with the rain I will be too busy."

Tayo nodded. He could hear his heart beating and he was breathing fast; something was shaking in his belly.

She had watched him all summer, whenever he had gone to Cubero with Josiah. She sat in the wicker rocking chair in the shade on the upstairs porch above the bar, and she stared down at him. She watched him while Josiah was inside buying a six-pack; Tayo tried to avoid her eyes, but she was a patient woman. She watched him steadily, rocking slowly in the chair, waiting for him to sneak a quick glance at her. She smiled down at him until Josiah reached the top of the stairs. Then she smiled at Josiah and said, "You have a fine nephew, Joseó," as she got up from the rocker and followed Josiah inside.

His hands felt slippery on the steering wheel, and he felt as if every curve in the road were slowing him down and he might never reach the place. The sun was hidden by the clouds, and he was not aware any more of the color of the land. As he got closer, he was afraid she wouldn't be there. He shifted down to second gear and crossed the cattle guard by the old graveyard. He was close enough then to feel afraid, so he repeated over and over inside his head that he was only delivering a message, and she might not be there anyway. Raindrops splattered across the windshield like flying bugs hitting head-on. He wanted to turn around. He took his foot off the gas pedal and looked for a place to turn around, but the road was narrow, and on either side the ditches were muddy and flowing with the run-off. Up ahead he could see the big cottonwood tree.

The rain rattled on the rusted tin roof, and rainwater leaked out of the rain gutter and splashed off the porch railing. He walked up the spiral staircase slowly, smelling wet adobe plaster and listening to the rain rattle the waxy green cottonwood leaves growing near the porch. A scratchy Victrola was playing guitars and trumpets; a man sang sad Spanish words. "Y volveré" were the only words Tayo could understand. He stood at the screen door and knocked, looking down at Josiah's note. He held it carefully

396

because his hands were sweaty and he didn't want to smear the writing. He wiped his hands on the thighs of his Levis while he waited. Nobody came to the door, but the music was playing loudly. He knocked on the screen door again, this time pounding it so hard that it bounced against the door frame. He waited, breathing hard, and felt the sweat run down his ribs like rainwater. He decided to push the note under the screen door; she would find it. He was kneeling to slide the note under the door when she came. He could smell her before he could even see her; the perfume smelled like the ivory locust blossoms that hung down from the trees in the spring. Her smell drifted out the screen on the air currents from the storm. The doorway at the back of the room had a long white curtain across it, and it swelled open as she came through. He looked at her through the sagging screen that had a fluffy ball of cotton stuck in the middle to scare the flies away. He saw her feet, the open-toe blue satin slippers and her painted toenails. The kimono was blue satin and it wrapped around her closely, outlining her hips and belly. He stood up quickly and felt his face get hot. He held out the note. She smiled, but she did not look at it. She looked at him.

"Come in," she said. She pointed to a blue armchair with dark wooden feet carved like eagle claws. The room smelled like the white clay the people used for whitewash. It was cool. The curtain at the back of the room drifted in a cool stream of air from the window or door behind it. The music came from behind the curtain too; the songs were soft and slow, without voices. Outside the thunder sounded like giant boulders cracking loose from the high cliffs and crashing into narrow canyons. Sometimes the room shook, and the panes of glass in the window behind him rattled. He watched her read the note and wondered what she kept behind the curtains. He could feel something back there, something of her life which he could not explain. The room pulsed with feeling, the feeling flowing with the music and the breeze from the curtains, feeling colored by the blue flowers painted in a border around the walls. He could feel it everywhere, even in the blue sheets that were stretched tightly across the bed. Somewhere, from another room, he heard a clock ticking slowly and distinctly, as if the years, the centuries, were lost in that sound. The rain pounded louder on the tin roof, and she looked up from the note then, at the screen door and the cottonwood tree outside, its leaves beaten flat by the downpour. The kimono was open slightly at the neck and he could see the light brown color of her skin. Her long brown hair was curled and piled on her head in long ringlets, the style of some past time. She did not look old or young to him then; she was like the rain and the wind; age had no relation to her. She got up from the edge of the bed and hooked the screen door. She closed the door and pushed the bolt forward. The music had stopped, and there was only the sound of the storm.

He dreamed it again and again, sinking and rolling with the light blue sheets twisted around his thighs and ankles, and the excitement of wet smells of rain, and their sweat. He wanted to lie like that forever.

L E S L I E   M A R M O N   **S I L K O**

She whispered in Spanish and touched him gently, rubbing his back and neck first, then brushing his ear and neck with her lips. She pressed against his chest and belly, and he clenched himself tight until he felt the warmth and softness of her legs and belly. Her sounds were gentle and the storm outside was loud. He could hear the rain rattling the roof and the sound of the old cottonwood tree straining in the wind. He moved his mouth over her face and slowly opened his eyes; she was smiling. He felt her shiver, and when he held her closer, he realized he was shaking too. Something was coiling tight. She breathed harder and he breathed with the same rhythm. She slid beneath him then, like a cat squeezing under a gate. She moved under him, her rhythm merging into the sound of the wind shaking the rafters and the sound of the rain in the tree. And he was lost somewhere, deep beneath the surface of his own body and consciousness, swimming away from all his life before that hour.

She sat with the sheets pulled around her and watched him get dressed. "I have been watching you for a long time," she said. "I saw the color of your eyes."

Tayo did not look at her.

"Mexican eyes," he said, "the other kids used to tease me."

The rain was only a faint sound on the roof, and the sound of the thunder was distant, and moving east. Tayo unbolted the door and opened it; he watched the rainwater pour out the rain gutter over the side of the long porch. "I always wished I had dark eyes like other people. When they look at me they remember things that happened. My mother." His throat felt tight. He had not talked about this before with anyone.

She shook her head slowly. "They are afraid, Tayo. They feel something happening, they can see something happening around them, and it scares them. Indians or Mexicans or whites—most people are afraid of change. They think that if their children have the same color of skin, the same color of eyes, that nothing is changing." She laughed softly. "They are fools. They blame us, the ones who look different. That way they don't have to think about what has happened inside themselves."

She was looking at him intently, and he felt uncomfortable. He walked over to the doorway, aware of the damp earth smell outside. He had one hand on the screen door, ready to leave.

"You don't have to understand what is happening. But remember this day. You will recognize it later. You are part of it now." She was looking up, at the pine vigas that held the roof. She turned her head and smiled at him. "Ah, Tayo," she said softly, and he felt that she cared a great deal about him.

"Good-bye," he said. He pushed the screen door open, into the cool damp air outside. "Good-bye, Tayo. Thank you for bringing the message."

The wind came up and fanned the fire. Tayo watched a red flame crawl out from under the white coals; he reached down for a piece of juniper and tossed it in. The fire caught. He rubbed pitch from the wood between his fingers and looked down at Gallup.

"I never told you about Emo," he said, "I never told you what happened to Rocky." He pointed at the lights below. "Something about the lights down there, something about the cars and the neon signs which reminds me of both of them."

"Yes," the old man said, "my grandmother would not leave this hill. She said the whole world could be seen from here."

"Rocky wanted to get away from the reservation; he wanted to make something of himself. In a city somewhere."

"They are down there. Ones like your brother. They are down there."

Leslie Marmon Silko's work reflects the mixed-blood's sense of dwelling at the edges of communities: "We are . . . Laguna, Mexican, White—but the way we live is like Marmons, and if you are from Laguna Pueblo, you will understand what I mean. All those languages, all those ways of living are combined, and we live somewhere on the fringes of all three." That experience of growing up around Laguna life without being fully immersed in it gives Silko's work a certain doubleness, a flexible narrative point of view. At times there's a distance, an ironic edge, a sense that she is writing about a tradition as much as out of it.

—Patricia Clark Smith and Paula Gunn Allen, in *The Desert Is No Lady:*

"He didn't make it though. I was supposed to help him, so he'd make it back. They were counting on him. They were proud of him. I owed them that much. After everything that happened. I owed it to them." He looked at the old man, but he was staring at the lights down below, following the headlights from the west until they were taillights disappearing in the east. He didn't seem to be listening.

"There are no limits to this thing," Betonie said. "When it was set loose, it ranged everywhere, from the mountains and plains to the towns and cities; rivers and oceans never stopped it." The wind was blowing steadily and the old man's voice was almost lost in it.

"Emo plays with these teeth—human teeth—and he says the Indians have nothing compared to white people. He talks about their cities and all the machines and food they have. He says the land is no good, and we must go after what they have, and take it from them." Tayo coughed and tried to clear the tightness from his throat. "Well, I don't know how to say this but it seems that way. All you have to do is look around. And so I wonder," he said, feeling the tightness in his throat squeeze out the tears, "I wonder what good Indian ceremonies can do against the sickness which comes from their wars, their bombs, their lies?"

The old man shook his head. "That is the trickery of the witchcraft," he said. "They want us to believe all evil resides with white people. Then we will look no further to see what is really happening. They want us to separate ourselves from white people, to be ignorant and helpless as we watch our own destruction. But white people are only tools that the witchery manipulates; and I tell you, we can deal with white people, with their machines and their beliefs. We can because we invented white people; it was Indian witchery that made white people in the first place.

Long time ago
in the beginning
there were no white people in this world
there was nothing European.
And this world might have gone on like that
except for one thing:
witchery.
This world was already complete
even without white people.
There was everything
including witchery.
Then it happened.
These witch people got together.
Some came from far far away
across oceans
across mountains.
Some had slanty eyes
others had black skin.
They all got together for a contest
the way people have baseball tournaments nowadays
except this was a contest
in dark things.

So anyway
they all got together
witch people from all directions

witches from all the Pueblos
and all the tribes.
They had Navajo witches there,
some from Hopi, and a few from Zuni.
They were having a witches' conference,
that's what it was
Way up in the lava rock hills
north of Canoñcito
they got together
to fool around in caves
with their animal skins.
Fox, badger, bobcat, and wolf
they circled the fire
and on the fourth time
they jumped into that animal's skin.

4 0 1

L E S L I E   M A R M O N   **S I L K O**

But this time it wasn't enough
and one of them
maybe a Sioux or some Eskimos
started showing off.
"That wasn't anything,
watch this."

The contest started like that.
Then some of them lifted the lids
on their big cooking pots,
calling the rest of them over
to take a look:
dead babies simmering in blood
circles of skull cut away
all the brains sucked out.
Witch medicine
to dry and grind into powder
for new victims.

Others untied skin bundles of disgusting objects:
dark flints, cinders from burned hogans where the dead lay
Whorls of skin
cut from fingertips
sliced from the penis end and clitoris tip.

Finally there was only one
who hadn't shown off charms or powers.
The witch stood in the shadows beyond the fire
and no one ever knew where this witch came from
which tribe
or if it was a woman or a man.
But the important thing was
this witch didn't show off any dark thunder charcoals
or red ant-hill beads.
This one just told them to listen:
"What I have is a story."

At first they all laughed
but this witch said
Okay
go ahead

4 0 2

laugh if you want to
but as I tell the story
it will begin to happen.

Set in motion now
set in motion by our witchery
to work for us.

Caves across the ocean
in caves of dark hills
white skin people
like the belly of a fish
covered with hair.

Then they grow away from the earth
then they grow away from the sun
then they grow away from the plants and animals.
They see no life
When they look
they see only objects.
The world is a dead thing for them
the trees and rivers are not alive
the mountains and stones are not alive.
The deer and bear are objects
They see no life.

They fear
They fear the world.
They destroy what they fear.
They fear themselves.
The wind will blow them across the ocean
thousands of them in giant boats
swarming like lava
out of a crushed ant hill.

4 0 3

They will carry objects
which can shoot death
faster than the eye can see.

They will kill the things they fear
all the animals
the people will starve.

L E S L I E   M A R M O N   S I L K O

They will poison the water
they will spin the water away
and there will be drought
the people will starve.

They will fear what they find
They will fear the people
They kill what they fear.

Entire villages will be wiped out
They will slaughter whole tribes.

Corpses for us
Blood for us
Killing killing killing killing.

And those they do not kill
will die anyway
at the destruction they see
at the loss
at the loss of the children
the loss will destroy the rest.

Stolen rivers and mountains
the stolen land will eat their hearts
and jerk their mouths from the Mother.
The people will starve.

They will bring terrible diseases
the people have never known.
Entire tribes will die out
covered with festered sores
shitting blood
vomiting blood.
Corpses for our work

Set in motion now
set in motion by our witchery
set in motion
for work for us.

They will take this world from ocean to ocean
they will turn on each other

they will destroy each other
Up here
in these hills
they will find the rocks,
rocks with veins of green and yellow and black.
They will lay the final pattern with these rocks
they will lay it across the world
and explode everything.

Set in motion now
set in motion
To destroy
To kill
Objects to work for us
objects to act for us
Performing the witchery
for suffering
for torment
for the still-born
the deformed
the sterile
the dead.
Whirling
whirling
whirling
whirling
set into motion now
set into motion.

So the other witches said
"Okay you win; you take the prize,
but what you said just now—
it isn't so funny
It doesn't sound so good.
We are doing okay without it
we can get along without that kind of thing.
Take it back.
Call the story back."

But the witch just shook its head
at the others in their stinking animal skins, fur and feathers.

L E S L I E   M A R M O N   S I L K O

It's already turned loose.
It's already coming.
It can't be called back.

SMOKE RISING

LUCI ⸮ TAPAHONSO

Tapahonso's work is highly autobiographical, infused and shaped by her beliefs and identity as a Navajo woman. In her poetry she attempts to reflect the "natural rhythms" of her world, frequently emphasizing the Southwest, community and familial relationships, and various aspects of Navajo society and culture. Sáanii Dahataal: The Women Are Singing, *for example, relates trips between New Mexico and Kansas, during which the narrator reminisces about her upbringing and the Navajo nation.*

Essay by

BLANCHE COX CLEGG

Tapahonso is also known for using "Red English," a combination of English and Navajo vocabulary and syntax, in her works. For instance, she writes of her uncle in the poem "Hills Brothers Coffee": " . . . then he sees the coffee can. / Oh, that's the coffee with / the man in the dress, like a church man. / ah-h, that's the one that does it for me. / very good coffee. / / I sit down again and he tells me / some coffee has no kick but / this one is the one. / It does it good for me."

Praised for her feminist and individualist sensibilities, her depictions of Navajo traditions and humor, and her ability to sensitively convey her multifaceted identity to diverse audiences, Tapahonso has recognized: "I know that I cannot divide myself or separate myself from [my birthplace, Shiprock, New Mexico]—my home, land, and my people. And that realization is my security and my mainstay in my life away from there."

4 0 7

P E R S O N A L   S T A T S

Navajo poet and short story writer.

Born: *c. 1953, in Shiprock, New Mexico.*

Partnerships: Married Earl Ortiz (an artist); children: Lori Tazbah, Misty Dawn.

Education: Participated in a training program for investigative journalism at the National Indian Youth Council; University of New Mexico, 1980.

Career: Writer and poet. Served on the board of directors of the Phoenix Indian Center, 1974.

Address: University of Arizona Press, 1230 N. Park Ave., Suite 102, Tucson, AZ.

In 1864

From *Sáanii Dahataal: The Women Are Singing*, The University of Arizona Press, copyright © 1993 by Luci Tapahonso

> In 1864, 8,354 Navajos were forced to walk from Dinetah to Bosque Redondo in southern New Mexico, a distance of three hundred miles. They were held for four years until the U.S. government declared the assimilation attempt a failure. More than 2,500 died of smallpox and other illnesses, depression, severe weather conditions, and starvation. The survivors returned to Dinetah1 in June of 1868.

While the younger daughter slept, she dreamt of mountains,
the wide blue sky above, and friends laughing.

We talked as the day wore on. The stories and highway beneath
became a steady hum. The center lines were a blurred guide.
As we neared the turn to Fort Sumner[2] I remembered this story:

A few winters ago, he worked as an electrician on a crew
installing power lines on the western plains of New Mexico.
He stayed in his pickup camper, which was connected to a generator.
The crew parked their trucks together and built a fire in the center.
The nights were cold and there weren't any trees to break the wind.
It snowed off and on, a quiet, still blanket. The land was like
he had imagined from the old stories—flat and dotted with shrubs.
The arroyos and washes cut through the soft dirt.
They were unsuspectingly deep.
During the day, the work was hard and the men were exhausted.
In the evenings, some went into the nearby town to eat and drink
a few beers. He fixed a small meal for himself and tried to relax.

4 0 8

Then at night, he heard cries and
    moans carried by the wind
and blowing snow. He heard the
    voices wavering and rising
in the darkness. He would turn
    over and pray, humming songs
he remembered from his child-
    hood. The songs returned to
    him
as easily as if he had heard them
    that very afternoon.
He sang for himself, his family,
    and the people whose spirits
lingered on the plains, in the
    arroyos, and in the old
    windswept plants.
No one else heard the thin wailing.
After the third night, he unhooked
    his camper, signed his time
    card,
and started the drive north to
    home. He told the guys,
"Sure, the money's good. But I miss
    my kids and it sure gets lonely
out here for a family man." He
    couldn't stay there any longer.
The place contained the pain and cries of his relatives,
the confused and battered spirits of his own existence.

After we stopped for a Coke and chips, the storytelling resumed:

My aunt always started the story saying, "You are here
because of what happened to your great-grandmother long ago."

They began rounding up the people in the fall.
Some were lured into surrendering by offers of food, clothes,
and livestock. So many of us were starving and suffering
that year because the bilagáana[3] kept attacking us.
Kit Carson and his army had burned all the fields,
and they killed our sheep right in front of us.
We couldn't believe it. I covered my face and cried.

*The more I learned about poetics
and theory, and the more I read what are considered the classics in poetry . . . I realized there was
a really strong connection between literary forms
and the oral Navajo tradition. . . . Once that revelation became clear to me, it was a freeing experience. I saw that the possibilities were really endless, because I grew up in a home, like many
Navajo homes, filled with storytelling. Prayer was
a ritual—songs and chants. Oration was part of
our daily life. When babies are born, or someone
dies, people stand up and literally orate.*

**—Luci Tapahonso, "A Part of Place," in the *Chicago Tribune*,
September 5, 1993.**

409

LUCI TAPAHONSO

Though many American Indian writers are to some extent cut off from tribal origins and can only grasp a tribal identity by an act of will, the tension inherent in that awareness is apt to be the source of their artistic strength. Luci Tapahonso's power, however, resides in the fact that she is fully conscious, no matter how far she might travel, of being a Navajo who is unable to be anything else. . . . For Tapahonso, the Navaho earth is itself a source of language . . . . "This land . . . is full of stories which hold the spirits of the people," she says in "Just Past Shiprock," a poem about hearing the story of a little girl who died and was buried on the trail and is now a part of the land that holds her memory.

—Robert L. Berner, in a review of *Saanii Dahataal: The Women Are Singing,* in *World Literature Today,* Summer 1993.

All my life, we had sheep. They
   were like our family.
It was then I knew our lives were
   in great danger.
We were all so afraid of that man.
   Redshirt,[4] and his army.
Some people hid in the foothills of
   the Chuska Mountains
and in Canyon de Chelly. Our
   family talked it over,
and we decided to go to this
   place. What would our lives
be like without sheep, crops, and
   land? At least, we thought
we would be safe from gunfire and
   our family would not starve.

The journey began, and the soldiers were all around us.
All of us walked, some carried
   babies. Little children and the
   elderly
stayed in the middle of the group.
   We walked steadily each day,
stopping only when the soldiers
   wanted to eat or rest.
We talked among ourselves and
   cried quietly.
We didn't know how far it was or
   even where we were going.
All that was certain was that we
   were leaving Dinetah, our home.

410

As the days went by, we grew more tired, and soon,
the journey was difficult for all of us, even the military.
And it was they who thought all this up.

We had such a long distance to cover.
Some old people fell behind, and they wouldn't let us go back to help them.
It was the saddest thing to see—my heart hurts so to remember that.
Two women were near the time of the births of their babies,
and they had a hard time keeping up with the rest.

Some army men pulled them behind a huge rock, and we screamed out loud
when we heard the gunshots. The women didn't make a sound,
but we cried out loud for them and their babies.
I felt then that I would not live through everything.
When we crossed the Rio Grande, many people drowned.
We didn't know how to swim—there was hardly any water deep enough
to swim in at home. Some babies, children, and some of the older men
and women were swept away by the river current.
We must not ever forget their screams and the last we saw of them—
hands, a leg, or strands of hair floating.

There were many who died on the way to Hwééldi.[5] All the way
we told each other, "We will be strong as long as we are together."
I think that was what kept us alive. We believed in ourselves
and the old stories that the holy people had given us.
"This is why," she would say to us. "This is why we are here.
Because our grandparents prayed and grieved for us."

LUCI TAPAHONSO

Poetry

One More Shiprock Night, illustrated by Earl P. Ortiz, Tejas Art Press, 1981.

Seasonal Woman, drawings by R. C. Gorman, Tooth of Time Books, 1982.
A Breeze Swept Through, West End Press, 1987.

Sáanii Dahataal: The Women Are Singing, University of Arizona Press, 1993.

The car hums steadily, and my daughter is crying softly.
Tears stream down her face. She cannot speak, Then I tell her that
it was at Bosque Redondo the people learned to use flour and now
fry bread is considered to be the "traditional" Navajo bread.
It was there that we acquired a deep appreciation for strong coffee.
The women began to make long, tiered calico skirts
and fine velvet shirts for the men. They decorated their dark velvet
blouses with silver dimes, nickels, and quarters.
They had no use for money then.
It is always something to see—silver flashing in the sun
against dark velvet and black, black hair.

Notes

1. "Dinetah" means "Navajo country" or "homeland of The People."
2. Fort Sumner was also called "Bosque Redondo" owing to its location.
3. "Bilagáana" is the Navajo word for Anglos.
4. Kit Carson's name was "Redshirt" in Navajo.
5. Hwééldi is the Navajo name for Fort Sumner.

HILLS BROTHERS COFFEE

From *Sáanii Dahataal: The Women Are Singing*, The University of Arizona Press, copyright © 1993 by Luci Tapahonso

My uncle is a small man.
In Navajo, we call him, "shidá'í,"
     my mother's brother.

He doesn't know English,
     but his name in the white way is Tom Jim.
     He lives about a mile or so
     down the road from our house.

One morning he sat in the kitchen,
drinking coffee.
> I just came over, he said.
> The store is where I'm going to.

He tells me about how my mother
> seems to be gone
every time he comes over.
> Maybe she sees me coming
> then runs and jumps in her car
> and speeds away!
> he says smiling.

We both laugh—just to think of my mother
jumping in her car and speeding.

I pour him more coffee
and he spoons in sugar and cream
until it looks almost like a chocolate shake.
Then he sees the coffee can.
> Oh, that's that coffee with the man in a dress,
> like a church man.
> Ah-h, that's the one that does it for me.
> Very good coffee.

I sit down again and he tells me,
> Some coffee has no kick.
> But this one is the one.
> It does it good for me.

I pour us both a cup
and while we wait for my mother,
his eyes crinkle with the smile and he says,
> Yes, ah yes. This is the very one
> (putting in more sugar and cream).

So I usually buy Hills Brothers Coffee.
Once or sometimes twice a day,
I drink a hot coffee and

> it sure does it for me.

"The way one talks . . . is a
direct reflection of the people who raised her. . . .
People are known . . . by their use of language."

—**Luci Tapahonso, in her preface to** ***Sáanii Dahataal***

4 1 3

LUCI   TAPAHONSO

GERALD  VIZENOR

Vizenor is a prolific author whose novels, poems, essays, and stories draw heavily upon his experiences as a mixed-blood Anishinabe (Chippewa). His career has been as varied as his writings: he has worked as an editorial writer for the Minneapolis Tribune, served in the U.S. Army during the early 1950s, organized an Indian Studies program at Bemidji State University in Minnesota, and taught at a number of universities, including the University of California, Berkeley. Vizenor's childhood was marred by poverty, violence, and abandonment, as his mother shuttled him between his grandmother, foster homes, and an alcoholic stepfather. As a means of coping with his chaotic upbringing, Vizenor cultivated a vivid fantasy life, populated, in his words, by "benign demons and little woodland people."

Essay by

BRETT A. LEALAND

415

Elements of Anishinabe folklore, which he first heard during childhood visits to his grandmother, would later figure prominently in his works. For example, Vizenor often incorporates the trickster figure, named Naan-abozho in Anishinabe. Possessed of insatiable appetites and fond of buffoonery and playing tricks, Naanabozho is essentially amoral; he violates the most sacred tribal taboos while performing benevolent and heroic acts on a whim. Vizenor often emphasizes that the trickster is capable of compassion and has stated that he represents "a spiritual balance in a comic drama rather than the romantic elimination of human contradictions and evil."

While Vizenor has published numerous novels, he began his career as a poet. Most of his poems, which are collected in such volumes as *Raising the Moon Vines* and *Empty Swings*, are haikus, a form which Vizenor has characterized as "intuitive, a manner of meditation at a dreamscape." Vizenor challenges conventional notions about contemporary Native American life in his essays and autobiographical memoirs. In *Crossbloods: Bone Courts, Bingo, and Other Reports*, for example, he argues against the tendency to view crossbreeds as inferior and suggests that mixed heredity is an ideal vantage for understanding the arbitrary and fictive nature of cultural identity. Vizenor has also been critical of those who believe that the "purity" of tribal culture is at stake in the struggle for political autonomy.

For Vizenor, assimilation of Native Americans into contemporary American culture is already a reality, and if actively embraced within a multicultural framework, will inevitably enrich tribal heritage. Critics frequently characterize Vizenor's fiction as postmodern because of the author's use of experimental narrative structures, word play, and complex symbols and imagery. In his novels and short stories Vizenor also attempts to blend written and oral literary traditions and to incorporate Native American myths and legends. For example, in his short story collection *Landfill Meditation* Vizenor blurs fact and fiction to challenge generalizations about Native Americans, and in *The Heirs of Columbus* he uses fantasy and satire to rewrite the myth of Christopher Columbus from a Native American perspective. Concerning Vizenor's literary career, A. LaVonne Brown Ruoff has stated: "Both a compassionate trickster and a formidable warrior in the word wars, Vizenor is a fine storyteller and acute commentator on the hypocrisies of modern society."

SANTA MARIA CASINO

From *The Heirs of Columbus*, Wesleyan University Press, copyright © 1992 by Gerald Vizenor

Christopher Columbus saw a blue light in the west, but "it was such an uncertain thing," he wrote in his journal to the crown, "that I did not feel it was adequate proof of land." That light was a torch raised by the silent hand talkers, a summons to the New World. Since then, the explorer has become a trickster healer in the stories told by his tribal heirs at the headwaters of the great river.

The Admiral of the Ocean Sea, confirmed in the name of the curia and the crown, was an obscure crossblood who bore the tribal signature of survivance and ascended the culture of death in the Old World. He landed at dawn with no missionaries or naturalists and heard the thunder of shamans

Chippewa novelist, short story writer, poet, nonfiction writer, scriptwriter, editor, and educator.

Born: October 22, 1934, in Minneapolis, Minnesota.

Partnerships: Married Judith Helen Horns, 1959 (divorced, 1968); married Laura Jane Hall, 1981; children: (first marriage) Robert Thomas.

Education: Attended New York University, 1955–56; University of Minnesota, B.A., 1960, graduate study, 1962–65; additional graduate study at Harvard University.

Career: Ramsey County Corrections Authority, St. Paul, MN, group worker, 1957–58; Capital Community Center, St. Paul, roving group worker, 1958; Minnesota Department of Corrections, Minnesota State Reformatory, St. Cloud, corrections agent, 1960–61; *Minneapolis Tribune*, Minneapolis, MN, staff writer, 1968–70; Park Rapids Public Schools, Park Rapids, MN, teacher trainer, 1971; instructor at Lake Forest College, Lake Forest, IL, and Bemidji State University, Bemidji, MN, 1971–73; University of California, Berkeley, lecturer, 1976–80; University of Minnesota, Minneapolis, professor of American Indian studies, 1980–87; University of California, Santa Cruz, professor of literature, 1987–90; University of California, Berkeley, professor of Native American studies. Kresge College, acting provost, 1990; University of Oklahoma, David Burke Chair of Letters, 1991. *Address:* Native American Studies, 3415 Dwinelle Hall, University of California, Berkeley, CA 94720.

---

in the coral and the stone. "No sooner had we concluded the formalities of taking possession of their land than people began to come to the beach," he wrote in his journal on October 12, 1492, at Samana Cay.

Columbus unfurled the royal banner, and the green cross of the crown shivered on the wind over the island the tribe had named *Guanahaní*. He was blinded by the white sand, the broken sun on the water. He showed his sword to a painted servant on the beach, "and through ignorance he grabbed it by the blade and cut himself."

"In order to win their friendship, since I knew they were a people to be converted and won to our holy faith by love and friendship rather than by force, I gave some of them red caps and glass beads which they hung around their necks," he wrote about his first encounter with tribal people in the New World. "They ought to make good and skilled servants, for they repeat very quickly whatever we say to them," but he misconstrued a tribal pose and later traced his soul to the stories in their blood. "They all go naked as their mothers bore them, including the women, although I saw only one very young girl."

At Samana Cay the great adventurer was touched by a hand talker, a silent tribal wanderer, who wore a golden braid in her hair and carried two wooden puppets. That night she danced with the blue puppets on the sterncastle. The *Santa María* was brushed with a blue radiance.

Columbus and the sailors were haunted by the wild puppets and roused by a golden shimmer on the night water. Samana was an island in the ocean sea that would be imagined but never possessed in the culture of

4 1 7

You can't understand the world without telling a story. There isn't any center to the world but a story. I want to distinguish "story." It's not a rehearsed or repeated story, it's a visual reference to experience. In fact I don't know many people, Indian people, who don't tell stories; I mean it's really extraordinary that people don't. . . .

—**Gerald Vizenor in *Winged Words: American Indian Writers Speak,* by Laura Cotelli, University of Nebraska Press, 1990.**

death. Five centuries later the crossblood descendants of the explorer and the hand talker declared a new tribal nation.

"Samana swam out to touch the man from heaven that first night in our New World and here we are on radio," said Stone Columbus.

Columbus was a seasonal voice on late night talk radio because of his surname and the curious stories he told about his inheritance. "She was a natural healer, a tribal hand talker, blessed with silence, and she discovered the incredible truth that the great explorer was tribal and he carried our stories in his blood."

The Heirs of Christopher Columbus are serious over their names and resurrections; the heirs come together at the stone tavern each autumn to remember the best stories about their strain and estate, and the genetic signature that would heal the obvious blunders in the natural world.

The stone tavern, that wondrous circle of warm trickster stones, has been located for more than a hundred generations on a wild blue meadow near the headwaters of the Mississippi River.

The Anishinaabe, the woodland tribe that founded this obscure tavern, the oldest in the New World, remember that Naanabozho, the compassionate tribal trickster who created the earth, had a brother who was a stone: a bear stone, a human stone, a shaman stone, a stone, a stone, a stone.

Naanabozho was the first human born in the world, and the second born, his brother, was a stone. The trickster created the new earth with wet sand. He stood on his toes as high as he could imagine, but the water rose closer to his nose and mouth. He could dream without a mouth or nose, but he would never leave the world to the evil gambler and his dark water. The demons in the water caused him to defecate, and with pleasure, but his shit would not leave; several turds floated near his mouth and nose.

Naanabozho was at the highest point on the earth and could not move, so he invented meditation with trickster stories and liberated his mind over his own excrement. The trickster created this New World with the sand a muskrat held in her paws.

4 1 8

The Heirs of Christopher Columbus created one more New World in their stories and overturned the tribal prophecies that their avian time would end with the arrival of the white man. The heirs warm the stones at the tavern with their stories in the blood. The tavern is on the natural rise of a meadow, and tribal panic holes are sown near the mount. The House of Life is on the descent to the headwaters, the burial ground for the lost and lonesome bones that were liberated by the heirs from museums.

The stones create a natural theater, an uncovered mount that is never touched by storms, curses, and disease; in the winter the stones near the headwaters are a haven for birds, animals, humans, and trickster stories of liberation.

Stone Columbus heard the summer in the spring once more on the occasion of his third resurrection. That season the rush of aspen touched him as a child on his first return from a furnace in a government school; he came back a second time in the arms of the notorious ice woman, and then he drowned in his bingo caravel and heard the push of bears. None of these

GERALD **VIZENOR**

Poetry

Born in the Wind, privately printed, 1960.

The Old Park Sleepers, Obercraft, 1961.

Two Wings the Butterfly (haiku), privately printed, 1962.

South of the Painted Stone, Obercraft, 1963.

Raising the Moon Vines (haiku), Callimachus, 1964.

Seventeen Chirps (haiku), Nodin, 1964.

Empty Swings (haiku), Nodin, 1967.

(Contributor) Kenneth Rosen, editor, *Voices of the Rainbow*, Viking, 1975.

Matsushima: Pine Islands (haiku), Nodin, 1984.

Novels

Darkness in Saint Louis Bearheart, Truck Press, 1973.

Griever: An American Monkey King in China, Fiction Collective, 1987.

The Heirs of Columbus, Wesleyan University Press, 1992.

Dead Voices: Natural Agonies in the New World, University of Oklahoma Press, 1992.

Other

Thomas James White Hawk, Four Winds, 1968.

(Editor) *Escorts to White Earth, 1868–1968: 100 Year Reservation*, Four Winds, 1968.

The Everlasting Sky, Crowell, 1972.

Anishinabe Nagomon: Songs of the Ojibwa, Nodin, 1974.

Anishinabe Adisokan: Stories of the Ojibwa, Nodin, 1974.

Tribal Scenes and Ceremonies (editorial articles), Nodin, 1976.

(Contributor) Chester Anderson, editor, *Growing up in Minnesota* (autobiographical stories), University of Minnesota Press, 1976.

Wordarrows: Indians and Whites in the New Fur Trade (stories), University of Minnesota Press, 1978.

(Contributor) Jane Katz, editor, *This Song Remembers* (autobiographical stories), Houghton, 1980.

Summer in the Spring: Ojibwa Songs and Stories, Nodin, 1981.

Earthdivers: Tribal Narratives on Mixed Descent (stories), University of Minnesota Press, 1981.

The People Named the Chippewa: Narrative Histories, University of Minnesota Press, 1984.

Crossbloods: Bone Courts, Bingo, and Other Reports (essays), University of Minnesota Press, 1990.

Interior Landscapes: Autobiographical Myths and Metaphors, University of Minnesota Press, 1990.

Landfill Meditation (short stories), Wesleyan University Press, 1991.

Manifest Manners: Postindian Warriors of Survivance (essays), Wesleyan University Press, 1994.

Shadow Distance: Gerald Vizenor Reader (selected fiction and essays), Wesleyan University Press, 1994.

---

stories would be true if he had not inherited an unwonted surname and the signature of survivance from the Admiral of the Ocean Sea.

The Heirs of Columbus celebrated the quintessence of their inheritance that season; a blue radiance warmed the tavern stones. The heirs told their stories about creation, the bear codex and hand talkers, the ice woman and moccasin games, panic hole tricksters and saints, the bingo caravel, and the third death and resurrection of the sovereign mariner Stone Columbus.

4 2 0

Christopher Columbus appeared in the dreams of the heirs; the stories that were told at the headwaters were bounden ceremonies, remembrance in the blood, because the bear codex, the last record of their signature of survivance, their blood histories, had been lost at sea. No others on the reservation were visited in dreams or stories by the great explorer; rather, those who revealed their dreams in his name were shunned at first. Later, when the caravels turned a fortune on sovereign bingo, the heirs were embraced as the cash would flow.

Stone Columbus was heartened by his esoteric genetic signature and the stories in his blood; he was a crossblood and his spiritual distance from the tribe seemed to be as natural as the reasons his namesake lost gold, gods, and glories, in the radiance of a hand talker. To be sure, the personal miseries and public troubles with white men over the centuries were blamed on the visions of the crossblood shamans and the estranged stories the heirs told at the stone tavern. The heirs were burdened with the withering ironies of those who had never beheld resurrections in their stories.

The *Santa María Casino*, the decorated bingo flagship, was anchored on the international border near Big Island in Lake of the Woods. The casino was an enormous barge that had been decked for games of chance on the ocean seas of the woodland. The *Niña*, a restaurant, and the *Pinta*, a tax free market, were simulated caravels anchored and moored on the border near the casino.

The *Santa María* was christened and launched as soon as the ice broke in the spring. Stone built a wide cantilevered sterncastle and a cabin that overlooked the spacious casino; on one level he heard the seasons on the lake, and on the lower level he watched the players in the lounge. The two caravels were fitted and christened by early summer in time for the tourists and their search for gold and tribal adventures.

The Fourth of July that year was not a celebration of tribal liberation or independence. Stone was arrested at dawn and detained on warrants that charged him with violations of state tax and gambling laws; the flagship and the caravels were confiscated and towed to a public dock. The next morning, however, a federal judge reversed the state court order; she agreed to review the issues of tribal sovereignty. Our tribal mariner of chance was back on the ocean sea, anchored once more to his stories at the border.

In the first two summers on the water he made a fortune on games and waited for the court to rule on his right to operate a casino as a new reservation moored to an anchor as long as the waters flow in the New World. Border patrols from both countries circled the "dirty mary," copied boat and airplane numbers, estimated the tax free cash flow, and anticipated the court decision that would sink the savage *Santa María Casino*.

Beatrice Lord, the federal judge, ruled in favor of the unusual casino and sanctioned the reservation on an anchor; she so admired the imagination and certitude of the founder that she announced the court decision from the wild sterncastle of the *Santa María Casino* on Columbus Day.

"The federal court finds in favor of Stone Columbus," the judge said over a loudspeaker: Thousands of people in canoes, pontoon boats, and launches heard the voice of the court waver over the water. "The notion of tribal sovereignty is not confiscable, or earth bound; sovereignty is neither fence nor feathers. The essence of sovereignty is imaginative, an original tribal trope, communal and spiritual, an idea that is more than metes and bounds in treaties." The court vacated the claims of the state and ruled that an anchor and caravel is as much a tribal connection to sovereignty as a homestead, mineral rights, the sacred cedar, and the nest of a bald eagle.

GERALD   VIZENOR

"The *Santa María* and the other caravels are limited sovereign states at sea, the first maritime reservations in international waters," the judge announced. "Moreover, the defendant was wise to drop his anchors on the border, knowing, as he must, that future appeals and other remedies could reach the International Court of Justice at The Hague."

The sovereign casino was a natural sensation that summer. Network television reported on the court decision, "the tribe that was lost no more," and pursued the genetic theories of the crossblood founder of the "new casino tribe" who traced his descent to the great adventurer Christopher Columbus.

Stone was pleased to pose on television with Felipa Flowers, the trick-ster poacher who repatriates tribal remains and sacred pouches from muse-ums, and Miigis, their luminous child, but he would never speak to a cam-era; however, he was eager to be heard on national talk show radio. Felipa, Miigis, Stone, and Admire, the mongrel with the blue tongue, lived on the *Santa María Casino*. The mongrel was a healer, she whistled and barked on radio, but she shied at television cameras.

"Radio is real, television is not," he reminded the radio listeners. His grandparents listened to talk radio late at night on the reservation; the bold lies and arguments over the truth that he heard as a child hurried his sense of adventure, imagination, and the stories in his blood.

Stone was heard by millions of people late at night on talk radio that wild summer. The crossblood of the northern air told his stories about the stone tavern, his resurrections, and the genetic signature of the heirs that would heal the nation. He spoke from the sterncastle of his casino; a flotilla of canoes, powerboats, and floatplanes from the cities circled the *Santa María*. The gamblers were white, most of them were on vacation, urban adventurers who would lose at bingo and slot machines with pleasure on a moored reservation.

"Admiral Luckie White is on the air . . . "

"Stone Columbus is here as usual, and who you hear is what you see," he said that summer night from the sterncastle of the *Santa María Casino*.

"Admiral Luckie White is on the air, your late night host and voice of the night on Carp Radio." The radio was heard in four directions from enor-mous loudspeakers on the masts of the casino and the caravels. "Columbus is back to answer your questions and mine tonight. Here we go once more with the truth in the dark, so, how do you expect our listeners to buy the sto-ries that your brother is a stone, a common rock?"

"Stone is my name, not my brother, and we are not common," said Stone Columbus. His voice was a primal sound that boomed over the black water. "The stone is my totem, my stories are stones, there are tribal stones, and the brother of the first trickster who created the earth was a stone, stone, stone."

"Really, but how can you be a stone, a real stone, and be talking on radio?" she asked, and then paused for a commercial. The talks from the casino two or three times a week had attracted new listeners and many eager advertisers. Carp Radio had discovered a new world on the *Santa María Casino*.

"Stones hold our tribal words and the past in silence, in the same way that we listen to stories in the blood and hold our past in memories," he said, and waved to several people boarding the caravel.

"Stone, listen, our listeners know you were born on a reservation, and we understand how proud you are to be an Indian, so how can you claim to be a direct descendant of a stone and Christopher Columbus?"

"Columbus was Mayan," said Stone.

"You must be stoned," she said, and laughed on the air. Her voice bounced on the water, and the boats rocked with laughter near the casino. Admire barked at the boats and healed the night. "Really, you must be stoned on that reservation boat, Columbus was Italian, not a Mayan Indian."

"The Maya brought civilization to the savages of the Old World and the rest is natural," said Stone. "Columbus escaped from the culture of death and carried our tribal genes back to the New World, back to the great river, he was an adventurer in our blood and he returned to his homeland."

"His homeland, now wait a minute, this is serious radio."

"My stories are evermore serious, serious, serious," he said and teased the sounds of the words. Admire whistled a tune from a familiar symphony based on tribal themes. Felipa laughed and inserted a tape cassette in the recorder and played the *New World* Symphony, by Antonín Dvořák.

Stone posed with Miigis that night as an orchestra leader on the stern-castle of the *Santa María Casino*. The mast was decorated with spirit catchers that held the wild beads of light from the boats on the lake. Felipa touched them from behind, the wondrous trickster on the ocean sea in a scarlet tunic, and her daughter in a blue robe. Admire heard her own bark echo on the loudspeaker; she bounced in a circle on the deck of the casino.

"Mayan genes, give me a break," said Admiral White.

4 2 3

"The truth is in our genes," said Stone.

"Right, we are what our genes must pretend."

"We are the tribal heirs of the great explorer," said Stone.

"What are you playing?"

"The *Santa María Overture*," said Stone.

"No, that's Dvořák," said Luckie White.

"Dvořák was at the headwaters," said Stone.

"Please, tell our listeners why."

"Dvořák heard tribal music in the stones," said Stone.

"What about Columbus?"

"He sought gold and tribal women," said Stone.

"So, what did he find?"

"He found his homeland at the headwaters."

"Really, so what's the real story?"

"Samana, the golden healer," said Stone.

"The truth at last, but first a commercial announcement from those wise companies that buy our time and make the truth possible in the dark," said Admiral White.

"Samana is our hand talker, the golden woman of the ocean seas and sister to the fish, and she touched his soul and set the wounded adventurer free on October 28, 1492, at Bahia de Bariay in Oriente Province, Cuba," he said, and smiled over the dates and names.

Felipa danced on the deck that warm night; she was touched by the memories of his stories, the sound of his creation. She could hear the end of the culture of death on the sterncastle of the casino, and she sensed the last of the heartsore stories of a broken civilization.

"Stone, wait a minute, you leap from stones, to genes, to goldfish, to dates and places, and back again, so take your time now and spell it out in your own words to our listeners," said Admiral White.

"October 29, 1492, at Rio de la Luna."

"You changed the date."

"Columbus is ever on the move in our stories," said Stone.

"This is a good time for a commercial."

424 Stone connected the tape recorder to the loudspeakers and turned the volume higher with the allegro con fuoco of the *New World* Symphony. The moon was a wicked sliver in the west; on the water the moon was shredded on the breeze. Felipa undressed and dove into the black water. Stone dove into her wake and swam at her side to the island. They made love on a granite boulder; the mosquitos sounded louder in their heat. They heard the bears, the breath of bears, and warm paws on the stone. Later, a cool wind touched them; the ice woman lived in a cave on the other side of the island.

"The ice woman saved me once," he said on the granite. Stone touched her breasts and moved closer to the heat of her thighs. "I crashed through the thin ice, the paper ice that teased me to rush in the spring, and sank deeper and deeper in the cold clear water. I could see the hole in the ice above me, and the veins on the underside of the ice, but my arms were numbed, my vision blurred, and the last breath of cold water was ecstatic. The ice woman brought me back, and that was my second resurrection."

The *Santa María Casino* paid high stakes to hundreds of winners and earned millions besides, and the tax free market caravel was a second gold mine. Stone earned more than a million dollars a season, and there were four summers in the name of the great explorer. Even the restaurant caravel turned a profit on pretentious bad taste, a commodities menu of fry bread, oatmeal, macaroni, and glorified wild rice.

Stone Columbus was the proud mariner on a moored reservation, a trickster creation on an ocean sea in the new tribal world. He heard the seasons turn from the wild sterncastle of the *Santa María Casino.* Summer touched the spring, and he discovered gold in the name of his blood and survivance. He heard the blue puppets dance on the decks, and then, late one night in a thunderstorm, at the crowing point of his casino glories and stories, the casino and the caravels were cracked by lightning.

Felipa and Miigis were on shore and survived the storm. The few gamblers in the casino were able to abandon the reservation and rode the storm in their own boats. The spirit catchers on the mast burned, and the blue medicine poles were overturned and crashed into the casino; the cantilevered sterncastle burst at the seams. Admire, a blue light in the water, was rescued by a woman in a powerboat.

Throughout his work, Vizenor demonstrates remarkable range and penetrating insight. His strength is his ability to depict with sharp accuracy and wry humor the contrarieties in Indian-White relations. Both a compassionate trickster and formidable warrior in the word wars, Vizenor is a fine storyteller and acute commentator on the hypocrisies of modern society. By exposing the sham of contemporary "Pan-Indianness," Vizenor encourages tribal people and humankind as a whole to abandon this artificial world of chicken feathers, plastic bear claws, and imitation turquoise to follow tribal tricksters and shamans, whose visions and dreams will lead us back to traditional tribal values.

—A. LaVonne Brown Ruoff, "Woodland Warrior: An Introduction to the Works of Gerald Vizenor," in *MELUS,* Spring–Summer, 1986.

GERALD VIZENOR

The *Santa María* lost her anchor and moorings as a sovereign casino; she bashed on a granite reef, the beam groaned and the flagship sank near the island, the sudden end of a new reservation. The great trickster explorer discovered gold and then drowned in his scarlet tunic; he washed ashore a rich man with thousands of bingo cards.

Stone was broken and lost on the cold granite; his black hair was mussed with weeds and wild tinsel. The bears pushed the seasons down to the shore at dawn and pawed the remains of the casino and the caravels; the spirit catchers, macaroni, and polyurethane were lost on the woodland sea in the last thunderstorm of the season.

Samana, the crossblood black bear and lonesome hand talker on the island, hauled the mariner to a granite boulder. She teased his ears with her nose and blew on his eyes and mouth; when she blew harder the other bears danced on the mount near shore. Samana was a shaman, as her mother was a bear, and her touch would heal the heir with stories in the blood. Stone heard the wild dance of blue puppets on the stones.

Samana touched his head and the bears pushed him back from death with a blue radiance; the stones were warmed on the shore and held his graven image. He was a hand talker in the maw of the bear. She was his heart and memories; she teased his third resurrection in the stone.

ANNA LEE WALTERS

A prolific writer who works in many literary genres, Walters has used her Native American background to make tribal perspectives accessible to non-Native audiences. Born and raised in Pawnee, Oklahoma, Walters was educated in Santa Fe, New Mexico. She later married a Navajo and has spent several years on the Navajo reservation in Arizona. Walters states: "I write about things I know, people I know. I write because of my need to write. It is my 'true' love." Her collection of eight short stories, The Sun Is Not Merciful, *addresses such themes as cultural- and self-identity, physical and spiritual survival, and the ways in which cultural differences affect individuals' perceptions of the world.*

In *Ghost Singer,* a contemporary horror novel, Walters creates a complex story of physical and metaphysical conflict that takes place at the Smithsonian Institution. *Talking Indian: Reflections on Survival and Writing* incorporates essays, stories, poems, and photographs to delineate personal and cultural history, while the children's book *The Two-Legged Creature: An Otoe Story* relates an Indian legend of how humankind became separated from the animals, save the horse and dog. Walters has also coauthored a textbook, contributed to and edited several books and periodicals, and published a book cataloging the David T. Vernon Collection of American Indian art objects at Grand Teton National Park.

Critical reaction to Walters's work has been generally positive, with many critics stating that her works successfully present the connected-

Pawnee/Otoe-Missouria novelist, essayist, short story writer, author of children's books, poet, and editor.

Born: September 9, 1946, in Pawnee, Oklahoma.

Partnerships: Married Harry Walters (a museum curator); children: two sons.

Education: Attended College of Santa Fe, 1972–74.

Career: Institute of American Indian Arts, Santa Fe, NM, library technician, 1968–74; Dineh Coopera-

tives, Chinle, AZ, technical writer, 1975; Navajo Community College, Tsaile, AZ, technical writer for curriculum development, 1976–84; Navajo Community College Press, Tsaile, director. Also worked at National Anthropological Archives, Smithsonian Institution.

Address: Home—Navajo Reservation of Arizona. Office—Navajo Community College Press, Tsaile, AZ 86556.

ness—particularly between past and present, and art and life—that pervades traditional Native American culture. Walters has also been praised for her effective blending of various literary and artistic genres, her realistic depiction of Native American culture, and her focus on spiritual concerns. As Joseph Bruchac has stated: "The enduring presence of the sacred in American Indian life has always been the underlying message in the writing of Anna Lee Walters."

THE WARRIORS

From *The Sun is Not Merciful*, Firebrand Books, copyright © 1985 by Anna Lee Walters

In our youth, we saw hobos come and go, sliding by our faded white house like wary cats who did not want us too close. Sister and I waved at the strange procession of passing men and women hobos. Just between ourselves, Sister and I talked of that hobo parade. We guessed at and imagined the places and towns we thought the hobos might have come from or had been. Mostly they were White or Black people. But there were Indian hobos, too. It never occurred to Sister and me that this would be Uncle Ralph's end.

Sister and I were little, and Uncle Ralph came to visit us. He lifted us over his head and shook us around him like gourd rattles. He was Momma's younger brother, and he could have disciplined us if he so desired. That was part of our custom. But he never did. Instead, he taught us Pawnee words. "*Pari* is Pawnee and *pita* is man," he said. Between the words, he tapped out drumbeats with his fingers on the table top, ghost dance and round dance songs that he suddenly remembered and sang. His melodic voice lilted over

428

us and hung around the corners of the house for days. His stories of life and death were fierce and gentle. Warriors dangled in delicate balance.

He told us his version of the story of *Pahukatawa,* a Skidi Pawnee warrior. He was killed by the Sioux, but the animals, feeling compassion for him, brought *Pahukatawa* to life again. "The Evening Star and the Morning Star bore children and some people say that these offspring are who we are," he often said. At times he pointed to those stars and greeted them by their Pawnee names. He liked to pray for Sister and me, for everyone and every tiny thing in the world, but we never heard him ask for anything for himself from *Atius,* the Father.

"For beauty is why we live," Uncle Ralph said when he talked of precious things only the Pawnees know. "We die for it, too." He called himself an ancient Pawnee warrior when he was quite young. He told us that warriors must brave all storms and odds and stand their ground. He knew intimate details of every battle the Pawnees ever fought since Pawnee time began, and Sister and I knew even then that Uncle Ralph had a great battlefield of his own.

As a child I thought that Uncle Ralph had been born into the wrong time. The Pawnees had been ravaged so often by then. The tribe of several thousand when it was at its peak over a century before were then a few hundred people who had been closely confined for more than a hundred years. The warrior life was gone. Uncle Ralph was trapped in a transparent bubble of a new time. The bubble bound him tight as it blew around us.

Uncle Ralph talked obsessively of warriors, painted proud warriors who shrieked poignant battle cries at the top of their lungs and died with honor. Sister and I were little then, lost from him in the world of children who saw everything with children's eyes. And though we saw with wide eyes the painted warriors that he fantasized and heard their fierce and haunting battle cries, we did not hear his. Now that we are old and Uncle Ralph has been gone for a long time, Sister and I know that when he died, he was tired and alone. But he was a warrior.

The hobos were always around in our youth. Sister and I were curious about them, and this curiosity claimed much of our time. They crept by the house at all hours of the day and night, dressed in rags and odd clothing. They wandered to us from the railroad tracks where they had leaped from slow-moving boxcars onto the flatland. They hid in high clumps of weeds and brush that ran along the fence near the tracks. The hobos usually traveled alone, but Sister and I saw them come together, like poor families, to share a can of beans or a tin of sardines that they ate with sticks or twigs. Uncle Ralph also watched them from a distance.

One early morning, Sister and I crossed the tracks on our way to school and collided with a tall, haggard whiteman. He wore a very old-fash-

I was brought up in Oklahoma. I went to public schools, and in that whole educational setting there was very little reference to tribal people in Oklahoma. That really had an impact on me. It motivated me to do something about it . . . . When you're a young person and you go through that kind of environment, where all the popular and classical literature says that Indian people are "bad," or that it was God's will that Indian people be conquered, or when there's the implication that all the "real" Indians are gone, Indian children are being told that they are not there, that they don't matter! That's very, very destructive.

—Anna Lee Walters and Rhoda Carroll, in an interview in *American Indian Quarterly,* Winter 1992.

ioned pin-striped black jacket covered with lint and soot. There was fright in his eyes when they met ours. He scurried around us, quickening his pace. The pole over his shoulder where his possessions hung in a bundle at the end bounced as he nearly ran from us.

"Looks just like a scared jackrabbit," Sister said, watching him dart away.

That evening we told Momma about the scared man. She warned us about the dangers of hobos as our father threw us a stern look. Uncle Ralph was visiting but he didn't say anything. He stayed the night and Sister asked him, "Hey, Uncle Ralph, why do you suppose they's hobos?"

Uncle Ralph was a large man. He took Sister and put her on one knee. "You see, Sister," he said, "hobos are a different kind. They see things in a different way. Them hobos are kind of like us. We're not like other people in some ways and yet we are. It has to do with what you see and feel when you look at this old world."

His answer satisfied Sister for a while. He taught us some more Pawnee words that night.

Not long after Uncle Ralph's explanation, Sister and I surprised a Black man with white whiskers and fuzzy hair. He was climbing through the barbed-wire fence that marked our property line. He wore faded blue overalls with pockets stuffed full of handkerchiefs. He wiped sweat from his face. When it dried, he looked up and saw us. I remembered what Uncle Ralph had said and wondered what the Black man saw when he looked at us standing there.

"We might scare him," Sister said softly to me, remembering the whiteman who had scampered away.

Sister whispered, "Hi," to the Black man. Her voice was barely audible.

"Boy, it's sure hot," he said. His voice was big and he smiled.

"Where are you going?" Sister asked.

"Me? Nowheres, I guess," he muttered.

"Then what you doing here?" Sister went on. She was bold for a seven-year-old kid. I was older but I was also quieter. "This here place is ours," she said.

He looked around and saw our house with its flowering mimosa trees and rich green mowed lawn stretching out before him. Other houses sat around ours.

"I reckon I'm lost," he said.

Sister pointed to the weeds and brush further up the road. "That's where you want to go. That's where they all go, the hobos."

I tried to quiet Sister but she didn't hush. "The hobos stay up there," she said. "You a hobo?"

He ignored her question and asked his own. "Say, what is you all? You not Black, you not White. What is you all?"

Sister looked at me. She put one hand on her chest and the other hand on me. "We Indians!" Sister said.

He stared at us and smiled again. "Is that a fact?" he said.

"Know what kind of Indians we are?" Sister asked him.

He shook his fuzzy head. "Indians is Indians, I guess," he said.

Sister wrinkled her forehead and retorted, "Not us! We not like others. We see things different. We're Pawnees. We're warriors!"

I pushed my elbow into Sister's side. She quieted.

The man was looking down the road and he shuffled his feet. "I'd best go," he said.

Sister pointed to the brush and weeds one more time. "That way," she said.

He climbed back through the fence and brush as Sister yelled, "Bye now!" He waved a damp handkerchief.

Sister and I didn't tell Momma and Dad about the Black man. But much later Sister told Uncle Ralph every word that had been exchanged with the Black man. Uncle Ralph listened and smiled.

Months later when the warm weather had cooled and Uncle Ralph came to stay with us for a couple of weeks, Sister and I went to the hobo place. We had planned it for a long time. That afternoon when we pushed away the weeds, not a hobo was in sight.

ANNA LEE **WALTERS**

For a long time now, over four hundred years, Indians have been trying to tell our colonizers and other folks in this country something, many things. Some of these things are very political, cultural, spiritual, economic, but mostly we've been talking about how to survive, how to get along or how we've gotten along. Mostly this telling has to do with a difference in viewing the world, a true difference in reality that goes deep—deeper than skin color, poverty, land rights, extermination or reclamations, although these are big factors in our lives. In the writing of her stories Anna Lee Walters has chosen by birth, by vision and telling, to speak about and through this difference.

—Jo Whitehorse Cochran, "One with the People," in *Women's Review of Books,* May 1986.

The ground was packed down tight in the clearing among the high weeds. We walked around the encircling brush and found folded cardboards stacked together. Burned cans in assorted sizes were stashed under the cardboards, and there were remains of old fires. Rags were tied to the brush, snapping in the hard wind.

Sister said, "Maybe they 're all in the boxcars now. It's starting to get cold."

She was right. The November wind had a bite to it and the cold stung our hands and froze our breaths as we spoke.

"You want to go over to them boxcars?" she asked. We looked at the Railroad Crossing sign where the boxcars stood.

I was prepared to answer when a voice roared from somewhere behind us.

"Now, you young ones, you git on home! Go on! Git!"

A man crawled out of the weeds and looked angrily at us. His eyes were red and his face was unshaven. He wore a red plaid shirt with striped gray and black pants too large for him. His face was swollen and bruised. An old woolen pink scarf hid some of the bruise marks around his neck, and his topcoat was splattered with mud.

Sister looked at him. She stood close to me and told him defiantly, "You can't tell us what to do! You don't know us!"

He didn't answer Sister but tried to stand. He couldn't. Sister ran to him and took his arm and pulled on it. "You need help?" she questioned.

He frowned at her but let us help him. He was tall. He seemed to be embarrassed by our help.

"You Indian, ain't you?" I dared to ask him.

(With Peggy V. Beck) *The Sacred: Ways of Knowledge, Sources of Life* (textbook), Navajo Community College Press, 1977.

(Editor) Chester Hubbard, Haz Agii BoHo Aah, *The Learning of that Which Pertains to the Home*, Navajo Community College Press,1977.

(Editor) *Navajo Weaving: From Spider Woman to Synthetic Rugs*, Navajo Community College Press, 1977.

The Sun Is Not Merciful (stories), Firebrand Books, 1985.

Ghost Singer (novel), Northland Publishing, 1988.

The Spirit of Native America: Beauty and Mysticism in American Indian Art (museum catalog), Chronicle Books, 1989.

Talking Indian: Reflections on Survival and Writing (essays, autobiography, poems, stories), Firebrand Books, 1992.

(Editor) *Neon Pow-Wow: New Native American Voices of the Southwest* (anthology), Northland Press, 1993.

The Two-Legged Creature: An Otoe Story (children's book), illustrated by Carol Bowles, Northland Press, 1993. Work represented in anthologies, including *Warriors of the Rainbow*, Viking, 1975; *The Third Woman*, Houghton, 1978; and *Coyote Was Here: Essays on Contemporary Native American Literary and Political Mobilization*, edited by Bo Schöler, University of Aarhus, 1984. Contributor to periodicals, including *Book Forum*.

He didn't answer me but looked at his feet as if they could talk so he wouldn't have to. His feet were in big brown overshoes.

"Who's your people?" Sister asked. He looked to be about Uncle Ralph's age when he finally lifted his face and met mine. He didn't respond for a minute. Then he sighed. "I ain't got no people," he told us as he tenderly stroked his swollen jaw.

"Sure you got people. Our folks says a man's always got people," I said softly. The wind blew our clothes and covered the words.

But he heard. He exploded like a firecracker. "Well, I don't! I ain't got no people! I ain't got nobody!"

"What you doing out here anyway?" Sister asked. "You hurt? You want to come over to our house?"

"Naw," he said. "Now you little ones, go on home. Don't be walking round out here. Didn't nobody tell you little girls ain't supposed to be going round by themselves? You might git hurt."

"We just wanted to talk to hobos," Sister said.

"Naw, you don't. Just go on home. Your folks is probably looking for you and worrying bout you."

433

I took Sister's arm and told her we were going home. Then we said "Bye" to the man. But Sister couldn't resist a few last words, "You Indian, ain't you?"

He nodded his head like it was a painful thing to do. "Yeah, I'm Indian."

"You ought to go on home yourself," Sister said. "Your folks probably looking for you and worrying bout you."

A N N A   L E E   **W A L T E R S**

His voice rose again as Sister and I walked away from him. "I told you kids, I don't have no people!" There was exasperation in his voice.

Sister would not be outdone. She turned and yelled, "Oh yeah? You Indian ain't you? Ain't you?" she screamed. "We your people!"

His topcoat and pink scarf flapped in the wind as we turned away from him.

We went home to Momma and Dad and Uncle Ralph then. Uncle Ralph met us at the front door. "Where you all been?" he asked looking toward the railroad tracks. Momma and Dad were talking in the kitchen.

"Just playing, Uncle," Sister and I said simultaneously.

Uncle Ralph grabbed both Sister and I by our hands and yanked us out the door. "*Awkuh!*" he said, using the Pawnee expression to show his dissatisfaction.

Outside, we sat on the cement porch. Uncle Ralph was quiet for a long time, and neither Sister nor I knew what to expect.

"I want to tell you all a story," he finally said. "Once, there were these two rats who ran around everywhere and got into everything all the time. Everything they were told not to do, well they went right out and did. They'd get into one mess and then another. It seems that they never could learn."

At that point Uncle Ralph cleared his throat. He looked at me and said. "Sister, do you understand this story? Is it too hard for you? You're older."

I nodded my head up and down and said, "I understand."

Then Uncle Ralph looked at Sister. He said to her, "Sister, do I need to go on with this story?"

Sister shook her head from side to side. "Naw, Uncle Ralph," she said.

"So you both know how this story ends?" he said gruffly. Sister and I bobbed our heads up and down again.

We followed at his heels the rest of the day. When he tightened the loose hide on top of his drum, we watched him and held it in place as he laced the wet hide down. He got his drumsticks down from the top shelf of the closet and began to pound the drum slowly.

434

"Where you going, Uncle Ralph?" I asked. Sister and I knew that when to took his drum out, he was always gone shortly after.

"I have to be a drummer at some doings tomorrow," he said.

"You a good singer, Uncle Ralph," Sister said. "You know all them old songs."

"The young people nowadays, it seems they don't care bout nothing that's old. They just want to go to the Moon." He was drumming low as he spoke.

"We care, Uncle Ralph," Sister said.

"Why?" Uncle Ralph asked in a hard, challenging tone that he seldom used on us.

Sister thought for a moment and then said, "I guess because you care so much, Uncle Ralph."

His eyes softened as he said, "I'll sing you an *Eruska* song, a song for the warriors."

The song he sang was a war dance song. At first Sister and I listened attentively, but then Sister began to dance the man's dance. She had never danced before and tried to imitate what she had seen. Her chubby body whirled and jumped the way she'd seen the men dance. Her head tilted from side to side the way the men moved theirs. I laughed aloud at her clumsy effort, and Uncle Ralph laughed heartily, too.

Uncle Ralph went in and out of our lives after that. We heard that he sang at one place and then another, and people came to Momma to find him. They said that he was only one of a few who knew the old ways and the songs.

When he came to visit us, he always brought something to eat. The Pawnee custom was that the man, the warrior, should bring food, preferably meat. Then, whatever food was brought to the host was prepared and served to the man, the warrior, along with the host's family. Many times Momma and I, or Sister and I, came home to an empty house to find a sack of food on the table. Momma or I cooked it for the next meal, and Uncle Ralph showed up to eat.

As Sister and I grew older, our fascination with the hobos decreased. Other things took our time, and Uncle Ralph did not appear as frequently as he did before.

Once while I was home alone, I picked up Momma's old photo album. Inside was a gray photo of Uncle Ralph in an army uniform. Behind him were tents on a flat terrain. Other photos showed other poses but only in one picture did he smile. All the photos were written over in black ink in Momma's handwriting. *Ralphie in Korea,* the writing said.

Other photos in the album showed our Pawnee relatives. Dad was from another tribe. Momma's momma was in the album, a tiny gray-haired woman who no longer lived. And Momma's momma's dad was in the album; he wore old Pawnee leggings and the long feathers of a dark bird sat upon his head. I closed the album when Momma, Dad, and Sister came home.

Momma went into the kitchen to cook. She called me and Sister to help. As she put on a bibbed apron, she said, "We just came from town, and we saw someone from home there." She meant someone from her tribal community.

A N N A L E E **W A L T E R S**

"This man told me that Ralphie's been drinking hard," she said sadly. "He used to do that quite a bit a long time ago, but we thought it had stopped. He seemed to be all right for a few years." We cooked and then ate in silence.

Washing the dishes, I asked Momma, "How come Uncle Ralph never did marry?"

Momma looked up at me but was not surprised by my question. She answered, "I don't know, Sister. It would have been better if he had. There was one woman who I thought he really loved. I think he still does. I think it had something to do with Mom. She wanted him to wait."

"Wait for what?" I asked.

"I don't know," Momma said, and sank into a chair.

After that we heard unsettling rumors of Uncle Ralph drinking here and there.

He finally came to the house once when only I happened to be home. He was haggard and tired. His appearance was much like that of the white-man that Sister and I met on the railroad tracks years before.

I opened the door when he tapped on it. Uncle Ralph looked years older than his age. He brought food in his arms. *Nowa,* Sister," he said in greeting. "Where's the other one?" He meant my sister.

"She's gone now, Uncle Ralph. School in Kansas," I answered. "Where you been, Uncle Ralph? We been worrying about you."

He ignored my question and said, "I bring food. The warrior brings home food. To his family, to his people." His face was lined and had not been cleaned for days. He smelled of cheap wine.

I asked again, "Where you been, Uncle Ralph?"

He forced himself to smile. "Pumpkin Flower," he said, using the Pawnee name, "I've been out with my warriors all this time."

He put one arm around me as we went to the kitchen table with the food. "That's what your Pawnee name is. Now don't forget it."

"Did somebody bring you here, Uncle Ralph, or are you on foot?" I asked him.

"I'm on foot," he answered. "Where's your Momma?"

I told him that she and Dad would be back soon. I started to prepare the food he brought.

Then I heard Uncle Ralph say, "Life is sure hard sometimes. Sometimes it seems I just can't go on."

"What's wrong, Uncle Ralph?" I asked.

Uncle Ralph let out a bitter little laugh. "What's wrong?" he repeated. "What's wrong? All my life, I've tried to live what I've been taught, but Pumpkin Flower, some things are all wrong!"

He took a folded pack of Camel cigarettes from his coat pocket. His hand shook as he pulled one from the pack and lit the end. "Too much drink," he said sadly. "That stuff is bad for us."

"What are you trying to do, Uncle Ralph?" I asked him.

"Live," he said.

He puffed on the shaking cigarette a while and said, "The old people said to live beautifully with prayers and song. Some died for beauty, too."

"How do we do that, Uncle Ralph, live for beauty?" I asked.

"It's simple, Pumpkin Flower," he said. "Believe!"

"Believe what?" I asked.

He looked at me hard. "*Awkuh!*" he said. "That's one of the things that is wrong. Everyone questions. Everyone doubts. No one believes in the old

A N N A   L E E   **W A L T E R S**

ways anymore. They want to believe when it's convenient, when it doesn't cost them anything and they get something in return. There are no more believers. There are no more warriors. They are all gone. Those who are left only want to go to the Moon."

A car drove up outside. It was Momma and Dad. Uncle Ralph heard it too. He slumped in the chair, resigned to whatever Momma would say to him.

Momma came in first. Dad then greeted Uncle Ralph and disappeared into the back of the house. Custom and etiquette required that Dad, who was not a member of Momma's tribe, allow Momma to handle her brother's problems.

She hugged Uncle Ralph. Her eyes filled with tears when she saw how thin he was and how his hands shook.

"Ralphie," she said, "you look awful, but I am glad to see you."

She then spoke to him of everyday things, how the car failed to start and the latest gossip. He was silent, tolerant of the passing of time in this way. His eyes sent me a pleading look while his hands shook and he tried to hold them still.

When supper was ready, Uncle Ralph went to wash himself for the meal. When he returned to the table, he was calm. His hands didn't shake so much.

At first he ate without many words, but in the course of the meal he left the table twice. Each time he came back, he was more talkative than before, answering Momma's questions in Pawnee. He left the table a third time and Dad rose.

Dad said to Momma, "He's drinking again. Can't you tell?" Dad left the table and went outside.

Momma frowned. A determined look grew on her face.

When Uncle Ralph sat down to the table once more, Momma told him, "Ralphie, you're my brother but I want you to leave now. Come back when you're sober."

He held a tarnished spoon in mid-air and put it down slowly. He hadn't finished eating, but he didn't seem to mind leaving. He stood, looked at me with his red eyes, and went to the door. Momma followed him. In a low voice she said, "Ralphie, you've got to stop drinking and wandering—or don't come to see us again."

He pulled himself to his full height then. His frame filled the doorway. He leaned over Momma and yelled, "Who are you? Are you God that you will say what will be or will not be?"

Momma met his angry eyes. She stood firm and did not back down.

438

His eyes finally dropped from her face to the linoleum floor. A cough came from deep in this throat.

"I'll leave here," he said. "But I'll get all my warriors and come back! I have thousands of warriors and they'll ride with me. We'll get our bows and arrows. Then we'll come back!" He staggered out the door.

In the years that followed, Uncle Ralph saw us only when he was sober. He visited less and less. When he did show up, he did a tapping ritual on our front door. We welcomed the rare visits. Occasionally he stayed at our house for a few days at a time when he was not drinking. He slept on the floor.

He did odd jobs for minimum pay but never complained about the work or money. He'd acquired a vacant look in his eyes. It was the same look that Sister and I had seen in the hobos when we were children. He wore a similar careless array of clothing and carried no property with him at all.

The last time he came to the house, he called my by my English name and asked if I remembered anything of all that he'd taught me. His hair had turned pure white. He looked older than anyone I knew. I marvelled at his appearance and said, "I remember everything." That night I pointed out his stars for him and told him how *Pahukatawa* lived and died and lived again through another's dreams. I'd grown, and Uncle Ralph could not hold me on his knee anymore. His arm circled my waist while we sat on the grass.

He was moved by my recitation and clutched my hand tightly. He said, "It's more than this. It's more than just repeating words. You know that, don't you?"

I nodded my head. "Yes, I know. The recitation is the easiest part but it's more than this, Uncle Ralph."

He was quiet, but after a few minutes his hand touched my shoulder. He said, "I couldn't make it work. I tried to fit the pieces."

"I know," I said.

"Now before I go," he said, "do you know who you are?"

The question took me by surprise. I thought very hard. I cleared my throat and told him, "I know that I am fourteen. I know that it's too young."

"Do you know that you are a Pawnee?" he asked in a choked whisper.

"Yes Uncle," I said.

"Good," he said with a long sigh that was swallowed by the night.

Then he stood and said, "Well, Sister, I have to go. Have to move on."

"Where are you going?" I asked. "Where all the warriors go?" I teased.

He managed a smile and a soft laugh. "Yeah, wherever the warriors are, I'll find them."

A N N A   L E E   **W A L T E R S**

I said to him, "Before you go, I want to ask you . . . Uncle Ralph, can women be warriors too?"

He laughed again and hugged me merrily. "Don't tell me you want to be one of the warriors too?"

"No, Uncle," I said, "Just one of yours." I hated to let him go because I knew I would not see him again.

He pulled away. His last words were, "Don't forget what I've told you all these years. It's the only chance not to become what everyone else is. Do you understand?"

I nodded and he left.

I never saw him again.

The years passed quickly. I moved away from Momma and Dad and married. Sister left before I did.

Years later in another town, hundreds of miles away, I awoke in a terrible gloom, a sense that something was gone from the world the Pawnees knew. The despair filled days, though the reason for the sense of loss went unexplained. Finally, the telephone rang. Momma was on the line. She said, "Sister came home for a few days not too long ago. While she was here and alone, someone tapped on the door, like Ralphie always does. Sister yelled, 'Is that you, Uncle Ralphie? Come on in.' But no one entered."

Then I understood that Uncle Ralph was dead. Momma probably knew too. She wept softly into the phone.

Later Momma received an official call confirming Uncle Ralph's death. He had died from exposure in a hobo shanty, near the railroad tracks outside a tiny Oklahoma town. He'd been dead for several days and nobody knew but Momma, Sister, and me.

Momma reported to me that the funeral was well attended by the Pawnee people. Uncle Ralph and I had said our farewells years earlier. Momma told me that someone there had spoken well of Uncle Ralph before they put him in the ground. It was said that "Ralphie came from a fine family, an old line of warriors."

440

Ten years later, Sister and I visited briefly at Momma's and Dad's home. We had been separated by hundreds of miles for all that time. As we sat under Momma's flowering mimosa trees, I made a confession to Sister. I said, "Sometimes I wish that Uncle Ralph were here. I'm a grown woman but I still miss him after all these years."

Sister nodded her head in agreement. I continued. "He knew so many things. He knew why the sun pours its liquid all over us and why it must do just that. He knew why babes and insects crawl. He knew that we must live beautifully or not live at all."

Sister's eyes were thoughtful, but she waited to speak while I went on. "To live beautifully from day to day is a battle all the way. The things that he knew are so beautiful. And to feel and know that kind of beauty is the reason that we should live at all. Uncle Ralph said so. But now, there is no one who knows what that beauty is or any of the other things that he knew."

Sister pushed back smokey gray wisps of her dark hair. "You do," she pronounced. "And I do, too."

"Why do you suppose he left us like that?" I asked.

"It couldn't be helped," Sister said. "There was a battle on."

"I wanted to be one of his warriors," I said with an embarrassed half-smile.

She leaned over and patted my hand. "You are," she said. Then she stood and placed one hand on her bosom and one hand on my arm. "We'll carry on," she said.

I touched her hand resting on my arm. I said, "Sister, tell me again. What is the battle for?"

She looked down toward the fence where a hobo was coming through. We waved at him.

"Beauty," she said to me. "Our battle is for beauty. It's what Uncle Ralph fought for, too. He often said that everyone else just wanted to go to the Moon. But remember, Sister, you and I done been there. Don't forget, after all, we're children of the stars."

441

ANNA LEE **WALTERS**

JAMES WELCH

Essay by

BRETT A. LELAND

A Saturday Review critic made this prediction in a review of James Welch's first book of poetry, Riding the Earthboy 40: *"His poems are alert, sorrowful, and true. For a young man he is very strong. . . . If Welch stays put in his own life, I think his strengths should develop; his voice is clear, laconic, and it projects a depth in experience of landscape, people, and history that conveys a rich complexity. You realize his is not looking at a thing, but seeing into it—which is vision."*

Welch's promise was realized in his first novel, *Winter in the Blood,* the story of a young Indian living on a reservation in Montana. The unnamed narrator is, like Welch, part Blackfoot and part Gros Ventre Indian. He describes himself as a "servant to a memory of death." Both his father and brother are dead; in the course of the novel, his beloved grandmother dies as well. In the *New York Times Book Review,* Reynolds Price described the narrator's life as a "black sack tied firmly shut." But just as the story "threatens to die in its crowded sack," Price wrote, "it opens onto light—and through natural, carefully prepared, but beautifully surprising narrative means; a recovery of the past; a venerable, maybe lovable, maybe usable past. . . . "

Welch's next work, *The Death of Jim Loney,* about an alienated, alcoholic half-breed of both white and Indian parentage, continues the themes of identity and purpose set down in *Winter in the Blood. Fools Crow,* Welch's acclaimed third novel, marks a change in direction for the author, telling the story of a band of Blackfoot Indians in Montana Territory in the 1870s. The book follows the life of Fools Crow, who grows from a reck-

I have seen poems about Indians written by whites and they are either sentimental or outraged over the condition of the Indian. There are exceptions . . . but for the most part only an Indian knows who he is . . . and hopefully he will have the toughness and fairness to present his material in a way that is not manufactured by conventional stance.

—James Welch, in *South Dakota Review,* 1971.

less young warrior to become the tribe's medicine man. A vision Fools Crow has of his tribe's bleak future foreshadows the end of the entire Indian prairie culture—a culture already threatened by disease, the extinction of the buffalo herds, and the encroachment of white settlers.

Welch's ability to recapture the Blackfeet way of life, especially its spiritual aspects, was a strength of the novel. Reviewing *Fools Crow* in the *Washington Post Book World,* Dennis Drabelle declared: "If *Fools Crow* succeeds . . . it does so because Welch, himself part Blackfoot, manages to convey a sense of his people's world view." Peter Wild of the *New York Times Book Review* agreed, noting that "the book becomes a series of dreams acted out, a chronicle of the Indians' visions as applied to daily life." And Lewis D. Owens, writing in the *Los Angeles Times Book Review,* stated: "In this novel, Welch is remembering the world of his ancestors, putting that world together again in a way that will tell both author and reader what has been lost and what saved."

Owens argued that Welch's work was significant for other reasons as well. "Perhaps the most profound implication of this novel," Owens suggested, "is that the culture, the world-view brought so completely to life in *Fools Crow,* is alive and accessible in the self-imagining of contemporary Blackfeet and other American Indians. In recovering the world found in this novel, Welch serves as storyteller, bearer of oral tradition and definer of what it means to be Indian today."

After the success of *Fools Crow,* Welch returned to a contemporary setting for his next novel, *The Indian Lawyer,* a tale of corruption involving prominent Indian attorney Sylvester Yellow Calf. Yellow Calf, a leading congressional candidate who also serves on the Montana prison parole board, falls victim to a blackmail scheme after he is seduced by the wife of a prison inmate whose case is under study by the parole board. Afraid that he has compromised his personal ethics as well as his political standing, Yellow Calf drops out of the congressional race and begins a law practice on the reservation where he was born.

Critics determined that *The Indian Lawyer* accurately reflects the conflicts that exist between white and Indian cultures. In the *Washington*

444

Blackfeet/Gros Ventre novelist and poet.

Born: 1940, in Browning, Montana.

Education: Attended Blackfeet and Fort Belknap reservation schools and later Northern Montana College, and Minnesota University; University of Montana, B.A.

Career: Poet and novelist. Visiting Professor at University of Washington and Cornell University; served on Montana State Board of Pardons; served on literature panel of National Endowment for the Arts; has also worked as laborer, forest service employee, firefighter, and counselor for Upward Bound.

Address: Home—Roseacres Farm, Rt. 6, Missoula, MT 59801. Office—c/o W. W. Norton and Co., 500 Fifth Ave., New York, NY 10110.

Agent: Ellen Levine.

Post Book World, Walter Walker remarked: "The concept of a man caught between two worlds is fresh and alive when it comes to American Indians, and Welch handles that beautifully, as he does his physical descriptions of virtually every location in the book." Walker also believed, however, that the novel's weak storyline undermined the author's message, stating: "Like many a human being, *The Indian Lawyer* starts off with great promise and ends marred by the scars of what might have been." He continued: "James Welch clearly had a very serious idea in mind that is all but lost in the banality of his plot."

Welch acknowledges that his work as a novelist places him in a small, select group of Indian writers. He told Will Nixon of *Publishers Weekly* that finding good fiction by Indian authors is difficult, adding, "I think Indians tend toward poetry instead. A lot of people have said that poetry more approximates the rhythms of their own traditions, such as songs. And Indians prefer to write poetry because they have something to say about their culture and society and it's harder to be political and polemical in fiction." Welch, though, seems committed to using the novel as a showcase for what Nixon called the author's "real subject . . . the American Indian's search for identity in his native land."

445

THANKSGIVING AT SNAKE BUTTE

From *Riding the Earthboy 40,* World Publishing, copyright © 1971 by James Welch

In time we rode that trail
up the butte as far as time
would let us. The answer to our time
lay hidden in the long grasses
on the top. Antelope scattered

Novels
Winter in the Blood, Harper, 1974.
The Death of Jim Loney, Harper, 1979.
Fools Crow, Viking, 1986.
The Indian Lawyer, Norton, 1990.

Poetry
Riding the Earthboy 40, World Publishing, 1971.

Other
(Editor with Ripley S. Hugo and Lois M. Welch) *The Real West Marginal Way: A Poet's Autobiography*, Confluence Press (nonfiction), 1986.

Also author of introduction to *Death and the Good Life*, by Richard Hugo, Clark City Press, 1991; contributor of poetry to periodicals, including *New American Review*.

through the rocks before us, clattered
unseen down the easy slope to the west.
Our horses balked, stiff-legged,
their nostrils flared at something unseen
gliding smoothly through brush away.

On top, our horses broke, loped through
a small stand of stunted pine, then jolted
to a nervous walk. Before us lay
the smooth stones of our ancestors, the fish,
the lizard, snake and bent-kneed

bowman—etched by something crude,
by a wandering race, driven by their names
for time: its winds, its rain, its snow
and the cold moon tugging at the crude figures
in this, this season of their loss.

Winter In The Blood

Harper & Row, copyright © 1974 by James Welch

Part Four—38

"Hello," he said. "You are welcome."

"There are clouds in the east," I said. I could not look at him.

"I feel it, rain tonight maybe, tomorrow for sure, cats and dogs."

The breeze had picked up so that the willows on the irrigation ditch were gesturing in our direction.

S M O K E   R I S I N G

"I see you wear shoes now. What's the meaning of this?" I pointed to a pair of rubber boots. His pants were tucked inside them.

"Rattlesnakes. For protection. This time of year they don't always warn you."

"They don't hear you," I said. "You're so quiet you take them by surprise."

"I found a skin beside my door this morning. I'm not taking any chances."

"I thought animals were your friends."

"Rattlesnakes are best left alone."

"Like you," I said.

"Could be."

I pumped some water into the enamel basin for Bird, then I loosened his cinch.

"I brought some wine." I held out the bottle.

"You are kind—you didn't have to."

"It's French," I said. "Maybe out of roses."

"My thirst is not so great as it once was. There was a time . . . " A gust of wind ruffled his fine white hair. "Let's have it."

I pressed the bottle into his hand. He held his head high, resting one hand on his chest, and drank greedily, his Adam's apple sliding up and down his throat as though it were attached to a piece of rubber. "And now, you," he said.

Yellow Calf squatted on the white skin of earth. I sat down on the platform on which the pump stood. Behind me, Bird sucked in the cool water.

"My grandmother died," I said. "We're going to bury her tomorrow."

He ran his paper fingers over the smooth rubber boots. He glanced in my direction, perhaps because he heard Bird's guts rumble. A small white cloud passed through the sun but he said nothing.

"She just stopped working. It was easy."

His knees cracked as he shifted his weight.

"We're going to bury her tomorrow. Maybe the priest from Harlem. He's a friend . . . "

He wasn't listening. Instead, his eyes were wandering beyond the irrigation ditch to the hills and the muscled clouds above them.

Something about those eyes had prevented me from looking at him. It had seemed a violation of something personal and deep, as one feels when he comes upon a cow licking her newborn calf. But now, something else,

447

[There] is a characteristic shape to Welch's fiction—a three-part story of estrangement, of search for self, and of return to the Indian world. Each hero, the nameless narrator of Winter in the Blood *and Jim Loney of* The Death of Jim Loney, *is cut off from everything except the pain of his consciousness. In his pain, each looks inward seeking to define his identity. The inward turn prompts a return to the reservation and a search for one's personal and ancestral past. For Welch, the hero's identity can never be defined in isolation; it stands in relation to his identity as Indian. One might rework Welch's idea to assert: "Whites have to adopt an identity; Indians already have one."*

—"Beyond Assimilation: James Welch and the Indian Dilemma," in *North Dakota Quarterly,* Spring 1985.

his distance, made it all right to study his face, to see for the first time the black dots on his temples and the bridge of his nose, the ear lobes which sagged on either side of his head, and the bristles which grew on the edges of his jaw. Beneath his humped nose and above his chin, creases as well defined as cutbanks between prairie hills emptied into his mouth. Between his half-parted lips hung one snag, yellow and brown and worndown, like that of an old horse. But it was his eyes, narrow beneath the loose skin of his lids, deep behind his cheekbones, that made one realize the old man's distance was permanent. It was behind those misty white eyes that gave off no light that he lived, a world as clean as the rustling willows, the bark of a fox or the odor of musk during mating season.

I wondered why First Raise had come so often to see him. Had he found a way to narrow that distance? I tried to remember that one snowy day he had brought me with him. I remembered Teresa and the old lady commenting on my father's judgment for taking me out on such a day; then riding behind him on the horse, laughing at the wet, falling snow. But I

448

couldn't remember Yellow Calf or what the two men talked about.

"Did you know her at all?" I said.

Without turning his head, he said, "She was a young woman; I was just a youth."

"Then you did know her then."

"She was the youngest wife of Standing Bear."

I was reaching for the wine bottle. My hand stopped.

"He was a chief, a wise man—not like these conniving devils who run the agency today."

"How could you know Standing Bear? He was Blackfeet."

"We came from the mountains," he said.

"You're Blackfeet?"

"My people starved that winter; we all starved but they died. It was the cruelest winter. My folks died, one by one." He seemed to recollect this without emotion.

"But I thought you were Gros Ventre. I thought you were from around here."

"Many people starved that winter. We had to travel light—we were running from the soldiers—so we had few provisions. I remember, the day we entered this valley it began to snow and blizzard. We tried to hunt but the game refused to move. All winter long we looked for deer sign. I think we killed one deer. It was rare that we even jumped a porcupine. We snared a few rabbits but not enough . . . "

449

"You survived," I said.

"Yes, I was strong in those days." His voice was calm and monotonous.

"How about my grandmother? How did she survive?"

He pressed down on the toe of his rubber boot. It sprang back into shape.

"She said Standing Bear got killed that winter," I said.

"He led a party against the Gros Ventres. They had meat. I was too young. I remember the men when they returned to camp—it was dark but you could see the white air from their horses' nostrils. We all stood waiting, for we were sure they would bring meat. But they brought Standing Bear's body instead. It was a bad time."

I tapped Yellow Calf's knee with the bottle. He drank, then wiped his lips on his shirt sleeve.

"It was then that we knew our medicine had gone bad. We had wintered some hard times before, winters were always hard, but seeing Standing Bear's body made us realize that we were being punished for having left our home. The people resolved that as soon as spring came we would go home, soldiers or not."

"But you stayed," I said. "Why?"

He drew an arc with his hand, palm down, taking in the bend of the river behind his house. It was filled with tall cottonwoods, most of them dead, with tangles of brush and wild rose around their trunks. The land sloped down from where we were sitting so that the bend was not much higher than the river itself.

"This was where we camped. It was not grown over then, only the cottonwoods were standing. But the willows were thick then, all around to provide a shelter. We camped very close together to take advantage of this situation. Sometimes in winter, when the wind has packed the snow and blown the clouds away, I can still hear the muttering of the people in their tepees. It was a very bad time."

"And your family starved . . . "

"My father died of something else, a sickness, pneumonia maybe. I had four sisters. They were among the first to go. My mother hung on for a little while but soon she went. Many starved."

"But if the people went back in the spring, why did you stay?"

"My people were here."

"And the old—my grandmother stayed too," I said.

"Yes. Being a widow is not easy work, especially when your husband had other wives. She was the youngest. She was considered quite beautiful in those day."

"But why did she stay?"

He did not answer right away. He busied himself scraping a star in the tough skin of earth. He drew a circle around it and made marks around it as a child draws the sun. Then he scraped it away with the end of his stick and raised his face into the thickening wind. "You must understand how people think in desperate times. When their bellies are full, they can afford to be happy and generous with each other—the meat is shared, the women work and gossip, men gamble—it's a good time and you do not see things clearly. There is no need. But when the pot is empty and your guts are tight in your belly, you begin to look around. The hunger sharpens your eye."

"But why her?"

"She had not been with us more than a month or two, maybe three. You must understand the thinking. In that time the soldiers came, the people had to leave their home up near the mountains, then the starvation and the death of their leader. She had brought them bad medicine."

"But you—you don't think that."

"It was apparent," he said.

"It was bad luck; the people grew angry because their luck was bad," I said.

"It was medicine."

I looked at his eyes. "She said it was because of her beauty."

"I believe it was that too. When Standing Bear was alive, they had to accept her. In fact, they were proud to have such beauty—you know how it is, even if it isn't yours." His lips trembled into what could have been a smile.

"But when he died, her beauty worked against her," I said.

"That's true, but it was more than that. When you are starving, you look for signs. Each event becomes big in your mind. His death was the final proof that they were cursed. The medicine man, Fish, interpreted the signs. They looked at your grandmother and realized that she had brought despair and death. And her beauty—it was as if her beauty made a mockery of their situation."

"They can't have believed this . . . "

"It wasn't a question of belief, it was the way things were," he said. "The day Standing Bear was laid to rest, the women walked away. Even his other wives gave her the silent treatment. It took the men longer—men are

4 5 1

not sensitive. They considered her the widow of a chief and treated her with respect. But soon, as it must be, they began to notice the hatred in their women's eyes, the coolness with which they were treated if they brought your grandmother a rabbit leg or a piece of fire in the morning. And they became ashamed of themselves for associating with the young widow and left her to herself."

I was staring at the bottle on the ground before me. I tried to understand the medicine, the power that directed the people to single out a young woman, to leave her to fend for herself in the middle of a cruel winter. I tried to understand the thinking, the hatred of the women, the shame of the men. Starvation. I didn't know it. I couldn't understand the medicine, her beauty.

"What happened to her?"

"She lived the rest of the winter by herself."

"How could she survive alone?"

He shifted his weight and dug his stick into the earth. He seemed uncomfortable. Perhaps he was recalling things he didn't want to or he felt that he had gone too far. He seemed to have lost his distance, but he went on: "She didn't really leave. It was the dead of winter. To leave the camp would have meant a sure death, but there were tepees on the edge, empty— many were empty then."

"What did she do for food?"

"What did any of us do? We waited for spring. Spring came, we hunted—the deer were weak and easy to kill."

"But she couldn't hunt, could she?" It seemed important for me to know what she did for food. No woman, no man could live a winter like that alone without something.

As I watched Yellow Calf dig at the earth I remember how the old lady had ended her story of the journey of Standing Bear's band.

There had been great confusion that spring. Should the people stay in this land of the Gros Ventres, should they go directly south to the nearest buffalo herd, or should they go back to the country west of here, their home up near the mountains? The few old people left were in favor of this last direction because they wanted to die in familiar surroundings, but the younger ones were divided as to whether they should stay put until they got stronger or head for the buffalo ranges to the south. They rejected the idea of going home because the soldiers were there. Many of them had encountered the Long Knives before, and they knew that in their condition they wouldn't have a chance. There was much confusion, many decisions and indecisions, hostility.

Finally it was the soldiers from Fort Assiniboine who took the choice away from the people. They rode down one late-spring day, gathered up the survivors and drove them west to the newly created Blackfeet Reservation. Because they didn't care to take her with them, the people apparently didn't mention her to the soldiers, and because she had left the band when the weather warmed and lived a distance away, the soldiers didn't question her. They assumed she was a Gros Ventre.

A gust of wind rattled the willows. The clouds towered white against the sky, but I could see their black underbellies as they floated toward us.

The old lady had ended her story with the image of the people being driven "like cows" to their reservation. It was a strange triumph and I understood it. But why hadn't she spoken of Yellow Calf? Why hadn't she mentioned that he was a member of that band of Blackfeet and had, like herself, stayed behind?

A swirl of dust skittered across the earth's skin.

"You say you were just a youth that winter—how old?" I said.

He stopped digging. "That first winter, my folks all died then."

But I was not to be put off. "How old?"

"It slips my mind," he said. "When one is blind and old he loses track of the years."

"You must have some idea."

"When one is blind . . . "

"Ten? Twelve? Fifteen?"

" . . . and old, he no longer follows the cycles of the years. He knows each season in its place because he can feel it, but time becomes a procession. Time feeds upon itself and grows fat." A mosquito took shelter in the hollow of his cheek, but he didn't notice. He had attained that distance. "To an old dog like myself, the only cycle begins with birth and ends in death. This is the only cycle I know."

I thought of the calendar I had seen in his shack on my previous visit. It was dated 1936. He must have been able to see then. He had been blind for over thirty years, but if he was as old as I thought, he had lived out a lifetime before. He had lived a life without being blind. He had followed the calendar, the years, time—

4 5 3

I thought for a moment.

Bird farted.

And it came to me, as though it were riding one moment of the gusting wind, as though Bird had had it in him all the time and had passed it to me in that one instant of corruption.

"Listen, old man," I said. "It was you—you were old enough to hunt!"

But his white eyes were kneading the clouds.

I began to laugh, at first quietly, with neither bitterness nor humor. It was the laughter of one who understands a moment in his life, of one who has been let in on the secret through luck and circumstance. "You . . . you're the one." I laughed, as the secret unfolded itself. "The only one . . . you, her hunter . . . " And the wave behind my eyes broke.

Yellow Calf still looked off toward the east as though the wind could wash the wrinkles from this face. But the corners of his eyes wrinkled even more as his mouth fell open. Through my tears I could see his Adam's apple jerk.

"The only one," I whispered, and the old man's head dropped between his knees. His back shook, the bony shoulders squared and hunched like the folded wings of a hawk.

"And the half-breed, Doagie!" But the laughter again racked my throat. *He wasn't Teresa's father; it was you, Yellow Calf, the hunter!*

He turned to the sound of my laughter. His face was distorted so that the single snag seemed the only recognizable feature of the man I had come to visit. His eyes hid themselves behind the high cheekbones. His mouth had become the rubbery sneer of a jack-o'-lantern.

And so we shared this secret in the presence of ghosts, in wind that called forth the muttering tepees, the blowing snow, the white air of the horses' nostrils. The cotton woods behind us, their dead white branches angling to the threatening clouds, sheltered these ghosts as they had sheltered the camp that winter. But there were others, so many others.

Yellow Calf stood, his hands in his pockets, suddenly withdrawn and polite. I pressed what remained of the bottle of wine into his hand. "Thank you," he said.

"You must come visit me sometime," I said.

"You are kind."

I tightened the cinch around Bird's belly, "I'll think about you," I said.

"You'd better hurry, he said. "It's coming."

I picked up the reins and led Bird to the rotting plank bridge across the irrigation ditch.

He lifted his hand.

ROBERTA HILL WHITEMAN

A highly respected poet, Whiteman is the author of the verse collection Star Quilt, *in which she uses vivid imagery, personal reminiscence, and a sincere and distinctive voice to treat such subjects as love, family life, and humankind's relationship to the natural world. Critical reaction to this volume has been positive, with commentators praising Whiteman's meticulous observations, her use of both simple and rhetorical language, and her capacity to form meaningful connections between seemingly disparate elements. Laurie Brown has asserted: "[These] poems attempt to connect what is human with the recurrent patterns of the natural world. The result is both personal and mythic, linking Whiteman's heritage as a member of the Oneida tribe with her role as daughter, mother, wife. Her voice, like prayer, invokes a world omnipresent but invisible."*

Essay by

ROBERTA KAPLAN

GELATT

455

A *Publishers Weekly* review of *Star Quilt* stated: "[Whiteman's] consciousness is so closely united with the dramatic landscapes of her youth that nothing happens in her poems without its reflection in the natural world. Her several elegies are as quietly affirmative as her love poems, and though her diction and style, combining simplicity and grandeur, are distinctly her own, the voice in this book also strikes us as ancestral Native American. Behind all these single moments of celebration is a mystical vision in which the spirit of the earth unfolds a life as infinitely good as it is endlessly mysterious. Whiteman catches that mystery."

Oneida poet.

Born: 1947.

Partnerships: Married Ernest Whiteman (an artist), 1980; children: Jacob, Heather, Melissa.

Education: University of Wisconsin, B.A.; University of Montana, M.F.A., 1973; University of Minnesota, Ph.D.

Career: Poets-in-the-School Program, various locales including Minnesota, Arizona, and Oklahoma, instructor; University of Wisconsin, Eau Claire, American literature instructor.

Address: 3354 Runway F, Eau Claire, WI 54601.

DREAM OF REBIRTH

From *Star Quilt*, Holy Cow! Press, copyright © 1984 by Roberta Hill Whiteman

We stand on the edge of wounds, hugging canned meat,
waiting for owls to come grind
nightsmell in our ears. Over fields,
darkness has been rumbling. Crows gather.
Our luxuries are hatred. Grief. Worn-out hands
carry the pale remains of forgotten murders.
If I could only lull or change this slow hunger,
this midnight swollen four hundred years.

Groping within us are cries yet unheard.
We are born with cobwebs in our mouths
bleeding with prophecies.
Yet within this interior, a spirit kindles
moonlight glittering deep into the sea.
These seeds take root in the hush
of dusk. Songs, a thin echo, heal the salted marsh,
and yield visions untrembling in our grip.

4 5 6

I dreamed an absolute silence birds had fled.
The sun, a meager hope, again was sacred.
We need to be purified by fury.
Once more eagles will restore our prayers.
We'll forget the strangeness of your pity.
Some will anoint the graves with pollen.
Some of us may wake unashamed.
Some will rise that clear morning like the swallows.

A Nation Wrapped in Stone

for Susan Iron Shell

When night shadows slipped across the plain, I saw a man
beside his horse, sleeping where neither man nor horse
had been. I've prayed
to a star that lied. The spirits near the ceiling of your room,
did they leave on horseback, turning dew into threads
by moonlight?
In wild stretch of days, you didn't fear ashes or weeping.
We, left behind, can't warm sunlight.
Isaac, you left with the wind.

The chokecherry grows slower. I held your trembling wife,
and windows trembled in our north room. The creek gnaws

ROBERTA HILL **WHITEMAN**

Star Quilt (poems), illustrated by Ernest Whiteman, Holy Cow! Press, 1984.

Work represented in *Carriers of the Dream Wheel: Contemporary Native American Poetry*, edited by Duane Niatum, Harper & Row, 1975; *The Third Woman: Minority Women Writers* *of the United States*, edited by Dexter Fisher, Houghton, 1980; and *Harper's Anthology of Twentieth Century Native American Poetry*, edited by Niatum, Harper & Row, 1988.

Work in Progress

Researching a history of the Oneida migrations; verse collection tentative-ly titled *Philadelphia Flowers* is sched-uled to be published by Holy Cow! Press.

remaining snow. Our blood runs pale.
You taught us to be kind to one another. Now we wake, questioning
our dreams. Nighthawks in warm fog. A nation wrapped in stone.
What do nurses
know of hay, of scents that float broken between canyons,
of strength in a worn face? You wept love, not death.
Around your bed, owls stood.

The north wind hunts us with music, enough pain
to set fires in ancient hills. West winds growl
around Parmelee.
The tanned, uneven banks will hold more frost. Unlike dust,
we cannot die from tears. You've settled
on a quiet prairie. Shrouded eyes
in thickets give a reason to contain
the heavy rind. We are left with grief, sinking boneward,
and time to watch rain soak the trees.

STAR QUILT

4 5 8

These are notes to lightning in my bedroom.
A star forged from linen thread and patches.
Purple, yellow, red like diamond suckers, children

of the star gleam on sweaty nights. The quilt unfolds
against sheets, moving, warm clouds of Chinook.
It covers my cuts, my red birch clusters under pine.

Under it your mouth begins a legend,
and wide as the plain, I hope Wisconsin marshes

S M O K E   R I S I N G

promise your caress. The candle
  locks

us in forest smells, your cheek
  tattered
by shadow. Sweetened by wings,
  my mothlike heart
flies nightly among geraniums.
We know of land that looks lonely,
but isn't, of beef with hides of
  velveteen,
of sorrow, an eddy in blood.

Star quilt, sewn from dawn light
  by fingers
of flint, take away those touches
meant for noisier skins,

anoint us with grass and twilight
  air,
so we may embrace, two bitter
  roots
pushing back into the dust.

For most of my life I felt this sense of exile and alienation and a fear. A lot of prejudice, growing up in an area in which there is a lot of prejudice I think affects people in that way. But there is this sense of home and of completeness that I also feel. Somehow I think that part of the writing is to set the record straight—for myself, to explain things for myself as if I were still a child inside. And I question it and I have to get it right. I have this feeling too, that other people have this same sense. They want to understand, they want to set it straight.

—Roberta Hill Whiteman with Joseph Bruchac, in an interview in *Survival This Way: Interviews with American Indian Poets* by Joseph Bruchac, Sun Tracks and The University of Arizona Press, 1987.

459

R O B E R T A   H I L L   **W H I T E M A N**

INDEX